THE KITCHEN GARDEN GROWER'S GUIDE

A PRACTICAL VEGETABLE AND
HERB GARDEN ENCYCLOPEDIA

STEPHEN ALBERT

Copyright © 2008 Stephen Albert
All rights reserved.

ISBN: 1-4196-5579-5
ISBN-13: 9781419655791
Library of Congress Control Number: 2008905152

Visit www.booksurge.com to order additional copies.

Written and edited by Stephen Albert
Art direction and cover photographs by Anna Heath
Photographer Bethany Lowe

Text and photographs copyright 2008 by Stephen Albert

Stephen Albert is editor-in-chief of HarvestToTable.com

All rights reserved. No part of this book may be reproduced without written permission from the author, except by a reviewer, who may quote brief passages or reproduce illustrations in a review with appropriate credits; nor may any part of this book be reproduced, stored in a retrieval system, or transmitted in any form or by any means—electronic, mechanical, photocopying, recording, or other—without written permission from the author.

Disclaimer:
The information in this book is true and complete to the best of our knowledge. Great care has been taken to be as accurate as possible. All information is made without guarantee on the part of the author or publisher. This book is for educational purposes only. It is not intended as a substitute for the advice of a health care professional. The author and publisher disclaim any liability in connection with any errors or omissions or for the use of this information. Neither the author nor the publisher can be held responsible for claims arising from the mistaken identity of plants or their inappropriate use. The author and publisher do not assume responsibility for any sickness, death, or other harmful effects resulting from eating or using any plant described in this book. There are thousands of varieties of vegetables, fruits, and herbs; we have not addressed all of them. The author and publisher cannot be held responsible for not including all of the food varieties available.

Table of Contents

List of Vegetable and Herb Entries by Common Name | 2

List of Vegetable and Herb Entries by Botanical Name | 3

Note on Common and Botanical Names | 5

Introduction | 7

Kitchen Garden Grower's Guide to Vegetables and Herbs | 11 to 357

Growing Season Information for the United States and Canadian Provinces | 359

Growing Zones throughout the World | 368

Glossary | 371

Bibliography | 385

Index | 389

Acknowledgments | 403

About the Author | 405

We Want to Hear from You | 407

Common Names of Vegetables and Herbs

Artichoke 11
Arugula 17
Asparagus 21
Basil 27
Beans 31
Beets, Beet Greens 39
Broccoli 45
Brussels sprout 51
Cabbage 57
Cardoon 63
Carrots 67
Cauliflower 73
Celeriac 79
Celery 83
Chard 89
Chervil 93
Chicory: Belgian Endive
and Witloof 97
Chinese leaves: Bok Choy,
Pei Tsai, Napa Cabbage, Michihili 103
Chives 109
Cilantro 113
Collards, Collard Greens 117
Sweet Corn 121
Corn salad, Mâche 127
Cress 131
Cucumber 135
Dill 141
Eggplant 145
Endive, Escarole 151
Florence fennel 155
Garlic 159
Horseradish 165
Kale 169
Kohlrabi 173
Leeks 177

Lettuce 181
Marjoram 187
Melons 191
Mesclun 197
Mint 201
Mustard Greens 205
Okra 209
Onions 213
Oregano 221
Parsley 225
Parsnips 229
Peas 233
Peppers 241
Potatoes 249
Radicchio 257
Radishes 261
Rhubarb 267
Rosemary 271
Rutabaga 275
Sage 279
Salsify 283
Savory 287
Shallots 291
Sorrel 295
Spinach 299
Summer Squash 305
Winter Squash and Pumpkin 311
Strawberries 317
Sunchokes 321
Sunflowers 325
Sweet potatoes 329
Tarragon 335
Thyme 339
Tomatoes 343
Turnips 355

Botanical Names of Vegetables and Herbs

Abelmoschus esculentus (Okra) 209
Allium cepa (Onions) 213
Allium cepa var. *ascalonicum* (Shallots) 291
Allium porrum and *A. ampeloprasum* (Leeks) 177
Allium sativum (Garlic) 159
Allium schoenoprasum (Chives) 109
Allium tuberosum (Garlic chives) 109
Anethum graveolens (Dill) 141
Anthriscus cerefolium (Chervil) 93
Apium graveolens var. *dulce* (Celery) 83
Apium graveolens var. *rapaceum* (Celeriac) 79
Armoracia rusticana (Horseradish) 165
Artemisia dracunculus (Tarragon) 355
Asparagus officinalis (Asparagus) 21
Beta vulgaris (Beets, beet greens) 39
Beta vulgaris var. *cicla* (Chard) 89
Brassica juncea var. *rugosa* (Mustard greens) 205
Brassica napus (Rutabaga) 275
Brassica oleracea var. *acephala* (Collards) 117
Brassica oleracea var. *acephala* (Kale) 169
Brassica oleracea, var. *botrytis* (Cauliflower) 73
Brassica oleracea var. *capitata* (Cabbage) 57
Brassica oleracea var. *gemmifera* (Brussels sprout) 51
Brassica oleracea var. *gongylodes* (Kohlrabi) 173
Brassica oleracea var. *italica* (Broccoli) 45
Brassica rapa var. *chinensis* (Chinese leaves, bok choy) 103
Brassica rapa var. *pekinensis* (Chinese leaves, pe-tsai, Napa cabbage) 103
Brassica rapa var. *rapa* (Turnip) 355
Capsicum annuum (Sweet peppers) 241
Capsicum chinense, Capsicum frutescens (Hot peppers) 241
Cichorium endivia (Endive, Escarole) 151
Cichorium intybus (Radicchio) 257
Cichorium intybus var. *foliosum* (Chicory: Belgian Endive and Witloof) 97

Coriandrum sativum (Cilantro) 113
Cucumis melo (Melons) 191
Cucumis sativus (Cucumber) 135
Cucurbita maxima, Cucurbita moschata, Cucurbita pepo (Winter squash) 311
Cucurbita pepo (Summer squash) 305
Cynara cardunculus (Cardoon) 63
Cynara scolymus (Artichoke) 11
Daucus carota sativus (Carrots) 67
Eruca sativa (Arugula) 17
Foeniculum vulgare var. *azoricum* (Florence fennel) 155
Fragaria vesca (Alpine Strawberry) 317
Helianthus annuus (Sunflowers) 325
Helianthus tuberosus (Sunchokes) 321
Ipomoea batatas (Sweet potatoes) 329
Lactuca sativa (Lettuce) 181
Lepidium sativum (Cress) 131
Lycopersicon esculentum (Tomato) 343
Mentha species (Mint) 201
Ocimum basilicum, Ocimum cispum, Ocimum minimum (Basil) 27
Origanum majorana (Marjoram) 187
Origanum vulgare (Oregano) 221
Pisum sativum (Edible-pod peas) 233
Pisum sativum var. *macrocarpon* (Shell peas) 233
Pastinaca sativa (Parsnips) 229
Petroselinum crispum (Curly leafed parsley) 225
Petroselinum neapolitanum (Flat or plain leafed parsley, also called Italian parsley) 255
Phaseolus vulgaris (Beans) 31
Raphanus sativus (Radishes) 261
Rheum rhabarbarum syns. *Rheum* x *cultorum, Rheum* x *hybridum* (Rhubarb) 267
Rorippa microphylla (Cress) 131
Rorippa nasturtium-aquaticum (Watercress) 131
Rosmarinus officinalis (Rosemary) 271
Rumex acetosa and *Rumex scutatus* (Sorrel) 295

Salvia officinalis (Sage) 279
Satureja hortensis (Summer savory);
S. montana (Winter savory) 287
Solanum melongena (Eggplant) 145
Solanum tuberosum (Potatoes) 249
Spinacea oleracea (Spinach) 299
Thymus vulgaris (Thyme) 339
Tragopogon porrifolius (Salsify) 283
Valerianella locusta (Corn salad, Mâche) 127
Zea mays var. *rugosa* (Sweet corn) 121

Note on Common Names and Botanical Names

Plants in this book are organized alphabetically by their common names. For each plant, first the common name in English is given followed by the common name used in other languages followed by the plant's Latin botanical name. While common names are widely used, one plant may have several common names, or its common name may be different in other parts of the world, or the common name may refer to a different plant in another part of the world.

Botanical names are an important way to identify plants specifically. A plant's botanical name includes two words in Latin form. The first word is the name of the genus and the second is the name of the species. Together they provide a specific universally recognized name for every plant.

Plants are sometimes reclassified and long established names are changed. This happens when research determines that a plant has been incorrectly identified or that its classification has changed. This book uses current names. Where there has been a recent change in the botanical name, the former name is shown in parenthesis.

Introduction

This is a book for the kitchen gardener and cook, a simple, easy-to-use guide to bring fresh, inexpensive, and healthy food from your garden to your table.

If you've ever thought you ought to cook and eat more fresh vegetables and herbs, and if you've ever thought you'd like to grow your own great-tasting food, then this book is for you.

A kitchen garden produces vegetables, salad greens, herbs, and small fruits for the home table. It's a garden situated close to the kitchen that offers the best ingredients fresh-picked at the peak of ripeness and ready to be used.

Whether you are starting a kitchen garden for the first time or an old-hand at gardening, this book has got information you can use today. Here is an easy-to-use, how-to-grow guide for the most commonly grown and used kitchen garden crops. Here you will find all you need to grow more than 80 different edible plants. This is an encyclopedia of the most common kitchen garden plants easily grown in temperate, cold, and subtropical climates.

This book does not require cover-to-cover reading. You can use it as you need it. You can turn to the vegetable or herb in question and get the answer you need today. This book provides answers to both basic and in-depth growing questions. You will learn where to plant, when to plant, how to plant, how to grow, and how to care for your crops. You will learn when to harvest and how to store and how to prepare your crops—from harvest to table.

Here's what you will find in these pages:

- Plants ordered alphabetically by their common name and a second table of contents which lists each plant alphabetically by its botanical name.

For each plant entry:

- The common name, Latin botanical and family name, and the plant's names common in other parts of the world.

- An identifying photograph and description of the plant part used and most commonly seen at harvest or in the market.
- A brief description of kitchen preparation.
- The plant's origin and history.
- Each plant's garden growing characteristics: form, height, breadth, root depth, bloom time and flower, and edible parts.
- Season and climate requirements.
- Site requirements: soil preparation and amendments as well as container growing suggestions.
- Planting and growing specifics in checklist form: planting depth, germination and growing soil temperatures required, days to germination and maturity, sowing time, transplanting time, plant spacing, water and light and nutrition requirements, cropping and rotation suggestions, propagation, and greenhouse and colframe growing suggestions to extend the season.
- Garden care: mulching, pinching and pruning suggestions and organic weed, pest, and plant disease solutions for each plant.
- Harvest and storage specifics: when to harvest, how to harvest, and how to store each crop.
- All measurements are given in both English standard and metric conversion.

At the end of the book, you will find additional helpful information:

- A list of first and last frost dates and the number of days in the growing season, zone classifications, and yearly minimum temperature averages for 228 cities and towns in the United States and Canada and also the growing zones and average minimum average temperatures for major temperate regions around the world.
- A glossary of plant and garden terms used in this book.
- A bibliography of other helpful garden books.
- An index to all of the plants and gardening terms throughout the book.

Your health and your family's health begin with the food you eat and the exercise you take. A kitchen garden will give you and your family both recreational exercise and fresh, healthy, tasty food.

Your kitchen garden starts here. Happy Gardening!

P.S. And don't forget, if you ever need answers to other kitchen or garden questions, please don't hesitate to contact us at HarvestToTable.com.

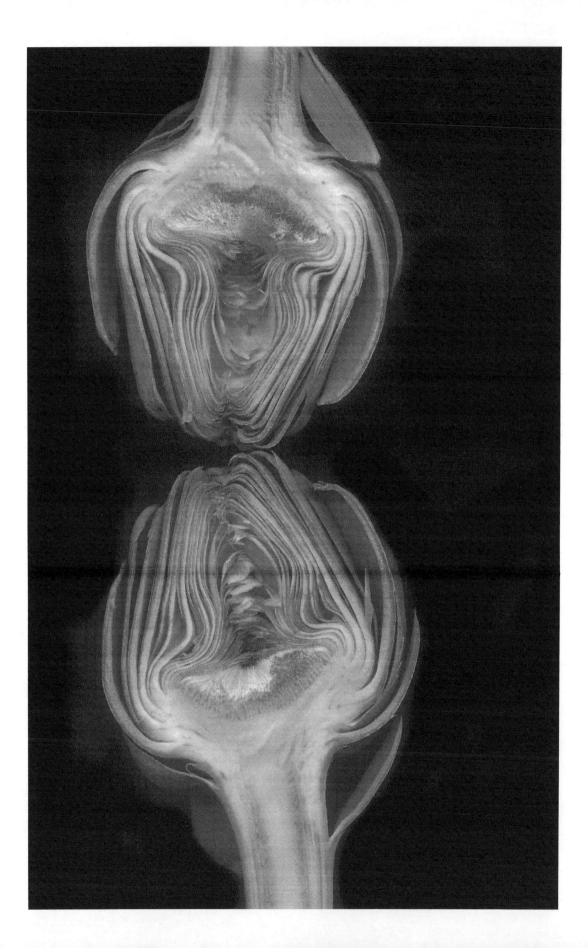

Artichokes

Common names: Artichoke, globe artichoke
World names: chao xian ji, yang ji (Chinese); artichaut (French); Artischocke (German); carciofo (Italian); chousen azami (Japanese); alcachofra (Portuguese); alcachofera (Spanish)
Botanical name: *Cynara scolymus*
Pronounced Sin-uh-ruh SKOLL-ih-mus
Family: Sunflower family—*Asteraceae (Compositae)*

ABOUT

Type of plant: Perennial that will live to 15 years, but usually bears for 3–4 years. Sometimes planted as an annual in cold-winter regions; planted in autumn for a spring harvest

Origin: Southern Europe, Mediterranean; perhaps derived from wild cardoon. Grown by the ancient Greeks and Romans before spreading to the rest of Europe.

Description: Thistle-like fountain shape with large, coarse silvery-gray-green, deeply-lobed frond-like leaves.

Height: 36–60 inches (90–152 cm)

Breadth: 60–72 inches (152–183 cm)

Root depth: More than 48 inches (122 cm)

Bloom time and flower: Usually mid-autumn, but bloom time may vary. Flowers are lavender to purple-blue thistles, 4–6 inches (10–15 cm) across forming at the top of stalks. This plant usually does not flower the first year.

Edible parts: Immature flower buds and receptacle of the flower buds (the soft part at base of leaves or bract). The base is sometimes called the "heart." Buds weigh up to 1 pound (0.45 kilogram).

KITCHEN

Serve: Artichokes are always eaten cooked. Once cooked, they can be served hot, warm or cold. Pull off each leaf; dunk it in the sauce; put it in your mouth and pull, scraping the tender flesh through your teeth. Cut the tender nut-flavored bottom into bite-sized pieces, dunk in sauce and eat. Serve with béchamel, butter, or hollandaise sauce.

BASICS

Seed planting depth: ¼ inch (6 mm)

Germination soil temperature: 70–80°F (21–27°C); optimum 75°F (24°C)

Days to germination: 10–14

Sow indoors: 10 weeks before last frost

Transplant outdoors: 6–8 week old plants when temperatures reach 50°F (10°C)

Crown planting depth: Set crowns just above the soil surface

Soil pH range: Near-neutral, 6.0–6.8

Growing soil temperature: 60–75° F (16–24°C)

Spacing of plants: 6 inches (15 cm) apart in every direction; thin successful plants to 4 feet (122 cm) apart.

Water: Keep the soil moist.

Light: 8 hours or more each day

Nutrients: Mix a small amount of nitrogen fertilizer such as blood meal into the soil before planting then work in lots of well-rotted manure or compost.

Rotating crops: Avoid following Jerusalem artichokes or sunflowers.

Companion crops: Perennial vegetables such as asparagus, also sunflower, tarragon, and brassicas or cabbage family plants

Incompatible crops: Vines

Propagation: Usually by offshoots (suckers) or divisions or by seed. (Seed may not breed true. Thus plants started from seed may be inferior to parent plants.)

Seed viability: 6 years

Seeds weight: 10,000 per ounce (333 per gram)

THE SITE

Artichokes prefer cool, moist summers and mild winters. They grow best in areas where the mean temperature is between 55°–60°F (13°–18°C). Growth zones 8–9 are good. Avoid planting artichokes in areas with fewer than 100 frost free days. In growth zones 5–7, mulch or heap leaves or straw above the roots during winter. In coldest regions, bring the roots inside during winter and keep them moist and cool. In hot, dry regions, buds may become tough or open too soon and may not be edible.

Container growing: Use a large container, such as a half barrel, at least 36–38 inches (90–96 cm) wide and just as deep.

PLANTING

Sow seed indoors 6–8 weeks before the last spring frost. Sow seed ¼ inch (6 mm) apart and ¼ inch (6 mm) deep in lightly moistened soil-less mix in a flat or cell container. Germinate seed at 70–80°F (21–27°C). When seedlings can be handled, transplant them to 4 inch (10 cm) deep pots and grow in full sun at 60–70°F (15–21°C) day and 50–60°F (10–15°C) night. After the soil has warmed and plants have developed four true leaves, transplant 6–8 week old plants to the garden. Transplants will need 8–10 days of temperatures around 50°F (10°C) to induce early budding.

Bud or division planting time in mild-winter climates: Set out bud or root divisions or plants in late winter or early spring, about 2 weeks before the last frost. Use a trowel to slice 10 inch (25 cm) tall suckers off the parent plant, each with a section of root. Plant the sucker in a 4-inch (10 cm) hole. Set root shanks vertically with bud shoots just above the soil.

Planting time in cold-winter climates: Plant the sucker in a pot to over-winter and root out indoors. Then set out in the garden about two weeks before the last frost. Set crowns just above the soil surface. When sowing seed, allow 4 feet (1.2 m) between plants. Consider plant placement in the garden with mature plant size in mind.

GROWING

Water: Keep the soil moist. Never allow roots to dry out, but do not saturate the ground or leave standing water either.

Mulch: Mulch heavily when plants are 6–8 feet (1.8–2.4 m) high. Also apply mulch over the winter.

Nutrients: Mix a small amount of nitrogen fertilizer such as blood meal into the soil before planting then work in lots of well-rotted manure or compost. Fertilize in spring and autumn with a low-nitrogen fertilizer such as fish emulsion or compost tea or top dress with a layer of well-rotted manure or compost in spring. In summer, apply a fish emulsion at 10–day intervals.

Propagation: Usually by offshoots (suckers) or divisions or by seed. (Seed may not breed true. Thus plants started from seed may be inferior to parent plants.)

CARE

- Cut harvested stalks and leaves to the ground after all artichokes have been picked. This will force new growth.
- In growing zones 7–8, over winter crowns in the ground if they are protected. Before the first freeze, cut plants back to about 10 inches (25 cm) and mulch the crowns with 12–inch (30 cm) deep mound of straw or leaves. Cover the mulched crowns with a basket or cardboard box. Remove this winter protection in the spring when small tufts of leaves emerge from the old crown.
- Dig up and thin plants every 3–4 years to avoid overcrowding and decline.

- Harvest buds in early spring then prune the plants back by one-third to encourage a second crop for harvest in autumn.

Pests: Aphids, plume moths, slugs, snails. Handpick snails and slugs. Knock off aphids using a strong jet of water. Plume moth may be a problem in commercial artichoke growing areas. To deter gophers, grow plants in a raised bed lined with hardware cloth.

Diseases: Curly dwarf (virus), crown rot (Southern blight), verticillium wilt. Crown rot, a fungus disease, may occur where plants have to be covered in winter or where drainage is poor. To avoid this problem avoid standing water and wet conditions. Don't mulch until the soil temperature drops to 40°F (5°C), and don't leave mulch in place longer than necessary in the spring. Avoid handling the plants when wet. Destroy or dispose of affected plants. Plant disease resistant varieties. Control viruses by controlling aphids and leafhoppers. Remove and destroy infected plants.

HARVEST

Artichokes may bear edible buds during the first year about 150–180 days after the seed is sown. Usually the first harvest will occur during the second year. For plants grown from offshoots or suckers, edible buds may come in 50 to 100 days.

- Harvest artichokes mid-summer to mid-autumn. Use a knife to cut off plump buds leaving an inch of stem attached to the bud. Cut off buds when they are about the size of an apple and before the scales have begun to open. Younger buds on lateral shoots are most tender and can be eaten whole. Hot weather will cause the buds to open and as a result the edible leaf bract will become tough the leathery. Two and three-year-old plants may produce a good crop of buds in early summer. After early summer harvest when leaves start to yellow, prune plants back by a third to get an autumn crop.

Storage: Refrigerate fresh artichokes for 1–2 weeks. Freeze or pickle artichoke hearts after cooking. Pickle whole small artichokes less then 3 inches (7.5 cm) in diameter.

VARIETIES

Choose from these artichoke varieties: 'Green Globe' is ready for harvest the second summer after seeding; 'Imperial Star' produces the first season, about 180 days from seed to harvest; 'Violetto' has purplish elongated buds.

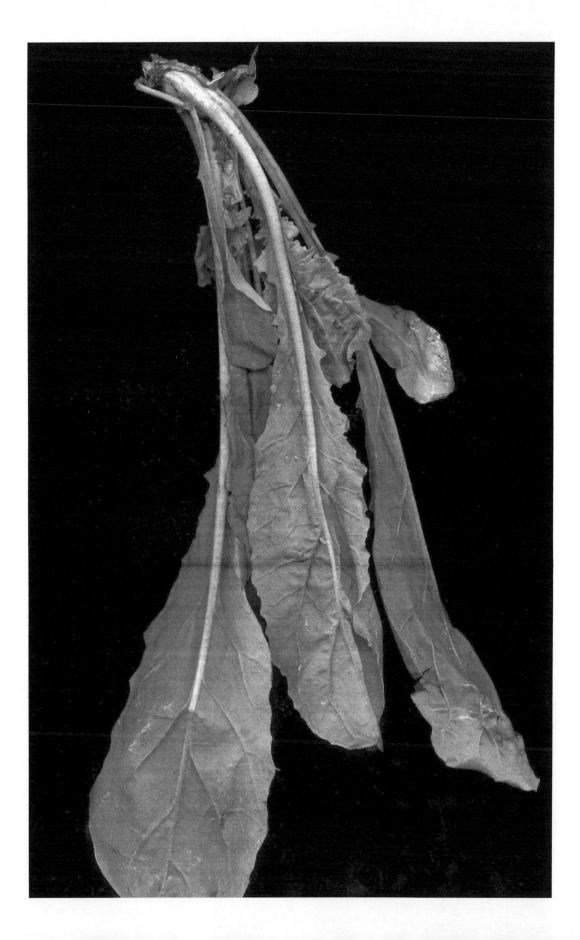

Arugula

Common names: rocket, garden rocket, rocket salad, roquette
World names: zi ma cai (Chinese); roquette (French); Rauke (German); rucola (Italian); roketsuto (Japanese); rúgula (Portuguese); arúgula (Spanish)
Botanical name: *Eruca sativa*
Pronounced eh-ROO-kuh sa-TY-vuh
Family: Mustard or cabbage family—*Brassicaceae (Cruciferae)*

ABOUT
Type of plant: Annual, cool season
Origin: Southern Europe and Western Asia. Arugula was used by the ancient Romans.
Description: Forms a rosette of deeply lobed blue-green leaves 1–4 inches (2.5–10 cm) long, similar to small mustard leaves. Leaves and flowers resemble those of the radish or turnip. Plant becomes erect when heat triggers bolting.
Height: 12–24 inches (30–60 cm)
Breadth: 6–12 inches (15–30 cm)
Bloom time and flowers: Late spring to late summer; flower stalks with sprays of white flowers
Edible parts: Leaves, flowers

KITCHEN
Serve: Arugula leaves can be eaten raw or cooked. Use arugula as a seasoning in broths, salads, mayonnaise, sandwiches, potato salads, and pasta. Arugula flowers are edible and can be used to garnish salads.

BASICS
Seed planting depth: ¼ inch (6 mm)
Germination soil temperature: 40–55°F (4–13°C)
Days to germination: 5–7
Sowing indoors: Late fall to early spring
Sowing outdoors: As soon as the soil can be worked in spring
Days to maturity: 40 days; thinnings may be harvested in three weeks.
Soil pH range: 6.0–7.0
Growing soil temperature: 50–65°F (10–18°C)

ARUGULA

Spacing of plants: Direct seed in 2–4 inches (5–10 cm) wide band, about 30 seeds per 12 inches (30 cm) for salad mix. When seedlings are 3 inches (7.5 cm) tall, thin to 6 inches (15 cm) apart. Can also be broadcast with other greens.
Water: Moderate and even
Light: Full sun as well as half-day sun or partial shade. Avoid hot, dry positions.
Nutrients: Low nitrogen, phosphorus and potassium
Rotating crops: Avoid following plants of the cabbage family.
Companion crops: Can be followed by or preceded by other vegetables and also is a good intercropping choice.
Incompatible crops: Pole beans, strawberries
Propagation: Seed
Seed viability: 5 years
Seed weight: 15,000 seeds per ounce (530 seeds per gram)

SITE

Best climate: Zones 3–6 in spring and autumn. In milder climates, grow as a winter vegetable.
Frost tolerance: Will tolerate frost
Soil preparation: Humus-rich, moist soil. Work finished compost into the top 3 inches (7.5 cm) of the bed.

PLANTING

Sow seed ¼ inch (6 mm) deep.
Spring planting time: Direct seed in spring as soon as the soil can be worked. Seed germinates quickly in cold soil. Light frost will not harm the seedlings. Growing in warm temperatures causes leaves to be bitter and pungent.
Autumn planting time: Sow last crop 30 days before the first-frost date.
Reverse season planting: Plant in late autumn in the subtropics.
Winter planting: Will bear through the winter in a coldframe or unheated greenhouse.
Planting time in cold-winter regions: Sow seed indoors and set out as soon as ground can be worked.
Succession planting: Follow early spring crop every 2–3 weeks for a continuous harvest. Continue planting until about a month before the average first frost date.
Intercropping and relay cropping: This fast growing plant is suited for intercropping and relay planting.

GROWING

Water: Keep soil moist
Nutrients: Nitrogen, phosphorus, and potassium needs are low

CARE

Care: If temperatures rise, shade plants to avoid bolting.

Common problems: Don't plant arugula too late in spring; it will bolt in warm weather before reaching harvestable size. Direct-seed or set out seedlings one to two months before the first autumn frost to avoid bolting.

Pests: Flea beetles. Cover plants with floating row covers. Use yellow sticky traps to help control pests.

Diseases: Rarely bothered by diseases.

HARVEST

Arugula is ready for harvest 40 days after sowing. Pick young, tender leaves when they are 2–3 inches (5–7.5 cm) long. Pick large leaves from the bottom of plant. Clip individual leaves for cut-and-come-again harvest. New leaves will sprout from the center crown. Harvest whole plants by pulling out plants or cutting the whole plant just above the root. Older, larger leaves will have a sharp taste.

Storage: Use arugula fresh for best taste.

VARIETIES

Choose from these arugula varieties: 'Astro' and 'Runway' are early arugula varieties and very good growers. Also try 'Rocket' and 'Italian Wild Rustic'.

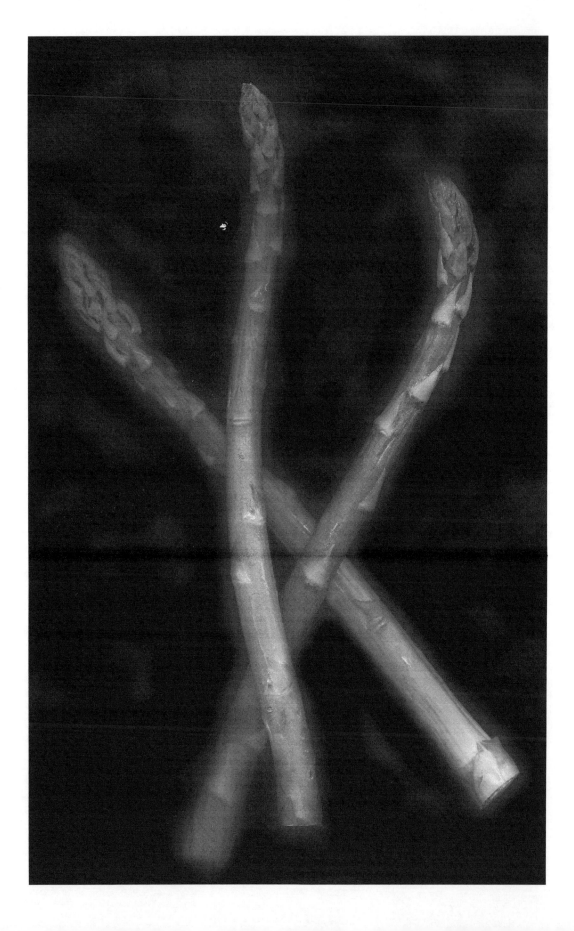

Asparagus

Common name: Asparagus

World names: long xu cài, lu san (Chinese); asperge (French); Spargel (German); asparago (Italian); asuparagasu (Japanese); espargo (Portuguese); espárrago (Spanish)

Botanical name: *Asparagus officinalis*

Pronounced uh-SPAIR-uh-gus oh-FISH-ih-nal-is

Family: *Asparagaceae (Liliaceae)*

ABOUT

Type of plant: Perennial. Asparagus is one of the earliest crops in spring.

Origin: Eastern Mediterranean. The asparagus has been grown for harvest from the time of the ancient Greeks.

Description: Tiny, fern-like leaves on tall fern-like fronds emerging from an underground rhizome or "crown." Female plant has red berries.

Height: 36–60 inches (90–152 cm)

Spread: 24–48 inches (60–122 cm)

Root depth: Up to 6 feet (1.8 m) horizontally, 6–8 feet (1.8–2.4 m) deep

Bloom time and flower: Summer. Insignificant white to green flowers. Older asparagus varieties, such as 'Mary Washington', have male and female flowers on separate plants. The male flower is larger and longer than the female.

Edible parts: Young, tender, green shoots, called spears. Spears are young leaf stalks that grow from roots.

KITCHEN

Serve: Asparagus can be eaten raw, parboiled, steamed, boiled, baked, roasted, and grilled.

BASICS

Seed planting depth: ¼–½ inch (6–13 mm)

Germination soil temperature: 77°F (25°C)

Days to germination: 14–18

Sow indoors: 8 weeks before last frost

Plant outdoors: 3 weeks before last frost

Time to maturity: Third year after planting

Soil pH range: 6.5–7.0

Growing soil temperature: 60–70°F (16–24°C)

Spacing of plants: 12–18 inches (30–45 cm) apart in all directions

Water: Heavy

Light: 8 hours per day is best; will accept 4–8 hours

Nutrients: Heavy feeder

Rotating crops: Avoid following onion family plants.

Companion crops: Tomatoes, parsley, and basil

Incompatible crops: Root vegetables such as carrots, onions, chives, garlic, leeks, or potatoes

Propagation: Division or separation of dormant roots called crowns. Divide plants in late winter or early spring. Seed: pre-soak seed for 24 to 48 hours before sowing.

Seed viability: 3 years

Seeds weight: 1,400 per seeds ounce (47 per gram)

SITE

Asparagus is a perennial. Plant it where it can produce undisturbed for 15 to 20 years. Place the asparagus bed where it will not be shaded by taller plants or buildings. An asparagus bed should have deep, loose, well-drained soil high in organic matter, that is fertilized with compost or aged manure. In heavy soil, plant asparagus in a raised bed to improve drainage. Lay crowns at ground level, rather than in trenches, and mound soil over them.

Greenhouse or container growing: Asparagus requires a cold period to induce dormancy. It is difficult to provide appropriate conditions in a greenhouse or container.

PLANTING

Sowing seed:

- Soak seed for 48 hours at 85–90°F (31°C) before sowing.
- Indoors: Sow seeds in flats ¼ to ½ inch (6–13 mm) deep; transplant when one year old.
- Transplant by digging a trench 12 inches (30 cm) or more wide and deep and add organic matter until the trench is about 8 inches (20 cm) deep.
- Direct seeding: seeds are drilled 1–2 inches (2.5–5 cm) deep in a trench 6–8 inches (15–20 cm) below ground level.

Planting crowns:

- Plant in trenches 8–10 inches (20–25 cm) deep and 12 inches (30 cm) or more wide. Space crowns 8 inches (20 cm) apart for slender spears to 14 inches (36 cm) apart for thick spears. Trenches should be 4–6 feet (1.2–1.8 m) apart. Place loose, manure-enriched soil at the bottom of the trench. Situate crowns and then cover them with 2 inches (5 cm) of soil. After the shoots emerge in spring and begin to grow, gradually fill in the remainder of the trench with soil, but never fully cover the growing tips. Fertilize with abundant compost.

GROWING

Water needs: Asparagus require heavy watering during the growing season. Soak the roots whenever the soil begins to dry out, but avoid over-watering as plants can not tolerate water-logged soils. Do not water during the winter.

Mulch: Use straw, hay, or leaf mulch over the winter and remove in spring. Use compost or leaf mulch during the growing season through mid-summer. Mulch will help to control weeds and keep the soil from drying out.

Nutrients: Heavy feeder. Apply 8 inches (20 cm) or more of rich compost or rotted manure in the spring before the spears begin to emerge. Regular applications of compost or well-rotted manure will provide plants with a steady source of nutrients. Apply a balanced organic fertilizer every two years once the plants are established. After harvest, fertilize with fish emulsion.

CARE

- Add rich compost or well-rotted manure to beds before spears emerge in the spring and then again after the last harvest, or dig in well-rotted manure alongside the rows during the growing season.
- Keep asparagus beds free of weeds. Weeds compete for nutrients, water, and light.
- Cut back ferns to 1 inch (2.5 cm) in autumn after the fronds have died back naturally; before the fronds turn brown, they are feeding the roots.
- Weed out volunteer plants from older variety females that set seed. Asparagus does not like competition, even from its own kind.
- In severe winter climates, mulch with organic matter.
- Heavy hay, straw or leaf mulch may be applied in mid-summer to control weeds, conserve water, and moderate soil temperature.
- If bud-forming tops are allowed to go to seed, the buds will sprout feathery, fern-like foliage.
- Clear debris from asparagus beds in autumn so that asparagus beetles can not over winter there. Exclude beetles in the spring by knocking them off of plants and excluding them with row covers.
- When plants turn brown in late autumn, cut the stems to the ground. Add a blanket of well-rotted manure or compost as asparagus is a heavy feeder. Then protect the plants through the winter with heavy hay or straw mulch. In the spring, pull the mulch away. If you don't cut dead stalks away let them stand in place until spring.

Pests: Aphids, spotted asparagus beetles, asparagus miners, spotted cucumber beetles, Japanese beetles, slugs, snails, spider mites.
- When the stems turn brown in early winter, cut them off at ground level. This will remove the asparagus beetles' over-wintering habitat. You can reduce the damage from over wintering asparagus beetles by burning or hot-composting old asparagus foliage and also by cultivating asparagus beds shallowly before applying mulch in the autumn. Lightly cultivate the beds again in spring before the plants begin to grow.
- Use row covers to exclude beetles or handpick and destroy. Spray away aphids with a stream of water. Handpick slugs and snails.

Diseases: Asparagus rust
- Rust: avoid planting asparagus in low-lying areas where there is heavy dew and morning fog. Use rust-resistant cultivars. Dispose of or hot-compost old or infected foliage. Discard the soil immediately surrounding the plant or soil clinging to the roots.
- Reduce disease by removing asparagus ferns in late autumn at the first sign of frost.

HARVEST

Do not harvest asparagus spears the first year. Allow the plants to develop a strong root system. Grown from seed, the first crop will come during the third year. Some cultivars may be picked sparingly for 1–2 weeks in the second year. Started from one-year-old roots, the first crop will come in the second year.

Harvest mid to late spring 2–3 years after planting seed. The first harvest (from 2-year-old plants) is very short, just 3 to 4 weeks. Harvest in third year is longer, as long as 6–10 weeks.
- When spears are ¼ – ¾ inch (6–19mm) in diameter and about 5–8 inches (13–20 cm) long, snap off tender young shoots at the base. Harvest daily before the stems toughen and the scales at the tips begin to open. Snap stalks instead of cutting them. This will limit the spread of fusarium by contaminated knives.
- Stop the harvest when the stalks start coming up pencil-thin, less than ½ inch (13 mm) in diameter. Then allow the shoots to grow for the rest of the season forming a bushy plant 5–8 feet (1.5–2.4 m) high. Trim the plant back to the ground in autumn. If you harvest all of the spears, you risk killing the plant.

Autumn harvest: When spears emerge in the spring, harvest only half of the bed. Allow the other half to leaf out. When the plant reaches full size cut it back to the ground. A second harvest of spears will emerge in autumn.

Blanching: Hill soil over spears or grow under opaque buckets or row covers.

VARIETIES

Choose from these asparagus varieties: 'Martha Washington' and 'Mary Washington' are traditional open-pollinated asparagus types; all-male varieties which produce larger spears include: 'Jersey Giant', 'Jersey Knight' and 'Greenwich'; in mild winter regions, grow 'UC157'.

Basil

Common name: Basil, sweet basil, St. Josephwort
World names: luo le, yu xiang cai (Chinese); basilic (French); Basilikum (German); babui tulsi (Hindi); basilico (Italian); bajiru (Japanese); kemangi, selaseh (Malay) alfavaca (Portuguese); albahaca (Spanish); horapha (Thai)
Botanical name: *Ocimum basilicum, Ocimum cispum, Ocimum minimum*
Pronounced OS-i-mum ba-SIL-i-kum
Family: Mint family—*Lamiaceae* (*Labiatae*)

ABOUT

Type of plant: Annual, warm season
Origin: Africa, tropical and subtropical Asia, India, Middle East, Central America; cultivation dates to early history.
Description: Shiny succulent with toothed, pointed oval, bright green or purple leaves 2–3 inches (5–7.5 cm) long on bushy stems. Leaves have a fresh, strong, clove-like scent. There are at least 30 varieties of basil.
Form: Upright
Height: 12–24 inches (30–60 cm)
Breadth: 8–18 inches (20–45 cm)
Root depth: 8–12 inches (20–30 cm)
Bloom time and flowers: Mid to late summer. Green-leaved varieties have small, scented, whitish blooms, in circular clusters of six on green spikes. Purple-leafed varieties have pink-purple flowers.
Edible parts: Leaves

KITCHEN

Serve: Use basil fresh or dried to add a mild, sweet flavor to soups, salads, stews, fish, meat, sauces, and eggs. Use basil fresh with ripe tomatoes adding a little oil and lemon juice.

BASICS

Seed planting depth: ⅛ inch (3 mm)
Germination soil temperature: 70–85°F (21–29°C)
Days to germination: 7–14
Sow indoors: 4–6 weeks before last frost
Sow outdoors: Spring to late summer

Days to maturity: 50–60 after direct seeding; 30 after transplanting
Soil pH range: 6.0–6.5
Growing soil temperature: 75–85°F (24–29°C)
Spacing of plants: 10–12 inches (25–30 cm) apart after thinning
Water: Light and even
Light: Full sun
Nutrients: Low nitrogen, phosphorus, and potassium
Rotating crops: Avoid rotating with marjoram or oregano.
Companion crops: Plant basil near tomatoes and peppers to enhance their growth.
Incompatible crops: Cucumber, rue, snap beans. Basil is said to lower cabbage yields and cause a higher incidence of whiteflies in snap beans.
Seed viability: 5 years; store in an airtight container in cool, dark place
Seed weight: 22,400 seeds per ounce (790 per gram)

SITE

Sow basil seed at a depth of ⅛ inch (3 mm).
Best climate: Zones 4–10. This plant thrives on heat and full sun.
Frost tolerance: Tender
Light: Full sun
Soil preparation: Loose, humus-rich, moist, well-drained soil
Container growing: Basil grows easily in containers.

PLANTING

Spring planting time: Indoors: Sow seed 2–3 weeks before the last expected frost. Transplant the seedlings outside 2–4 weeks after the last frost.
- Outdoors: Sow seed 1–3 weeks after danger of frost has passed. Plants started in the spring that are pinched back regularly will thrive all season.

Autumn planting time: Plant 80 days before the first expected frost.
Succession planting: Every two weeks to ensure a steady supply of leaves

GROWING

Water: Keep the soil moist for quick growth. Mulch with compost to retain soil moisture.
Nutrients: Spray plants with liquid seaweed extract two or three times during the growing season.

CARE

Water at midday, not in the evening. Pinch out flower stems as they form. Plants stop producing new growth when flowering begins.
Pruning or pinching: Keep plants pinched back for full growth. Prune or pinch back basil before it flowers. Cut the main stem from the top leaving at least one node with two

young shoots. Pinch off blossoms as they appear. Flowering will affect leaf growth and the oil content of the leaves. Pinching may be required every 2 or 3 weeks.

Pests: Japanese beetles, slugs, snails. Exclude beetles with row covers or hand pick and destroy. Hand pick slugs and snails.

Diseases: Botrytis rot (gray mold), damping-off, fusarium wilt. Use a commercial fungicide containing baking soda against botrytis. Ensure good soil drainage to counter damping-off and fusarium wilt. Remove and destroy infected plants.

HARVEST

Basil is ready for harvest 50–60 days after seeding. Harvest leaves every week during the summer. Pick leaves when young for best flavor. Cut leaves just above a leaf node. Harvest basil in the early morning just as the dew evaporates. Harvest the whole plant before the first frost.

Storage: Wash and pat dry. Place leaves in a single layer on a screen in a dry indoor place and dry then for 5 to 7 days. Store in an air-tight container in a cool, dark place.

VARIETIES

Choose from these basil varieties: 'Genovese' is an Italian green variety; 'Dark Opal', 'Red Rubin', 'Purple Ruffles' are purple-leafed varieties.

Beans

Common names: Snap bean, green bean, French bean, wax bean, Romano bean, string bean, stringless bean
- Dry beans: Pinto, white, navy, red kidney. Called dry beans because the mature seeds are generally dried before they are eaten. Dry beans are sometimes called soup beans because they are used in soup.
- Shell beans: also referred to as horticultural bean, French flageolet, French horticultural. Also called borlotto or cranberry bean. Sometimes referred to as "shellies." Some dry beans are good when harvested at the green shelling stage (thus called shell beans) and cooked like green lima beans.

World names: si ji dou, cai dou (Chinese); haricot (French); Gartenbohne, Stangenbohne, Fasiole (German); fagiolo (Italian); ingen mame (Japanese); kachang bunchis (Malay); judia (Spanish)
Botanical name: *Phaseolus vulgaris*
Pronounced fa-ZEE-o-lus vul-GAY-riss
Family: Legume family—*Fabaceae (Leguminosae)*

ABOUT

Type of plant: Annual, tender warm season
Origin: South Mexico, Central America. Beans have been cultivated for more than 7,000 years.
Description: Leaves composed of three leaflets on bush or vine; pods round, flat or curved in shape, 3–8 inches (97–20 cm) long, pencil thickness to about ¾ inch (2 cm) in diameter, colored green, yellow, purple, red or green flecked with purple.
Forms: Pole, bush, intermediate
Height: Pole 8–15 feet (2.4–4.5 m); Bush 10–24 inches (25–60 cm)
Spread: Pole 8–12 inches (20–30 cm); Bush 6–8 inches (15–20 cm)
Root depth: 36–48 inches (90–122 cm)
Bloom time and flower: Summer; pale yellow, lavender or white flowers
Edible parts: Immature seeds and seed pods

KITCHEN

Serve: Eat edible pod snap beans raw or lightly cooked. Use snap beans in casseroles, braises, soups, and quiches. Use fresh shelled beans in soups, stews, salads, and vegetable side dishes. Dried beans can be soaked overnight and served as a vegetable side dish or added to salads, soups, stews, and stir-fries, or used as a main dish.

BASICS

Seed planting depth: 1 inch (2.5 cm) in early spring; 1½–2 inch (3.8–5 cm) in autumn
Germination soil temperature: 60–85°F (18–29°C); optimum 65°F (18°C); maximum of 75°F (24°C). Beans will not germinate properly if planted too deeply or too early in cold, wet ground. (Plant beans when late-leafing trees—oaks, hickories, and pecans—uncurl new spring foliage.)
Day to germination: 4–10
Sow indoors: Not recommended
Sow outdoors: Spring when the soil reaches 60°F (16–18°C)
Growing soil temperature: 70–80°F (21–27°C)
Soil pH range: 6.0–6.8
Days to maturity: Bush: 45–60 days. Pole: 60–85 days
Spacing of plants: Pole: 6 inches (15 cm) apart in all directions; Bush 2–4 inches (5–10 cm) apart in all directions
Planting pole beans: Sow after you have installed a pole or trellis on which they can climb. Sow pole beans 6 inches (15 cm) apart around the pole, later thin to 3 seedlings.
Water: Light, even, and regular water from germination to flowering. More water later after flowering.
Light: Full sun
Nutrients: Low nitrogen, moderate phosphorus and potassium
Rotating crops: Follow a bean crop with a high nitrogen requiring crop such as lettuce, squash, broccoli, Brussels sprouts, cabbage, cauliflower, or collards.
Companion crops:

- Bush beans: carrot, celery, chard, corn (corn rows can be wind breakers for dwarf beans), cucumber, eggplant, peas, potatoes, radish, rosemary, strawberries, and summer savory, but not onions.

- Pole beans: corn, rosemary, summer savory, scarlet runner beans, sunflowers

Incompatible crops: Beets, all brassicas or cabbage family plants, onions
Propagation: Seed
Seed vitality: 3 years
Seed weight: 30–65 seeds per ounce (1–2 per gram)

SITE

Best climate: Growing zones 3–11. Cold climates may require a quick-maturing cultivar.
Frost tolerance: None
Site selection: Consider a raised bed if the soil does not warm quickly in the spring. Colder clay loam soils can delay the emergence of early varieties, particularly white seeded types.

Allow 5–7 days longer for the emergence in cold, wet soils as opposed to sandy loam. Do not choose a site where beans will cast a shadow on other crops.
Soil preparation: Humus-rich, loose, well-drained soil. Add nitrogen-fixing bacteria in gardens that have not been planted with vegetables before.

PLANTING

Sow bean seeds 1 inch (2.5 cm) deep in early spring; 1½–2 inch (3.8–5 cm) deep in autumn. To help prevent disease and speed germination, soak seed in compost tea for 25 minutes before sowing.

Spring planting time: Direct sow 1–2 weeks after the last expected frost when the soil has warmed to at least 60°F (16°C). Do not disturb the roots when transplanting.

- For the quickest harvest, plant bush green or wax variety snap beans after the last frost; the harvest will come all at once in 6 to 8 weeks.

Autumn planting time: 12 weeks before the first expected frost

Planting time in mild-winter and reverse-season climates: Autumn through late winter

Succession planting:

- Bush beans are usually determinate with one week or two period of harvest; plant a new crop every 10 days through mid summer for a continuous harvest.
- Pole beans are usually indeterminate with a continuous harvest over 6–8 weeks when beans are picked every day or two. Pole beans take longer to come to harvest, but the period of harvest also is longer. Make several plantings 3–4 weeks apart, ending 8 weeks before the first expected autumn frost.

Seed color and planting: Do not plant white seeded beans too early; wait until the soil has warmed. White seeds can transmit water too fast which will crack the cotyledons (seed leaves) reducing seed vigor and germination. Black and tan seed are better able to regulate water uptake in cool, wet soils preventing the cracking of cotyledons.

Crop rotation and nitrogen fixation: To aid your garden soil's ability to produce leafy greens, rotate beans with leafy greens from one season to the next. Working with soil-borne bacteria, beans (and certain other legumes such as soybeans and peas) take nitrogen from the air and store it in nodules on their roots. (Nitrogen is an important element needed by plants for growth; but most plants are unable to directly benefit from nitrogen in the atmosphere.) The process of drawing nitrogen from the air and converting it into plant useable soil nitrogen is called nitrogen fixation. Nitrogen fixed in bean root nodules is stored there until it is needed for growth. Beans require nitrogen from the soil for only a few weeks after germination. Shortly after germination, *Rhizobia* bacteria begin to grow in colonies in the root nodules of beans. The bacteria converts nitrogen in the air into soil nitrates which beans then use for continued growth. Importantly, some of that nitrogen is added back into the soil thus restoring soil nitrogen depleted by plantings of lettuce, cabbage, or other leafy greens which are heavy nitrogen users. To encourage nitrogen fixation, bean seeds can be

dampened and then dusted with *Rhizobia* bacteria powder and then planted in warm soil. The use of high nitrogen fertilizers may prevent nitrogen fixation.
Nutrients: Low nitrogen, moderate phosphorus, and potassium. In rich soils, top-dress with compost or bone meal at flowering time. Use low nitrogen compost. Avoid using green manure or fertilizers that are high in nitrogen.
Container growing: Choose bush varieties for containers.
Container size: 8 inches (20 cm) wide, 8–10 inches (20–25 cm) deep

CARE
Water: Beans prefer light, even water. Increase water from flowering to the formation of the first pods. Increase water from the beginning to the end of harvest. Avoid overhead watering.
Care:
- Avoid cultivating too deeply near beans. The root system is shallow and widespread.
- Keep soil moist during flowering and pod formation.
- Mulch beans to prevent weed and cultivation damage and to cut down on watering.
- Provide good air circulation to help prevent blights, mosaic disease, and anthracnose
- Do not cultivate after a rain or too early in the morning when plants are wet. This may cause bean rust, anthracnose, or blight and helps to spread mosaic.
- Till or spade under plant debris in autumn to destroy disease organisms.
- Plant disease resistant varieties when available.
- Remove and destroy infected plants.
- Do not plant beans or other legumes in the same place more than once every 3 years.

Common problems:
- Seeds sown too early in cold or wet soil may rot before germinating.
- Blossoms may drop off if the summer is too hot.
- Mildew can occur where the summer is cool and foggy.

Pests: Aphids, bean leaf beetles, beet and potato leafhoppers, cabbage loopers, corn earworms, cucumber beetles, cutworms, flea beetles, Japanese beetles, leaf-footed bugs, leaf miners, Mexican bean beetles, root-knot nematodes, seed corn maggots, slugs, tarnished plant bugs, thrips, webworms, weevils, whiteflies, wireworms.
- Handpick and destroy beetles, larvae, and egg clusters.
- Row covers help exclude insect pests.
- Ladybugs and lacewings (beneficial insects) eat the eggs of beetles.
- Use rotenone (1% solution), pyrethrins, or neem to control Mexican bean beetles.

Diseases: Anthracnose, bacterial blight, bacterial wilt, bean rust, common mosaic, curly top, downy mildew, fusarium root rot, seed rot, crown rot (Southern blight), white mold, and yellow mosaic.
- Provide good air circulation to help prevent blights, mosaic disease, and anthracnose.
- Do not cultivate after a rain or too early in the morning when plants are wet. This may

cause bean rust, anthracnose, or blight and helps to spread mosaic.
- Till or spade under plant debris in autumn to destroy disease organisms.
- Plant disease resistant varieties when available.
- Remove and destroy infected plants.
- Do not plant beans or other legumes in the same place more than once every 3 years.

HARVEST
- **Snap beans:** Pick snap beans when they are pencil size in diameter before they begin to bulge. Daily harvesting will encourage extended production of new flowers and of new pods.
- **Shell beans:** At 30–40 days from seeding, pods of shell beans will be flat, not plump. Pick slender, immature pods green. Beans for shelling reach their best flavor before they begin to dry. (Fully mature pods will become slightly lumpy and change from a green pod to red, cream, and yellow streaked. These beans can then be used as dry beans.) Slender-podded French filet beans produce light crops. Filet beans should be picked daily to ensure tender pods and good flavor. Complete the harvest of shell beans within three days in hot weather and five days in cool weather to ensure that they do not become oversized or tough.
- **Dry beans:** Harvest late summer until first frost. Beans should remain on the bush until leaves have withered and fallen and the pods turn dry or begin to shatter. Pick pods or pull out the plants when pods are completely dry. Fully dry pods will split open naturally to reveal the dried beans. To test if dry beans are ready for harvest, bite a couple of seeds; if they hardly dent they are dry and ready to harvest. In moist climates or where weather is rainy, pick pods as soon as they begin to wither.

Threshing methods for dry beans:
- Shell pods individually.
- Hold several plants by the roots then knock back and forth inside a barrel or dry, clean trash can.
- Place dry plants in a closed bag then step on and off the bag.
- Use a threshing machine.

Storage:
- **Snap beans:** Store in the vegetable compartment of the refrigerator for 1–1½ weeks, or blanched and frozen for up to 3 months. Do not wash beans until you are ready to cook them. Freeze, can, dry, or pickle beans.
- **Shell beans:** Use fresh; not recommended for freezing or canning. Shell beans must be picked regularly when pods are young to avoid toughness.
- **Dry beans:** Unshelled beans can be kept up to one week in the refrigerator. Dried shelled beans can be stored in a cool, dry place for 10–12 months. Store dry beans in fabric bags

with good air circulation, not in plastic or glass containers. If there is any sign of weevils (small holes in beans), put beans in a jar or heavy bag and place the container in the freezer for a few hours.

VARIETIES
Choose from these bean types and varieties:

Snap beans: 'Blue Lake' and 'Kentucky Wonder' are classic bush or pole varieties. 'Emerite' is a French filet pole bean. 'Romano' is a bush or pole Italian green bean.
Shell beans: 'Borlotto' has a red and cream pod. 'Chevrier' is a French flageolet bean. 'French Horticulture' is a classic shell bean.
Dried beans: 'Great Northern White' is a classic shellie. 'Jacob's Cattle' is a white bean splashed with maroon, and 'Vermont Cranberry' is a red bean speckled with brown.
Lima bean: 'Fordhook 242', 'Henderson bush' are bush limas; 'King of the Garden' is a pole lima.
Fava bean: 'Broad Windsor' is a classic fava bean. 'Aguadulce', 'Con Amore', 'Loretta'. 'Sweet Lorraine', 'Windsor Long Pod'.
Chickpea: 'Chickpea', 'Garbanzo', 'Gram', 'Kabuli Black'.
Soybean: 'Early Hakucho' and 'Envy' are green-seeded soybeans.

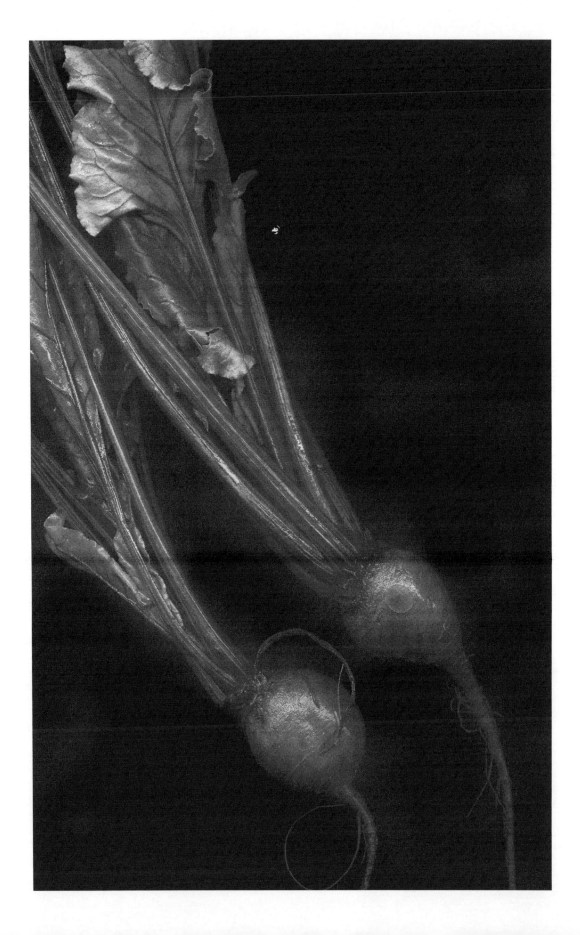

Beets and Beet Greens

Common name: Beet, beetroot
World names: tian cai (Chinese); betterave (French); Rote Bete, Rote Rübe (German); barbabietola rossa (Italian); biitsu (Japanese); beterraba (Portuguese); remolacha (Spanish)
Botanical name: *Beta vulgaris* var. *esculenta*
Pronounced BAY-tuh vul-GAY-riss
Family: Beet family—*Chenopodiaceae*

ABOUT

Type of plant: Biennial grown as an annual, cool season
Origin: Southern Europe, North Africa. The ancient Romans ate beets. Beets became a popular garden crop in the sixteenth century.
Description: Thick bulb-shaped roots either round or cylindrical as large as 4–10 inches (10–25 cm) in diameter, best when 1–3 inches (2.5–7.5 cm) in diameter. Leaves grow from the crown on short stems to 15 inches (38 cm) high. Second year growth of fruiting stem is 24–48 inches (60–122 cm) high. Root flesh can be gold, yellow, white or concentric pink and white stripes.
Height: 6–12 inches (15–30 cm)
Spread: 4–8 inches (10–20 cm)
Root depth: 24–60 inches (60–122 cm)
Bloom time and flower: Beets usually produce an enlarged root the first season and a flower stalks the second year after over-wintering.
Edible parts: Roots; leaf tops (greens)

KITCHEN

Serve: Beets can be eaten raw or cooked. Beet greens and thinnings can be eaten raw in salads. Beet greens can be cooked much like spinach.

BASICS

Seed planting depth: ¼–½ inches (6–13mm)
Germination soil temperature: 55–80°F (13–27°C). Will germinate in temperatures as low as 50°F (10°C) and as high as 90°F (32°C).
Days to germination: 4–10 at 45–70°F (7–21°C) soil temperature
Sowing indoors: 5 weeks before last frost
Sowing outdoors: 2–4 weeks before last frost

Days to maturity: 49-91
Soil pH range: 6.5-7.5
Growing soil temperature: 65-75°F (18-24°C)
Spacing of plants: 2-4 inches (5-10 cm) apart in all directions; thin seedlings when they have 3-4 leaves and are 4-6 inches (10-15 cm) tall.
Nutrients: Moderate feeder with low nitrogen requirement
Rotating crops: Avoid following spinach or Swiss chard.
Companion crops: bush bean, cabbage family, corn, leek, lettuce, lima bean, onion, radish
Incompatible crops: mustard, pole bean
Propagation: Seed. Soak seed in tepid water for 2-3 hours before sowing to encourage germination.
Seed vitality: 4 years
Seeds weight: 2,000 seeds per ounce (67 per gram)

SITE

Beets grow in all climate zones but best in growth zones 5-10. Where summers are hot (growing zones 8 and warmer), grow beets as an autumn, late winter, and early spring crop. Cool weather produces the best flesh color. Weather fluctuations will cause "zoning" or white rings in the roots. Beets grown in warm weather are lighter colored and have less sugar.
Frost tolerance: Hardy, will withstand some short-term sub-freezing temperatures
Soil preparation: Beets prefer light, loamy, well-drained soil free of clods and stones and high in organic matter. Mix well-rotted manure and compost as deep as 9 inches (23 cm). Stone free soil will allow for uniform development of roots.
Container growing: Choose a container at least 6-12 inches (15-20 cm) wide and deep.

PLANTING

Sow seed ¼-½ inches (6-13mm) deep. Soak seed in tepid water for two or three hours before sowing to encourage germination.
Spring planting time: Sow early crops under cover.
- **Indoors in early spring:** Sow indoors 5-6 weeks before transplanting.
- **Outdoors:** Direct seed 2-4 weeks before the last expected frost when the soil has warmed to at least 45°F (7°C) and become workable.

Autumn planting time: 8-10 weeks before the first expected frost
Planting time in reverse-season climates: Plant year-round avoiding hot summer months.
Succession planting: Plant beets every 2-3 weeks until midsummer or until daily temperatures reach 80°F (27°C). (Plants will become too tough or stringy if sown mid-summer or later.) Resume planting 8-10 weeks before the first frost for late-autumn or winter harvest. Crops will be slow to mature when days grow shorter. In mild-winter areas,

successive plantings can be made year-round. In reverse-season climates, plant in autumn after daily temperatures has fallen below 80°F (27°C).

GROWING

Water: Keep soil evenly moist to prevent wilting and interior discoloring. Water over head to keep both tops and roots crisp. Tough beets are caused by insufficient or irregular watering.

Nutrients: Heavy feeder. A humus-rich soil will need no amendments during the season.

Side dressing: When seedlings are 3–4 inches (7.5–10 cm) tall give them a light feeding with fish emulsion. Or apply blood and bone meal or cottonseed meal in a band parallel to the crop rows about 2 inches (5 cm) from the seedlings.

CARE

- Weed and cultivate when soil begins to dry. Weed competition will interfere with water uptake.
- Watch for boring pests, especially when plants reach maturity.
- To produce bright red beets, sprinkle the growing bed lightly with Epsom salts, a spoonful per foot (28 cm).
- The seed of some beet varieties may contain a cluster or ball of 2–6 seeds; so seedlings must be thinned early. Cultivars that produce single or mono-germ seed need little or no thinning.

Pests: Beet leafhoppers, beet webworms, carrot weevils, potato flea beetles, spinach flea beetles, spinach leafminers.

- Leaf miners leave irregular gray streaks on the undersides of the leaves. Look for tiny oblong eggs, which are white and yellow and are laid in straight rows on the undersides of leaves. Pick off infested leaves and stems.
- Floating row covers or cheesecloth placed early in the season will discourage insects.

Disease: Leaf spot, scab, yellows

- Discourage leaf spot by not growing beets where they or their relatives, such as spinach and chard, have been grown in the previous year. Avoid wetting foliage and crowding plants. Thin plants to allow air circulation.
- Scab: raised brown rough spots on mature roots—can occur after prolonged hot, dry periods. Irrigate regularly and check the soil for a deficiency of the nutrient boron.
- Control aphids to avoid the spread of yellows (leaves yellow starting at tips and margins).

HARVEST

Pull beetroots 7–13 weeks after sowing. Roots are best tasting when bulbs are 1–3 inches (2.5–7.5 cm) in diameter. Carefully pull up or fork to lift the entire plant then rinse thoroughly to remove soil and then dry. Twist off green tops leaving 2 inches (5 cm) of

stem above shoulder to avoid "bleeding" or loss of interior juice. Late summer sowings can be left in the ground until the first light frost. In warm climates, some beets may be left in the garden to over-winter.
- Beet greens: Seedlings can be harvested when they are 4–5 inches (10–13 cm) tall. Greens taste best when they are young and tender.

Storage: Store beets in a plastic bag in the refrigerator for one to three weeks. Store roots in moist sand or damp sawdust at 32° (0°C) at 95% humidity for up to 3 months. Also preserve by canning or pickling for storage up to 1 year. Beets can over winter in the ground in warm climates.

VARIETIES

Choose from these beet types and varieties: round red beet favorites are 'Detroit Dark Red', and 'Crosby's Egyptian'; main-crop beets include 'Red Ace', and 'Scarlet Supreme'; miniature beets include 'Kleine Bol' ('Little Ball'), and 'Gladiator'; specialty beets include 'Chioggia', an heirloom with pink and white rings; 'Forono' has long deep purple roots; 'Golden Beet' has yellow flesh. For beet greens try 'Big Top'. Try 'Lutz Green Leaf' for winter beet greens.

Broccoli

Common name: broccoli, spouting broccoli, Italian broccoli, calabrese, brocks
World names: yang hua ye cai, kai-lan-fa (Chinese); chou brocoli, brocoli (French); Brokkoli (German); cavolo broccolo (Italian); bróculos (Portuguese); brócoli, bróculi (Spanish)
Botanical name: *Brassica oleracea* var. *italica*
Pronounced BRASS-ih-kuh oh-leh-RAY-see-uh ih-TAL-ih-kuh
Family: Mustard family or cabbage—*Brassicaceae (Cruciferae)*

ABOUT

Type of plant: Biennial grown as an annual, hardy cool season
Origin: Eastern shores of the Mediterranean and in Italy and from there broccoli spread to the rest of Europe. The ancient Romans developed broccoli from wild cabbage.
Description: Branching form with broad leaves and a thick stalk. Tight clusters of tiny blue-green flower buds grow at the stalk ends and are referred to as "heads." There are early, midseason, and late varieties.
Height: 18–24 inches (45–60 cm) with central stalk to 36 inches (90 cm) tall and 6 inches (15 cm) wide
Breadth: 15 inches (38 cm)
Root depth: 18–36 inches (45–90 cm)
Bloom time and flower: Spring; yellow flowers on green, purple, or white stalks
Edible parts: Flower buds, stems, leaves

KITCHEN

Serve: Broccoli can be served raw as an appetizer with a dressing or cut up on a salad. Cooked broccoli is good warm or cold when still slightly firm or crunchy.

BASICS

Seed planting depth: ¼–½ inch (6–13 mm)
Germination soil temperature: 50–85°F (10–29°C); optimum temperature 77°F (25°C)
Days to germination: 7–10
Sow indoors: 6–8 weeks before last frost
Sow outdoors: Early summer for fall crop
Days to maturity: 78–98
Soil pH range: 6.0–6.8

Growing soil temperature: 65–75°F (18–24°C)
Spacing of plants: 14–18 inches (35–45 cm) apart in all directions
Water: Roots should not dry out during the summer. Do not over water.
Light: Full sun; tolerates partial shade
Nutrients: Heavy feeder; avoid excessive nitrogen
Rotating crops: Avoid following cabbage family plants
Companion crops: Artichoke, bush beans, beets, carrots, celery, chard, cucumbers, herbs, lettuce, mint, nasturtium, onion family, oregano, peas, potatoes, rosemary, sage, spinach, tomatoes
Incompatible crops: Pole lima and snap beans, strawberries
Propagation: Seed
Seed vitality: 3 years
Seeds weight: 8,000 per ounce (282 per gram)

SITE

Broccoli grows best in growth zones 3–11. Plant spring and autumn crops where the weather in those seasons is cool. Grow as a winter crop in mild-winter climates. Broccoli is best when it matures in cool weather with an average mean temperature of 59°F (15°C).
Frost tolerance: Hardy, will withstand some sub-freezing temperatures
Soil preparation: Broccoli prefers humus rich, moist, well-drained soil. Early season crops do best in sandy loam, loam, or silt loam. Change planting location annually to avoid soil nitrogen depletion.
Container planting: Use container 20 inches (51 cm) deep

PLANTING

Sow broccoli seed ¼–½ inch (6–13 mm) deep. Broccoli cultivars are classified as early, midseason, and late. Early varieties are the quickest to mature. Early and midseason varieties require a cold period for flowering. The late or over-wintering varieties do not require cold temperatures for flowering. Broccoli matures quickly so both early and late crops are possible in one growing season.
Spring planting time: Grow broccoli from seed in regions where the season is long enough to grow corn. Broccoli tends to bolt in high temperatures.
Short growing season planting: Transplanting is best in cold or short season climates. Start seedlings indoors 6–10 weeks before the last frost. Sow in flats ¼ inch (6mm) deep, cover lightly. Transplant into 2¼ or 3 inch (6 or 8 cm) containers or place plants 2 inches (5 cm) apart in flats when the plant is 5–6 weeks old or 5 inches (13 cm) tall. Plant seedlings outdoors 2–4 weeks before the last frost. Young plants can withstand a frost but not a hard freeze. Before transplanting small plants are hardened by gradual exposure to lower temperatures for a period of about 10 days. Plants also can be hardened by withholding water.
- Transplanting seedlings to the garden may help avoid irregular germination. Irregular

germination due to soil crusting may result in lack of uniformity of head size. Transplant seedlings into seed beds outdoors in late spring at about the fourth or fifth leaf stage.

Autumn crop planting time: Sow seed 14–17 weeks before the first expected frost. Shade young plants if summers are hot and the average temperatures is more than 85°F (29°C).

Mild-winter planting time: Plant in late summer, autumn, winter, or early spring.

Succession planting: Sow broccoli in succession from spring to early summer for summer and autumn crops. Plant early, midseason, and late-flowering varieties for a year-round harvest. If the summers do not get too hot (average temperature over 85°F/29°C), plant additional broccoli one month after the first planting, otherwise, wait until autumn to plant again. Broccoli tends to bolt in high temperature.

Rotating crops: Avoid following broccoli with cabbage family plants.

GROWING

Nutrients: Broccoli is a heavy feeder. Add compost to the soil before planting. Apply two light applications of blood and bone meal, or liquid fertilizer during the growing season.

Side dressing: When buds begin to form, side-dress the plant with compost, fish emulsion, seaweed, or other liquid fertilizer every 2–3 weeks. Avoid excessive nitrogen.

CARE

Common problems: In warm areas, spring broccoli will bolt at the onset of hot weather. Choose quick-maturing varieties in warm regions. Spring-grown broccoli heads may be smaller than those grown in autumn.

Avoid: Overhead watering.

Pests: Aphids, cabbage loopers, cabbage root maggots, cutworms, diamondback moths, flea beetles, harlequin bugs, imported cabbageworms, mites, root flies, slugs, weevils, whiteflies.

- Cardboard "collars" at the base of plants will deter cutworms.
- Floating row covers placed on the day of planting will deter flea beetles, cabbage worms, and root maggots.
- Spray or dust with Bacillus thuringiensis (Bt) to deter cabbageworms.
- A small planting of Chinese cabbage nearby will draw flea beetles away from broccoli.

Diseases: Black rot, clubroot, damping-off, downy mildew, fusarium wilt, leaf spot, root rot, yellows.

- Use disease resistant varieties and avoid working with plants when they are wet.
- Use clean starting mixes. Clean planting beds at the end of the season to deter soil-borne diseases.
- To help avoid soil-borne diseases, do not plant broccoli or other cabbage-family plants in the same spot more than once every 3 years.
- Deter clubroot by adding lime to raise the soil's pH.

HARVEST

Broccoli will mature 78–98 days after direct seeding and 60–80 days after transplanting. Start harvesting as soon as the first heads form but before flowering; dots of yellow indicate that a shoot is about to flower. Cut the main or central head when it is 3–4 inches (7–10 cm) in diameter and the flower buds are still tight and green, not yellow. Cut side shoots when they are 4 inches (10 cm) long. After the main harvest, harvest secondary side shoots regularly to encourage continued production. Harvest with a knife, cutting the main stem 6 inches (15 cm) below the head.

Storage: Broccoli will keep in the refrigerator crisper section for 10–14 days. Dry thoroughly before refrigeration. Store frozen broccoli (after blanching) for up to three months.

VARIETIES

Spring or early broccoli varieties include 'Early Dividend', 'Early Emerald', 'Early Packman', and 'Green Comet'. Summer broccoli varieties: 'Genji', 'Mariner', 'Saga', and 'Small Miracle'. Autumn or winter varieties: 'Arcadia', 'Marathon', 'Pirate', 'Saga'. 'Romanesco' produces light green heads. 'Spring Raab' is a broccoli raab variety. (Broccoli raab has 6- to 9-inch (15 cm-22 cm) stalks with clusters of tiny broccoli-like buds.)

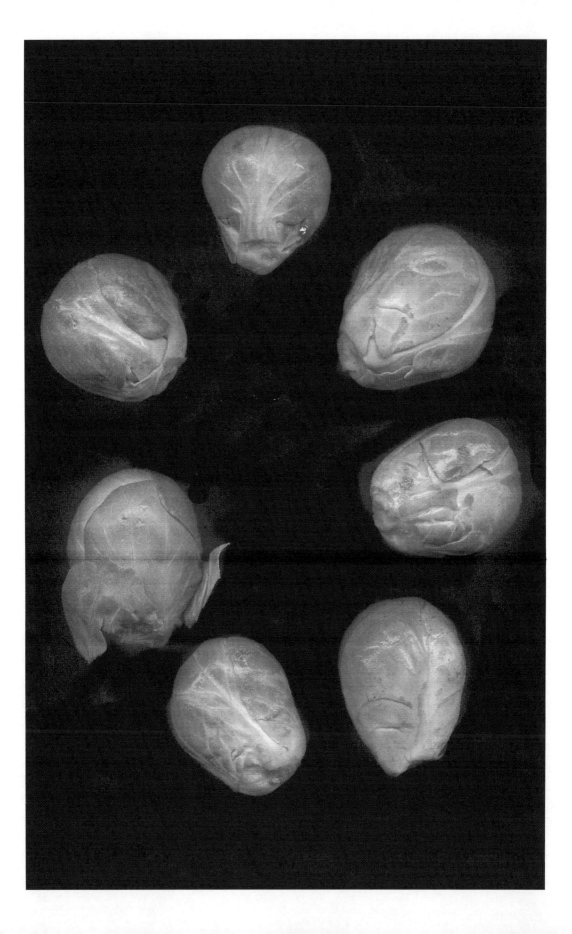

Brussels Sprouts

Common name: Brussels sprouts, sprouts; includes red Brussels sprouts (Rubine)
World names: bao zi gan lai (Chinese); chou de Bruxelles (French); Rosenkohl, Kohlsprossen (German); cavolo di Bruxelles (Italian); couve de Bruxelas (Portuguese); col de Bruselas (Spanish)
Botanical name: *Brassica oleracea* var. *gemmifera*
Pronounced BRASS-ih-kuh oh-leh-RAY-see-uh jem-MIF-er-uh
Family: Mustard family or cabbage—*Brassicaceae (Cruciferae)*

ABOUT
Type of plant: Biennial grown as an annual, cool season
Origin: Europe, Mediterranean. Brussels sprouts are named after the city in Belgium. Brussels sprouts were developed at the beginning of the nineteenth century.
Description: Leggy, thick stalked plant with large, broad leaves. Cabbage-shaped buds called sprouts or heads 1–2 inches (2.5–5 cm) in diameter grow in the axils of the lower leaves. The edible heads form the first season and go to seed during the second season.
Height: 36–48 inches (90–122 cm)
Breadth: 24 inches (60 cm)
Root depth: 18–36 inches (45–90 cm)
Bloom time and flower: Yellow flowers form in the second year
Edible parts: Sprouts (swollen buds)

KITCHEN
Serve: Brussels sprouts are only eaten cooked. Serve Brussels sprouts as a vegetable side dish on their own or with butter or a béchamel sauce. They can also be served au gratin or added to soups, stews, or stir-fries. Brussels sprouts can be puréed with potatoes.

BASICS
Seed planting depth: ¼–½ inch (6–12 mm)
Germination soil temperature: 50–85°F (10–29°C); optimum 70°F (21°C)
Days to germination: 3–10
Sow indoors: 4–6 weeks before last frost
Sow outdoors: Early summer for fall crop in warm areas
Days to maturity: 100–110 days for seeds; 80–90 days for transplants
Soil pH range: 5.5–6.8

BRUSSELS SPROUTS

Growing soil temperature: 60–65F (16–18C)
Space of plants: 2 inches (5cm) apart in each direction; thin seedlings to 12–18 inches (30–45 cm) apart
Water: Regular water; keep soil evenly moist
Light: Full sun
Nutrients: Heavy feeder; mix in compost before planting.
Rotating crops: Avoid following cabbage family plants
Intercropping: Plant with fast-growing crops such as radishes or lettuces.
Companion crops: Artichoke, beets, celery, herbs, onions, peas, spinach and potatoes
Incompatible crops: Kohlrabi, all pole beans, strawberries, tomatoes
Propagation: Seed
Seed viability: 5 years; store in an airtight container in a dark, cool place.
Seed weight: 7,000 seeds per ounce (250 per gram)

SITE

Brussels sprouts grow best in growth zones 4–7; growth zone 8 as a winter vegetable; generally unsuited to warmer regions.
Frost tolerance: Hardy, can take some sub-freezing temperatures. Late winter cultivars can stand minimum temperatures as low as 14°F (-10°C).
Soil preparation: Brussels sprouts prefer moist, humus rich, fertile soil, not overly acidic. Early spring crops do best in rich sandy loam, loam, or silt loam.
Container growing: Choose a container 12 inches (30 cm) wide and 12 inches (30 cm) deep.

PLANTING

Sow Brussels sprouts seeds ¼–½ inch (6–12 mm) deep.
Planting time: Brussels sprouts require a long growing season. They do best when matured in cool weather and are not recommended where summers are long, hot, and dry.

- Sow seed in late spring at least 120 days before the first expected autumn frost. Start seeds indoors if necessary; transplant 4–6 weeks later when plants are 5 inches (13 mm) tall after hardening for 5–6 days. Harden by gradual exposure to lower temperatures or by withholding water. Both methods can be used together.

Planting time in short-season regions: Set out transplants when sowing other spring crops.
Planting time in mild-winter or reverse-season regions: Sow seed in late summer or autumn after late summer heat has ended for winter to spring harvest.
Succession planting: A second planting can be direct sown four months before the first frost date.

GROWING

Brussels sprouts are heavy feeders; mix compost into the soil before planting.

Side dressing: Apply fish emulsion, seaweed, or other liquid fertilizer every 2–3 weeks. Use balanced organic fertilizers as heads begin to form and avoid excessive nitrogen.

CARE
- Water at the base of plants, and keep the soil free of weeds by mulching.
- Use bird netting over the top of plants to stop birds from harvesting the crop.
- Pinch off top leaves to encourage side growth.
- To prevent sprout heavy plants from tipping before harvest, shore up the soil around each plant stem one month after planting.

Pests: Aphids, cabbage loopers, cabbage butterflies, cabbage root maggots, cabbageworms, flea beetles, harlequin bugs, mites, root flies, slugs, thrips, weevils, whiteflies.
- Control cutworms, cabbage loopers, and cabbageworms with Bacillus thuringiensis (Bt).
- Use row covers from planting time to exclude flea beetles, cabbageworms, and root maggots. Small yellow moths flying around Brussels sprouts are the adult form of the cabbage looper and imported cabbageworm. They lay eggs.
- Aphids can be deterred by keeping plants well watered and by spraying them away with a stream of water.

Diseases: Black rot, clubroot, damping off, downy mildew, fusarium wilt, leaf spot, root rot, yellows.
- Rotate with non-cabbage-family crops to avoid soil-borne fungal and viral diseases. Don't plant in the same place more than once every 4 years.
- Plant disease resistant varieties when available.
- Ensure good drainage and avoid constant wet conditions.
- Water from below. Avoid handling plants when they are wet.
- Remove and destroy any infected plants.

HARVEST

Brussels sprouts are ready for harvest 100–110 days after sowing seeds and 80–90 days after putting out transplants. Harvest Brussels sprouts after frost and through mid-winter in most areas and through the winter where the cold is not severe. Pick when sprouts are firm and well formed about 1–1½ inches (25–38 mm) in diameter, usually when big leaves have started to yellow. Break off the leaf below the sprout and then snap off the sprout. Snap off small sprouts from the bottom of the plant first. Leave small sprouts on upper stems until they mature. Remove leaves below the harvest. Upper sprouts continue to form and enlarge as the lower ones are harvested; sprouts mature from the bottom up. There are 50–100 harvestable sprouts per plant.
- To encourage rapid development of upper sprouts, pinch the stalk back at about 20 inches (50 cm). Upper and lower sprouts will mature at about the same time though the yield may be smaller.

- The sweetest flavor comes after a light frost; water the evening before harvesting for mild flavor.
- Young leaves found growing between sprouts may be eaten as greens.

Storage: Refrigerate for 3–4 weeks at 32°F (0°C) at 95–98% relative humidity. Freeze (after blanching) for up to 4 months. Don't wash sprouts until you are ready to use them.

VARIETIES

Choose from these Brussels sprouts varieties: 'Jade Cross Hybrid' and 'Oliver' are heat tolerant; 'Valiant' has excellent flavor; 'Prince Marvel' is a favorite; 'Long Island Improved' and 'Catskill' (a dwarf variety) are good autumn growers.

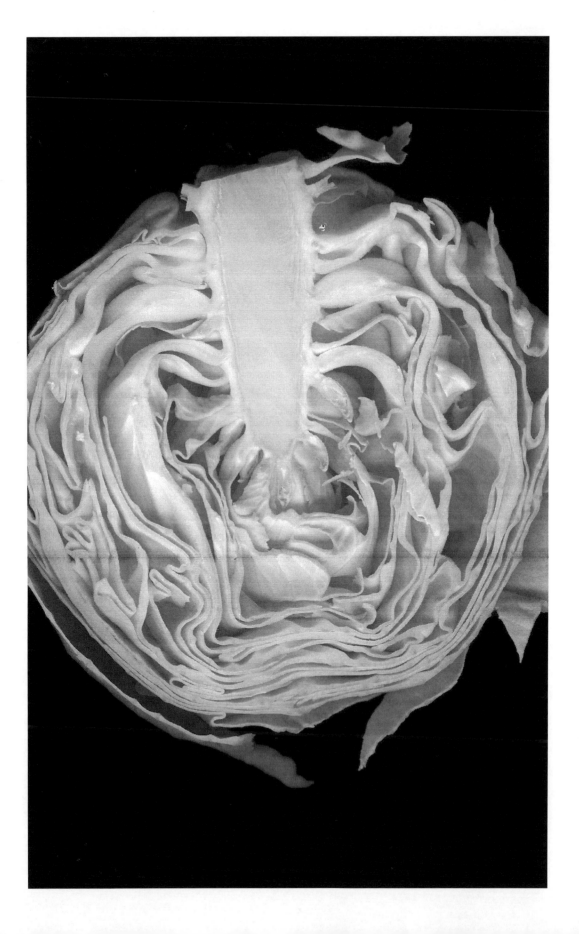

Cabbage

Common name: Cabbage
World names: gan lan, lan cai (Chinese); chou cabas, chou blanc (French); Kopfkohl (German); cavolo cappuccino (Italian); couve de repolho, couve de cabeça (Portuguese); col, repollo, berza camún (Spanish)
Botanical name: *Brassica oleracea* var. *capitata*
Pronounced BRASS-ih-kuh oh-leh-RAY-see-uh kap-ih-TAY-ta
Family: Cabbage or mustard family—*Brassicaceae (Cruciferae)*

ABOUT

Type of plant: Biennial usually grown as an annual, cool season
Origin: Southern Europe, Mediterranean region; in cultivation for more than 4,000 years
Description: Terminal bud or head of curled or ruffled leaves in a variety of colors—green, blue-green, red, purple, or blue. Head shapes vary from round, pointy, and flat. Green-leafed cabbage is the most common. Savoy or crinkle-leafed cabbage is milder in flavor.
Height: 12–15 inches (30–38 cm)
Breadth: 24–42 inches (60–107 cm)
Root depth: As deep as 18–36 inches (45–90 cm) but most of the roots will be found in the upper 12 inches (30 cm)
Bloom time and flower: Blooms in warm weather; flowers are yellow and usually not seen.
Edible parts: Leafy heads, greens

KITCHEN

Serve: Cabbage can be eaten raw or cooked. Raw cabbage can be sliced, shredded or chopped to be used in salads or to make coleslaw. Cooked cabbage can be steamed, braised, sautéed, or stuffed. It can be added to soups, stews, stir-fries, and stuffings.

BASICS

Seed planting depth: ¼ inch (6 mm)
Germination soil temperature: 45–90°F (7–32°C); optimum 70°F (21°C)
Days to germination: 5–10
Sow indoors: 4–6 weeks before last frost
Sow outdoors: 10–12 weeks before first frost for fall crop

CABBAGE

Days to maturity: 70–120 days for seed; early varieties 7–8 weeks from transplant; late varieties 3–4 months from transplant
Soil pH range: 6.5–7.5
Growing soil temperature: 65–75°F (18–24°C)
Spacing of plants: Sow 1 inch (2.5 cm) apart in all directions; thin plants to 15–24 inches (30–60 cm) apart. Wide spacing produces bigger heads.
Water: Heavy from planting to head formation, moderate late in the season.
Light: Full sun; light shade in hot climates
Nutrients: Heavy feeder, high in nitrogen, phosphorus, and potassium.
Rotating crops: Avoid following cabbage family plants (broccoli, cauliflower, Brussels sprouts, kale) for three years.
Intercropping: Use a fast-growing crop like radishes, beets or carrots until midseason.
Companion crops: Beets, catnip, bush beans, carrots, celery, cucumbers, dill, lettuce, mint, nasturtium, onions, potatoes, rosemary, sage, spinach, thyme
Incompatible crops: Pole beans, strawberries, or tomatoes
Propagation: Seed. Soak seed in 122°F (50°C) water for 25 minutes before planting to eliminate soil-borne diseases.
Seed viability: 5 years; store in airtight container in cool, dark place.
Seed weight: 7,000 seeds per ounce (250 per gram)

SITE

Cabbage grows best in growth zones 3–11. Cabbage does best when it matures in cool conditions.
Frost tolerance: Hardy; withstands some sub-freezing temperatures
Soil preparation: Cabbage prefers medium light, fertile, well-drained soil; add compost or rotted manure before planting. Spring plantings do best in lighter, sandier soils. Autumn plantings do best in soil that contains more clay.
Container planting: Use a container 8–10 inches (20–25 cm) wide, 12 inches (30 cm) deep

PLANTING

Soak cabbage seed in 122°F (50°C) water for 25 minutes before planting to eliminate soil-borne diseases.
Planting time in cold-winter climates: Sow cabbage in early spring for early summer harvest or late summer for autumn harvest. Cabbage matures best in cool weather. Sow seed indoors 5–7 weeks before the last frost. Transplant seedlings to the garden after 4–5 weeks when they are 4–6 inches (10–15 cm) tall, but first harden them off for 5–7 days in a coldframe. Or direct sow cabbage in the garden between 4–6 weeks before the last expected frost and up to 2–3 weeks after the last frost. Use floating row covers to protect the start of early crops.

Planting time in mild-winter climates: Sow in autumn, winter, and spring. Seed may be sown in late summer for a winter or spring harvest.

Planting time in reverse-season climates: Plant in autumn after the summer heat has passed. Continue to plant throughout the winter. Avoid plantings that will mature in hot, dry weather.

Early spring planting: Choose a fast-maturing early or midseason variety and start the seeds indoors.

Starting seed indoors: Sow in flats or cell packs, two or three seeds per inch (2.5 cm). Grow in the greenhouse or under fluorescent light illuminated 14–16 hours a day. Thin seedlings to one plant per inch (2.5 cm). For an autumn harvest, direct sow 13–14 weeks before the first expected frost.

Autumn harvest sowing: Start longer maturing varieties in midsummer or later to mature in autumn.

Succession plantings: Plant transplants 2 months after the first planting and then again in late summer to get three harvests of cabbage in one growing season.

GROWING

Water: Cabbage requires heavy water from planting to head formation, moderate water late in the season. Do not let cabbage wilt. Uneven water, such as a heavy watering after a dry period, may cause stunted or cracked heads. Avoid overhead watering to control diseases. Water at the base of plants and keep the soil moist, and mulch to keep the soil moist and cool.

Splitting: Early varieties may split or bust at maturity from rapid growth as a result of heavy irrigation following a dry spell.

Nutrients: Heavy feeder, high in nitrogen, phosphorus, and potassium. When plants are established use a high nitrogen fertilizer.

Side dressing: Apply fish emulsion or compost tea 3 weeks after planting, and then again every 3–4 weeks, or use 1 tablespoon of blood meal mixed in 1 gallon (4 liter) of water. If leaves start to yellow, give plants manure tea.

CARE

- Keep soil free of weeds by mulching.
- Sever roots on one side of the cabbage plant when the head is fully formed to slow maturity and prevent the head from splitting.
- Remove decaying leaves as they appear.
- Excess fertilizer or severe flooding will cause heads to lose their roundness as they begin to mature. This may result in pointed, loose heads.

Pests: Aphids, birds, cabbage loopers, cabbage root maggots, cabbage worms, flea beetles, harlequin bugs.

- Aphids are a sign of heat or water stress; hose them off with a strong spray from the garden hose.
- Protect cabbage from birds with netting. Remove the netting when plants are about 8 inches (20 cm) high.
- Use row covers and Bacillus thuringiensis (Bt) to control cabbage worms and loopers; larvae eat holes in leaves.
- Prevent cabbage root fly larvae called cutworms from entering the soil by placing a 12-inch (30 cm) square of black plastic directly over the roots of the plant with a hole cut in the center for the emerging plant. Or use a paper collar 2 inches (5 cm) in diameter and 2 inches (5 cm) high pressed ½ inch (1 cm) into soil. Loosen the soil around plants and pick out cutworms by hand. Look for cutworms in the early morning.
- Control red and black-spotted harlequin cabbage bug by hand-picking or spraying with a soap mixture.
- Use row covers to protect plants from aphids, cabbage loopers, imported cabbage worms and root maggots.

Diseases: Black rot, cabbage yellows, clubroot, damping off, downy mildew
- Prevent black rot, the blackening of the leaf veins, by soaking seed in hot-water before sowing.
- Prevent cabbage yellows by planting resistant varieties.
- Prevent clubroot through garden sanitation and adding lime to the soil to raise the pH above 7.
- Rotate cabbage-family plantings to avoid soil-borne diseases.
- Destroy infected plants.
- Pull up all cabbage family weeds such as mustard and shepherd's purse.
- Control disease by not growing cabbage or any other member of the Brassica family, such as broccoli, cauliflower or kale, in the same location years after year. Rotate crops on a 3-year cycle.

HARVEST

Cabbage will be ready for harvest 70–120 days from sowing; 50–100 days after transplanting. Cut cabbage at the base of the stalk when heads are firm, filled out, and 4–10 inches (10–25 cm) in diameter. Young, small cabbages are tastier. Harvest cabbages before they reach maturity. To produce up to five smaller heads within six weeks of harvest, cut stalk squarely then cut a shallow slit across the top of the stump. Harvest and store before heavy frost.

Storage: Use cabbage fresh or refrigerate at 32°F (0°C) for one to two weeks. Green and actively growing heads store best. Store only disease-free heads. Cabbage can be dried and frozen. Cabbage can be canned as sauerkraut.

VARIETIES

Cabbages are classified according to the season in which they are harvested or their shape. Choose cultivars for specific garden conditions and climate. For autumn harvest, choose a midseason, late-season, or storage variety.

Early Season Green: 'Charmant', 'Dynamo', 'Early Jersey Wakefield', 'Farao'.
Midseason: 'Blue Vantage', 'Copenhagen Market', 'Fortuna', 'Tendersweet'.
Winter or Late-Season Green: 'Brunswick', 'Danish Ballhead', 'Gloria', 'January King', 'Late Flat Dutch', 'Storage No. 4'.
Red Cabbage: 'Rona', 'Ruby Ball', 'Regal Red' (midseason), 'Red Perfection' (late season).
Savoy Cabbage: 'Savoy King' and 'Savoy Chieftain'. Savoy or crinkle-leafed cabbage is milder in flavor than round-head cabbage.

Cardoon

Common name: Cardoon, wild artichoke
World names: cardoon (French, Portuguese); Karden (German); cado, cardi (Italian, Spanish), cardone (Italian)
Botanical name: *Cynara cardunculus*
Pronounced SIN-uh-ruh
Family: Sunflower family— *Asteraceae (Compositae)*

ABOUT
Type of plant: Perennial in mild regions, annual in cold regions
Origin: Southern Europe, Central Asia. Cardoon is related to the artichoke, both members of the thistle family. Cardoon came into wide cultivation during the Middle Ages.
Description: Arching form from a basal rosette of leaf stalks. Leaves are deeply cut similar to the artichoke. Mostly spiny, felted, and heavy bristled flower head is also similar to the artichoke.
Height: 48–72 inches (122–183 cm)
Breadth: 48–60 inches (122–153 cm)
Root depth: Long tap root
Bloom time and flower: Summer; purple thistle-like flowers
Edible parts: Fleshy base of thick leaf stalks

KITCHEN
Serve: Raw cardoon can be chopped into salads, but taste a piece to make sure it is not bitter. If the taste is bitter, pre-cook the stalks, chill then serve.

BASICS
Seed planting depth: ¼ inch (6 mm)
Germination soil temperature: 75°F (24°C)
Days to germination: 10–14
Sow indoors: 10 weeks before last frost
Plant outdoors: After frost danger is past
Days to maturity: 120–150 cool sunny days
Soil pH range: 6.0–7.0
Growing soil temperature: 55–60°F (13–18°C)
Spacing of plants: 20 inches (51 cm) apart in all directions

Watering: Moderate and even
Light: Full sun
Nutrients: Moderate nitrogen, phosphorus, and potassium
Rotating crops: Avoid following Jerusalem artichokes or sunflowers
Companion crops: Sunflower, tarragon, and brassicas or cabbage family plants
Propagation: Seed or rooted offshoots
Seed viability: 6 years; store in airtight container in a cool, dark place.
Seed weight: 540 seeds per ounce (20 per gram)

SITE

Cardoon grows best in mild regions, growth zones 5–10.
Frost tolerance: Will withstand light frost
Soil preparation: Cardoon prefers humus-rich, well-drained soil.
Container growing: Cardoons do not grow well in containers.

PLANTING

Sow cardoon seed ¼ inches (6 mm) deep.
Planting time in mild-winter climates: Sow seed or plant root offshoot in spring
Planting time in cold-winter climates: Sow seeds indoors 10 weeks before the last frost; set plants out after the last frost. May not reach full height where growing season is short, but will still supply usable stalks.

GROWING

Water: Keep soil moist.
Nutrients: Feed weekly with fish emulsion.

CARE

Blanch for mild flavor and tender interior tissue. Blanch when the plant is about 36 inches (90 cm) tall, 4–6 weeks before harvesting, or a month before the first autumn frost. To blanch, tie the leaves together in a bunch and wrap paper or burlap around the stems, or hill the soil around the stems.
Pests: Aphids. Pinch out infested foliage or hose the aphids off.
Diseases: Crown rot. Provide good drainage and avoid overly wet conditions.

HARVEST

Cardoon will be ready to harvest 120–150 cool sunny days after sowing, 4-6 weeks after blanching. Cut bunched stalks at the soil surface. Harvest blanched stalks as needed until the first hard freeze is near, then bank the plant with earth or straw to prolong harvest into winter
Storage: Wrap, and refrigerate stalks; they will keep for 1–2 weeks. Freeze to preserve.

VARIETIES

A favorite cardoon variety is 'Large Smooth'.

Carrots

Common name: Carrot
World names: hu luo bo (Chinese); carotte (French); Möhre, Karotte (German); gajar (Hindi); carota (Italian); cenoura (Portuguese); zanahoria (Spanish)
Botanical name: *Daucus carota sativus*
Pronounced DAW-kus ka-RO-tuh sa-TY-vus
Family: Carrot and parsley family—*Apiaceae (Umbelliferae)*

ABOUT
Type of plant: Biennial grown as an annual, cool season
Origin: Afghanistan to eastern Mediterranean. Carrots have been cultivated for thousands of years. The orange carrot was developed in Holland and France.
Description: Finely divided fern-like leaves sprout in a circle from a swollen, fleshy orange or yellow taproot 3 inches (8 cm) in diameter and reaches 3–12 inches (7.5–30 cm) in length depending on the variety.
Height: 12–18 inches (30–45 cm)
Breadth: 12 inches (30 cm)
Root depth: Short taproot but some fibrous roots can reach down to 60 inches (152 cm)
Bloom time and flower: Blooms white flowers the second year on 24–48 inch (60–122 cm) high stems which bear flower and seed.
Edible parts: Roots

KITCHEN
Serve: Serve carrots raw or cooked.

BASICS
Seed planting depth: ¼–½ inches (6–12 mm)
Germination soil temperature: 50–75°F (10–24°C)
Days to germination: 6
Sow indoors: Not recommended
Sow outdoors: Early spring to midsummer
Days to maturity: 50–80 days; 30–40 days for baby carrots
Soil pH range: 5.5–6.8
Growing soil temperature: 65–75°F (18–24°C)
Spacing of plants: 2 inch (5 cm) apart in all directions.

CARROTS

Water: Moderate
Light: Full sun
Nutrients: Light feeder
Rotating crops: Avoid rotating with celery, dill, fennel, parsley, parsnip
Intercropping: Plant with fast growing radishes which will emerge first and break up crusted surface soil.
Companion crops: Beans, Brussels sprouts, cabbage, chives, leaf lettuce, leeks, onions, peas, peppers, radishes, rosemary, sage, tomatoes
Incompatible crops: Celery, dill, parsnip
Propagation: Seed
Seed viability: 3 years; store in airtight container in a cool, dark place.
Seed weight: 19,600 seed per ounce (690 per gram)

SITE

Carrots grow best in growth zones 3–12. Plant quick-maturing cultivars in cold regions.
Frost tolerance: Hardy; will tolerate light frosts as seedlings or as mature plants.
Soil preparation: Carrots prefer deep, loose, light, sandy loam, free of clods and rocks, with good moisture-holding capacity; this will ensure straight, smooth roots. In heavy or shallow soil, plant round or half-long varieties. Do not mix fresh manure into the planting bed.

- In poor or rocky soil, dig a V-trench and fill it with friable soil or grow carrots in a container. Carrots will not grow straight if they hit a stone. Carrots do not grow well in poorly drained soil.
- Use a raised bed if it is difficult to improve your planting bed.

Container growing: Standard and large varieties of carrots will not thrive in containers, but short or finger varieties can be grown. Choose a container at least 10–12 inches (25–30 cm) deep.

PLANTING

- Space carrots in beds 2 inches (5 cm) apart in all directions. Seed is very small and difficult to see; mix seed half-and-half with fine sand to help avoid over-seeding.
- Do not allow the soil to crust prior to emergence. Crusted soil can result in irregular germination which may cause variations in the maturity and length of the roots at harvest time.
- Thin plants to 2–4 inches (5–10 cm) apart in beds and 2 inches (5 cm) apart in rows.

Planting time: Early spring. Sow seed 2–4 weeks after the last frost. Plant a quick maturing variety for summer eating. Plant winter storage varieties after the soil warms at about the same time tomatoes are planted.
Planting time in cold-winter climates: Make last sowing 70 days before first frost.
Planting time in reverse-season climates: Autumn, winter, and early spring
Succession planting: At three-week intervals until three months before the first autumn frost; sow seed when the previous planting is up and growing.

GROWING

Water: Carrots prefer even moisture. Do not over-water them.
- Low moisture grown carrots have a strong and pungent flavor.
- Continuously wet soil can cause root rot and poor root color.
- Over-watered young seedlings may result in short stubby roots.
- Too little moisture will result in stress and forked roots.
- Keep soil surface moist. Do not allow soil to crust before the emergence of seedlings which will take 1–3 weeks depending on temperature and moisture.
- To avoid weather stress problems over the course of the growing season, make successive sowings every seven days.

Nutrients: Carrots are light feeders; too much top growth may mean too much nitrogen. Fertilize twice during the growing season applying fish emulsion: first, three weeks after germination, and again when carrots are 6–8 inches (15–20 cm) tall.

Temperature note: Bolting to seed is usually caused by low or high air temperature stress at the 5–8 leaf stage. There is little root enlargement and very little top growth when the temperature dips to between 40–50°F (4–10°C). Also, top growth is reduced and the roots become strong flavored when the mean air temperature rises above 82°F (28°C). Carrots will be bland tasting and small if the soil temperature rises above 70°F (21°C).
- To avoid total crop loss as the result of temperature fluctuations make several sowings 7 days apart.

CARE

- Apply mulch around plants after they are 2–3 inches (5–7.5 cm) tall to keep soil moist and inhibit weeds.
- During the growing period, lightly mound or hoe soil over any exposed root crowns to prevent greening at the top of the carrot root.
- Thin plants when they are 1–2 inches (2.5–5 cm) tall, then later when they appear crowded.

Common problems: Twisted roots indicate inadequate thinning. Forked or deformed roots indicate that the seedbed was not free of stones or clods. Split roots indicate that heavy rain or irrigation followed a dry period. Hairy roots indicate excessive fertility. Do not use high-nitrogen fertilizer or fresh manure on carrot beds.

Pests: Aphids, carrot rust flies, carrot weevils, cutworms, flea beetles, leafhoppers, maggots, nematodes, parsley caterpillars, slugs, snails, weevils, wireworms.
- Exclude adult rust fly and other insects with floating row covers. Carrot rust fly, a dark-green fly, lays eggs in the soil near carrot, celery, or parsnip plants. Larvae dig through the soil to the tip of the root and eat their way upward. Crops planted after late spring and harvested before late summer often escape damage without protection.

Diseases: Blights, leaf spot, damping off, soft rot, yellows.

- Rotate plantings to avoid bacterial diseases. Practice 3-year crop rotations. Blights can reduce yield and quality. Copper fungicide can be used as a preventive measure for the control of blights.
- Blight appears as brown-black dark spots edged with yellow on leaf margins. Leaflets may shrivel and die. Hot water seed treatment: 126°F (52°C) for 25 minutes.
- Carrot scab, a bacterial disease, can be avoided by seed treatment and use of disease-free planting beds.
- Mosaic, a viral disease, is aphid transmitted. Control aphids by spraying off with water.
- Yellows are leafhopper transmitted. Plant resistant varieties. Spray with insecticidal soap.
- Soft rot, a bacterial disease, is caused by excessively high soil moisture.

HARVEST

Harvest carrots 50–80 days after sowing; 30–40 days for baby carrots. Harvest carrots late spring onwards. Dig up roots any time after they become brightly colored. They should be flavorful at this stage. Pull roots when the ground is moist to avoid breaking them, or dig them up with a garden fork.
- Usually, tapered varieties are ready to eat at about finger length and round varieties are ready to eat when they are about ¾ inch (19 mm) across. Short, round varieties generally are easier to grow and tend to be sweeter than the tapered varieties.
- In cold-winter climates, complete the harvest before the first hard frost. Roots can be taken up after frost but before the ground freezes.
- In hot-weather climates, complete the harvest before the hottest weather arrives.
- A harvest period lasts about 3 weeks, perhaps longer in cool, autumn weather. Roots left in the ground too long may crack or their taste and appearance may decline.

Storage: Store carrots at 32–34°F (0–1°C) with high humidity. Remove tops and store washed or unwashed. Carrots keep well in perforated plastic bags or storage bins in the refrigerator or a cold storage area. Roots store best with the tops removed to avoid the translocation of moisture and nutrients. Store in the refrigerator for 1–3 months; frozen after slicing and blanching for up to 6 months; or pickled in vinegar brine (after boiling) for up to 1 year.
- In mild climates, carrots can be left in soil until ready for use.

VARIETIES

Carrots come in various colors: white, yellow, purple and red. 'Nantes' is medium length and cylindrical. 'Shipping' or 'Imperator' are extra long and grow best in deeply worked soil. 'Chantenays' is top-shaped and suitable for shallow and heavy soil. 'Danvers Half Long' is sweet and cylindrical. 'Lady Finger', 'Short 'n Sweet', and 'Thumbelina' are baby or mini varieties.

Early-harvest carrots include 'Danvers Half Long', 'Scarlet Nates', and 'Chantenays'. Choose 'Napoli' and 'Ithaca' for summer or autumn sowing and later harvest.

Cauliflower

Common name: Cauliflower
World names: cai hua, gai lan hua (Chinese); chou-fleur (French); Blumenkohl (German); cavolo broccolo, cavolfiore (Italian); couve-flor (Portuguese); coliflor (Spanish)
Botanical name: *Brassica oleracea* var. *botrytis*
Pronounced BRASS-ih-kuh oh-leh-RAY-see-uh boh-TRY-tis
Family: Cabbage or mustard family—*Brassicaceae (Cruciferae)*

ABOUT

Type of plant: Biennial grown as an annual, cool season
Origin: Eastern end of the Mediterranean. Cauliflower has been in cultivation for at least 2,500 years. It was popularized in France in the mid-sixteenth century.
Description: Single-stalked fleshy stem with many small, tightly formed, white or cream colored curd-shaped flower heads surrounded by large green leaves. Heads can also be green (often called 'Romanesco' or romanesco broccoli) or purple (called purple Cape broccoli). Broccoflower is a hybrid cross between broccoli and cauliflower with characteristics of both and a distinctive green head. All require warm weather to begin growth followed by cool temperatures at harvest.
Height: 18–24 inches (45–61 cm)
Breadth: 24–30 inches (24–76 cm)
Root depth: 18–36 inches (45–90 cm)
Bloom time and flower: Edible flower buds form a solid head, sometimes called a curd, which may be white, purple, or green
Edible parts: Curds or heads which are aborted flower buds

KITCHEN

Serve: Serve cauliflower raw or cooked. Serve cooked cauliflower as vegetable side dish or add it to soups, stews, pasta, omelets, soufflés, or quiches.

BASICS

Seed planting depth: ¼–½ inches (6–13 mm)
Soil temperature for germination: 70–90°F (21°C); optimum 70°F (21°C)
Days to germination: 4–10
Sow indoors: 4–6 weeks before last frost
Sow outdoors: From last frost to late spring

CAULIFLOWER

Days to maturity: 70–120
Soil pH range: 6.4–7.4
Growing soil temperature: 60–75°F (16–24°C); optimum 65°F (18°C)
Spacing of plants: 15 inches (37.5 cm) apart in staggered pattern
Watering: Moderate and even
Light and situation: Full sun. Avoid hot and dry sites.
Nutrients: Heavy feeder
Rotating crops: Avoid following cabbage family crops. Precede cauliflower with a nitrogen-fixing cover crop.
Companion crops: Aromatic plants, artichoke, bush beans, beets, carrots, cucumbers, celery, dill, lettuce, mint, nasturtium, garlic, onion family plants, peas, potatoes, rosemary, sage, spinach
Incompatible crops: Pole beans, strawberries, tomatoes
Propagation: Seed
Seed viability: 5 years; store in airtight container in a cool, dark place.
Seeds weight: 6,000–9,000 seeds per ounce (210–320 per gram)

SITE

Grow cauliflower in growth zones 3–11. Grow spring and autumn crops in cool-spring areas; winter crop in mild climates.
Frost tolerance: Cauliflower is half-hardy and will withstand some light freezing.
Soil preparation: Cauliflower prefers light, humus-rich, moist but well-drained soil with plenty of calcium and well-rotted manure or compost worked in.
Container growing: Minimum container depth 20 inches (51 cm)

PLANTING

Cauliflower prefers slow, steady growth. The time of planting and weather conditions during the growing season will affect the results. Hot weather can result in stem rot. A long dry spell can cause cauliflower to bolt or button up. Start cauliflower in flats. Move the seedlings from flats to 2-inch (5 cm) containers as soon as they can be handled.
Early spring planting for harvest before hot weather: Spring planted cauliflower must be started early under protection, transplanted to the open before the danger of frost is over, and grown rapidly to produce its edible heads before hot weather ruins it.
Mid-autumn to late-autumn planting for a spring harvest: In mild-winter climates, autumn planted cauliflower will reach maturity in a more leisurely course, and the flavor will be superior to the summer crop.
Planting in cold-winter climates: For autumn harvest, sow in late spring to midsummer. Sow indoors 4–6 weeks before the last frost. Do not set out too early; severe frost may cause the plant to form a button instead of a full-sized head.

Planting in mild-winter climates: For winter harvest, sow seed or set out plants in late summer to late winter, after the summer heat has ended. Sow 90–120 days before the first autumn frost. Plants started indoors can be set out when the seedlings are 4–5 weeks old.

Planting in reverse-season climates: Plant in late autumn to early winter for a winter crop. Sow seeds in flats 4–6 weeks before you intend to set out plants. A late summer planting will be ready to harvest by late winter or early spring.

Succession planting: To prevent the chance of unfavorable weather conditions destroying an entire crop, sow seed in successive plantings a week apart or transplant 4–5 -week-old plants on a weekly basis.

Planting by seasonal variety or type:
- **Early or snowball type:** The maximum temperature for curd formation is 66–77°F (20–25°C); optimum is about 68°F (17°C). There is little difference in the quality of the curds at 57–68°F (14–20°C); but above 68°F (20°C) the quality is poor.
- **Mid-spring to late-spring type:** Planted for a late summer and autumn harvest.
- **Late or winter type:** Requires a period of cold temperatures to induce heading. Winter types must be sown early so that plants are mature enough for cold weather to trigger the formation of flower heads. (Vernalization is the term used to describe flowering induced by cold temperatures.)
- **Intermediate type:** Will form heads at temperatures below 50°F (10°C).

GROWING

Water: Keep the soil moist particularly early in season and during warm weather. Even watering is important for undisturbed growth.

Nutrients: Feed cauliflower every 3–4 weeks with fish emulsion, compost tea, or use 1 tablespoon (15 ml) of blood meal in 1 gallon (3.8 liters) of water.

CARE

Keep soil moist by mulching around plants. Cultivate to keep beds free of weeds.

Blanching: Improves flavor and quality of curd. Blanching is the process of limiting the amount of light that contacts a developing head. Blanch when small white heads about 2–3 inches (5–7.5 cm) wide become visible through the leaves. Fold the outer leaves over the head and tie or pin them at the top with a rubber band, twine or a clothes pin to preserve the white curd color. Blanching is not necessary, but it may help prevent curd yellowing due to exposure to sunlight and may result in better head quality especially when curds develop during hot weather.

Common problems:
- **Buttoning:** Low temperatures or excessive dry or wet periods will cause tiny curds or buttons to form before enough leaves appear.

- **No head formed:** High temperatures will keep plants in the vegetative stage until temperatures fall to optimum levels.
- **Riceyness:** Heads look like a pot of boiled rice. This is caused by low temperatures just after planting or a late supply of nitrogen to the plants.
- **Discolored heads:** Keep heads shaded during the vegetative phase before curds are formed. Discoloring may also be caused by poor harvest techniques.

Pests: Aphids, cabbage butterflies, cabbage loopers, cabbage root maggots, cutworms, diamondback moths, cabbage worms, flea beetles, harlequin bugs, mites, root flies, slugs, snails, striped flea beetles, weevils.

- Cabbage worms can be controlled early with row covers or spray or dust with Bacillus thuringiensis (Bt).
- Flea beetles on young plants are controlled with row covers. Older, vigorous plants can withstand flea beetle attack.
- Cutworms and cabbage maggots are deterred by plastic collars set around the plants. Also, loosen the soil around the plants and pick out cutworms and cabbage maggots by hand (early morning is a good time to look for cutworms).
- Red and black-spotted harlequin cabbage bugs can be controlled by hand-picking or spraying with a soap mixture.

Diseases: Black rot, clubroot, damping off, downy mildew, leaf spot, root rot, seed rot, yellows, fusarium wilt.

- Rotate cabbage-family plantings to avoid soil-borne diseases.
- Destroy infected plants as soon as they are discovered. Sanitation and rotation of crops are the most effective ways to eliminate plant diseases.
- Ensure proper drainage; avoid constantly wet conditions; don't work with plants when they are wet.

HARVEST

Cauliflower matures 70–120 days after sowing; 55–80 days after transplanting.

Harvest time can depend upon the type and variety. Cut when heads are firm and tight and reach 4–8 inches (10–20 cm) in diameter and curds have not become loose or become coarse or started to separate. Cut the stalk just below the head. In warm weather, harvest about 4 days after tying leaves for blanching. In cool weather, harvest about 10 days after tying leaves for blanching.

Storage: Store heads unwashed and wrapped in plastic in the refrigerator. Freeze (after blanching) for up to 4 months; pickled in vinegar and brine and canned for up to 1 year.

VARIETIES

Popular cauliflower varieties include 'Snowball', 'Snow King', and 'Snow Crown' or hybrids such as 'Early White Hybrid' and 'Snow Crown Hybrid'; 'Fremont' is self blanching; green heads are often called 'Romanesco' or romanesco broccoli, 'Chartreuse' is a green head variety; purple heads are called purple Cape broccoli, one variety is 'Purple Head'. Broccoflower is a hybrid cross between broccoli and cauliflower with characteristics of both and a distinctive green head.

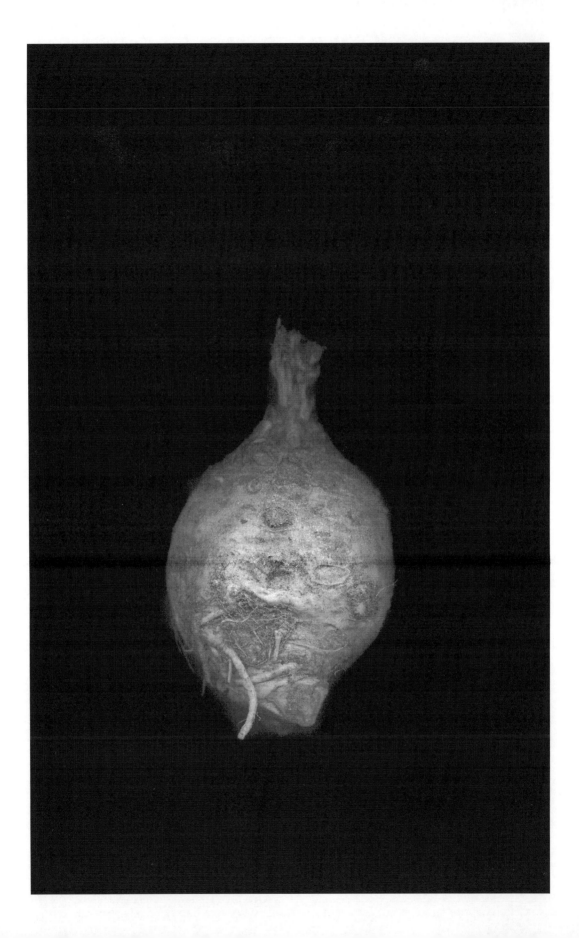

Celeriac

Common name: Celery root, knob celery, turnip-rooted celery
World names: sai kan choi (Chinese); ćeleri rave (French); Sellerie (German); sèdano (Italian); oranda mitsuba (Japanese); apío (Spanish)
Botanical name: *Apium graveolens* var. *rapaceum*
Pronounced AY-pee-um gruh-VEE-o-lenz ruh-PAY-see-um
Family: Carrot and parsley family—*Apiaceae (Umbelliferae)*

ABOUT
Type of plant: Biennial grown as an annual, cool weather
Origin: Mediterranean region
Description: In the first year, the plant has above ground leaves similar to the carrot. These dark green leaves sprout from the root on hollow stems. The stem is very short and does not elongate during the first year. After low temperatures induce flowering the stems and plant grow several feet (from 1–2 m) in height. As the plant grows, a turnip-like, white, globe-shaped root or knob forms just above the ground.
Height: 12 inches (30 cm)
Breadth: 12 inches (30 cm)
Root depth: 18–24 inches (45–60 cm)
Bloom time and flower: Small yellow flowers in the second year
Edible parts: Large, rounded roots

KITCHEN
Serve: Celeriac can be served raw or cooked. Use raw as a flavoring in salads, soups, and stews. Cook alone or with other vegetables: allow 10 to 15 minutes when boiling and 12 to 18 minutes when steaming.

BASICS
Seed planting depth: ¼–½ inch (5–10 mm)
Germination soil temperature: 55–61°F (13–16°C)
Days to germination: 10–20 days at temperature of 65°F (18°C)
Sow indoors: 10 weeks before last frost
Sow outdoors: Not recommended
Days to maturity: 90–120 days

CELERIAC

Soil pH range: 5.8–6.8
Growing soil temperature: 50–65°F (10–18°C)
Spacing of plants: 15–26 inches (38–66 cm) apart in all directions
Water: Heavy and even
Light: Full sun; tolerates lights shade
Nutrients: Heavy feeder
Companion crops: Lettuce, spinach, and English peas, but not pumpkins, cucumbers, tomatoes, or squash
Incompatible crops: None
Propagation: Seed
Seed viability: 5 years; store in airtight container in a cool, dark place.
Seed weight: 56,000 seeds per ounce (1,975 per gram)

SITE

Celeriac grows best in growth zones 4–10, except where summer temperatures fall below 55°F (13°C).
Frost tolerance: Can withstand increasingly severe frost for the last 30–45 days
Soil preparation: Celeriac prefers humus rich, moisture-retentive soil with plenty of well-rotted manure or compost. Fertile soil is necessary for mild taste.
Container growing: Celeriac can be grown in a container.

PLANTING

Plant celeriac seed ¼–½ inch (5–10 mm) deep. Seed should be covered and kept moist. If soil dries out, germination will be delayed.
Planting time in cold-winter climates:

- Start indoors 6–8 weeks before the last spring frost. Set out seedlings in early spring after they have formed two true leaves and the plant is 3 inches (8 cm tall), about 2–4 weeks before the last frost. Set plant 6–8 inches (15–20 cm) apart in rows 24–36 inches (60–90 cm) apart. Irrigate to keep soil moist.

- Indoors: Sow about 6 seeds per inch (2.5 cm) ⅛ inch (3 mm) deep and keep soil moist and temperatures 70–75°F (21–24°C) if possible. Seeds require a temperature of 55–61°F (13–16°C) to germinate. Seedlings emerge in 2–3 weeks and then the temperature can be reduced to 60–70°F (16–21°C).

- Bolting is caused by exposure of young plant to temperatures below 55°F (13°C) for 10 days or more. Harden plants before transplanting by reducing water for 7–10 days. Do not harden off plants by lowering temperatures.

Planting time in mild-winter climates: Autumn, winter, and early spring
Planting time in reverse-season climates: Not recommended for reverse-season climates because of its low tolerance for heat and dry conditions. Experiment by trying late autumn

planting, sowing seeds indoors about 3 months before outdoor planting and transplanting when 5–6 leaves have emerged.

GROWING

Water: Keep soil moist. For succulent and tender stalks, high soil moisture is necessary. Provide extra moisture in the last month before harvest as the most rapid growth occurs at this time. Inadequate moisture will produce small, tough, or fibrous plants.

Nutrients: Celeriac is a heavy feeder; apply liquid fertilizer or mulch with organic compost a month after transplanting and water in. Feed every 2–3 weeks during the growing season with compost tea or fish emulsion or use 1 tablespoon blood meal mixed into 1 gallon (3.7 liters) of water.

CARE

Keep beds weed free. Do not disturb the shallow root system when weeding.

Physiological disorders: Blackheart, the dying of the growing point, is caused by a calcium deficiency. Cracked stem is caused by a boron deficiency. Brown checking is caused by low boron in conjunction with excess potassium. Yellowing of the leaf blades is caused by low magnesium in the soil.

Pests: Aphids, cabbage loopers, celery worms, slugs, weevils, spider mites, wireworms, leafhoppers, cut worms, armyworms, whiteflies, nematodes.

- Use row covers in early spring; later handpick parsley worms or celery worms.
- Spray away aphids with a steady stream of water.
- Spray plants with an insecticidal soap.

Diseases: Blight, damping off, leaf spot, mosaic

- Control blights with fungicides that contain copper and rotate crops.
- Celery mosaic—mottled leaves, twisted stems, dwarfing—is a viral disease transmitted by aphids. Control pests.

HARVEST

Celeriac will be ready for harvest 90–120 days after sowing. Cut stems close to the knobby root when the root reaches 2–3 inches (5–7.5 cm) across and before outer petioles become pithy. Use a garden fork to lift roots. Harvest before the ground freezes.

Storage: Refrigerate for up to one week, or store in a cold, moist place for 2–3 months.

VARIETIES

Improved celeriac varieties are 'Brilliant' and 'Mentor'. 'Diamant' is a favorite.

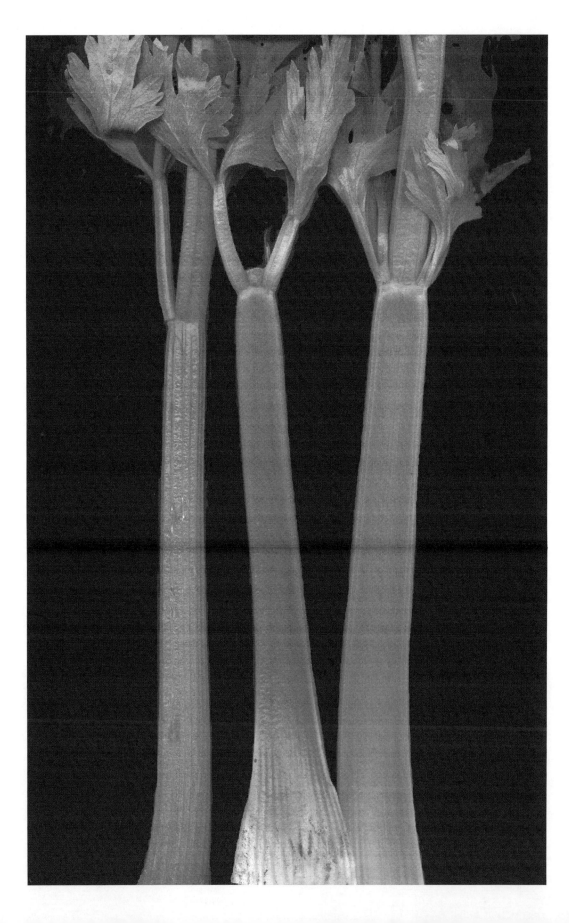

Celery

Common name: Celery
World names: sai kan choi (Chinese); ćeleri (French); Sellerie (German); sèdano (Italian); oranda mitsuba (Japanese); apío (Spanish)
Botanical name: *Apium graveolens* var. *dulce*
Pronounced AY-pee-um gruh-VEE-oh-lenz
Family: Carrot and parsley family—*Apiaceae* (*Umbelliferae*)

ABOUT

Type of plant: Biennial grown as an annual completing its life cycle in a year if plant is subjected to low temperatures during development
Related varieties: *Apium* var. *secalinum* (Chinese celery); *Apium* var. *rapaceum* (turnip-rooted celery)
Origin: Europe. Celery was first cultivated in Italy late in the sixteenth century. Mild-tasting celery descended from a harsh-tasting ancestor that once grew wild in marshes throughout Europe and Asia.
Description: Tight rosette of 8- to 18-inch (20–40 cm) stalks topped with many divided leaves. Celery consists mainly of leaves above ground—similar to the carrot—until vernalization when the stalks elongate to about 24 inches (60 cm) in length. Small yellow flowers followed by fruit or celery seed develop.
Height: 16 inches (41 cm)
Breadth: 8–12 inches (20–30 cm)
Root depth: 6–19 inches (15–45 cm)
Bloom time and flower: Summer; small yellow flowers look like coarse Queen Anne's lace carried on a tall stalk.
Edible parts: Leaf talks (celery), leaves (Chinese celery), root (celeriac), fruit ("celery seeds")

KITCHEN

Serve: Celery can be served raw or cooked. Serve raw celery as a snack, appetizer or in a salad. Use celery leaves and stems to flavor soups, sauces, stews, pasta, tofu, quiches, omelets, and rice.

CELERY

BASICS

Seed planting depth: ⅛ inch (3 mm)
Germination soil temperature: 55–75°F (13–24°C). Soak seeds in water overnight before sowing.
Days to germination: 10
Sow indoors: 10 weeks before last frost
Sow outdoors: Not recommended
Days to maturity: 120–180 days from seed to harvest
Soil pH range: 5.8–6.8
Growing soil temperature: 60–70°F (16–21°C)
Spacing of plants: 6–8 inches (15–20 cm) apart in all directions after thinning at about the 4–6 leaf stage.
Water: Heavy and even
Light: Full sun; tolerates lights shade
Nutrients: High nitrogen, phosphorus and potassium
Rotating crops: Avoid following lettuce or cabbage.
Companion crops: Beans, brassicas or cabbage family plants, tomatoes, lettuce, spinach, English peas
Incompatible crops: Carrots, cucumbers, parsley, parsnips, pumpkins, squash
Propagation: Seed. Seeds need light to germinate.
Seed viability: 5 years; store in an airtight container in a cool, dark place.
Seed weight: 76,000 seeds per ounce (2,683 per gram)

SITE

Celery grows best in growth zones 5–10. Celery prefers cool summer regions except where summer temperatures fall below 55°F (13°C). Autumn and winter crops can be grown in mild-winter climates.
Frost tolerance: Hardy. Protect transplants from temperatures below 60°F (16°C)
Soil preparation: Celery prefers humus-rich, light and well-drained soil. Work in well-rotted manure or compost.
Container growing: Self-blanching varieties can be grown in containers.

PLANTING

Planting by celery type: There are two types of celery: blanching and self-blanching.
- Blanching varieties require the exclusion of sunlight from their leaf stalks in order to blanch or turn white. To blanch celery do the following: (1) plant seed in a trench that is 12 inches (30 cm) deep by 18 inches (45 cm) wide; (2) midseason: gather stalks into a bunch and tie the top with string and then wrap the stalks with wax paper to prevent soil from getting between the stalks; (3) two months before harvest, fill the trench with soil up to the bottom of the leaves; (4) mound soil around the base of the plant every 3 weeks to keep the plants upright. Another way to blanch or whiten stalks is to set a bottomless

milk carton or plastic cylinder around plants to exclude light from stalks; however, leaves must have sunlight.
- Self-blanching varieties spontaneously lose the chlorophyll in their leaf stalks and therefore do not require trenches and the blanching process. Self-blanching varieties are easier to grow but the harvest is limited.

Planting time in cold-winter climates: Sow seed indoors 4–6 weeks before the last spring frost. Set out seedlings when they reach 3 inches (8 cm) tall about the time of the last frost. Harden plants before transplanting by reducing water for 7–10 days. Do not harden off celery plants by lowering temperatures. Use row covers to keep plants warm for a month after transplanting, if necessary.

Autumn planting time: Sow seed 19 weeks before the first expected frost.

Planting time in mild-winter climates: Plant in flats in early spring where winters are mild; for late winter crops start seed in the summer. Set out plants in autumn, winter, and early spring. Celery may not do well in reverse-season climates because of its low tolerance for heat and dry conditions.

Succession planting: Set out transplants every month

GROWING

Water: Keep soil moist. High soil moisture is necessary to grow succulent, tender stalks. Even moisture is particularly important in the last month before harvest during the period of most rapid growth.

Nutrients: Celery is a heavy feeder. About 2–3 weeks before planting, apply a 4-inch (10 cm) layer of well-rotted manure or compost to the soil and then work it 12 inches (30 cm) into soil.

Side dressing: Mulch with organic compost a month after transplanting and water in.

Feed every 2–3 weeks during the growing season; side-dress with compost tea or fish emulsion or use 1 tablespoon (15 ml) blood meal mixed into 1 gallon (3.8 liters) of water.

CARE

- Avoid direct sun and excessive heat.
- Water when the soil is dry to the touch.
- Roots grow close to the surface so be careful when weeding.
- Blanch when plants reach about 12 inches (30 cm) tall by mulching with soil or straw or by wrapping with paper.
- Bolting is caused by exposure to temperatures below 55°F (13°C) for 10 days or more.

Physiological disorders: Blackheart, the dying of the growing point, is caused by a calcium deficiency. Cracked stem is caused by a boron deficiency. Brown checking is caused by low boron in conjunction with excess potassium. Yellowing of the leaf blades is caused by low magnesium in the soil.

CELERY

Common problems: Excessive heat and inadequate moisture will result in stringy celery.
- Bolting is caused by exposure to temperatures below 55°F (13°C) for 10 days or more. Harden plants before transplanting: reduce water for 7–10 days. Do not harden off celery plants by lowering temperatures.

Pests: Aphids, cabbage loopers, celery worms, slugs, weevils, spider mites, wireworms, leafhoppers, cut and armyworms, whiteflies, nematodes.
- Use row covers to exclude pests.
- Handpick parsley worms or celery worms (green caterpillars with yellow and black bands).
- Spray persistent pests with insecticidal soap.

Diseases: Blight, damping off, leaf spot.
- Rotate plantings to avoid blight problems.
- Early blight and late blight caused by fungi can be controlled by the use of fungicides, some of which contain copper. Solarize the soil and remove infected plants.
- Celery mosaic—mottled leaves, twisted stems, dwarfing—is a viral disease transmitted by aphids. Spray aphids away with a steady stream of water.
- Yellows are a viral disease transmitted by leafhoppers. Spray with insecticidal soap. Plant resistant varieties.

HARVEST

Harvest celery in the autumn before the first frost or earlier. Harvest should begin before outer stalks turn pithy. Cut the entire plant at the root. Outer stalks can be harvested individually when the plant reaches 12–18 inches (30–45 cm) in height; this will allow for the continued production of stalks from the inside out. To intensify flavor, withhold water for 2 days before harvest. Flavor and water storage may be enhanced by watering 4–8 hours prior to harvest.

Storage: In the refrigerator at 32°F (0°C) at 95–98% humidity for 4–6 weeks.

VARIETIES

Choose from these celery varieties: 'Golden Self-Blanching' is tender and mild without blanching. 'Tall Utah 52–70' has long, dark, green stalks. 'Tendercrisp' has pale green stalks.

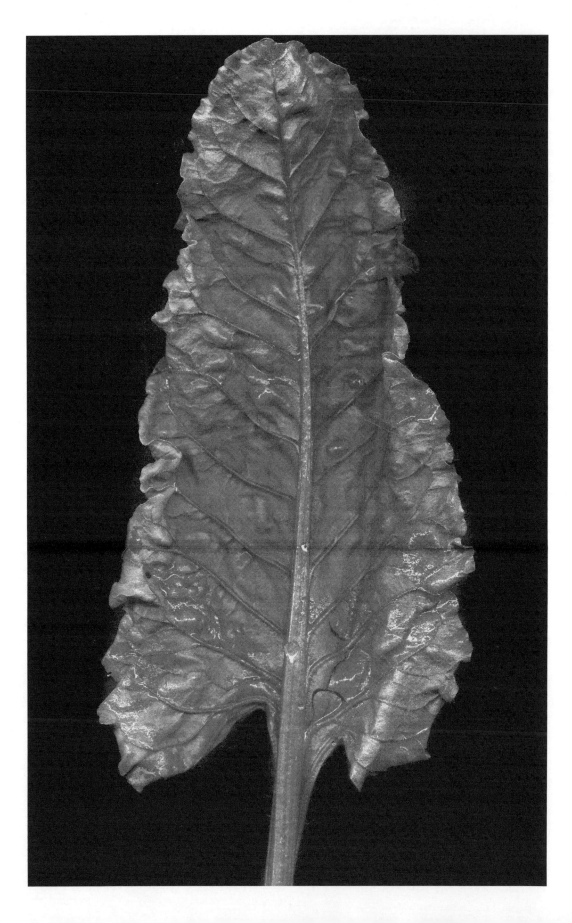

Chard

Common names: Swiss chard, spinach beet, leaf beet, sea kale, Swiss beet, sea kale beet, silver beet, Indian spinach
World names: hou pi cai (Chinese); bette, bette à couper (French); Mangold, Schnittmangold (German); bietola (Italian); acelga (Portuguese, Spanish)
Botanical name: *Beta vulgaris* var. *cicla*
Pronounced BAY-tuh vul-GAR-is SIH-kluh
Family: Beet family—*Chenopodiaceae*

ABOUT
Type of plant: Biennial grown as an annual, cool season
Origin: Europe, Mediterranean. The general cultivation of chard came during the Middle Ages.
Description: Deep green leaves and white ribs and stems or deep green leaves and beet red ribs and stems (stalks called "chards"). Similar to a beet without a bottom. Rainbow chard has multicolored stems of chartreuse, pink, orange, magenta, cherry, yellow and white stems with green leaves.
Height: 12–16 inches (30–40 cm)
Breadth: 6 inches (15 cm)
Root depth: Taproot to 42 inches (107 cm) with laterals spreading to 60 inches (152 cm)
Bloom time and flower: Summer; inconspicuous greenish flowers on slender clusters
Edible parts: Leaves, stalks

KITCHEN
Serve: Serve chard raw or cooked. Use cooked, chopped chard leaves in recipes calling for spinach.

BASICS
Seed planting depth: ½–¾ inches (13–19 mm)
Germination soil temperature: 50–85°F (10–29°C)
Days to germination: 7
Sow indoors: 1–2 weeks before last frost
Sow outdoors: After last frost
Days to maturity: 45–55
Soil pH range: 6.0–6.8; will grow in soil with up to 7.5 pH

CHARD

Growing soil temperature: 40–80°F (4–27°C); will tolerate light
Spacing of plants: 1–2 inches (2.5–5 cm); thin successful plants to 8–12 inches (20–30 cm) apart in all directions
Water: Moderate and even
Light: Full sun, or in warm areas, partial shade
Nutrients: Low nitrogen, moderate phosphorus and potassium
Rotating crops: Follow legumes. Avoid following beets, spinach, orach.
Companion crops: Cabbage, chicory, garlic, leeks, legumes, mustard, onions
Incompatible crops: Beets, orach, spinach
Propagation: Seed
Seed vitality: 4 years; store in airtight container in a cool, dark place.
Seeds weight: 1,500 seeds per ounce (53 per gram)

SITE

Chard grows best in growth zones 2–10; grow as a winter vegetable in mild areas, but chard can withstand some hot weather.
Frost tolerance: Will tolerate considerable heat as well as light frost
Soil Preparation: Chard prefers well-drained soil.
Container growing: Grows well when planted in wide rows in a square or rectangular container or 3–4 plants in a container at least 8 inches (20 cm) deep.

PLANTING

Sow seed ½–¾ inches (13–19 mm) deep spaced 1–2 inches (2.5–5 cm) apart; thin successful plants to 8–12 inches (20–30 cm) apart.
Planting to harvest leaves for salad mix: Sow in 2–4 inch (5–10 cm) wide band, 1 inch (2.5 cm) apart; clip leaves in about 5 weeks.
Planting time in cold-winter climates: Spring to early summer; sow 2 weeks after all danger of frost has passed for summer and autumn crops. Plant indoors in early spring for transplanting out in mid-spring.
Planting time in mild-winter climates: For spring and early summer harvest, sow in late winter or early spring. For autumn and winter harvest, sow in late summer to early autumn. Where temperatures do not fall below 25°F (-3.9°C), sow in early autumn or late winter.
Planting time in reverse-season climates: Autumn after summer heat has passed for winter harvest.
Succession planting: If you harvest the entire plant, not just its outer stalks, plant anew after each harvest from summer through early autumn.

GROWING

Water: Keep soil moist; do not let chard wilt. Mulch to keep soil moist and cool.

Nutrients: Low applications of nitrogen; moderate application of phosphorus and potassium.

Side dressing: Feed every 4–6 weeks with fish emulsion or compost tea.

CARE

- Keep soil moist and weed free.
- Water stress causes tough stems.
- If the plant begins to bolt, pinch back the central stalk to slow maturation.
- Inspect frequently for chewing and sap-sucking insect pests.
- Apply well-rotted manure every 4–6 weeks.

Pests: Aphids, cabbage worms, flea beetles, leaf miners, nematodes.

- Use row covers to deter flea beetles.
- Control aphids by pinching out the affected area or spraying away with a strong stream of water.
- Pick off the older leaves where you see that miners have laid rows of pearl-white eggs.

Diseases: Leaf spot, downy mildew

- Plant in well-draining soil. Rotate crops. Remove and destroy infected plants.

HARVEST

Chard will be ready for harvest 45–55 days after sowing when plants are 6 inches (15 cm) in height. Begin harvest at one end of the row; thin or cut outer leaves at the base of the stalk, slightly above the soil, moving down the row in succession. The first plants will be ready to harvest again when the end of the row is reached. Or slice off whole plant 2 inches (5 cm) above base and it will grow a new set of leaves. For "cut-and-come-again" crop, harvest by cutting leaves and allowing roots to remain and grow a new crop for another harvest. Chard will rejuvenate itself for several pickings after its leaves are harvested before finally bolting into a flowering stalk.

Storage: Rinse and dry cut leaves thoroughly before storing in vegetable compartment of refrigerator for 2–3 weeks. Chard also may be stored in the freezer for up to 6 months after removing the stem and center rib, blanching, and chilling in an ice water bath. You can freeze leaves in the same way as you would spinach.

VARIETIES

Choose from these chard varieties: 'Charlotte' has large, cherry red stalks; 'Rhubarb' has red ribs; 'Bright Lights' and 'Rainbow' have rainbow colored stalks; 'Bright Yellow' has lemon colored stalks; 'Fordhook Giant' is a long time favorite with thick stalks and tasty leaves; 'Argentata' is crisp and flavorful.

Chervil

Common name: Chervil, salad chervil, sweet cicely
World names: cerfeuil (French); Gartenkerbel (German); perifollo (Spanish)
Botanical name: *Anthriscus cerefolium*
Pronounced an-THRIS-kus ser-ee-ih-FOH-lee-um
Family: Carrot and parsley family—*Apiaceae (Umbelliferae)*

ABOUT
Type of plant: Perennial herb usually grown as an annual; hardy cool-season
Origin: Russia. Chervil was brought to France during the Middle Ages.
Description: Bright green, fine-textured, fern-like leaves forming a basal rosette resemble carrot tops. Foliage turns pink in autumn.
Height: Fern-like foliage to 6 inches (15 cm), umbels 12–24 inches (30–60 cm) tall
Breadth: 12–18 inches (30–45 cm).
Root depth: Forms a taproot
Bloom time and flower: Summer; small, white blossoms in umbrella-shaped clusters
Edible parts: Leaves, fresh or dried

KITCHEN
Serve: Use chervil leaves fresh or dried. Chop fresh leaves into salads, sauces, or soups. Use fresh with fish (especially salmon), asparagus, potatoes, and also in vinegars and butters. For cooked dishes, add chervil at the last moment; the flavor dissipates with cooking.

BASICS
Seed planting depth: Sow seeds on the surface or in furrows 1 inch (2.5 cm) deep
Germination soil temperature: 55–75°F (13–24°C)
Days to germination: 7–12
Sow indoors: Late winter to early spring
Sow outdoors: Early spring and early fall
Day to maturity: 50–60
Soil pH range: 6.0–6.7
Growing soil temperature: 55–60°F (13–16°C)
Spacing of plants: 6 inches (15 cm), thin to 9–12 inches (23–30 cm) in all directions
Water: Light

Light: Full sun to partial shade; shade in the afternoon in hot areas
Nutrients: Moderate nitrogen, phosphorus, and potassium
Companion crops: Asparagus, corn, pepper, tomatoes
Incompatible crops: None
Propagation: Seed; requires light to germinate; readily self-sows in hot, dry conditions
Seed viability: 3 years; store seed in an airtight container in a cool, dark place.
Seed weight: 18,000 per ounce (635 per gram)

SITE

Best climate: Zones 3–7; prefers cool, moist weather; goes to seed quickly in hot weather
Frost tolerance: Tender
Soil preparation: Moist, well-drained, humus-rich soil
Container growing: Grows and produces well in a container at least 12 inches (30 cm) deep. Does not require a lot of sun; will grow in an east window indoors.

PLANTING

Sow seeds on the surface or in furrows 1 inch (2.5 cm) deep, but do not cover with soil, instead cover seed with cheesecloth or agricultural fleece.
Spring planting time: Direct sow after last spring frost; transplants poorly
Autumn planting time: Sow in late summer for autumn crop. Chervil may self-sow over the winter.
Succession planting: Sow a few seeds every 2 weeks from early until mid-summer, or until the weather is hot. Once established, chervil reseeds itself each year if flowers are left to mature in the garden.
Planting time in cold-winter climates: Sow in spring
Planting time in mild-winter climates: Sow in autumn

GROWING

Water: Keep soil moist
Nutrients: Light feeder. Spray plants with a liquid seaweed extract 2–3 times during the growing season.

CARE

Care: Pinch out flower stalks to encourage leafy growth and prolonged growth. For fresh leaves year-round, over-winter in a coldframe or grow indoors.
Pests: Aphids, earwigs, parsley caterpillars.
- Mulch to prevent earwig damage. Use rolled up wet newspaper to attract and trap and dispose of earwigs.
- Use row covers to exclude caterpillars.
- Spray aphids away with a steady stream of water.

Diseases: No serious disease problems

HARVEST

Snip chervil leaves continuously beginning 6–8 weeks after sowing or once plants reaches 4 inches (10 cm) tall. Harvest leaves before flowering,
Storage: Best fresh; freeze or dry leaves; preserve in butter or oil

VARIETIES

Chervil comes in flat and curly-leaf types. Curly-leaf chervil may taste slightly bitter. 'Brussels Winter' is a large leaf variety.

Chicory: Belgian Endive and Witloof

Common name: Chicory, Belgian endive, witloof (white leaf), witloof chicory, heart of chicory, asparagus chicory, succory, Italian dandelion
Botanical names: *Cichorium intybus* var. *foliosum* (grown as a salad vegetable, similar to endive)
Pronounced sih-KO-ree-um in-TY-bus
World names for *Cichorium intybus* var. *foliosum*: chicorée (French); Salatzichorie, Chicorée (German); radicchio (Italian); archicoria (Spanish). (Note: These common names may be confused with the common names for endive and radicchio. *Cichorium intybus* var. *foliosum* is sometimes used in the same way as endive, *Cichorium endiva*.)
Botanical name of related chicory variety, sometimes called "coffee chicory": *Cichorium intybus* var. *sativum* (grown for its roots, dried and ground, and used as a coffee substitute)
World names for *Cichorium intybus* var. *sativum*: ku ju (Chinese); chicorée à café (French); Wurzelzichorie, Kaffeezichorie (German); cicoria (Italian); kiku nigana (Japanese); escarola (Spanish).
Family: Sunflower family—*Asteraceae (Compositae)*

ABOUT

Type of plant: Biennial or perennial, best in cool season
Origin: Asia, Mediterranean, Europe; long used in Italy from early Roman times.
Description: Belgian endive, witloof, witloof chicory, or heart of chicory is grown for its elongated, blanched leaves. Seeds are sown in spring; plants mature in autumn; the green leaf tops are trimmed to an inch (2.5 cm) of the stem in winter; the plant is lifted and buried diagonally in moist sand in a cool, dark growing area; the new growth or leaf heads (called chicons) grow tight and elongated and blanched white in the dark.
Height: 24–48 inches (60–122 cm)
Breadth: 6 inches (15 cm)
Root depth: Long taproot
Bloom time and flower: Pale blue bachelor button-like flowers open in the morning and close in the evening during the second year
Edible parts: Leaves; chicons (the whitened, compact, leafy shoots that are lifted, forced and blanched); dried, ground roots can be used as a coffee substitute.

KITCHEN

Serve: Serve Belgian endive raw or cooked. Combine Belgian endive raw in salads with other greens. Braise or steam Belgian endive and serve with béchamel sauce or top with butter and season with herbs.

BASICS

Seed planting depth: ¼ inch (6 mm)
Germination soil temperature: 60–70°F (16–21°C)
Days to germination: 10–14
Sowing indoors: Year-round for indoor growth
Sowing outdoors: After the last frost in spring
Soil pH range: 5.0–6.8
Growing soil temperature: 50–85°F (10–29°C)
Days to maturity: 120 days for roots; add 3–4 weeks to blanch cylindrical sprouts called chicons
Spacing of plants: 3–4 inches (7.5–10 cm); thin plants when first true leaves appear to 6–12 inches (15–30 cm) apart in all directions
Light: Full sun; partial shade in midsummer
Water: Keep soil moist; dry soil may result in bolting.
Nutrients: Moderate nitrogen, phosphorus, and potassium
Rotating crops: Do not follow escarole or endive.
Companion crops: Leafy green vegetables; including lettuce and spinach
Incompatible crops: Beans
Propagation: Seed
Seed viability: 6 years; store in an airtight container in a cool, dark place.
Seed weight: 14,430 seeds per ounce (510 per gram)

SITE

Best climate: Growing zones 4–10; grow as a winter vegetable in mild areas. Some cultivars are suited for autumn planting for spring harvest in areas as cool as zone 5.
Soil preparation: Humus-rich, well-drained supplemented with well-rotted manure or organic compost
Container growing: Plant 3 plants in a 5-gallon (19 l) container. The container should be a minimum of 8 inches (20 cm) wide and 12 inches (30 cm) deep.

PLANTING

Sow chicory seed ¼ inch (6 mm) deep.
Planting time: Sow outdoors in early spring or early summer to mature by autumn; requires a long growing season. Roots may be dug in 120 days, after the first autumn frost.
Planting time in cold-winter climates: Spring and early summer

Planting time in mild-winter climates: Autumn and winter
Planting time in reverse-season climates: Winter. Cooler temperatures produce a sweeter crop while warmer temperatures produce a slightly bitter flavor

CARE

Keep soil moist; cultivate to control weeds; protect plants from heat by installing shade cover fabric. Add well-rotted manure or organic compost to soil before planting.
Forcing or blanching for C. *intybus* var. *foliosum* for chicons:

- **Outdoor blanching or forcing:** In late autumn or early winter about 120 days after sowing, force or blanch in trenches, coldframes, or containers. Two methods: 1) Lift the mature plant carefully, remove green leaves about 1 inch (2.5 cm) above ground level or root shoulder leaving the root 8–9 inches (20–22 cm) long. Replant the root covering the stump with soil forming a ridge about 6 inches (15 cm) high. Chicons will re-sprout from the root stump and force their way through the soil. These blanched shoots or chicons are then harvested. 2) Dig a trench 6–8 inches (18–20 cm) deep. Trim long, fleshy roots opposite the growing point to about ½ inch (13 mm) above the shoulder; replant roots closely packed in the upright position; cover the tops with moist finely aggregated soil, peat, sand, or combinations of the three or cover with a layer of straw mulch. Cover the trench with an opaque material that will allow sprout or shoot growth of at least 16 inches (40 cm) above the trench. Grow shoots on in the temperature range of 41–70°F (5–21°C), optimum 64°F (18°F). Keep the soil moist throughout growth for another 20–22 days until the chicons are ready for harvest.

- **Indoor blanching or forcing:** (Use this method when garden soil is heavy or winter weather is severe.) As above, dig up the plant in late autumn or early winter; cut off leaves to 1 inch (2.5 cm) above the root shoulder. Replant the roots upright in a large container filled with soil leaving the shoulders or crown slightly exposed; cover the container with an inverted pot or box or opaque material to block out the light. Keep the soil moist and maintain a temperature of 50–64°F (10–18°C). Harvest the chicons in 3–4 weeks by cutting the blanched shoots (chicons) just above the soil. Cover the roots again and the stumps may re-sprout to give second crops of smaller chicons. To store roots for forcing later: Lay them flat in boxes with moist sand between each of the layers and keep them in a frost-free shed or cellar until they are needed.

- **Tying outer leaves together to blanch or force:** Tie the outer leaves together at the top of the developing heads (or hearts) about 100 days after sowing or 2–3 weeks before you wish to harvest chicons. In humid areas, blanching by tying outer leaves may cause inside leaves to rot.

Common problems: Water well and provide shade in hot spells to prevent brown, crisp ends on leaves.

Pests: Aphids, slugs.

• Control slugs with shallow pans of beer set into the soil or hand pick and destroy.

• Spray away aphids with a strong, steady stream of water.

Diseases: Provide good air circulation to avoid molds.

HARVEST

Belgian endive or chicons are ready for harvest about 120 days after sowing. See forcing or blanching above: Cut when the chicons—the tight, pale-green succulent heads are tightly formed and 3–5 inches (7.5–12 cm) in diameter. If only the leaves are cut, the plant will re-sprout and provide a continuous harvest.

Storage: Will keep in the vegetable compartment of refrigerator for 1 week; roots 4–5 months.

VARIETIES

Belgian endive varieties include: 'Flash', 'Galla', 'Red C', 'Witloof Robin', 'Witloof Zoom'.

Chinese Leaves: Bok Choy, Pei Tsai, Napa Cabbage, Michihili

Types of Chinese leaves: The term "Chinese leaves" or "Chinese cabbage" is often loosely used to refer to several different members of the *Brassica* or cabbage or mustard family. There are three general types of Chinese leaves or Chinese cabbages: the "loose-headed", the "hearted' or "barrel-shaped", and the "tall cylindrical".

- **The loose- or open-headed type** of Chinese leaves or cabbage has a lax demeanor with outwardly floppy textured leaves. The best known of this type are bok choy and pei tsai.

Bok choy or **pak choi** has smooth, rounded stalks that bear a resemblance to chard or celery without the grooves. The leaves of bok choy are large and spoon-shaped like the leaves of spinach. Bok choy has crunchy stalks that are mild and juicy sweet. The leaves are tender and crisp with a subtle peppery flavor. ("Choy" means "vegetable" or "cabbage".)

Pei Tsai is loose headed and does not form a heart. Pei tsai is slightly cylindrical with a ruffled appearance and grows to about 12 inches (30 cm) tall. This cabbage has a tangy sweet but not spicy flavor and is favored by home gardeners who benefit from its cut and come again harvest.

- **The hearted or barrel-shaped type** of Chinese leaves form a compact head with tightly wrapped leaves around a dense heart. These are commonly referred to as Napa cabbage.

Napa Cabbage, also called che-foo or wong bok, is stout to about 10 inches (25 cm) tall. Napa cabbage—which is named after the Napa Valley in California where it was first commercially planted in the United States—is the most popular of Chinese leaves. Napa is a tender and very sweet-tasting cabbage.

- **The tall cylindrical type** of Chinese leaves has long, upright leaves that form a tapering head. These varieties are generally referred to as chihili or 'Michihili' (also spelled Michihli), the name of one popular tall cylindrical variety.

Michihili or chihili type is a semi-heading cabbage—the leaves may turn slightly inward or outward—that looks something like a head of cos lettuce. Michihili can grow to 18 inches (45 cm) tall. It is mild flavored and can absorb the flavors of the vegetables, meats, and poultry it's cooked with. Michihili is often considered a form of Napa cabbage.

Botanical name for bok choy, pak choi: *Brassica rapa* var. *chinensis*
Pronounced BRASS-ih-kuh rap-a
Common name for bok choy, pak choi: Chinese white cabbage, pak choi or pac choi and bok choy ("choy" is Cantonese, also Romanized as "choi", means "vegetable"; "bok" or "pak" means "white.")
World names for bok choy, pak choi: pak choi, bok choi, bai cai, peh-chai (Chinese); chou pak choi (French); Chinakohl, Chinesischer Senfkohl, Pak-Choi (German); cavolo cinese (Italian); col chino (Spanish)

Botanical name for pe-tsai: *Brassica rapa* var. *pekinensis*
Common name for pe-tsai: Chinese cabbage, white cabbage, flowering cabbage, celery cabbage, pak choy, pe-tsai, Michihili, Napa cabbage, nappa, Asiatic cabbage
World names for pe-tsai: pe tsai, bai cai, huang ya cai (Chinese); chou de Pékin, chou pe-tsai (French); Pekingkohl (German); cavolo sedano (Italian); couve petsai (Portuguese); col petsai (Spanish)

Family: Cabbage or mustard family—*Brassicaceae (Cruciferae)*

ABOUT
Type of plants: Biennial grown as an annual, cool season
Origin: China and Eastern Asia. The varieties grown today derive from Japanese cultivars.
Height: Up to 20 inches (51 cm)
Breadth: 5 inches (13 cm) or more
Root depth: Shallow, 18–36 inches (45–90 cm)
Bloom time and flower: Blooms yellow flowers in the second year; flowering is induced by long days. Short days and warm temperatures keep the plant in the vegetative phase.
Edible parts: Leaves

KITCHEN
Serve: Chinese leaves can be steamed, boiled, quickly stir fried, or eaten raw. Cooked leaves and stalks add flavor to soups, stews, pasta dishes, and stir-fries.

BASICS
Seed planting depth: ¼ inch (6mm)
Germination soil temperature: 75–85°F (24–29°C).

Days to germination: 4–10
Sow indoors: 4–6 weeks before last frost
Sow outdoors: 10–12 weeks before first frost
Days to maturity: 65–70 after direct seeding; 40–50 after transplanting
Soil pH range: 6.5–7.5
Growing soil temperature: 45–75°F (7–24°C)
Spacing of plants: 4 inches (10 cm) apart; thin plants to 12–18 inches (30–45 cm) apart in all directions
Water: Moderate and even, water frequently
Light: Full sun to part shade in hot climates; needs at least 6 hours of sun a day.
Nutrients: Heavy feeder
Rotating crops: Avoid rotating with cabbage family crops
Companion crops: Beets, lettuce, onions, radishes, spinach
Incompatible crops: Tomatoes, peppers, okra, potatoes
Propagation: Seed
Seed viability: 3 years; store in airtight container in cool, dark place
Seed weight: 8,500 seeds per ounce (300 per gram)

SITE

Chinese cabbage requires a long, cool growing season. It will bolt to seed in excessive hot weather and the long day lengths of mid-summer.

Frost tolerance: Hardy; can survive subfreezing weather for short periods of time
Soil preparation: Chinese cabbage prefers humus-rich, well-drained soil and clay loam soils with good fertility
Avoid: Planting in exposed, hot locations that receive more than 6 hours per day of direct sunlight

PLANTING

Planting time in cold-winter climates: Direct seed in early to mid-summer for autumn harvest. Start seed indoors 2–3 weeks before last expected frost; transplant out in 1 month when the plants have about 10 leaves. Crop performs best in the gradually decreasing day length and temperatures of late summer. For spring and early summer planted crops, young plants may bolt to seed if exposed to frost for more than a week of sub 50°F (10°C) nights. Direct seed or transplant out after the last frost or protect the plants with fabric row cover. Some varieties planted in early spring will bolt with hot and lengthening days and are best planted in late-summer for autumn harvest. To avoid this, plant bolt-resistant varieties.
Planting time in mild-winter climates: Direct seed in early autumn for winter harvest.
Planting time in reverse-season climates: Autumn

GROWING

Water: Water frequently

Nutrients: A side dressing of aged manure can be dug in the early autumn.

Common problems: Subject to bolting when garden temperatures rise and daylight hours lengthen in mid-spring and early summer.

CARE

Pests: Aphids, flea beetles, cabbage worms, cabbage maggots, slugs.
- Spray aphids with a steady stream of water
- Cabbage worm can be controlled with Bacillus thuringiensis (Bt).
- Cover seed and seedlings with floating row cover from day of planting to deter flea beetles

Diseases: Yellows, clubroot, black rot
- Cut down disease by planting disease-resistant varieties.
- Avoid handling plants when wet.
- Practice preventive crop rotation and sanitation.

HARVEST

Chinese leaves will be ready for harvest 65–70 after direct seeding; 40–50 after transplanting. Harvest leaves summer to late autumn before hard freeze when the plant is at least 5 inches (12 cm) tall; pick outside leaves sparingly. Young leaves have the most subtle flavor.

Storage: Keep in refrigerator for about 1 month, or blanched and frozen for 3–4 months. Heads will store 1–2 months at 32°F (0°C) at 95% humidity. Napa or wong bok types are barrel shaped and usually store 2 months in horizontal position to prevent crushing the crowns. Michihili types—tall cylindrical varieties—do not store for long periods.

VARIETIES

There are several plants that go by the name of Chinese cabbage:
- **Bok choy** stalks are smooth and rounded and leaves are large and spoon-shaped. Try 'Joi Choi' which is heat and cold tolerant. 'Mei Qing Choy' is a 'baby bok choy'.
- **Napa cabbage** or **wong bok** or **che-foo** has a short, compact, broad but not tight head. Try 'Tokyo Giant', 'Tropical Pride', or 'Wintertime'.
- **Michihili** or **chihili**-type Napa cabbage has a large, oblong compact heart. Try 'Michihili', 'Market Pride', or 'Shaho Tsai'.
- **Pe-tsai** has broad yellowish green leaf stalks that develop into a densely packed, narrow, oblong, lettuce-like head. Pe-tsai is a name used to describe plants also known as Napa cabbage.

Chives

Common name: Chive, chives
World names: Chive: bei cong (Chinese); ciboulette, civette (French); Schnittlauch (German); cipoletta (Italian); cebolinha (Portuguese); cebollino (Spanish); **Garlic chive:** jiu cai (Chinese);ciboule de chine à feuilles larges (French); Chinesischer Schnittlauch, Schnittknoblauch (German); bawang kuchai (Malay); cive chino (Spanish).
Botanical name: Common chives or Europeans chives, *Allium schoenoprasum*; Chinese chives or garlic chives, *Allium tuberosum*.
Pronounced AL-lee-um skee-noh-PRAY-zum
Family: Onion family—*Alliaceae (Liliaceae)*

ABOUT

Type of plant: Perennial, hardy cool season
Origin: Europe, Asia, North America. Chives became widely cultivated after the Middle Ages.
Description: Common chives *(A. schoenoprasum)*: Clusters of slender, round and hollow grass-like leaves similar to clumps of onions rising from a fleshy base. Purple flower clusters.
- Garlic chives (*A. tuberosum*): flat, strap-like leaves, solid, not hollow, with clusters of white blooms. Grass-like leaves are often drooping.

Height: 12–18 inches (30–45 cm)
Breadth: 6–8 inches (15–20 cm)
Root depth: Shallow
Bloom time and flower: Late spring and early summer; lavender to purple, 1-inch (2.5 cm) globular flowers on stems to 24in (60cm)
Edible parts: Leaves; all plant parts are edible

KITCHEN

Serve: Chives are generally used as a fresh herb. Use chives raw or dried in salads, vegetables, poultry, fish, soups, sauces, eggs, cheeses, butters, or vinegars. Chives can be added to dishes both warm and cold.

BASICS

Seed planting depth: ½ inch (13 mm)

Germination soil temperature: 60–70°F (16–21°C); optimum 70°F (21°C)
Days to germination: 7–14
Days to maturity: 75–90 days; a year or more from sowing to form a harvestable colony
Soil pH range: 6.0–7.0
Growing temperature: 40–85°F (4–29°C); optimum 63–77°F (17–25°C)
Spacing of plants: 6 inches (15 cm) apart in all directions
Water: Keep soil moist; steady water
Light: Full sun to partial shade
Nutrients: Light feeder. Spray plants with liquid seaweed extract 2–3 times during the growing season.
Rotating crops: Do not follow or precede other onion family crops
Companion crops: Carrots, celery, grapes, peas, roses, tomatoes, cress, mint
Incompatible crops: Beans, peas
Propagation: Seed or division. Divide established clumps every 3 years in early spring.
Seed viability: 4 years; store in airtight container in a cool, dark place.
Seeds weight: 33,000 seed per ounce (1,155 per gram).

SITE

Best climate: Zones 3–9; evergreen in warm regions. (Garlic chives are hardy to zones 4–8)
Frost tolerance: Hardy; chives go dormant in cold-winter climates.
Soil preparation: Humus-rich, well-drained soil
Container growing: Start seeds in pots at least 6 inches (15 cm) deep in late summer and grow outdoors. Before frost, move plants indoors to a sunny windowsill.

PLANTING

Sow chive seed ½ inch (13 mm) deep.
Spring planting time: Sow outside late winter to early spring after the ground has warmed and is workable. Divide older clumps in the early spring every 3 years.
Planting time in reverse-season climates: Autumn.
Planting root divisions: Divide clusters with a sharp garden spade or shovel, trim green tops and expose 1 inch (2.5 cm) above the ground covering the rest of the plant with ½ inch (13 mm) of soil.

- Trim flowers as they appear to keep the plant from generating leaves for harvest.
- Protect plants from direct sun in hot climates with shade fabric installed on wooden supports.

CARE

- Trim flowers as they appear to keep the plant from generating leaves for harvest.
- Protect plants from direct sun in hot climates with shade fabric installed on wooden supports.

- In cold climates, trim chives to the ground in autumn and fertilize with organic compost in spring.

Pests: No serious pest problems.
Diseases: No serious disease problems.

HARVEST

Chives are ready for harvest 75–90 days after planting. When stems reach 3–4 inches (7.5–10 cm) tall, clip by one-third then allow the stems to grow on. Clip again by one-third when 5–8 inches (13–20 cm) in height. Stop harvesting 3 weeks before first frost date then allow flowering and expansion of the colony.

Storage: Use fresh or dried. Refrigerate in a sealed plastic bag to retain crispness for 7 days. Dry in a microwave or oven for winter use.

VARIETIES

Choose from these chive varieties: 'Ruby Gen' has gray-green foliage; 'Forescate' has rose-red flowers.

Cilantro

Common name: Cilantro and coriander come from the same plant. When the plant is cultivated for its pungent, aromatic leaves, it is called cilantro (in the Americas) or Chinese parsley. When it is cultivated for its citrus-flavored seeds, it is called coriander.
World names: hu sui, xiang sui, yan sui (Chinese); coriandre, persil arabe (French); Koriander (German); dhania, dhaanya (Hindi); coriandro (Italian); ketumbar, daun ketumbar (Malay); coriandro, cilantro (Spanish); phak chee (Thai)
Botanical name: *Coriandrum sativum*
Pronounced kor-ee-AN-drum sa-TY-vum
Family: Carrot and parsley family—*Apiaceae (Umbelliferae)*

ABOUT
Type of plant: Annual, hardy
Origin: Mediterranean, Europe, Asia Minor, Russia; in cultivation for more than 3,500 years
Description: Low growing, lower leaves are glossy and oval with shallow lobbing; upper leaves on side branches are finely divided and feathery resembling flat-leaved parsley.
Height: 12–21 inches (30–53 cm)
Breadth: 6–12 inches (15–30 cm)
Root depth: 8–18 inch taproot (20–45 cm)
Bloom time and flower: Spring to late summer; tiny white or pale-pinkish mauve flowers in umbels with enlarged outer flowers. Small rounded, ribbed beige seeds
Edible parts: Leaves, seeds

KITCHEN
Serve: Use cilantro leaves fresh in salads, salsas, marinades, stir-fries, rice, pastas, or vinegars and with fish and shellfish. Add leaves to guacamole or to Chinese soups and Asian chicken dishes. Use coriander seed to flavor confections, bread, cakes, biscuits.

BASICS
Seed planting depth: ½ inch (13 mm)
Germination soil temperature: 50–85°F (10–30°C)
Days to germination: 7–10
Sow indoors: Not recommended

CILANTRO

Sow outdoors: After the last frost and every 3 weeks until fall in cool regions; in autumn in warm regions
Days to maturity: 60–75
Soil pH range: 6.0–6.7
Spacing of plants: 6–8 inches (15–20 cm) apart in all directions
Light: Full sun to light shade
Water: Keep moist
Nutrients: Light feeder; low phosphorus and potassium needs; too much nitrogen will reduce flavor and cause plant to sprawl.
Rotating crops: Avoid rotating with other carrot family plants
Companion crops: Caraway, eggplant, fruit trees, potatoes, tomatoes
Incompatible crops: None
Propagation: Seed
Seed viability: 5 years; store an airtight container in dark, cool location
Seed weight: 2,100 seeds per ounce (74 per gram)

SITE

Best climate: Growing zones 2–9
Soil preparation: Humus rich, moist, well-drained soil
Container growing: Minimum soil depth of 8 inches (20 cm)

PLANTING

Sow cilantro seed ½ inch (13 mm) deep.
Spring planting time: Sow outdoors after danger of frost is past. Also sow in autumn. Self sows after flowering.
Succession planting: Sow every 2–3 weeks until late summer for a continuous supply of fresh leaves.

CARE

Weed growing bed thoroughly to prevent seedlings from being overcome by vigorous weeds.
Pests: No serious pest problems.
Diseases: No serious disease problems.

HARVEST

Cilantro is ready for harvest 60–75 days after seeding. Pick cilantro leaves at about 6 inches (15 cm) long.
Storage: Place stems in water and cover with a plastic bag to retain freshness.
Harvest coriander: After the plant goes to seed and the seeds turn yellowish-brown, bunch seed heads together, place upside down in a paper bag, then allow seeds to ripen until they drop into the bag.

Storage: In airtight containers in the refrigerator. Dried foliage is of lesser quality; freezes poorly.

VARIETIES

'Santo' is slow to bolt cilantro variety.

Collards, Collard Greens

Common name: Collards ("collard" is an American dialect corruption of the English word "colewort" which means a cabbage that does not heart and having loose leaves.)
World names: wu tou gan lai (Chinese); boerenkool (Dutch); chou cavalier, chou vert (French); Blattkohl, Kuhkohl (German); cavolo da foglia (Italian); couve forrageira (Portuguese); berza, col forrajera (Spanish)
Botanical name: *Brassica oleracea* var. *acephala*
Pronounced *BRASS-ih-kuh oh-leh-RAY-see-uh ay-SEF-uh-luh*
(Acephala means headless; thus this broad classification of cabbage family plants includes kale and collards.)
Family: Mustard or cabbage family—*Brassicaceae (Cruciferae)*

ABOUT
Type of plant: Biennial grown as an annual; hardy, cool season
Origin: Europe. Grown first by the Greeks and Romans; traveled to Britain by 400 B.C. Collards are a form of kale which is the oldest cultivated form of cabbage.
Description: Trunk like stems grow 2–4 feet tall topped with clusters of loosely arranged cabbage-like leaves to 18 inches (45 cm) long.
Bloom time and flower: Yellow or white flowers in the second year
Height: 24–30 inches (61–76 cm)
Breadth: 24 inches (61 cm)
Edible parts: Leaves

KITCHEN
Serve: Collards are served cooked. Cook collards like you would spinach: steamed, braised, stir-fried, sautéed, or added to soups.

BASICS
Seed planting depth: ¼–½ inch (6–13 mm)
Germination soil temperature: 65–85°F (18–29°C)
Days to germination: 5–10
Sow indoors: Not recommended
Sow outdoors: Early spring to midsummer
Soil pH range: 5.5–6.8
Days to maturity: 60–90 days

Growing soil temperature: 45–75°F (7–24°C); optimum 60°F (16°C)
Spacing of plants: 2 inches (5 cm) apart; thin plants to 15–18 inches (38–45 cm) apart in all directions
For salad mix: Sow in a 2–4 inch (5–10 cm) wide band; sow 60 seeds per foot (30 cm)
Water: Moderate
Light: Full sun
Nutrients: Low nitrogen, phosphorus, and potassium
Rotating crops: Avoid following cabbage family crops.
Companion crops: Tomatoes, southern peas, peppers
Incompatible crops: Celery, potatoes, yams
Propagation: Seed
Seed viability: 4 years; store in an airtight container in a cool, dark place.
Seeds per ounce: 7,000 seeds per ounce (250 per gram)

SITE

Collards grow best in growth zones 3 and warmer; use as a winter vegetable in mild areas.
Frost tolerance: Frost hardy; flavor improves as temperatures drop.
Soil preparation: Collards prefer medium light, well-drained soil, supplement with organic compost.
Container growing: A single plant should be planted in a 10-inch (25 cm) pot, 12 inches (30 cm) deep. In a large container allow 18–24 inches (45–60 cm) between plants.

PLANTING

Sow collard seeds ¼–½ inches (6–13 mm) deep. Direct-seeding too thickly may cause overcrowded and spindly plants. Thin plants first to 6 inches (15 cm), then 12 inches (30 cm), then 18 inches (45 cm) apart; thinnings can be served as greens.
Planting time in cold-winter climates: Spring planting: sow seed from 4 weeks before to 2 weeks after the last expected frost. Late summer planting: sow seed 8–10 weeks before the first expected frost. Collards grow well after the first frost.
Planting time in mild-winter climates: Set out plants or sow seeds in early spring or late summer to early autumn. Collards will tolerate summer heat, but prefer cool weather; mulch to keep the soil cool. Set out in summer for autumn and winter harvest; set out in early spring for spring into summer harvest.
Planting time in reverse-season climates: Sow in winter

GROWING

Water: Keep soil moist. Collards are shallow rooted.
Nutrients: Mix well-rotted manure into the soil before planting.
Side dressing: Feed every 3–4 weeks with fish emulsion or use 1 tablespoon (15 ml) blood meal mixed in 1 gallon (3.8 liters) of water or apply compost tea once a month.

CARE

Mulch surrounding soil with straw or place clear plastic on planting beds in autumn.

Common problems: Direct-seeding too thickly may cause overcrowded and spindly plants. Thin plants first to 6 inches (15 cm), then 12 inches (30 cm), then 18 inches (45 cm) apart; thinnings can be served as greens.

Pests: Aphids, cabbage loopers, cabbage worms, cutworms, flea beetles, harlequin bugs.

- Use row covers to protect young plants from flea beetles and cabbageworms.
- Control imported cabbage worm with Bacillus thuringiensis (Bt).
- Exclude pests with floating row covers. Spray away aphids with a steady stream of water.

Diseases: Avoid soil-borne diseases by rotating with other cabbage-family members.

HARVEST

Collards can be harvested 60–90 days after sowing. Clips individual leaves when they reach about 12 inches (30 cm) long. Do not disturb the central bud when picking the leaves. Cut after a frost for sweetest taste, but before a hard freeze. Pick leaves from the bottom up before they get old and tough. Harvest through the winter in most regions by using row covers to protect plants from hard freezes. Remove leaves by removing them from the outside of clusters.

Storage: Collards will keep in the refrigerator for about 1 week. Freeze, can or dry.

VARIETIES

Three favorite collard varieties are: 'Champion', 'Georgia', and 'Vates'.

Sweet Corn

Common name: Corn, sweet corn
World names: yu mi, yu shu shu (Chinese); mäis (French); Körnermais (German); anaaj (Hindi); granoturco (Italian); toumorokoshi (Japanese); jagung (Malay); milho (Portuguese); máiz (Spanish)
Botanical name: *Zea mays* var. *rugosa*
Pronounced ZEE-uh MAYZ
Family: Grass family—*Poaceae (Gramineae)*

ABOUT
Type of plant: Annual, tender, warm weather
Origin: Central America
Description: Grass-like stalk that grows 4–12 feet (1.2–3.6 m) high. Ears form on the side of the stalk about three-quarters of the way up. The top of the stalk terminates in a flowering plume or tassel (the male flower) that produces pollen. The pollen is carried by the wind and pollinates silky threads called silks or styles (the female flowers) on ears lower down the stalk. Each of the silks is connected to an under-fertilized kernel. The lower ears develop as many kernels as the number of silks that were pollinated. The kernels of sweet corn can be yellow, white, black, red or a combination of colors.
Height: 4–12 feet (1.2–3.6 m)
Breadth: 18–48 inches (45–122 cm)
Root depth: Shallow to18–36 inches (45–90 cm); some fibrous roots may extend to 7 -feet (2.1 m)
Bloom time and flower: Summer
Edible parts: Seed

KITCHEN
Serve: Corn is served cooked either on or off the cob. Kernels can be removed from the cob before or after cooking. Raw kernels can be added to soups, mixed with vegetables, stews, and relishes. Cooked kernels can be added to salads, omelets, pasta, risotto, salsa, or soups.

BASICS
Seed planting depth: 1 inch (2.5 cm)
Germination soil temperature: 65–85°F (18–29°C); optimum 72°F (22°C)
Days to germination: 4–10
Sow indoors: Not recommended

SWEET CORN

Sow outdoors: 1 week after last frost
Days to maturity: 60–100 frost free days
Soil pH range: 6.0–7.0
Growing soil temperature: 65–75°F (18–24°C)
Spacing of plants: 4–6 inches (10–15 cm) apart; thin to 12–18 inches (30–45 cm) apart in all directions
Light: Full sun
Water: Moderate until flowering; heavy from flowering to harvest
Nutrients: Heavy feeder
Rotating crops: Precede corn with a nitrogen fixing crop.
Companion crops: Bush beans, beets, cabbage, cantaloupe, cucumbers, melon, parsley, peas, potatoes, pumpkins, squash
Incompatible crops: Tomatoes, cane berries, pole beans
Propagation: Seed
Seed viability: 2 years; store in an airtight container in a cool, dark place
Seed weight: 156 seeds per ounce (5–6 per gram)

SITE

Corn grows best in growth zones 3–11.
Frost tolerance: Tender; injured by light frost.
Soil preparation: Grow corn in sandy loam for early crops. Grow in clay loam or peat and muck soils for later crops. Prepare planting bed in the autumn by working in 1 inch (2.5 cm) of organic compost or rotted manure. Mulch before a hard freeze and then remove the mulch in the spring.
Container growing: 21 inches (53 cm) wide, 8 inches (20 cm) deep container; grow at least 3 plants per container to assure pollination.

PLANTING

Planting time: Sow all corn varieties—early, midseason, and late—in spring, 2–3 weeks after the last frost. Sow 1–2 weeks earlier if the soil has first been warmed by covering with black plastic for a week or more in sunny weather.
Spacing of plants in rows: 12–18 inches (30–45 cm) apart in all directions
Spacing between rows: 36–40 inches (91–100 cm). Plant corn in blocks of four or more short rows since corn is pollinated by the wind. Try blocks of four short rows at least 24–36 inches (60–90 cm) apart to form a square. Too much space between rows will cause the pollen to drop between the rows, resulting in unpollinated ears.
Number of plants per square foot: 4.
Planting in "hills": Space hills or clumps 36 inches (90 cm) apart on all sides; plant 6–7 seeds in each hill; thin to the 3 strongest plants.
Best soil temperature for germination: 65–85°F (18–29°C); optimum 72°F (22°C)

Corn will not germinate below 50°F (10°C). Corn seed germinates poorly in cold, wet soil and may rot. Planting in cold soil risks poor stands. Fungicide treatment of seed is beneficial when planted in cool wet soil. Treated corn seeds will not germinate below 55°F (13°C) and there may be low germination under 60°F (16°C). Wait to sow treated seeds until soil temperature is over 55°F (13°C). Plant untreated seeds when the soil is warm, at lest 65°F (18°C).

Weeks to transplanting: 4

Succession planting: Make second planting 3 weeks after the first and a third planting 4 weeks later and so on. Two week planting intervals will extend the harvest. Or extend the harvest by planting early, mid-season, and late varieties.

GROWING

Water: Moderate water early; heavy water from flowering to harvest. Corn is sensitive to fluctuations in soil moisture because it is shallow rooted. Water when there is a sign of wilting. Keep soil moist when tassels appear and ears are forming. Water is most critical when corn is in tassel. Flooding will cause the plant stress at the tasseling and silking stages which may result in stalk rot, reduced plant height, ear development, and yield. Deep water when tassels emerge and repeat deep watering when silks form.

Nutrients: Heavy feeder (high in nitrogen, phosphorus, and potassium); apply well-rotted manure in the autumn, or compost a few weeks before planting.

Side dressing: Apply fish emulsion or compost tea twice during the growing season: first, one month after planting and again when the tassels appear. Feed with high nitrogen fertilizer when stalks are 12–15 inches (30–38cm) tall.

Pollination: Wind-pollinated. Pollen is produced by the tassel (the male flower) that forms at the top of each stalk of corn. The silks that emerge from the ears are the female flowers. Pollen from the tassels (male flowers) must fall into the corn silks (female flowers) to produce kernels. When a silk is pollinated it will grow a kernel. Wind blows the pollen from the tassel and gravity drops it onto the silks. Each silk that is pollinated results in a kernel of corn developing on the ear. After tassels and silks have formed, give the cornstalk a little shake to aid pollination. If pollination does not take place only the cob, not the kernels, will grow.

- For the best pollination and well-filled ears, plant corn in blocks of at least 4 rows.
- Pollination will occur whether the pollen falls on the silks of the same plant or on the silks of another plant nearby. This results in cross pollination.
- Avoid the cross-pollination of differing varieties by planting different varieties so that they mature at different times or separate the varieties by at least 25 feet (8 m). As an alternative, plant different varieties at 2-week intervals.
- Corn varieties which reproduce true to type from seeds year after year are referred to as "open-pollinated" or "standard." They are not affected by cross pollination.
- It does not make a difference where the pollen that pollinates an "open pollinated" variety comes from. Hybrid varieties of corn must be pollinated by like varieties.
- Hand-pollinate to guarantee seeds that will come true if more than one cultivar is being grown.

- Don't plant popcorn near sweet corn; pollen of one can affect characteristics of the other. Grow super sweet varieties at a distance from standard varieties.
- Pollination may be poor when the air temperature is more than 96°F (36°C), when there are hot dry winds, or when the plant is under moisture stress. Under normal temperatures, ears will be ready to harvest about 14–19 days after pollination.

Flowering requirements: Sweet corn is influenced by day length (photoperiod) and temperature. Short days of 8 hours or less and low mean temperatures of 72°F (22°C) or less can delay flowering.

CARE
Use short-season cultivars in colder regions.

Common problems:
- Ears that do not fill with kernels to the tip were not fully pollinated. Hand-pollinate by stripping pollen from the tassels and sprinkling it on the silks, especially on plants growing on the outside edges of the plot.
- Poor kernel development also may be caused by overcrowding, potassium deficiency, or dry weather.
- Poor pollination may occur when there are too few corn plants in the patch.
- Avoid planting in areas that do not receive at least 6 hours per day of direct sunlight.

Pests: Aphids, armyworms, corn earworms, corn maggots, corn rootworms, cucumber beetles, earwigs, garden webworms, corn borers, cutworms, wireworms, flea beetles, Japanese beetles, June beetles, leafhoppers, sap beetles, seed corn maggots, thrips, webworms, white grubs, wireworms, birds, raccoons.
- Plant in warm soil to avoid wireworms, which destroy seed.
- Late spring plantings are less prone to corn borers.
- Early plantings are less susceptible to corn earworms. Corn earworms deposit eggs on the developing silks; later small caterpillars follow the silks down into the ears, where they feed on the tips. Control earworms by dropping mineral oil into the immature ears as soon as the earworm's sticky frass is spotted on the silks, usually 3–7 days after silks appear.
- Rotate corn plantings and shred, bury, or compost crop debris to reduce over wintering worm pests.
- Protect seed and seedlings from birds by placing bird netting or chicken wire a few inches off the ground; keep in place until plants reach 6 inches (15 cm) in height.
- Control raccoons and most rodents by planting away from wooded areas or fencing the garden.
- Protect maturing ears from birds by slipping a paper bag over each ear; hold the bag in place with a rubber band.

Diseases: Bacterial wilt, mosaic virus, rust, corn smut, southern corn leaf blight, Stewart's wilt

- Corn smut is a fungus disease that attacks the kernels; kernels turn gray or black and grow about four times larger than normal. Destroy affected plants and rotate corn to a new location next season. Smut spores can survive in the soil for two years.
- Stewarts' wilt is a bacterial disease spread by flea beetles resulting in yellowing of the leaves and severe stunting of the whole plant. Plant resistant varieties and control flea beetles when they first appear.
- Destroy plants with mosaic virus, mottled green leaves and stunted growth.

HARVEST

Harvest corn 60–100 frost free days after planting, usually in autumn when silks begin to dry and turn brown and kernels growing 2 inches (5 cm) from the top of an ear yield a white milky fluid when pinched, usually about 18–24 days after silks first show. Check the crop when the ears are plump and the silks have withered. To check the crop, pull back husks and try popping a kernel with your thumbnail—milky juice means the corn is ready; watery juice means the corn is immature. If the fluid is watery, wait a few more days. If the fluid is gummy, you've waited too long. To harvest, pull the ear down and twist it free. Sugar content is highest in the morning. If you want to serve sweet corn at dinner, pick the corn in the early morning and refrigerate in the husk until supper. Low temperature decreases the rate of conversion of sugars into starch.

Baby Corn: Baby corn is corn harvested before it has matured. Plant corn seed 1–2 inches (2.5–5cm) apart and later thin seedlings to 4 inches (10cm) apart. Or, use normal spacing and harvest secondary ears as babies, leaving the top ears to mature. Harvest a few weeks after sowing just before or just as the silks emerge; eat whole, pickled or use in salads or Asian cuisine.

Storage: Keep corn in the refrigerator, for 2–4 days after plunging freshly picked ears into ice water to preserve the sweetness by slowing the conversion of the sugar in the kernels into starch. Store in the freezer for 3–6 months after blanching on the cob, plunging into an ice bath, and cutting the kernels from the cob.

VARIETIES

Choose from these sweet corn varieties: early planting and early harvest corn varieties include 'Early Sunglow' and 'Polar Vee'; midseason varieties include 'Golden Bantam' a classic yellow variety, 'Honey and Cream' which is bicolor white, and 'Indian Summer SH2' which is super sweet; late varieties include 'Country Gentleman' and 'Illini Xtra-Sweet SH2'; 'Silver Queen' is a classic white variety; for a small garden, choose 'Golden Midget', it has 3 foot stalks and 4 inch ears; also for small gardens, 'Tom Thumb'.

Corn Salad, Mâche

Common name: Corn salad, mâche, lamb's lettuce, field salad
World names: mâche (French); Feldsalad, Rapunzel, Ackersalat (German); Vogerlsalat (Austria); Nüsslisalat (Switzerland); valeriana (Italian)
Botanical name: *Valerianella locusta* (common or European corn salad)
Pronounced vuh-lair-ee-uh-NEL-luh loh-KOO-stuh
Family: Valerian family—*Valerianaceae*

ABOUT
Type of plant: Annual, tender, cool weather
Origin: Europe, North Africa, Asia Minor. Cultivated in Europe since Roman times.
Description: Rosettes of spoon-sized round or oval, grey-green leaves
Height: 3 inches (7.5 cm); Italian corn salad to 16 inches (41 cm)
Breadth: 4–6 inches (10–15 cm)
Root depth: Shallow to less than 1 inch
Bloom time and flower: Spring; inconspicuous flowers
Edible parts: Leaves

KITCHEN
Serve: Use mâche fresh in salads. It can be used in early spring in place of lettuce.

BASICS
Seed planting depth: ¼ inch (6 mm)
Germination soil temperature: 50–70°F (10–21°C)
Days to germination: 7–10
Sowing indoors: Late fall to late winter and grow indoors
Sowing outdoors: 4 weeks before last frost
Soil pH range: 6.0–7.0
Growing soil temperature: 50°–59°F (10–15°C)
Days to maturity: 60–75
Spacing of plants: 2 inches (5 cm); thin to about 4 inches (10 cm) apart in all directions
Water: Keep soil moist
Light: Full sun or partial shade
Nutrients: Low nitrogen, phosphorus, and potassium
Rotating crops: Avoid following radicchio, endive, escarole, artichokes

CORN SALAD, MÂCHE

Companion crops: Carrots, onions, strawberries
Incompatible crops: None
Propagation: Seed
Seed viability: 5 years; store in airtight containers in a dark, cool place.
Seed weight: 11,200 per ounce (395 per gram)

SITE

Best climate: Growing zones 2–6. Over winters in zones 5 and warmer; grow as a winter vegetable in mild areas.
Frost tolerance: Withstands light frost. Chilly nights sweeten flavor.
Soil preparation: Humus-rich, well-drained soil
Container growing: A good choice for container growing. Choose a container 8 inches (20 cm) wide, 12 inches (30 cm) deep

PLANTING

Sow corn salad seed ¼ inch (6 mm) deep.
Spring planting time: Early spring; sow 2–4 weeks before the last frost. Avoid plantings that will mature in hot weather.
Autumn planting time: Plant near first frost date; mulch lightly after hard freeze.
Planting time in cold-winter climates: Sow seed indoors 10 weeks before the last frost. Harvest from the coldframe or transplant to the garden after hardening-off seedlings.
Planting time in mild-winter climates: Sow in the autumn for winter and spring use.
Succession planting: Plant at 2 week intervals until early summer. Start succession planting again in autumn. Good cut-and-come-again crop.
Interplanting: Broadcast seed around onions, garlic, and later peppers. Good under crop for winter brassicas or cabbage family plants.

CARE

Corn salad will need partial shade in the heat of summer. Plant will go to seed in hot weather. Mulch corn salad lightly after a hard freeze. Remove the mulch in early spring.
Common problems: In colder winter areas, mulch heavily to avoid heaving of plants over winter.
Pests: No serious pest problems; fence out deer and rabbits.
Diseases: No serious disease problems.

HARVEST

Corn salad will be ready for harvest 60–75 days after sowing. Pinch off entire young rosettes at ground level or remove outside leaves. Some cultivars remain sweet even when in flower; taste to check.
Storage: Refrigerate unwashed leaves; wash when ready to use.

VARIETIES

Choose from these corn salad varieties: 'A Grosse Graine' is a French variety; 'Cavallo' is an early French variety; 'Broad Leaved' is a standard variety.

Cress

Common name: cress, garden cress, watercress, winter cress
World names cress and garden cress: jia du xing cai (Chinese); cresson alénois (French); Gartenkresse (German); crescione (Italian); agrião, mastruco (Portuguese); berro de huerta, berro alenois, mastuerzo (Spanish).
World names watercress: xi yang cai, dou ban cai (Chinese); cresson de fontaine (French); Brunnenkresse (German); crescione acquatico (Italian); mizu garashi (Japanese); selada air (Malay); agrião (Portuguese); berro (Spanish).
Cress and garden cress botanical name: *Lepidium sativum*
Watercress botanical name: *Rorippa nasturtium-aquaticum* (watercress), *R. microphylla* (winter watercress)
Family: Mustard or cabbage family—*Brassicaceae (Cruciferae)*

ABOUT
Type of plant: Perennial grown as a cool-season annual
Origin: Middle East and Europe; first mentioned in ancient Greek writings.
Description: Small, round, dark-green irregular compound leaves on stems slightly thicker than parsley
Height: 3–12 inches (7–30 cm)
Breadth: 6 inches (15 cm)
Root depth: 1–2 inches (2.5–5 cm)
Bloom time and flower: Summer; oblong clusters of white flowers
Edible parts: Leaves; stems

KITCHEN
Serve: Use raw garden cress or watercress to lend a peppery flavor to salads and sandwiches.

BASICS
Seed planting depth: Broadcast seeds over the area and cover with ⅛ inch (3 mm) of loose soil.
Germination soil temperature: 50–60°F (10–16°C)
Days to germination: 2–7
Sowing indoors: Grow in containers year-round

CRESS

Sowing outdoors: Spring, when soil becomes workable
Soil pH range: 6.2–6.8
Growing soil temperature: 50–75°F (10–24°C)
Days to maturity: *Garden cress*: 14–21 days to harvest with scissors. *Watercress*: 55–70 days.
Spacing of plants: *Garden cress*: Broadcast seed in 3 inch (7.5 cm) bands, 20 seed per inch (2.4 cm); thin to 3 inches (7.5cm) *Watercress*: Thin successful plants to 6–8 inches (15–20 cm) apart in all directions. For seedlings, transplant and space accordingly.
Light: Full sun
Water: Keep soil moist
Nutrients: Low nitrogen, phosphorus, and potassium
Succession planting: Sow every 2 weeks for a steady supply
Intercropping: With carrots, radishes and leafy vegetables
Rotating crops: Do not precede or follow with cabbage family crops
Companion crops: Bush beans, beets, carrots, celery, chamomile, cucumbers, dill, lettuce, mint, onion family, potatoes, rosemary, sage, spinach, thyme
Propagation: Seed, cuttings, divisions
Seed viability: 5 years; store in an airtight container in a cool, dark place.
Seed weight: 11,200 seeds per ounce (400 per gram)

SITE

Best climate: Growing zones 3 and warmer; grow as a winter vegetable in warmer areas or indoors in pots almost anywhere.
Soil preparation: *Garden cress*: Humus-rich, moist soil. Fast growing cress can be grown in a flat with soil or soilless mix for up to four successive cuts. Sow on a moist paper towel, in a saucer, or in a sprouter for one harvest. *Watercress*: Wet, humus-rich, well-limed soil, preferably at the edge of a stream or stream-fed pond. Watercress grows best in containers with a rich soil, sand, and compost mixture submerged in running water or artificial watercourses constructed for ornamental use. Prepare pots then submerge after planting.
Container growing: Watercress will grow in clay pots filled with porous planting medium that sit in fresh water, changed daily. Does not need to grow directly in water. Place 1 inch (2.5 cm) of charcoal in the base of pot 8 inches (20 cm) in diameter or more; then fill the pot with clean loam and compost at a ratio of 2:1; add a small handful of lime or dolomite. Keep pot cool and place a large saucer of fresh water underneath the pot to help maintain moisture.

PLANTING

Planting time for watercress and garden cress: Spring when soil becomes workable and water temperatures reaches 50°F (10°C). Start indoors 4–8 weeks before the last spring frost. Grow in pots, indoors or out. Set pots in pans of water and change the water daily.

Planting time for watercress in reverse-season climates: Late autumn for winter harvest

Planting time for early winter cress: Late summer for autumn and winter harvests; allow for new growth the following year. Not recommended for reverse-season climates. Sow through autumn and winter where frosts are mild.

CARE

- Watercress requires a moving, well-aerated supply of water in an area free from excessive sunlight; avoid locations contaminated by runoff from pastures or faulty sewage systems. Pinch main runners to limit spreading.
- Garden cress grows well in containers and on indoor windowsills. Fill flat or container with moist seed-starter mix, sprinkle seeds, cover with vermiculite or seed-starting mix; harvest after first true leaves appear. Can grow seed on damp cheesecloth; harvest in 2 weeks.

Pests: Possibly cabbage maggots, flea beetles, harlequin bugs, snails. But few pests if planted in running water.

Diseases: No significant diseases

HARVEST

Garden cress: Cut seedlings 10–21 days after sowing. Cut young seedlings when about 2 inches (5 cm) tall. Cut stems and leaves back to ½ inch (13 mm) stubs. Cut again after re-growth.

Watercress: Harvest before flowering; flavor deteriorates during flowering. Pick individual leaves and tender sprouts at the tips of runners.

Storage: In refrigerator for 3–5 days; stand stems in container of cold water and cover tops with plastic bag.

VARIETIES

Other garden cress varieties include common cress, broad leaf cress, French cress, curled cress, curly moss cress, land cress, mustard cress, upland cress, and peppergrass.

Broadleaf cress: considered best for salads. 'Cressida' and 'Persian' are flat leaf varieties, sometimes called peppercress.

Curly cress: also called cresson, curled cress, curlicress, fine curled cress, moss curled cress, extra-curled cress; resembles parsley or chervil with darker green thin stems with lacy foliage. 'Wrinkled Crinkled' is a curly type that is bolt resistant. 'Presto' is a ruffled cultivar.

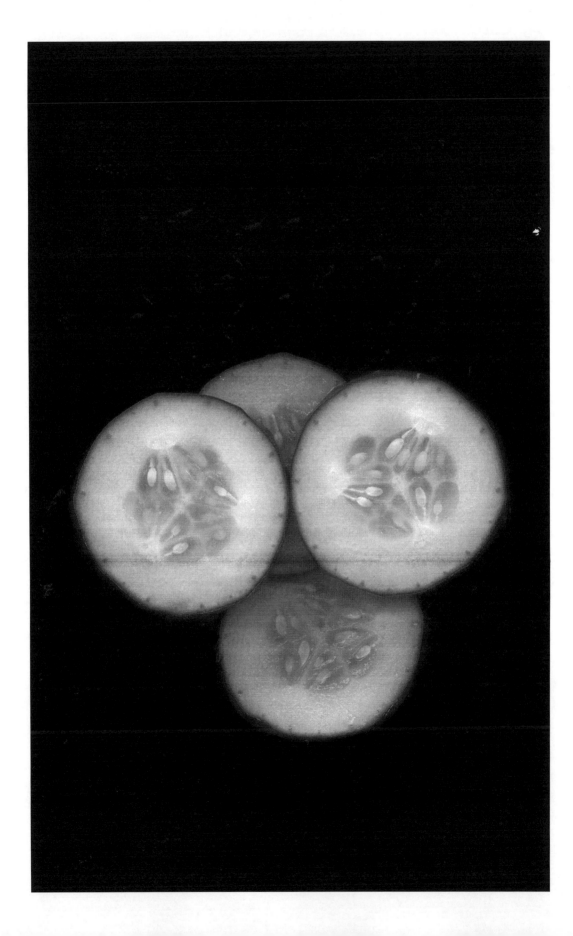

Cucumber

Common name: Cucumber; American pickling cucumber, American slicing cucumber, Middle Eastern cucumber, Oriental cucumber, European greenhouse cucumber
World names: huang gua (Chinese); concombre (French); Gurke (German); khira (Hindi); ketimum (Indonesian); cetriolo (Italian); kyu uri (Japanese); timun (Malay); pepino (Portuguese); pepino (Spanish); taeng kwaa (Thai)
Botanical name: *Cucumis sativus*
Pronounced kew-KEW-mis sa-TY-vus
Family: Cucurbits or gourd family—*Cucurbitaceae*

ABOUT

Type of plant: Annual, tender, warm season
Origin: Asia, the Himalayas. Grown in India 5,000 years ago then spread northeast into China and northwest into Greece and Rome
Description: Weak-stemmed trailing vine; large three- to five-angled leaves and stems are covered with short hairs; cylindrical fruit 4–6 inches (10–15cm) with smooth dark-green skin bearing prickly protrusions and a whitish crisp, juicy interior. Japanese cultivars may have smooth skinned fruit to 12 inches (30cm) long. Gherkins have short, stumpy fruit to 3 inches (7cm) long. Apple and lemon cucumbers are round, yellow-skinned and grow to 2½ inches (6 cm) in diameter.
Height: 3–10 feet (1–3 m); some compact bush cultivars to 8 inches (20cm)
Breadth: On ground, 12 to 20 square feet (3.6–6 m); on trellis, 12–15 inches (30–38cm)
Root depth: Taproot can grow from 24–36 inches (61–91 cm) deep; most roots are in the top 12 inches (20 cm)
Bloom time and flower: Summer; small yellow flowers
Edible parts: Fruits

KITCHEN

Serve: Cucumbers are usually eaten raw but may be cooked—prepared like squash. Cucumbers can replace squash in most recipes.

BASICS

Planting seed depth: ¾–1 inch (1.9–3.8 cm)
Germination soil temperature: 75–95°F (24–35°C); optimum 85°F (29°C)

CUCUMBER

Days to germination: 5–7; at 68°F (20°C) it takes 6–7 days for seedlings to emerge; this time is cut in half at 77°F (25°C)
Sow indoors: 3 weeks before last frost
Sow outdoors: After last frost
Days to maturity: 55–65 frost-free days
Soil pH range: 6.5–7.5
Growing soil temperature: 60–90°F (16–32°C); optimum 65–86°F (18–30°C);
Spacing of plants: 36 inch (90 cm); trellised 18 inch (45 cm) apart
Water: Moderate until flowering; heavy from flowering to harvest
Light: Full sun; will grow with just 5 hours of sun a day
Rotating crops: Avoid rotating with other cucumber family members
Companion crops: Bush beans, broccoli, cabbage family, corn, dill, eggplant, kale, lettuce, melon, nasturtium, peas, pumpkins, radish, squash, sunflower, tomatoes
Incompatible crops: Potatoes, herbs
Propagation: Seed. Each plant has separate male and female flowers. There may be 10 male flowers to every female flower. Male flowers bloom first; female flowers bloom about a week later. Only female flowers produce fruit. "Gynoecious" varieties produce more female flowers than male flowers. This helps to insure pollination and a greater yield. Seed packets usually declare if a variety is gynoecious.
Seed viability: 5 years; store in an airtight container in a cool, dark place.
Seeds weight: 985 seeds per ounce (35 per gram)

SITE

Cucumbers grow best in growth zones 4–12.
Frost tolerance: Very tender; need temperatures of 70°F (21°C) or warmer to grow well
Soil preparation: Cucumbers prefer well-drained sandy loam, supplemented with compost or well-rotted manure.
Planting site: If you allow cucumber vines to sprawl on the ground you will need about 9 square feet (2.7 sq m) per plant. Use hills if you allow the plants to sprawl. To grow vertically, place plants next to a fence or a trellis. Plant in rows if you grow cucumbers vertically.
Container growing: Container size: 8 inches (20 cm) wide, 12 inches (30 cm) deep. Use a trellis or support to increase yields.

PLANTING

Spring planting time:
- **Outdoors:** Direct sow seed in spring after all danger of frost has passed and soil has warmed to 70°F (21°C) for summer crop. Seed will not germinate at a soil temperature below 50°F (10°C). Seed germinates slowly at soil temperatures below 68°F (20°C).
- **Indoors:** Sow in peat pots 3–5 weeks before planting out. Transplant out after soil has

warmed and the weather settled and before sensitive roots become root bound. Indoors, keep temperature above 70°F (21°C) day and 60°F (16°C) night. Do not disturb roots when transplanting.

Autumn planting time: 11½ weeks before the first expected autumn frost

Succession planting: Plant cucumbers every 2 weeks until midsummer.

Mound planting: Sow 4–6 seeds 1 inch (2.5 cm) deep in mounds 16 inches (40 cm) in diameter, raised 10 inches (25 cm) above the soil surface, spaced 4–6 feet (1.2–1.8 m) apart. Compress soil firmly around seed. Thin to 2–3 seedlings per mound. Set trellises or support wires 18–24 inches (45–60 cm) in height.

GROWING

Water: Keep soil moist. Apply moderate water until flowering; heavy water from flowering to harvest. Yields increase if additional water is applied during the growing season. Avoid overhead watering.

Nutrients: Cucumbers are heavy feeders. They prefer ample amounts of phosphorus and potassium and a moderate amount of nitrogen. Add compost and phosphorus to the soil before planting.

Side dressing: Spray with fish emulsion or compost tea 1–2 times per month. Fertilize with blood meal during the period before blooming.

CARE

- Weed every 7–10 days or mulch.
- Trellis where space is limited. Trellis-grown cucumbers are straighter and more uniform in shape. Or use an A-frame support covered with netting or chicken wire to support the vines.

Pests: Aphids, cucumber beetles, cutworms (seedlings), flea beetles, mites, pickleworms, nematodes, slugs, snails, squash bugs, squash vine borers.

- Cucumber beetles carry cucumber bacterial wilt. The sudden collapse of plants indicates wilt disease. Straw mulch may help deter beetle attacks.
- Floating row covers will protect young plants from cucumber beetles; remove covers when plants bloom.
- Pinch out infested vegetation or hose off aphids or cucumber beetles.
- Successive plantings will extend the harvest even where beetles are a problem.
- Hand pick cutworms, slugs, snails, and squash bugs.

Diseases: Anthracnose, bacterial wilt, fusarium wilt, belly rot, cucumber wilt, downy mildew, powdery mildew, leaf spot, scab, curly top, cucumber mosaic, and squash mosaic virus.

- Plant disease resistant varieties.
- Remove and destroy infected plants.
- Trellising will improve air circulation and reduce mildew.

- Do not grow cucumbers or their relatives, such as squash and melons, in the same spot more often than once every 3 years.
- Commercial fungicide containing baking soda can be used to control mildew, anthracnose, and scab.

HARVEST

Cucumbers are ready for harvest 55–65 frost-free days after sowing, midsummer onwards. Harvest 3–4 times per week as fruit matures; this allows the setting of new flowers and fruit. Harvest when the fruit is dark green all over and before the fruits have fully elongated and the seeds are still succulent. Do not let fruit yellow on the vine; the plant will stop producing

Recommended harvest lengths:
- **Slicing cucumber varieties:** When the cucumber is 6–10 inches (15–25 cm) in length
- **Pickling (sweet or baby dills) cucumber varieties:** When 1–6 inches (2.5–15 cm) in length; (regular dills): when 3–4 inches (7.5–10 cm) in length
- **English or Armenian cucumber varieties grown in a hothouse or under glass:** When 12–15 inches (30–38 cm) in length.

Storage: Pickling and slicing cucumbers: in the refrigerator at 45–50°F (7–10°C) and 90% humidity for up to 2 weeks. Cucumbers held lower than 50°F (10°C) suffer chilling injury.

VARIETIES

Choose from these cucumber types and varieties:
Slicers: 'Marketmore', 'General Lee', 'Bush Champion', 'Salad Bush', 'Sweet Success'. A seedless type is 'Diva'. 'Socrates' is a seedless type for cool regions.
Picklers: 'Pickalot', 'Pioneer', 'Little Leaf', 'Northern Pickling'.
Others: 'Suyo Long" an Asian slicing; 'Lemon' is lemon shaped, 'Armenian'.
For containers: Grow varieties specifically developed for small spaces, 'Pot Luck', 'Bush Champion', 'Spacemaster', 'Patio Pik', 'Salad Bush'.

Dill

Common name: Dill
World names: aneth (French); Dill (German); aneto (Italian); eneldo (Spanish)
Botanical name: *Anethum graveolens*
Pronounced uh-NEE-thum gruh-VEE-oh-lenz
Family: Carrot and parsley family—*Apiaceae (Umbelliferae)*

ABOUT

Type of plant: Annual or biennial
Origin: Southwestern Asia. Dill has been used as a seasoning since ancient Egyptian times.
Description: Soft fern-like blue-green leaves resembles fennel. Flat, oval, light brown seeds.
Height: 24–48 inches (60–122 cm)
Breadth: 24 inches (60 cm)
Root depth: Long taproot
Bloom time and flower: Summer to autumn; tiny, highly aromatic, pale greenish yellow blooms, arranged in flat-headed clusters 8 inches (20 cm) across
Edible parts: Foliage and flowers

KITCHEN

Serve: Use fresh dill to season tomatoes, celeriac, beets, cucumbers, cabbage, fresh and sour cream, cream cheese, white sauces, melted butter, salad dressing, eggs, stews, and seafood. Use fresh dill at the end of cooking; it will lose flavor if overheated.

BASICS

Seed planting depth: ¼–½ inches (6–13 mm)
Germination soil temperature: 50–70°F (10–21°C)
Days to germination: 7–10
Sowing indoors: 4–6 weeks before planting out
Sowing outdoors: Every 3–4 weeks from spring until mid summer
Soil pH range: 6.0–6.5
Growing soil temperature: 60–80°F (16–27°C)
Days to maturity: 50–60

DILL

Spacing of plants: 8–10 inches (20–25 cm) apart in all directions if harvesting leaves; 10–12 inches (25–30 cm) if harvesting seeds.
Light: Full sun
Water: Keep soil moist
Nutrients: Light feeder. Spray plants with liquid seaweed extract 2–3 times during the growing season.
Rotating crops: Follow beets
Companion crops: All brassicas or cabbage family plants, fruit trees
Incompatible crops: Carrots, fennel (cross-pollinates with dill), tomatoes
Intercropping: Dill attracts beneficial insects including predatory wasps and flies.
Propagation: Seed
Seed viability: 5 years; store in an airtight container in a cool, dark place.
Seed weight: 13,630 seeds per ounce (480 per gram)

SITE

Best climate: Growing zones 2–9
Soil preparation: Light, sandy, humus-rich soil, moist but well-drained soil
Container growing: Yields well in a container minimum depth of 6–8 inches (15–20 cm)

PLANTING

Sow dill seed ¼–½ inches (6–13 mm) deep.
Spring planting time: Direct sow after the last spring frost, or start seeds indoors 2 weeks before the last frost; transplants poorly.
Autumn planting time: Sow seed in late summer, or allow spring-planted dill to self-sow for an autumn crop.
Planting in warm climates: Late summer through autumn
Succession planting: Sow seeds at 2–3 week intervals spring until midsummer for a continuous harvest through autumn.

CARE

Keep bed weed free. Protect from wind. Pinch off the earliest flower heads to prolong leaf quality.
Common problems: Easily cross pollinates with fennel resulting in a loss of flavor. Dill runs to seed quickly.
Pests: Carrot rust flies, parsley worms, tomato hornworms.
- Use row covers all season or yellow sticky traps to control carrot rust fly.
- Parsley caterpillar is the larva of the swallow tail butterfly; handpick larva off of plants if you don't want butterflies.
- Handpick tomato hornworms or spray with insecticidal soap.

Diseases: No serious disease problems

HARVEST

Dill will be ready for harvest 50–60 days after sowing. In spring and summer, clip fresh leaves at the stem as needed; do not cut more than one-fifth of the plant's foliage at one time. In summer, to collect seed cut flower heads before the seeds mature and shatter, about 2–3 weeks after bloom; hang upside down in a paper bag until the seeds dry and drop into the bag.

Storage: Refrigerate fresh leaves for 1 week. Dry chopped dill leaves on a nonmetallic screen. Freeze leaves or store dried foliage and seeds in an air-tight container.

VARIETIES

Choose from these dill varieties: 'Bouquet' is popular; 'Fernleaf' is a dwarf variety excellent for container growing; 'Superdukat' has intense flavor.

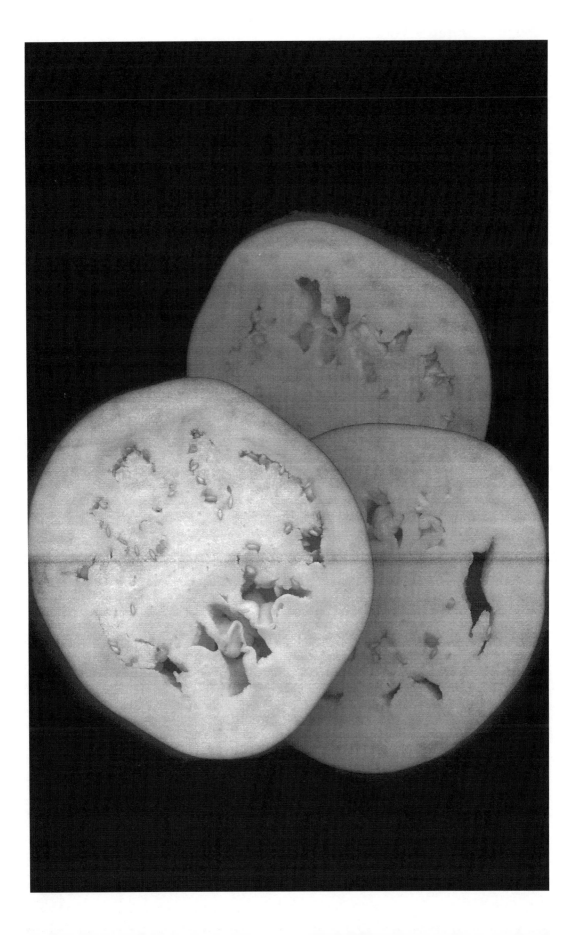

Eggplant

Common name: Eggplant, guinea squash
World names: qie zi, ai gua (Chinese); aubergine, melongène (French); Eierfrucht, Eierpflanz, Aubergine (German), baigan, brinjal (Hindi), melanzane (Italian); daimaru nasu (Japanese); berenjena (Spanish); makhua (Thai)
Botanical name: *Solanum melongena*
Pronounced so-LAY-num mel-on-GEE-nuh
Family: Nightshade or potato family— *Solanaceae*

ABOUT

Type of plant: Tropical perennial grown as an annual
Origin: India. First cultivated more than 2,000 years ago; introduced to Europe through Spain in the sixteenth century by the Arabs
Related plant: *Solanum integrifolium*, called tomato-fruited eggplant or gilos, is cultivated in Asia and Africa bearing red- and orange-fruited eggplants rarely exceeding 2 inches (5 cm) in diameter.
Description: Herbaceous perennial of indeterminate growth with large, lobed, velvety gray leaves 4–5 inches (10–12 cm) long. Large, egg-shaped fruit 5–12 inches (13–30 cm) long; skin is commonly deep purple, though some varieties are white, green, yellow, or mottled green; flesh is white. Each plant usually produces 3–4 well-developed fruits weighing up to 2 pounds (0.75 kg) or more each.
Height: 24–30 inches (60–76 cm)
Breadth: 24–36 inches (60–90 cm)
Root depth: 4–7 feet (1.2–2.1 m)
Bloom time and flower: Summer. Drooping flowers are violet to purple with yellow stamens, 1–2 inches (2.5–5 cm) across. In early cultivars, flowering begins after the sixth leaf has developed; in late cultivars flowering begins after 14 leaves are on the plant. Eggplant appears to be insensitive to day length for flowering.
Edible parts: Fruits. All other parts of the plant are poisonous.

KITCHEN
Serve: Eggplant is served cooked: baked, grilled, stewed, deep-fried.

EGGPLANT

BASICS

Seed planting depth: ¼ –½ inches (6–12 mm)
Germination soil temperature: 70–95°F (20–35°C); optimum 86°F (30°C)
Days to germination: 10–15
Sow indoors: 4–6 weeks before last frost
Sow outdoors: Not recommended
Days to maturity: 100–140 days from seed; 50–75 frost-free days for transplants
Soil pH range: 5.5–6.8
Growing soil temperature: 65–90°F (18–32°C)
Spacing of plants: 3–5 inches (7.5–13 cm); thin to 18–24 inches (45–60 cm) apart in all directions
Water: Heavy
Light: Full sun
Nutrients: Moderate nitrogen and high potassium and phosphorus
Rotating crops: Follow beans or peas
Companion crops: All beans, peas, peppers, potatoes, southern peas
Incompatible crops: Corn, fennel, tomatoes
Propagation: Seed, layering
Seed viability: 5 years; store in an airtight container in a cool, dark place
Seed weight: 5,600 eggplant seeds per ounce (200 per gram)

SITE

Eggplant grows best in growth zones 5–12. It is a perennial in growth zone 10.
Frost tolerance: Very tender
Soil preparation: Eggplant prefers light, humus-rich, well-drained, warm soil. Eggplant grows best in light sandy soils in early spring and loam for later crops. In high rainfall regions or in areas with poor drainage, grow in raised beds. Flooding causes root rot.
Container growing: Requires moist soil, full sun, weekly fertilizing. Choose space-saving varieties. Use a container at least 12 inches (30 cm) deep.

PLANTING

Spring planting time: 1–3 weeks after last expected frost. Seed will not germinate in cool soil.
Planting time in cold-winter climates: Sow indoors 6–8 weeks before planting out. Maintain soil temperature at 80–90°F (27–32°C) until seeds emerge and 70°F (21°C) after. After at least three true leaves form, thin to 2–3 inches (5–7.5 cm) apart in flats or transplant into 2–3 inch (5–7.5 cm) pots or plug trays. To harden plants reduce water and temperature to about 60°F (16°C) for about a week before planting out. Transplant outdoors when the daytime air temperature averages 70°F (21°C) and night temperatures remain above 55°F (13°C). Cold weather may weaken plants. Use row covers to control temperature and insects or warm the soil by covering with black plastic.

Autumn planting time: 14 weeks before the first expected frost
Succession planting: In long-season climates, two small plantings 4 weeks apart will lengthen the harvest. For short-season climates, plant fast-maturing varieties.
Weeks to transplanting: 6–14; when seedlings are at the 2–3 true-leaf stage
Layering: Stems can be rooted by layering; cover the stem with soil while still attached to the plant; adventitious roots form and emerge at the nodes. When well rooted the stem is cut off and transplanted.

GROWING
Water: Soak the soil deeply; water in basins around each plant.
Nutrients: Feed eggplant every 3–4 weeks with fish emulsion or compost tea. Use organic compost mulch to keep the soil moist and free of weeds.

CARE
- Pinch growing tips when plants are 6 inches (15 cm) high to encourage branching. Later clip several branches, to encourage larger fruit; thin fruit to one per branch.
- In hot regions, protect plants with shade covers or plant in early spring to avoid temperatures above 100°F (38°C).
- Long-fruit varieties are more resistant to extremely high temperatures; small egg-shaped and oval-type fruits cannot stand extremely high summer heat.
- In short or cool summer regions, plant eggplant in containers that allow the soil to retain heat and can be moved to protected locations.
- Stake or support foliage-bearing stems when plant becomes heavy with developing fruit.
- Poor fruit color may be caused by low soil moisture.

Common Problems: Provide adequate soil moisture and calcium to prevent blossom-end rot which shows up as a soft, brown spot at the blossom end of the fruit. Avoid planting where peppers, tomatoes, potatoes or eggplants were grown during the past 2 years. Avoid cool locations because blossoms will drop if temperatures fall below 50°F (10°C).

Pests: Lace bugs, aphids, cutworms, Colorado potato beetles, cucumber beetles, cutworms, flea beetles, harlequin bugs, lace bugs, leafhoppers, spider mites, nematodes, tomato hornworms, whiteflies.
- Use row covers to deter flea beetles or apply a light dusting of ground limestone.
- Check the underside of leaves for the orange egg masses of the Colorado potato beetle; crush eggs or control with Bacillus thuringiensis (Bt).
- Handpick Colorado potato beetles and hornworms off the plants.
- Place collars around plants at the time of transplanting to discourage cutworms.

Diseases: Anthracnose, bacterial wilt, botrytis fruit rot, blight, tobacco mosaic, verticillium wilt, fusarium wilt.
- Plant resistant varieties.

- Remove debris from garden, use a 3-year crop rotation, ensure well-drained soil and good air circulation.
- Rotate eggplant and other members of the nightshade (*Solanaceae*) family. Planting vegetables from other plant families to avoid soil-borne diseases such as verticillium wilt.
- Mildew will develop in too humid climates.

HARVEST

Eggplant will be ready to harvest 100–140 days from seed sowing; 50–75 frost-free days for transplants, midsummer onward. Pick when shiny, firm, and full-colored purple; overripe fruit will have a dull greenish-bronze color. Mature fruit is soft enough that thumb pressure will leave an indentation in the flesh of the fruit. Use shears to clip the fruit with stem attached. Harvest regularly to encourage further fruiting. Each plant usually produces 3–4 well-developed fruits; some varieties will produce up to 10 fruits. Prune back unproductive disease-free plants to stimulate new growth.

Storage: In refrigerator at 50–59°F (10–15°C) at 85–90% relative humidity for about 10 days without loss of quality. Storage below 50°F (10°C) will cause chilling injury.

VARIETIES

Choose from these eggplant types and varieties:

Oval fruits: 'Black Beauty' the classic purple-skinned variety; 'Dusky' is purple, and 'Rosa Bianca', heirloom with white skin and lavender streaks.

Long fruits: 'Ichiban', 'Agora', 'Pingtung Long'.

Container growing: 'Dusky,' 'Modern Midget,' 'White Egg,' 'New York Improved,' 'Early Black Egg,' 'Ichiban,' 'Green Goddess' 'Neon, Bambino,' 'Little Fingers,' 'Rosa Bianca,' 'Comprido Verde Claro'.

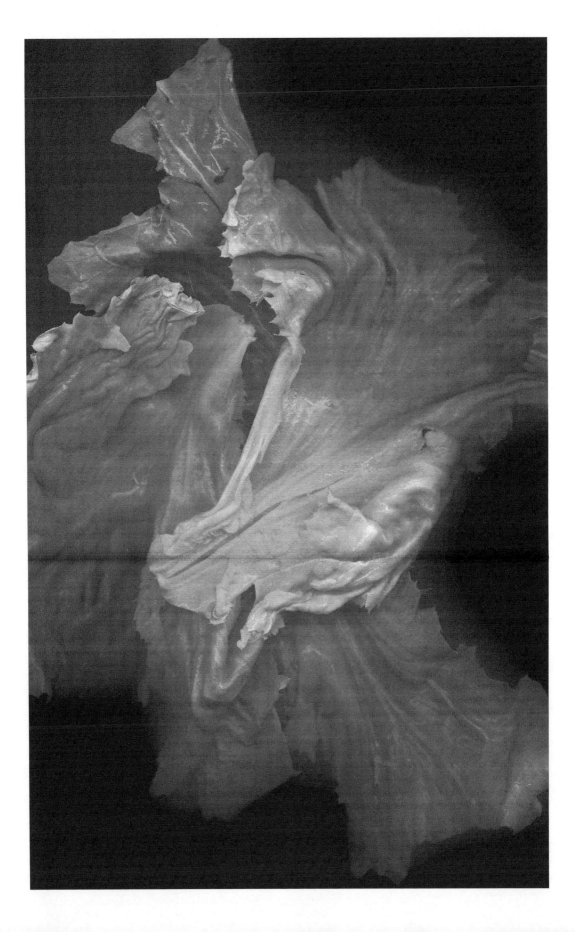

Endive, Escarole

Common name: endive, curly endive, curly chicory, frisee; escarole, broad-leaved endive, Batavian escarole, broad-leaved Batavian
World names: ku ju (Chinese); endive (French); Winterendivie, Escariol (German); indiva (Italian); kiku jisha (Japanese); escarola (Spanish)
Botanical name: *Cichorium endivia*
Pronounced sih-KOR-ee-um en-DY-vee-uh
Family: Sunflower family—*Asteraceae (Compositae)*

ABOUT
Type of plant: Annual or biennial, cool season
Origin: Mediterranean. Used as a vegetable in Europe since the fourteenth century.
Description:
- Endive or curly endive is a loose-headed plant with narrow serrated or ruffled-leaves light-green in the center graduating to dark-green on the outer leaves. Outside leaves taste slightly bitter; inner leaves are milder. Endive or curly endive has a sharp almost bitter taste.
- Escarole or broad-leafed endive is a smooth, broad-leaved plant. Outside leaves are dark to light green and inner leaves are creamy yellow. Escarole is usually less bitter than endive.

Height: 8–12 inches (20–30 cm)
Breadth: 12–15 inches (30–38 cm)
Root depth: 3–4 inches (7.5–10 cm)
Bloom time and flower: Blue flower but rarely allowed to flower
Edible parts: Leaves

KITCHEN
Serve: Serve escarole or curly endive alone or mixed with other greens or root vegetables. Escarole or broad-leafed endive is less bitter tasting than curly endive.

BASICS
Seed planting depth: ¼ inch (6 mm)
Germination soil temperature: 60–70°F (16–21°C)
Days to germination: 10–14

Sow indoors: 8 weeks before last frost
Sow outdoors: Spring to early summer and late summer to fall
Soil pH range: 5.0–6.8
Growing soil temperature: 50–80°F (10–27°C); optimum 60°F (16°C); plant may bolt if temperatures fall below 41°F (5°C); tolerates more heat than lettuce; grows faster in cold weather.
Days to maturity: 90–95 days from seed
Spacing of plants: 1–2 inch (2.5–5 cm) apart; thin successful plants to 6–12 inches (15–30 cm) apart in all directions
Water: Keep soil moist
Light: Full sun to part shade in warmer areas
Nutrients: Moderate nitrogen, phosphorus, and potassium
Rotating crops: Avoid following radicchio
Companion crops: Non-heading salad greens, radishes, turnips, parsnip.
Incompatible crops: Pumpkins, squash
Propagation: Seed
Seed viability: 6 years; store in an airtight container in a cool, dark place.
Seed weight: 14,430 seeds per ounce (510 per gram)

SITE

Best climate: Growing zones 4–10; grow as a winter vegetable in mild areas.
Frost tolerance: Tolerates light frost
Soil preparation: Well-drained, loose soil high in organic matter
Container growing: Good container plant. Use 6-inch (15 cm) pot or grow several plants on 10-inch (25 cm) centers in a large container.

PLANTING

Planting time in cold-season climates: Sow seed out from spring to summer or sow seed indoors 8 weeks before the last frost; set out plants 4 weeks before the last frost. Crop will be sweeter tasting if sown in early spring after the last frost. For winter harvest, sow about 2 months before the first autumn frost.
- Both curled and broad-leafed varieties will bear through hot weather reaching the peak of tastiness after the first autumn frost.
- Cooler temperatures produce a sweeter crop while warmer temperatures produce a slightly bitter flavor.

Planting time in warm-winter climates: Midsummer to early autumn, to produce the bitter-tasting crop preferred by some.
Succession plantings: From spring, sow every 3–4 weeks until the weather warms.
Planting time in reverse-season climates: Late autumn to harvest leafy greens throughout the winter.

ENDIVE, ESCAROLE

CARE
- Keep soil free of weeds
- Feed with fish emulsion every 3 weeks. Moderate nitrogen, phosphorus, and potassium

Common problems: Provide shade in hot spells to prevent brown, crisp ends on endive leaves.

Blanching to ensure a mild flavor:
- Encourage self-blanching by spacing plants closely at 8–10 inches (20–25 cm).
- Tie outer leaves loosely around the heart of the plant when 4–5 inches (10–13 cm) tall.
- When plants reach 12 inches (28 cm) across pull the outer leaves over the center and tie them up at the top (but not when wet to avoid decay); covered leaves will blanch to yellow to white.
- French-blanching technique: 3 days before harvest make sure the plant is dry then place a 4–8 inch (10–20 cm) cardboard disk, or invert a plate or margarine cup over the center of the plant

Pests: Aphids, armyworms, flea beetles, leafhoppers, slugs, snails.
- Control slugs with saucers of beer set into the soil or handpick and destroy. (They are attracted to the yeast in beer and will drown.)
- Exclude beetles and leafhoppers with floating row covers. Spray with insecticidal soap.
- Spray away aphids with a strong, steady stream of water.

Diseases: Downy mildew
- Provide good air circulation to avoid molds.
- Avoid blanching while foliage is wet, which will cause fungal disease.

HARVEST

Endive and escarole is ready for harvest 90–95 days after sowing, summer through winter. Cut outer leaves as needed or when leaves are 5–6 inches (12–15 cm) in length, cut 1 inch (2.5 cm). This will allow the plant to re-sprout and provide a continuous harvest.

Storage: In refrigerator for 2 weeks. Endive and escarole can not be frozen, canned or dried.

VARIETIES
- Curly endive: Try 'Green Curled', 'Green Curled Ruffec', or 'Frizz E'.
- Escarole or broad-leafed endive: Try 'Batavian Full-Heart' or 'Broad-leaved Batavian'.

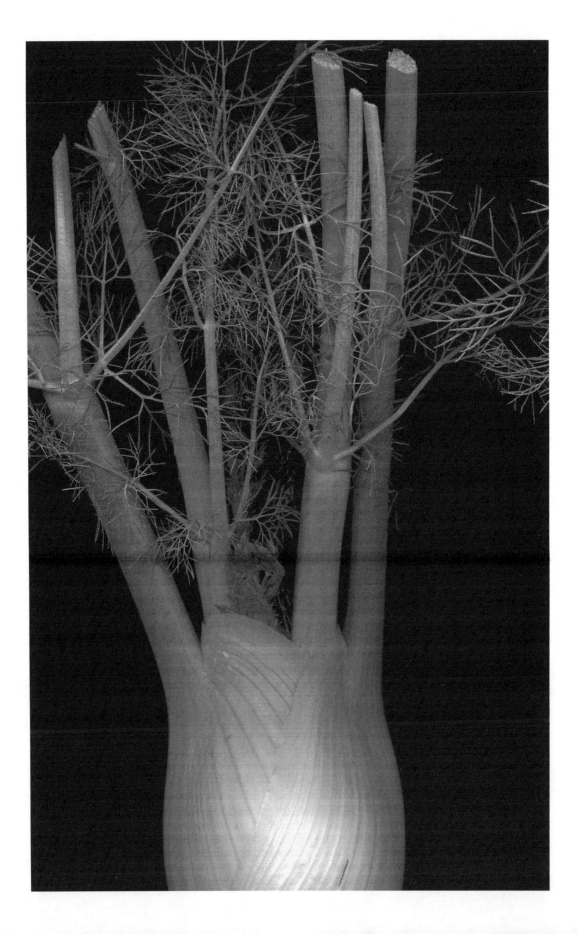

Florence Fennel

Common name: fennel, Florence fennel, finocchio (Italian), bulbing fennel
World names: hui xiang (Chinese); fenouil (French); Fenchel (German); finocchio (Italian); fenneru (Japanese); funcho (Portuguese); hinojo (Spanish); phak chi (Thai)
Botanical name: *Foeniculum vulgare* var. *azoricum* (grown as an annual for its edible leaf base, called Florence fennel or finocchio); *Foeniculum vulgare* (grown as a perennial for its flavorful seeds and young leaves)
Pronounced *feh*-NIK-yoo-lum vul-GARE-ee az-OR-ik-um
Family: Carrot and parsley family—*Apiaceae (Umbelliferae)*

ABOUT

Type of plant: Perennial grown as a summer annual, semi-hardy
Origin: Mediterranean. Used as a vegetable since ancient Roman times.
Description: Spreading-flattened bulb of leaf-stalk base with overlapping celery-like scales or stalks topped with fern-like leaves. Finely cut, aromatic, lime-green leaves turn dark green by autumn. Florence fennel is grown primarily for its bulbous base and leaf stalks which are used as a vegetable. The plain species is cultivated for its licorice flavored seeds and leaves.
Height: 24 inches (60 cm)
Breadth: 12–18 inches (30–45 cm)
Root depth: 4–5 inches (10–13 cm)
Bloom time and flower: Late summer; small, golden flower which appear in flat-topped umbels. Oval, ribbed brown seeds.
Edible parts: Enlarged leaf base and leaf stalks

KITCHEN

Serve: Use fennel raw or lightly cooked after removing the tough outer leaves.

BASICS

Seed planting depth: ¼ inch (6 mm)
Germination soil temperature: 65–75°F (18–24°C)
Days to germination: 7–14
Sow indoors: Not recommended
Sow outdoors: Early spring to midsummer

FENNEL

Days to maturity: 90–115 frost-free days
Soil pH range: 6.5–7.0
Growing soil temperature: 65°F (16°C)
Spacing of plants: 10–12 inches (25–30 mm) apart in all directions
Water: Light
Light: Full sun
Nutrients: Moderate nitrogen, low phosphorus, and potassium
Rotating crops: Avoid rotating with carrots, parsnips and other members of the carrot family.
Companion crops: Mints and members of the mint family
Incompatible crops: Do not grow near dill, as seeds cross-pollinate. Coriander is said to reduce fennel's seed production.
Propagation: Seed, division. Self seeds when established. Divide in autumn.
Seed viability: 4 years; store in an airtight container in dark, cool place.
Seed weight: 7,000 seeds per ounce (250 per gram)

SITE

Florence fennel will grow in all growth zones; grow as a winter vegetable in mild areas.
Frost tolerance: Tolerates light frost
Soil preparation: Fertile, humus-rich, well-drained soil

PLANTING

Plant Florence fennel seed ¼ inch (6 mm) deep.
Planting time in cold-winter climates: Sow early to midsummer or sow indoors 2–4 weeks before the last frost; transplant out when seedlings have no more than four leaves.
Planting time in warm-winter climates: Sow in spring for a summer crop. Sow in late summer for an autumn crop two months before the first frost.
- Plant early in warmer areas since it bolts quickly in hot weather.

Succession planting: Plant small, successive crops to prolong harvest.
Container growing: Plant in autumn, placing a single plant in a 6-inch (15 cm) pot or several on 8-inch (20 cm) centers in a large container.

GROWING

Water: Light but evenly moist
Nutrients: Light feeder. Moderate nitrogen, low phosphorus and potassium. Apply manure tea every 4–5 weeks.

CARE

- Blanch lower stems when bulb reaches the size of an egg.
- Remove seed stalks to increase production of stems and bulbs.
- Keep well weeded or mulch.

- Disturbing the roots will cause bolting.
- Self seeds when established. Divide in autumn.

Common problems: Florence fennel becomes woody when over mature.

Pests: Celery worms, parsley worms (green caterpillars with black and yellow stripes); remove by hand.

- Handpick parsley worms in the early morning. Encourage birds.

Diseases: No common diseases

HARVEST

Florence fennel will be ready for harvest 90–115 frost-free days after sowing. Cut the bulbous stalk just below the point where the individual stalks come together; cut when the bulb is 3 inches (7.5 cm) or more in diameter. Cut leaves as needed after they reach 18 inches (45 cm) long but before flowering.

Storage: Best used fresh. Refrigerate for up to one week.

VARIETIES

Choose from these Florence fennel varieties: 'Herald' for spring planting; 'Zefa Fino' has thick stalks and large bulb; 'Rudy' and 'Trieste' have large, flavorful bulbs.

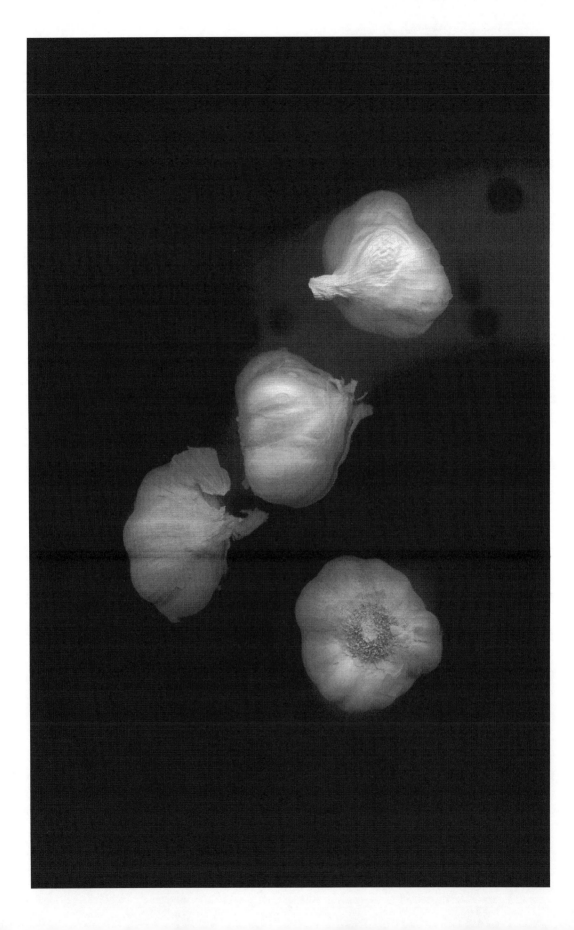

Garlic

Common name: Garlic
World names: suan (Chinese); ail blanc (French); Knoblauch (German); aglio (Italian); gaarikku (Japanese); bawang puteh (Malay); ajo (Spanish)
Botanical name: *Allium sativum*
Pronounced AL-lee-um suh-TEE-vum
Family: Onion family—*Alliaceae (Liliaceae)*

ABOUT

Type of plant: Perennial, cool season
Origin: Central Asia. Garlic has been in cultivation for more than 5,000 years.
Description: Solid, narrow, strap-shaped stalks atop an underground round, white papery sheathed bulb, or head, divided into a cluster of individual cloves.
Height: 12–24 inches (30–60 cm)
Breadth: 6–8 inches (15–20 cm)
Root depth: 4–5 inches (10–13 cm)
Bloom time and flower: Spring and summer; small, white to pinkish blossoms in terminal globular umbel atop a tall, central stalk
Edible parts: Cloves (sections of bulbs)

KITCHEN

Serve: Garlic is most commonly used as a condiment or seasoning. Use garlic as a flavoring agent in vinaigrettes, soups, vegetables, tofu, meats, stews, cold meats, and marinades.

BASICS

Clove planting depth: Regular garlic cloves 2 inches (5 cm) deep; plant elephant garlic cloves up to 4 inches (10 cm) deep.
Germination soil temperature: 55°F (13°C)
Days to germination: 7–14
Sow indoors: Not recommended
Plant outdoors: Late summer to autumn
Days to maturity: 90–100 days after spring planting; 8 months after autumn planting
Soil pH range: 4.5–8.3
Growing soil temperature: 45–85°F (7–29°C); optimum 70°F (21°C)

GARLIC

Spacing of plants: 4–8 inches (10–15 cm) apart; elephant garlic 12 inches (30 cm) apart in all directions
Water: Low
Light: Full sun
Nutrients: Moderate nitrogen, phosphorus, and potassium
Rotating crops: Do not follow any onion family crop.
Companion crops: Beets, brassicas or cabbage family plants, celery, chamomile, lettuce, summer savory, tomatoes, raspberry, strawberries, fruit trees
Incompatible crops: All beans, peas
Propagation: Grown vegetavtively from the cloves formed in each bulb. Seed clove size is important to yields. The yield of a large clove is usually greater than a medium-size clove which, in turn, is usually greater than a small-size clove. The largest cloves will produce the largest bulbs. Small center cloves are excellent for cooking. Small center cloves used as seed clove will produce small plants. Cloves should be chilled in storage at 41°F (5°C) for several months before planting.

SITE

Garlic grows best in growth zones 5–10.
Frost tolerance: Hardy
Soil Preparation: Garlic prefers humus-rich, well-drained, fertile soil. Best if soil is deeply cultivated at least 18–24 inches (45–60 cm). Supplement soil with organic compost that does not contain garlic or onion waste. Garlic should not be planted in beds recently planted with onions unless it is known that the onion crop was free of disease.

PLANTING

Garlic prefers short, cool days at the start of growth and long, warm days to produce bulbs. Garlic is usually planted in the cool of autumn or early spring allowing for the chilling required for bulbing. Bulb development begins after the plant is well established and the days are warmer and longer. Seed clove size is important to yields. The yield of a large clove is usually greater than a medium size clove which, in turn, is usually greater than a small clove. The largest cloves will produce the largest bulbs. Small center cloves are best used for cooking. Small center cloves used as seed clove will produce small plants. Cloves should be chilled in storage at 41°F (5°C) for several months before planting.
Planting depth: Regular garlic cloves 2 inches (5 cm) deep; plant elephant garlic cloves up to 4 inches (10 cm) deep. Set cloves pointed end up.
Planting time in cold-winter climates and in heavy, cold soils: Early spring up to 6 weeks before the last expected frost. Also plant in early autumn about 6 weeks before the soil freezes. Autumn-planted garlic yield bigger cloves than garlic planted in spring.
Planting time in mild-winter climates: Very early spring for harvest in late summer. Also plant in autumn for harvest the following mid- to late-summer.

Planting time in reverse-season climates: Winter

GROWING

Water: Garlic prefers steady water, but do not saturate the soil. Garlic is shallow rooted and requires irrigation in regions where rainfall is not adequate.

Nutrients: Add compost to the soil in the spring. Spray plants with liquid seaweed extract 2–3 times during the growing season. Nitrogen, phosphorus, and potassium needs are moderate.

CARE

- In spring, if seed stalks appear, pick them off promptly.
- In early summer, when flower stalks appear, pinch them back allowing the plant to devote its energy to developing bulbs.
- After flowers form and stems yellow, bend the stems sharply to the ground but do not break them. This is called "lodging." Lodging promotes bulb formation and the drying and withering of plant tops. Bulbs will grow before winter with little or no top growth. Discontinue regular watering about one month later, except in very hot, dry climates, where soil moisture should be maintained.
- In winter, mulch garlic beds heavily to prevent repeated freezes and thaws from heaving the bulbs.
- In short-season regions, plant cloves in small pots and place them into a coldframe until the end of winter. In spring, plant them out in the open.
- Small cloves found at the inside of softneck bulbs can be sown like beans for "garlic greens." Small cloves will produce small plants.
- Do not plant garlic in heavy, wet soils or in the same location in subsequent seasons.

Pests: Aphids, nematodes, thrips.

- Control aphids with a strong, steady stream of water.
- Plant nematode resistant varieties. Solarize the soil to control nematodes.
- Spray thrips with a hard stream of water or an insecticidal soap.

Diseases: Botrytis rot, white rot

- Control botrytis and other molds with a commercial fungicide that contains baking soda.

HARVEST

Harvest garlic in the summer, when tops have begun to yellow and are partially dry and bent to the ground or 2–3 weeks after lodging when heads are fully formed. Take up bulbs with spade or spading fork or when they pull up easily from the stem.

Curing: Remove any clinging soil and allow heads to dry (cure) for 3–4 weeks protecting heads from sunburn or from rainfall or dew and allowing good air circulation around the heads. Heads can be strung-up in bunches or placed on screens to dry. Outer skins will turn papery. Discard cloves that have blue-green spots or mold. Curing is complete when the skins are dry and the necks are tight.

Storage: Store cured garlic in a well-ventilated container or nylon net bag in a dry, cool, and dark place. Peeled garlic cloves can be canned or frozen. Partially dried garlic can be braided into strands for short-term storage. Bulbs may start to shrink if stored at temperatures above 77°F (25°C); cloves may sprout if temperatures fall to around 41°F (5°C).

TYPES

There are three botanical groups of garlic:
- **Softneck garlic including silverskin and artichoke garlic.** The necks of this garlic type are soft and pliable at maturity. Bulbs produce medium size cloves on the outside layer, plus 2–4 layers of small, inner cloves. The cloves overlap like artichoke scales. Softneck is the strongest-flavored garlic. It is less winter hardy than hardneck garlic but stores better. Softnecks are propagated by planting single cloves taken from around the edge of the bulb. 'Silverskin' is a soft-neck suited to cool climates. 'Red Toch' is softneck suite for warm climates.
- **Hardneck, stiffneck, or top-setting garlic, also referred to as Rocambole, serpent garlic, Ophio garilic, and Spanish garlic.** This garlic has a stiff central stem or "scape" or neck. This woody stem curls at the top forming a 360° coil. At the top of the scape a cluster of "bulbils" or miniature cloves forms. Hardneck bulbs form large outside cloves and no inner cloves. This garlic has a mild taste and is easy to peel. As the coiled scapes appear forming bulbils, they should be pinched off so that the underground bulbs reach full size. If the scapes are not removed, the underground bulbs will be about one-third smaller. This garlic is more cold hardy than softneck. The hardneck is propagated by planting the topset bulbils in the same way as onion sets. This perennial plant is usually left in the ground for two years before harvesting. The freshly snipped topset bulblets can be used in stir-fry. The botanical name of this type of garlic is *Allium* var. *ophioscorodon*.

  'German Porcelain' is a hard-neck type with white-wrapped cloves. 'Killarney Red' is a hardneck with pink-skinned cloves.
- **Elephant garlic.** Given this name because of its distinct size and taste. It has large fist-size bulbs. Elephant garlic is related to leeks. This plant produces very large bulbs weighing up to ½ pound (225 g) or more. The extra-large individual cloves have a very mild garlic taste and are easy to peel. This plant is not as hardy as other types of garlic but stores for 10–12 months. Space 8–12 inches (20–30cm) apart. The botanical name of this garlic is *Allium scorodoprasum*.

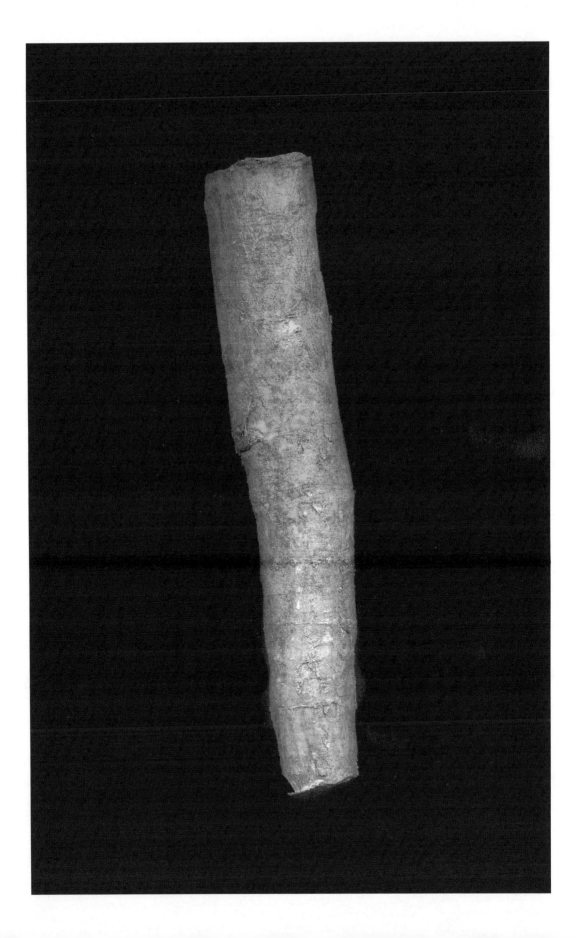

Horseradish

Common name: Horseradish.
World names: la gen (Chinese); raifort, grand raifort (French); Meerrettich, Kren (German); cren (Italian); hoosu radiishu, seiyou wasabi (Japanese); rábano picante (Spanish)
Botanical name: *Armoracia rusticana*
Pronounced arm-or-AY-see-a rus-tih-KAY-na
Family: Mustard or cabbage family—*Brassicaceae (Cruciferae)*

ABOUT
Type of plant: Perennial best grown as an annual
Origin: Southeastern Europe. Horseradish has been cultivated since Biblical times.
Description: Coarse looking plant grown for large white roots. Clumps of lobed or toothed leaves topped by cluster of small white flowers, each with four petals. Long, tapering parsnip-like root is brownish with rough skin and white interior.
Height: 12–30 inches (30–76 cm)
Breadth: 12–14 inches (30–35 cm)
Root depth: 5–10 feet (1.5–3 m)
Bloom time and flower: Summer; clusters of small white flowers, each with four petals
Edible parts: Roots

KITCHEN
Serve: Horseradish can be used fresh or pickled as a condiment or in sauces. You can grate, dice, julienne, or slice it. Use an inch or two at one time, just peel the section you will be grating.

BASICS
Root or crown planting depth: 3–4 inches (7.5–10 cm) deep; set root horizontally cover with 2 inches (5cm) of soil
Planting soil temperature: 45–85°F (7–29°C)
Days to germination: Not applicable; grow from roots
Sow indoors: Not applicable; a perennial that requires growing room
Transplant outdoors: Early spring
Days to maturity: 140–160 days
Soil pH range: 5.5–6.8

Growing soil temperature: 50–85°F (10–29°C); optimum 60°F (16°C)
Spacing of plants: 30–36 inches (76–90 cm) apart in all directions
Water: Low to moderate
Light: Shade to full sun
Nutrients: Low nitrogen, phosphorus, and potassium
Rotating crops: Perennial; grow in place
Companion crops: Potatoes, yams; best not grown with other crops
Incompatible crops: Beets
Propagation: Plant root (rhizome) or crown cuttings top side up. Use 6- to 8-inch (15–20 cm)-long root cuttings that are ½ inch (13 mm) wide. Each cutting must have at least one bud; mark the top side—that is the side nearest the soil surface—of each cutting. Remove any side shoots. Plant each root cuttings at a 30° angle or slant with the flat-cut end up.

SITE

Horseradish grows best in growth zone 3 and warmer. Horseradish prefers full sun and cool, moist conditions.
Soil preparation: Deep, well-drained soil. Spade the soil about 12 inches (30 cm) deep and work in compost and rotted manure and sand as needed to permit easy digging of roots at harvest.

PLANTING

Set out roots in late winter or early spring after all danger of frost has passed.
Planting note: Set wood, metal or masonry borders at least 24 inches (60 cm) deep around the planting bed to restrict the unintentional spread of horseradish. Pieces of harvested roots left in the soil are likely to take root. Due to its spreading form, consider planting horseradish in containers.
Container growing: Best grown in containers due to its spreading form. Plant needs downward space to accommodate its long, woody root.

GROWING

Keep the soil moist and fertilize monthly with organic compost.

CARE

Pests: Flea beetles, grasshoppers, leafhoppers.
- Use floating row covers to exclude flea beetles, grasshoppers.
- Control flea beetles with insecticidal soap and leafhoppers with yellow sticky traps.

Diseases: Roots may be susceptible to fungal disease; remove infected roots and plants and rotate crops on a 3-year cycle.

HARVEST

Horseradish will be ready for harvest 140–160 days after planting, usually in the autumn when leaves are about 12 inches (30 cm) long and roots are 3–4 inches (7.5–10 cm) in diameter and following the first hard frost. Carefully expose roots with a spading fork and cut out 12-inch (30 cm) sections; cover the remaining roots with soil for additional growth and later harvest. Roots that are over-wintered should be removed in the spring before a new season of growth begins. Harvest horseradish from the outside of the clump. Harvest large roots first. (Save the small roots in moist sand in a dark place to use for propagation next year.) Second-year and older roots develop tough fibers and are not as flavorful as newly grown roots.

Storage: Trimmed, washed roots can be stored in a glass jar or plastic bag for two weeks in the refrigerator. Store unwashed roots in the root cellar or damp sawdust for 10–12 months. The ideal storage temperature is 30–32°F (–1–0°C). To freeze, grate the roots and mix with vinegar and water.

VARIETIES

A favorite horseradish variety is 'Bohemian'.

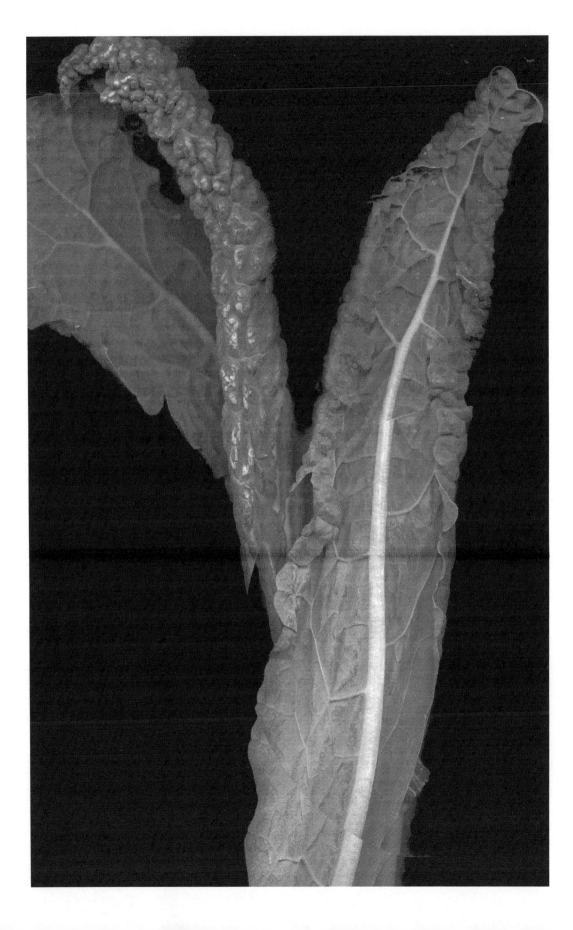

Kale

Common names: Kale, borecole, German greens
World names: wu tou gan lai (Chinese); boerenkool (Dutch); chou cavalier, chou vert (French); Blattkohl, Kuhkohl (German); cavolo da foglia (Italian); couve forrageira (Portuguese); berza, col forrajera (Spanish)
Botanical name: *Brassica oleracea* var. *acephala*
Pronounced BRASS-ih-kuh oh-leh-RAY-see-uh ay-SEF-uh-luh
Family: Cabbage or mustard family—*Brassicaceae (Cruciferae)*

ABOUT

Type of plant: Annual, hardy, cool season
Origin: Mediterranean. Grown by the Greeks and Romans before reaching northern Europe in the sixteenth century and later North America.
Description: A large cabbage-like curled leaf, usually soft green but also shades of blue-green and variegated shadings from red to white and yellow to white. Curly-leafed kales form compact; clusters of tightly curled leaves. 'Toscano' is non-curly kale.
Related plant: *Brassica oleracea* var. *sabellica* is known as curly kale, Portuguese kale or Scotch kale. This is a short-lived perennial with a single or branched stem with broad, oblong leaves that have crispy margins. The leaves are used in soups and as vegetable dishes.
Height: 8–12 inches (20–30 cm)
Breadth: 8–12 inches (20–30 cm)
Bloom time and flower: Summer of second year; yellow or white flowers
Edible parts: Leaves

KITCHEN

Serve: Kale is usually cooked and rarely eaten raw because of its strong pungent flavor. Small amounts of raw, young kale can be added to salads to add a spicy note. Steam kale and serve with butter, lemon juice, and chopped bacon.

BASICS

Seed planting depth: ½ inch (13 mm)
Soil temperature for germination: 40–70°F (4–21°C)
Days to germination: 5–7
Sow indoors: 6 weeks before last frost
Sow outdoors: Late spring or early summer in cool regions; early spring in warm regions

KALE

Days to maturity: 55–75 days after direct seeding; 30–40 days after transplanting
Soil pH range: 5.5–6.8
Growing soil temperature: 60–70°F (16–21°C); optimum 60°F (16°C)
Spacing of plants: 1 inch (2.5 cm) apart in all directions, thinning successful plants to 12 inches (30 cm) apart; or sow 3 seed every 8 inches (20 cm)
Water: Heavy during growing season; light after frost
Light: Full sun, tolerates partial shade
Nutrients: Moderate nitrogen, phosphorus, and potassium
Rotating crops: Avoid following cabbage family crops
Companion crops: Artichokes, beets, bush beans, celery, cucumbers, lettuce, herbs, onions, peas, potatoes, spinach
Incompatible crops: Pole beans, strawberries, tomatoes
Propagation: Seed
Seed vitality: 4 years
Seeds weight: 10,000 seeds per ounce (353 per gram)

SITE

Kale grows best in growth zones 3–11.
Frost tolerance: Very hardy; can tolerate frost and temperatures as low as 14°F (–10°C)
Heat tolerance: Will tolerate high summer temperatures but sweet flavor may turn bitter
Soil preparation: Kale prefers humus-rich, well-drained soil; best if previously manured, but will grow in poorer soils. For early spring crops rich sandy loam, loam, or silt loam is best. Accepts moderate applications of nitrogen, phosphorus and potassium.

PLANTING

Spring planting time: Sow seed 5 weeks before to 2 weeks after last expected frost for summer crop.
Planting in cold-climate regions: Start in seedbed for transplanting later. Before transplanting, harden off by gradual exposure to lower temperatures for a period of about 10 days or by withholding water for the same period or both.
Autumn planting time: 6–8 weeks before first expected frost. The flavor of the autumn crop is best after first frost.
Reverse climate planting: Grow in cooler months
Container growing: All varieties of kale can be grown in containers a minimum 8 inches (20 cm) wide, 8 inches (20 cm) deep

GROWING

Water: Keep the soil moist; water well in dry weather.
Nutrients: Heavy feeder. Apply compost one month before sowing.
Side dressing: Feed every 3–4 weeks with fish emulsion or use 1 tablespoon (15 ml) of blood meal mixed with 1 gallon (3.8 liters) of water

CARE

- After plants have reached 6 inches (15 cm) in height, pile straw around the stems to prevent direct contact with the soil.
- Avoid growing kale during the heat of summer. Heat will turn kale's sweetness bitter.

Pests: Aphids, cabbage loopers, cabbage maggots, diamondback moths, flea beetles, harlequin bugs, imported cabbage worms, Mexican bean beetles, mites, thrips, weevils.

- Control cutworms, cabbage loopers, and imported cabbage worms by spraying with Bacillus thuringiensis (Bt).
- Use row covers to exclude pests from seedlings.
- Inspect the undersides of leaves for cabbage butterfly egg clusters; wash infested plants with dilute soap solution to remove and kill the eggs.

Diseases: Alternaria leaf spot, black rot, clubroot, damping off, fusarium wilt

- Well-drained soil is less likely to harbor mold and fungus spores.
- Ensure good drainage. Don't work with plants when they are wet.
- Remove and destroy infected plants.

HARVEST

Kale will be ready for harvest 55–75 days after direct seeding; 30–40 days after transplanting. Kale is harvested from autumn through the winter to mid-spring in most areas. Harvest when leaves are 8–10 inches (20–25 cm) in length. Pick individual outside leaves when young and tender. Inside leaves are generally tastier than outside leaves. Cut the whole plant before it bolts; cut at the stalk about 2 inches (5 cm) above the soil leaving the roots in place. In mild climates, roots will sprout new heads in 1–2 weeks. Use row covers in severe climates. Flavor is greatly improved by frost.

Storage: In refrigerator at 32°F (0°C) at 95–98% relative humidity. Store in a plastic bag for 1–2 weeks, or blanched and frozen for up to 6 months.

TYPES AND VARIETIES

Choose from these kale types and varieties:

- **Curly-leafed kales** form compact; clusters of tightly curled leaves. 'Dwarf Blue Curled Vates', 'Dwarf Siberian' are compact varieties with curly leaves.
- **Tall kale varieties** include 'Lacinato' and 'Red Russian'.
- **Frilly leaf kales** include 'Winterbor' (green) and 'Redbor' (purple) for garnishes. 'White Peacock' and 'Red Peacock' have finely cut edges.
- **Related plant:** *B. o.* var. *sabellica* is known as curly kale, Portuguese kale or Scotch kale. This is a short-lived perennial with a single or branched stem with broad, oblong leaves that have crispy margins. The leaves are used in soups and as vegetable dishes.

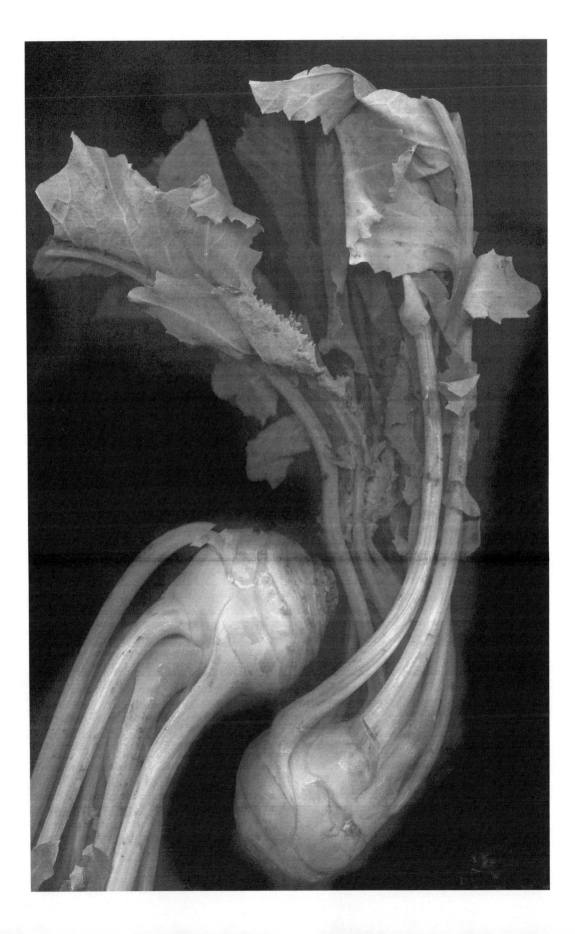

Kohlrabi

Common name: Kohlrabi, turnip-rooted cabbage, stem turnip, turnip cabbage
World names: cai tou, gai lan tou (Chinese); chou-rave (French); Kohlrabi (German); cavolo rapa (Italian); couve rábano (Portuguese); col rábano (Spanish)
Botanical name: *Brassica oleracea* var. *gongylodes*
Pronounced BRASS-ih-kuh oh-lehRAY-see-uh gon-gy-LOH-deez
Family: Cabbage or mustard family—*Brassicaceae (Cruciferae)*

ABOUT
Type of plant: Biennial grown as an annual, hardy cool season
Origin: Horticultural hybrid; kohlrabi originated in Europe as late as the sixteenth century although Pliny described a similar vegetable grown by the Romans in the first century. The name is derived from the German words Kohl (cabbage) and Rübi (turnip).
Description: Swollen stem resembles an above-ground turnip growing on a cabbage root. The swollen stem is white, purple, or green and is topped with a widely-spaced rosette of blue-green leaves. The interior flesh is apple-white.
Height: 9–12 inches (22–60 cm)
Breadth: 9–12 inches (22–60 cm)
Root depth: 7 to 8 ½ feet (2–2.6 m)
Bloom time and flower: Second year; yellow flowers
Edible parts: Enlarged bulb-like stem: the turnip-like globe which forms above the ground; leaf and leaf stalks

KITCHEN
Serve: Kohlrabi can be served raw, grated, sprinkled with salt, or cooked. Kohlrabi can be steamed, added to soups and stews, and stir-fried.

BASICS
Seed planting depth: ¼–½ inches (6–12 mm)
Germination soil temperature: 70–85°F (21–30°C)
Days to germination: 5–10
Sow indoors: Not recommended
Sow outdoors: 4 weeks before last frost for spring crops; early summer for fall crops
Days to maturity: 45–60 after direct seeding; 25–35 after transplanting

KOHLRABI

Soil pH range: 5.5–6.8
Growing soil temperature: 65–75°F (18–24°C); optimum 65°F (18°C)
Spacing of plants: 1 inch (25 mm); thin successful plants to 5–8 inches (13–20 cm) apart in all directions. Kohlrabi planted too close together will not get the light it needs for good bulb formation.
Water: Moderate and even
Light: Full sun, tolerates light shade
Nutrients: Moderate nitrogen, phosphorus and potassium
Rotating crops: Avoid following cabbage family crops.
Companion crops: Bush beans, beets, celery, cucumbers, herbs, lettuce, nasturtium, onions, potatoes
Incompatible crops: Pole beans, strawberries
Propagation: Seed
Seed vitality: 4 years; store in an airtight container in a cool, dark place.
Seed weight: 8,400 seeds per ounce (300 per gram)

SITE

Kohlrabi grows best in growth zones 3–11 and prefers cool temperatures.
Frost tolerance: Hardy
Soil preparation: Kohlrabi prefers loam rich in organic matter. Early spring crops do best in rich sandy loam, loam, or silt loam.

PLANTING

Cool-season crop: Two weeks after average last frost. In the Northern Hemisphere, grow as a winter crop in the southern temperate regions and as a summer crop in the northern temperate regions, and as a spring and autumn crop in the intermediate regions.
Spring planting time: 5 weeks before to 2 weeks after the last expected frost. For earliest crops, start indoors in flats or plug trays and transplant; does not transplant well. Rapid growth makes for best eating.
Autumn planting time: 10 weeks before the first expected frost
In reverse-season climates: In autumn for harvest in early winter; in early spring at higher elevations.
Succession planting: Where winter temperatures rarely fall below 30°F (–1°C), sow seeds at two-week intervals beginning in late summer
Container growing: Does not grow well in containers

GROWING

To be tender and tasty, kohlrabi must be grown quickly and without interruption.
Water: Keep soil moist.
Nutrients: Prefers moderate applications of nitrogen, phosphorus, and potassium. Top-dress the soil with organic compost after plants reach 4–5 inches (10–13 cm) in height.

Side dressing: Feed every three weeks with fish emulsion or use 1 tablespoon (15 ml) of blood meal to 1 gallon (3.8 liters) of water.

CARE
- Cultivate for weed control.
- Do not allow the stem to grow larger than an apple; it will become woody and lose flavor.
- Avoid handling the plants when wet.

Pests: Aphids, cabbage loopers, cabbage root maggots, imported cabbage worms, flea beetles, harlequin bugs.
- Control cutworms, cabbage loopers and imported cabbage worms by spraying with Bacillus thuringiensis (Bt).
- If white cabbage butterflies appear, inspect the undersides of leaves for egg clusters; wash infested plants with dilute soap solution to remove and kill the eggs.
- Exclude many pests with floating row covers early in the season.

Diseases: Yellows, clubroot, damping off, downy mildew, fusarium wilt
- Plant disease-resistant varieties.
- Make sure the planting bed is well drained. Avoid handling plants when wet.
- Remove and destroy infected plants.

HARVEST
Kohlrabi will be ready for harvest 45–60 after direct seeding; 25–35 after transplanting. Cut stems at soil level when they are about the size of an apple, 2–3 inches (5–7.5 cm) in diameter.

Storage: Kohlrabi will keep in refrigerator for 1–2 weeks at 32°F (0°C) at 95–98% relative humidity, or for 1-2 months in a cold, moist place. Kohlrabi can also be frozen.

VARIETIES
Choose from these kohlrabi varieties: 'Rapid' is an early variety; 'Grand Duke' is a midseason green hybrid; 'Purple Danube' and 'Purple Vienna' are favorites.

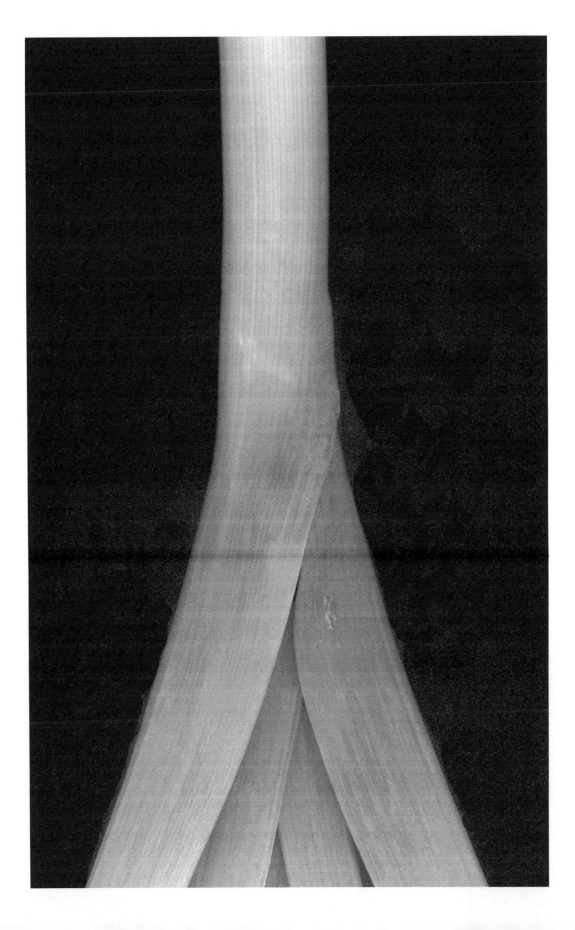

Leeks

Common name: Leek, leeks
World names: jiu cong, tai chung (Chinese); poireau (French); Porree, Lauch (German); porre (Italian); puerro (Spanish)
Botanical name: *Allium porrum* (cultivated) and *A. ampeloprasum* (wild species)
Pronounced AL-lee-um POR-rum
Family: Onion family—*Alliaceae* (*Liliaceae*)

ABOUT
Type of plant: Biennial grown as annual, hardy, cool season
Origin: Mediterranean, Egypt. Leeks have been cultivated since the time of ancient Egypt.
Description: Resembles a long, non-bulbing green onion with a white base, stem or stalk, topped with deep-green flat, fan-like foliage. Long-season leeks have thick, cylindrical stems with a fan of 1–1½ inches (2.5–3.8 cm) wide flat, dark green leaves. Short-season leeks have thinner stems.
Height: 18–24 inches (46–61 cm)
Breadth: 6–10 inches (15–25 cm)
Root depth: 6 inches (15 cm)
Bloom time and flower: Second year; small violet flowers borne in a rounded cluster
Edible parts: Stems

KITCHEN
Serve: Leeks can be used raw or cooked. Raw, finely chopped leeks are often added to salads—use in combination or as substitute for onions, shallots or chives. Leek greens are often used to add flavor to broth, stews and purees. Steam or braise leeks and serve chilled in a salad.

BASICS
Seed planting depth: ¼ inch (6 mm); germination is reduced significantly when planted ¾ inches (2 cm) deep.
Germination soil temperature: 50–75°F (10–24°C); optimum 77°F (25°C); above 81°F (27°C) germination is reduced
Days to germination: 8–16
Sow indoors: 4 weeks before last frost

LEEKS

Sow outdoors: Not recommended
Days to maturity: 120–170 days
Soil pH range: 6–6.8
Growing soil temperature: optimum 70°F (21°C)
Spacing of plants: 6 inches (15 cm) apart in all directions
Water: Moderate
Light: Full sun, tolerates partial shade
Nutrients: Moderate nitrogen, phosphorus, and potassium
Rotating crops: Avoid following onions, shallots, garlic, chives
Companion crops: Beets, carrots, celeriac, celery, garlic, onions, parsley, tomatoes
Incompatible crops: Beans, peas
Propagation: Seed
Seed vitality: 3 years; store in an airtight container in a cool, dark place.
Seeds weight: 10,000 seeds per ounce (350 per gram)

SITE

Leeks grow best in growth zones 3–10. Best in cool-summer climates. Grow as a winter vegetable in mild areas.
Frost tolerance: Very hardy; bulbs and leaves will tolerate freezing.
Soil preparation: Leeks prefer fertile, loose, humus-rich soil. Dig well-rotted manure or organic compost into the soil the autumn before planting.
Container growing: Leeks do not grow well in containers

PLANTING

Planting time: Sow seed indoors about four weeks before the last frost. Set out plants in spring through autumn where summers are cool.
Planting time in cold-winter climates: Set out plants in spring.
Indoor starting in cold-winter climates: Start indoors up to 12 weeks before the last spring frost. Sow seeds ⅛ inch (3 mm) deep, 1 inch (2.5 cm) apart, in flats filled with loose potting soil at least 3 inches (7.5 cm) deep. Transfer seedlings when about 2 inches (5 cm) tall to individual pots then harden them off in a cool 60–65°F (16–18°C) location.
Transplanting to garden: Set out plants in spring, at least a week after the last frost when seedlings are 6–12 inches (15–30 cm) tall and about the thickness of a pencil. Space them 2–4 inches (5–10 cm) apart in trenches 5 inches (13 cm) deep spaced 6–10 inches (15–25 cm) apart. Or drop seedlings in holes dibbled about 6 inches (15 cm) deep leaving just one or two leaves above the soil surface. Cover all but 1 inch (2.5 cm) or so of leaves. As leeks grow, fill in the trench gradually or, if planted on level soil, "hill" them by drawing soil up around the stems. Large transplants will grow the best leeks.
Planting time in mild-winter climates: Set out in spring where summers are cool; set out in autumn where summers are hot.
Planting time in reverse-season climates: Grow as a winter vegetable. Sow in autumn where summers are hot.

Succession Planting: For longer harvests, plant at 3 weeks intervals.

GROWING

Water: Keep soil moist to keep stems tender.
Nutrients: Allow moderate applications of nitrogen, phosphorus, and potassium.
Side dressing: Feed every two weeks with fish emulsion.

CARE

In colder climates, cover soil with mulch to insulate the plants.
Blanching: To increase the edible portion of the plant, stems are blanched. (Blanching will keep the stalks white and tender.) Stems are blanched by planting them in trenches and hilling up the soil (or sand or mulch) as they grow. During the growing period, hill the plants with soil two or three times forcing leaves higher up the plant and resulting in long, blanched stalks. Hill or fill in the trench as the plant grows. Hill to just below the leaf junctions. Do not hill plants higher than their leaf junctions or soil will lodge in the leek's leaves and stems.
Common problems: Short, tough stems indicate lack of moisture or fertility or inadequate hilling.
Pests: Thrips, root maggots.
- Control thrips by hosing them off the plants.
- Avoid root maggot damage by not planting where other onion family members have grown in previous years.

Diseases: Leeks have no serious diseases.

HARVEST

Leeks will be ready for harvest in 120–170 days after sowing, early autumn to late spring. Short-season leeks (with thinner stems) are harvested during the summer. Long-season varieties (with thick, cylindrical stems) are harvested from late summer through winter. Harvest when stems reach 1–2 inches (2.5–5 cm) in diameter and the leaves reach 6–8 inches (15–20 cm) in height. Lift with spading fork for use any time. Detach and replant offshoots.
Storage: Leeks do not store well; harvest as needed. Store leeks in the refrigerator for up to one week or in a cold, moist place for 2–3 months. In mild-winter areas, leeks can be left in the ground and used as needed.

VARIETIES

Choose from these leek varieties: 'American Flag' and 'Giant Musselburgh' are good choices; 'King Richard' is early maturing; 'Blue Solaise' is sweet tasting; 'Argenta', 'Unique', and 'Nebraska' are cold hardy.

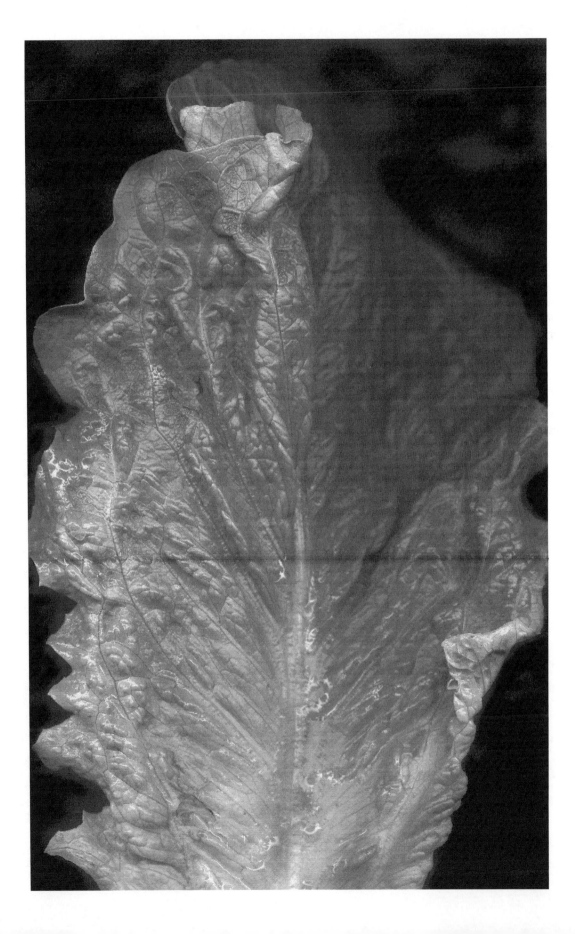

Lettuce

Common name: Lettuce
World names: sheng cai (Chinese); laitue (French); Kopfsalat, Gartensalat (German); lattuga (Italian); selada (Malay); alface (Portuguese); lechuga (Spanish)
Botanical name: *Lactuca sativa*
Pronounced lak-TOO-kuh suh-TY-vuh
Family: Sunflower family—*Asteraceae (Compositae)*

ABOUT

Type of plant: Annual, cool season
Origin: Mediterranean and the Near East. Lettuce was known in ancient Egypt and popular among the Romans.
Types of Lettuce:
- **Butterhead or Bibb:** Small, loosely-packed, green heads with soft-textured leaves; heads are a creamy-yellow at their centers. Range in size from miniatures of about 2 inches (10 cm) in diameter to large heads about 7 inches (18 cm) in diameter. Known for its smooth buttery taste. Perhaps the most popular lettuce grown in northern Europe. As easy to grow as leaf lettuce, much less fussy than iceberg.
- **Crisphead, Head or Iceberg Lettuce:** Solid, tightly folded head with crisp, pale green to greenish-white crinkly-edged leaves. The most common commercially grown lettuce. More difficult to grow in the home garden if the objective is tight, perfect heads such as those found in groceries. Plant early for best results although more tolerant of heat than leaf lettuces. Space 8–12 inches (20–30 cm) apart. Requires a monthly average temperature of 55–60°F (13–16°C); does well in mild climates over a long season.
- **Leaf or Looseleaf Lettuce:** Loose, circular rosette of leaves surrounding the central growth bud. Leaves branch out from the stalk without overlapping; they do not close tight to produce a heart. Grouped by leaf shape and color including yellow, green, red or purplish varieties. Margins can be smooth, ruffled, curled, variegated, or resemble oak leaves. Easy to grow in the home garden and less subject to bolting than headed varieties. Pick leaves as needed for salads without harvesting the whole plant. Space plants about 8 inches (20 cm) apart for full-size heads, or sow thickly (about ½ inch/13 mm apart) in a 2–4 inch (5–10 cm) wide band for clipping small, young leaves.
- **Romaine or Cos Lettuce:** Cos or romaine lettuce has erect, elongated leaves that form an upright, cylindrical or loaf-shaped head 8–9 inches (20–23 cm) tall; outer leaves are green and

heavy ribbed; inner leaves are whitish green. Center leaves are crisp and somewhat sweeter than other varieties. Romaine lettuce is usually planted for an autumn crop. Withstands heat fairly well but does not produce heads during warm weather. Tie leaves together in late summer to form elongated heads. The leaves will bunch as they mature. Space about 10 inches (25 cm) apart. Easy to grow. Harvestable at all stages of maturity. Cos varieties are very popular in the United States, southern Europe and Mediterranean countries.

- **Latin lettuce:** Elongated leaves that form a loose head. Grown mainly in the Mediterranean and South America.
- **Celtuce, stem or asparagus lettuce:** Celtuce or stem lettuce (*Lactuca sativa* var. *augustana*) is grown for its succulent, thick stem and tender leaves. Use raw or cooked. Thought to have originated in China.

Height: 4–8 inches (10–20 cm), depending upon variety
Breadth: 6–12 inches (15–30 cm), depending upon variety
Root depth: 18 inches (45 cm), but the taproot can grow to 60 inches (152 cm) long
Bloom time and flower: Summer, small yellow flowers
Edible parts: Leaves

KITCHEN

Serve: Lettuce is usually eaten raw in salads or sandwiches, but can also be quickly cooked.

BASICS

Seed planting depth: ¼–½ inch (6–13 mm)
Germination soil temperature: 45–75°F (7–24°C); optimum 68°F (20°C).
Days to germination: 2–10
Sow indoors: 4 weeks before transplanting
Sow outdoors: When soil can be worked
Soil pH range: 6.0–6.8
Growing soil temperature: 40–75°F (4–24°C)
Spacing of plants: Leaf, 6–9 inches (15–23 cm) apart in all directions after thinning; Head, 10–12 inches (25–30 cm); for salad mix and continuous harvest sow in 2–4 inch (5–10 cm) wide band, about 60 seeds per foot (28 cm).
Water: Light to moderate
Light: Full sun
Nutrients: High nitrogen, potassium, and phosphorus
Rotating crops: Avoid following radicchio, endive, escarole, artichokes
Companion crops: Good with all vegetables: particularly beets, all brassicas or cabbage family plants (except broccoli), carrots, cucumbers, onion family, pole lima beans, radishes, strawberries
Propagation: Seed
Seed vitality: 4 years; store in an airtight container in a cool, dark place.
Seed weight: 22,400 seeds per ounce (790 per gram)

SITE

Lettuce grows well in all growth zones; grow as a winter vegetable in mild areas.

Frost tolerance: Hardy

Light: Full sun in cool weather; partial shade in warm weather.

Container growing: Any variety grows well in containers. A single head of lettuce does well in a 6 inch (15 cm) pot; in a larger container allow 10 inches (25 cm) all around each plant.

PLANTING

Lettuce is a cool-weather crop that can be planted as early as the soil can be worked. It makes its best growth at temperatures of 60–65°F (16–18°C). Lettuce seed will germinate at soil temperature as low as 40°F (4°C), but poorly above 75–85°F (24–28°C) as seed will go temporarily dormant at temperatures above 75°F (24°C). If air temperatures fall below 30°F (-1°C), provide warmth with floating row covers.

Starting seed indoors: Sow 3–4 weeks before transplanting outdoors covering seeds with fine vermiculite; shade the flats on sunny, warm days if necessary to keep the soil surface cool, below 75°F (24°), until germination.

Transplanting: Harden seedlings by reducing water and temperature for 2–3 days before planting outdoors. Properly hardened transplants can survive temperatures as low as 20°F (-6°C).

Planting time in cold-winter climates: For spring crop, sow seed or set out plants in spring 4–6 weeks before the last frost date; make successive sowing or plantings until temperatures are 75°–80°F (24°–27°C). For autumn crop, sow or plant again in late summer and early autumn (until 6–8 weeks before the first frost).

Planting time in mild-winter climates: For autumn, winter, and spring crops, sow seed or set out plants from autumn through mid-spring until temperatures are 75°–80°F (24°–27°C).

Planting time in hot-summer climates: Early spring and again in late summer for an autumn crop. Cool nights are essential for quality lettuce production; high temperatures tend to produce bitter flavors. Careful variety selection is important for hot weather regions. Head lettuce is not usually a satisfactory crop in hot regions since it tends to go to seed quickly instead of forming heads. The leaf lettuces and Cos or Romaine lettuce can be grown to take the place of head lettuce.

Planting time in reverse-season climates: Winter. For succession harvesting, plant beds every 3–4 weeks throughout the growing season.

Succession planting: Plant lettuce every 10 days to 2 weeks. As the weather warms, shift to varieties that tolerate hot weather and are bolt resistant for the summer months. Lettuce can be grown through warm weather if shaded by agricultural fleece, cheesecloth, or other shading material. Plant several varieties at once for mixed salads.

Intercropping: Grow between slower maturing crops such as pole beans, cabbage, cauliflower, corn, cucumbers, eggplant, peppers, and tomatoes.

LETTUCE

GROWING

Water: Keep soil moist. Lack of moisture will cause plants to growth slowly and add a bitter taste to leaves. Mulch to help keep the bed consistently moist.

Nutrients: Tender, sweet lettuce comes with rapid growth, supply plenty of nitrogen and potassium. Add finished compost or well-rotted manure to the bed before planting. Feed every 2 weeks with fish emulsion or liquid kelp if growth seems slow. Calcium is important, especially for heading types; work bone meal into the soil to supply calcium.

Side dressing: To encourage rapid growth, add finished compost or well-rotted manure as a side dressing after seedlings appear or transplants are planted. Give compost tea or fish emulsion every few weeks until harvest. Or use a top dressing of blood meal or cottonseed meal.

CARE

- Avoid overhead watering in direct sun to prevent leaf burn.
- Protect from frost by covering with protective plastic or straw mulch whenever cool nighttime temperatures are expected.
- Erect shade covers made of porous shade cloth above each bed to prevent bolting, especially on hot, sunny days.
- Thin seedlings to encourage large-leafed plants and good head formation; unthinned plants can be harvested for "baby" salad greens.
- Keep soil moist and weed-free.

Common problems: Bitter leaves indicate heat and water stress, or over-mature lettuce. Plant small crops at frequent intervals.

Pests: Aphids, beet leafhoppers, cabbage loopers, cutworms, earwigs, flea beetles, leaf miners, millipedes, slugs, snails.

- Exclude pests by using floating row covers.
- Handpick slugs and snails and destroy.
- Attract and trap earwigs in wet rolled up newspaper.
- Spray pests with insecticidal soap.

Diseases: Bacterial soft rot, botrytis rot, damping off, downy mildew, fusarium wilt, lettuce drop, mosaic, pink rot, powdery mildew

- Rotate crops to avoid soil-borne diseases.
- Remove and destroy diseased plants.
- Ensure proper drainage and water plants from below.

Physiological disorders: Tip burn, russet spotting, rib discoloration

HARVEST

Use lettuce fresh as needed. Gather outer leaves first. The harvest is over when a central stem forms. For young and tender lettuce, harvest the entire plant early on.

- **Butterhead and Bibb harvest:** Cut after loose heads form, but before inner leaves turn yellow. Cut individual leaves with scissors 1 inch (2.5 cm) above roots, leaving the plants to re-sprout for a second harvest. To harvest the whole head, cut at the top of the stem, beneath the head. Roots left in the ground will sprout new foliage, but the second harvest will not be as tender as those first. Days to maturity: Leaf 40–50; head 70–75.

- **Crisphead harvest:** When heads are tight and turn yellowish-green, cut heads from the stem about 1 inch (2.5 cm) above the soil; remove any loose outer leaves. Days to maturity: 80–90.
- **Looseleaf harvest:** Thin or cut outer leaves 1–2 inches (2.5–5 cm) above the soil when the leaves are salad size and before they turn yellow or the plant bolts. Avoid cutting the central growth bud when harvesting outer leaves. The plant will grow to a second harvest. Days to maturity: 40–50.
- **Cos, Romaine harvest:** Once heads form, harvest individual leaves until the plant begins to bolt. Avoid cutting the central growth bud when harvesting the outer leaves. Harvest the entire plant by cutting the stem 1 inch (2.5 cm) above the soil before the leaves turn yellow or the plant bolts. Days to maturity: 80–85.

Storage all varieties: In the vegetable compartment of the refrigerator for 2–3 weeks.

VARIEITES

Choose from these lettuce types and varieties:
- **Butterhead or Bibb:** 'Bibb' ('Limestone'), 'Buttercrunch', 'Migonette' ('Manoa'); 'Boston' and 'Four Seasons' for early harvest. 'Summer Bibb' is heat tolerant. 'Bronze Mignonette' has frilly red-edged leaves. Use 'Tom Thumb' for interplanting. Plant 'Winter Marvel' and 'North Pole' in autumn.
- **Crisphead, Head or Iceberg Lettuce:** 'Great Lakes', 'Summertime', 'Nevada', 'Sierra', for cool regions, 'Rouge de Grenoblouse', is bolt resistant.
- **Leaf or Looseleaf Lettuce:** 'Black-Seeded Simpson', 'Green Ice', 'Lolla Rossa','Oak Leaf', 'Red Sails', 'Salad Bowl', 'Red Deer Tongue', 'Prizehead', 'Ruby'.
- **Romaine or Cos Lettuce:** 'Blushed Butter Cos', 'Little Gem', 'Medallion', 'Olga', 'Parris Island'. 'Rogue d'Hiver' can be planted in autumn with protection.

Marjoram

Common name: Marjoram, sweet marjoram, annual marjoram, knotted marjoram
World names: marjolaine (French); Majoran (German); maggiorana (Italian); amàraco (Spanish)
Botanical name marjoram: *Origanum majorana*
Pronounced or-IG-ah-num mah-jor-RAY-nuh
Family: Mint family—*Lamiaceae (Labiatae)*

ABOUT
Type of plant: Perennial grown as an annual
Origin: Turkey, North Africa and Southwestern Asia
Description: Fuzzy, oval gray-green leaves to 1 inch (2.5 cm) long on square stems
Height: 12–24 inches (30–60 cm)
Breadth: 6–8 inches (15–20 cm)
Root depth: 6–12 inches (15–30 cm)
Bloom time and flower: Late summer; inconspicuous white flower from clusters at the top of plant; clustered spikes open into tiny edible pink and white flowers. Unopened flower clusters resemble knots giving the common name knotted marjoram.
Edible parts: Leaves

KITCHEN
Serve: Add marjoram to salads, cheeses, fish, beef, pork, sausages, tomatoes, cabbage-family vegetables, potato soup, or vinegars. Add in the last few minutes of cooking, just before serving to veal and liver, in meat and egg dishes, and in poultry stuffings.

BASICS
Seed planting depth: ⅛–¼ inch (3–6 mm)
Germination soil temperature: 60–70°F (16–21°C)
Days to germination: 10–21
Sowing indoors: 4 weeks before setting out
Sowing outdoors: After the last frost in spring
Day to maturity: 50–60
Soil pH range: 6.0–7.0
Growing soil temperature: 55–80°F (13–27°C)

MARJORAM

Spacing of plants: 8–10 inches (20–25 cm) apart for marjoram; 18–24 inches (45–60 cm) for oregano
Light: Full sun to light shade
Water: Water sparingly
Nutrients: Low nitrogen, phosphorus, and potassium
Rotating crops: Avoid rotating oregano and marjoram with each other
Companion crops: Grow well with almost all vegetables and herbs
Incompatible crops: None
Propagation: Seed, division or cuttings
Seed vitality: 1–2 years
Seed weight: 120,000 seeds per ounce (4,236 per gram)

SITE

Best climate: Growing zones 9–10
Frost tolerance: Marjoram is tender; oregano is hardy to −30°F (−34°C)
Soil preparation: Light, well-drained soil
Container growing: Minimum soil depth of 6 inches (15 cm); will produce enough leaves to use as flavoring if grown in a 4-inch (10 cm) pot on a south window sill in the winter. Container grow as an annual or over-winter in an unheated garage or patio.

PLANTING

Sow marjoram seed 1/8 to 1/4 inch (3–6 mm) deep.
Spring planting time: Sow indoors 4 weeks before setting out; set plants outdoors after all danger of frost is past; sow in groups of three seeds.
Autumn planting time: Divide roots and bring indoors in pots to a cool location, replanting outdoors in early spring.
Winter growing: Grow in pot indoors in sunny windowsill.

CARE

Nutrients: Low nitrogen, phosphorus, and potassium
Side dressing: Spray plants with liquid seaweed extract 2–3 times during the growing season.
- Keep blossoms cutoff and plant trimmed to encourage fresh growth. Cut back severely just before blooming to induce bushy growth for harvest; use the prunings in cooking, or dry them for storage.

Pests: Aphids, spider mites, but generally no serious pest problems.
- Spray away aphids and mites with a strong stream of water from the garden hose.
- Spray spider mites with insecticidal soap.

Diseases: Botrytis rot, damping off, root rot where there is prolonged wet weather.
- Ensure good drainage and avoid over-watering.

HARVEST

Marjoram is ready for harvest 60 days after sowing. Cut fresh leaves when they are 4–6 inches (10–15 cm) long as needed for cooking; hang small bunches to dry.
Storage: Keep fresh in a plastic bag in the refrigerator for 3–4 days. Store dried in an airtight container. Freeze or dry leaves.

VARIETIES

Choose from these marjoram varieties: 'Aureum' is creeping golden marjoram; 'Aureum Crispum' has curly golden leaves; 'Compactum' is low growing; 'Thumbles Variety' is gold and green variegated; 'Kaliteri' has silver-gray leaves; 'White Anniversary' is tender with variegated green and white foliage. Italian oregano (*O.* x *majoricum*) is a pungent oregano and sweet marjoram hybrid.

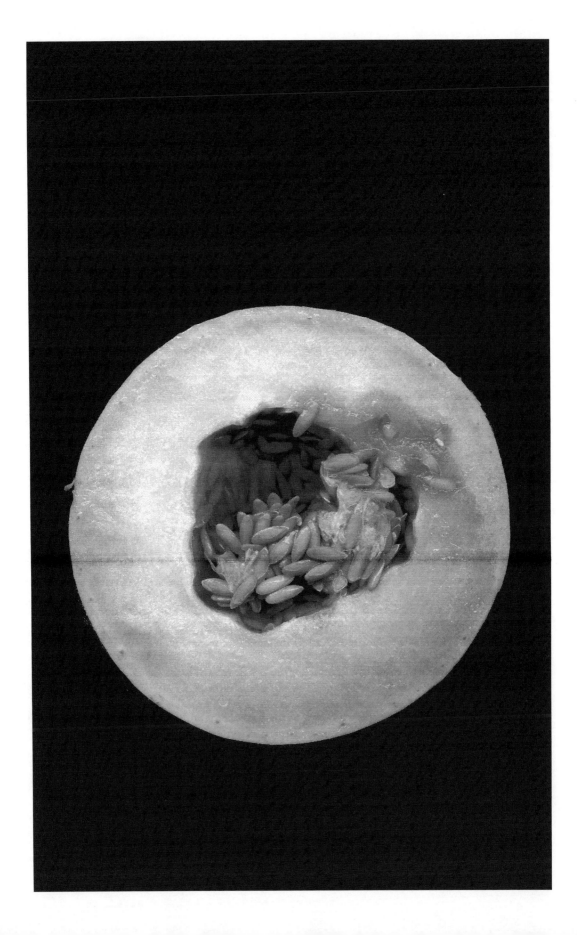

Melons

Common name: Melons
World names: xiang gua, tian gua (Chinese); melon (French); Melone (German); melone (Italian); blewah (Indonesian); buah semangka (Malay); melão (Portuguese); melón (Spanish); taeng lai (Thai)
Botanical name: *Cucumis melo*
Pronounced kewKEW-mis MEE-lo
There several botanical varieties of melons. Three are noted here:
- *Cucumis melo* var. *cantaloupesis:* the true cantaloupe and referred to as cantaloupe in Europe. Also referred to as a warm weather or summer melon.
- *Cucumis melo* var. *cantaloupesis* (also designated as *Cucumis melo melo* var. *cantaloupesis*) previously recognized as *Cucumis melo* var. *reticulatus*: the netted or nutmeg muskmelon, commonly called "cantaloupe" in North America. A warm weather, summer, or short season melon.
- *Cucumis melo* var. *inodorus:* includes honeydews, casaba melons and Crenshaw melons; all are referred to as late, winter, or long-season melons.

Family: Cucurbits or gourd family—*Cucurbitaceae*

TYPES OF MELONS

Summer Melons include true cantaloupes and muskmelons; round or oval in shape with a firm rind surrounding light-green, yellow, orange, or red flesh. The muskmelon has a rough, web-patterned rind and seldom exceeds 4 pounds (1.5 kg) in weight. Usually ready for harvest in about 3 months or at the end of summer.
- **True Cantaloupe:** hard, rough, scaled or warted-rinds (does not have a netted skin); medium round, oval, or globe-shaped; gray-green, yellow-tan and orange, or salmon-orange flesh; weighs about 2 pounds (.9 kg).
- **Muskmelon:** smooth, yellow-tan netted rinds; round, globular; salmon, white, or green flesh; weighs about 2–3 pounds (.9–1.3 kg).

Late or Winter Melons includes casaba, Charentai, Crenshaw, honeydew, and Persian; longer development cycle (3–4 months on average) than the so-called summer melons. Usually not ready to harvest until late autumn or early winter in most areas. Range in size from ½–30 pounds (.2–13 kg), can be round to oblong with exterior colors from shades of green and yellows to orange; interior flesh from greens and oranges to reds, yellows, and whites.

- **Casaba:** ribbed, rough, yellow-rind; greenish flesh; weighs about 5 pounds (2.2 kg).
- **Crenshaw:** smooth yellow-green skin; oval shape; pale green or salmon flesh; weighs about 6 pounds (2.7 kg).
- **Honeydew:** smooth, white rinds; green, white, orange, or pink-orange flesh; weighs about 3 pounds (1.3 kg).
- **Persian:** yellow-orange netted rinds; round shape; orange flesh; weighs about 7–8 pounds (3.1–3.6 kg).

ABOUT
Type of plant: Annual, warm season
Origin: Asia, tropical West Africa
Height: 24 inches (60 cm)
Breadth: Bush, 36–48 inches (.9–1.2 m); trailing or vine varieties: 30–40 square feet (9–12 m)
Root depth: Shallow, some to 48 inches (1.2 m)
Bloom time and flower: Summer; small yellow flowers
Edible parts: Fruit flesh

KITCHEN
Serve: Melons are usually eaten raw alone or in salads but also can be grilled.

BASICS
Seed planting depth: ½–1½ inches (13–38 mm)
Germination soil temperature: Seed will not germinate at soil temperatures lower than 65°F (18°C). Indoors maintain soil temperature of 80–90°F (27–32°C) until germination then lower the temperature to 75°F (24°C) for about a week following the appearance of the first true leaves.
Days to germination: 4–10
Sow indoors: 3 weeks before last frost
Sow outdoors: After last frost when soil temperature reaches 70°F (21°C)
Days to maturity: Summer melons: 70–120 days; Winter melons: 110–140 frost free days.
Soil pH range: 7.0–8.0
Soil growing temperature: 70–90°F (21–32°C)
Spacing of plants: Plant 2–3 seeds per 12 inches (30 cm), thin to 1 strong plant per 24–36 inches (60–90 cm) apart in all directions
Water: Moderate and even; low to none during ripening
Light: Full sun
Nutrients: Low nitrogen, high phosphorus and potassium
Rotating crops: Avoid following cucumbers, pumpkins, and summer and winter squash.
Companion crops: Corn, pumpkins, radishes

Incompatible crops: Do not grow near cucumbers or winter squash; melons will taste bitter if their blossoms are pollinated by either of these related plants.
Propagation: Seed
Seed vitality: 5 years; store in an airtight container in a cool, dark place.
Seed weight: 1,260 seeds per ounce (45 per gram)

SITE

Melons require 10–16 weeks of warm weather to mature. They grow best in growth zone 4 and warmer.
Frost tolerance: Tender; can not withstand frost or light freezes
Soil preparation: Melons prefer deep, light, well-drained sandy loam soil. Sandy loam is best for early crops. Clay soil is not recommended. Add abundant amounts of organic compost.
Container growing: Melons do not grow well in containers.

PLANTING

Sow melon seed ½–1½ inches (13–38 mm) deep. Sow seed or set out plants in spring 2 weeks after all danger of frost has passed and when the soil has warmed to 70°F (21°C). In reverse season regions, set out plants in midwinter for harvest in early summer.
Starting seed indoors: Sow seed indoors 3–4 weeks before you set out plants. Sow in 2–3 inch (5–7.5 cm) pots or cell packs. Sow 3 seeds per cell about ¼-inch deep. Keep temperature 80–90°F (27–32°C) until germination. Grow seedlings at 75°F (24°C). Handle young plants carefully and never let the soil dry out. Thin to 1 plant per pot. Reduce water and temperature for a week to harden seedlings.
Transplanting: After frost has passed, transplant seedlings 24–36 inches (60–90 cm) apart in rows 72 inches (180 cm) apart. Do not disturb roots when transplanting; water thoroughly.
Planting on mounds or hills: Prepare mounds 24–36 inches (60–90 cm) in height, 24–36 inches (60–90 cm) in diameter; space mounds 4–6 feet (1.2–1.8 m) apart. To support fruit, install tripod-shaped trellis or pole supports. Plant 4–5 seeds per hill; thin to the 2 strongest vines per hill. Use hot tents for extra early crops

GROWING

Water: Keep soil moist. Soil moisture is important in the early stages of growth and during pollination when fruits are setting. After pollination, the soil can dry between watering, but be consistent. Uneven watering leads to bitter melons. Limit water for one week before harvesting to concentrate sweetness.
Nutrients: Melons are heavy feeders; apply low amounts of nitrogen and high applications of phosphorus and potassium. Before planting, work compost or well-rotted manure into the planting bed.
Side dressing: Feed every 6 weeks with fish emulsion.

CARE

- Pinch back flowers to permit only 4 fruits to form per vine.
- Keep fruit off of damp soil by placing melons on a raised board preventing direct soil contact.
- Support fruit by installing a tripod-shaped trellis and placing the fruit in nylon netting suspended from the trellis.
- Do not allow fruit to stand in the garden beyond maturity, it will become mushy and seedy.
- Protect fruit from sunburn by shading them on the southwest side with a wooden shingle
- Use row covers in short season areas for early crops. Row covers will help ensure consistently warm conditions. Remove row covers when plants have female flowers (they look like tiny fruit at the base of the blossom). Removing row covers will allow for pollination by insects. Row covers also will protect crops from birds and some insects that may eat seedlings. Plastic mulch also will help warm the soil, speed harvest, and keep fruit from rotting.

Pests: Aphids, cucumber beetles, cutworms, flea beetles, leafhoppers, leaf miners, red spider mites, pickleworms, slugs, snails, squash bugs, vine borers, whiteflies. Soil pests include nematode, wireworm, and corn seed maggot.

- Control aphids by pinching out infested vegetation or hose them off the vines.
- Use floating row covers to exclude beetles. Cucumber beetles are unlikely to do much feeding damage, but they carry cucumber bacterial wilt.
- Hand pick slugs, snails, and squash bugs.
- Solarize the soil to control worms, nematodes, and maggots.

Diseases: Alternaria leaf spot, anthracnose, bacterial wilt, cucumber wilt, curly top, downy mildew, fusarium wilt, mosaic, powdery mildew, scab.

- "Sudden wilt" is a cold weather related stress that occurs in late summer when plants have a heavy set of ripening melons; plants suddenly wilt. Keep soil evenly moist.
- Melon seedlings can be attacked by root rot in cold, wet soil; older plants can be attacked by fusarium, phytophthora, alternaria, stem blight, and powdery and downy mildew.
- Viral diseases transmitted by aphids include watermelon mosaic and cucumber mosaic. Hose away aphids with a strong stream of water.
- Squash mosaic is seed borne and beetle transmitted. Exclude beetles with row covers.
- Curly top is transmitted by beet leafhoppers.
- Avoid overhead watering which can promote mildew.
- Plant disease resistant varieties.
- Remove and destroy infected plants.
- Place fruit on an aluminum reflector to enhance heat in colder climates; this also will protect melons from soil-borne fungal diseases.

HARVEST

Melons are ready for harvest 70–140 frost free days after sowing depending upon variety. Harvest melons when stems have turned brown and the stem-hold has a strong, sweet aroma. Gently press your thumb between the fruit and the base of the stem; if the stem parts away easily, the melon is ripe.

- Cantaloupes are ripe when they slip easily from the stem.
- Casaba and honeydew melons are ripe when the skins turn from greenish white to yellowish white and feel slightly sticky. A slight aroma will emanate from the blossom end when ripe.
- Crenshaw and Persian melons are ripe when they develop a fruity scent.

Storage: In refrigerator at 45–50°F (7–10°C) and 80% humidity for 2–4 weeks; some sweetness and flavor will be lost after a few days. Following harvest, cantaloupes should be cooled as rapidly as possible to about 50°F (10°C). Cooling rapidly decreases the respiration rate and loss of sugars.

VARIETIES

Choose from these melon types and varieties:

True Cantaloupe: 'Charentais' is a small, early melon. 'Savor' has sweet, orange flesh.
Muskmelon: Try 'Ambrosia', juicy, sweeet and mildew resistant. 'Passport' is green-fleshed variety. 'Sweet 'n Early' is good in short-season regions.
Crenshaw: 'Burpee's Early Hybrid' is pink fleshed. 'Morning Dew' is suited for warm regions.
Honeydew: Try 'Honey Pearl'.
Casaba: 'Casaba Golden Beauty' is spicy sweet.

Mesclun

Mesclun crops can be selected from the following greens and herbs: Common name *(botanical name):* Anise hyssop (*Agastache foeniculum*); Arugula (*Eruca stiva*); Basil (*Ocimum basilicum*); Beet greens (*Beta vulgaris*); Bok choy (*Brassica rapa*, Chinensis group); Chervil (*Anthriscus cerefolium*); Chive (*Allium schoenoprasum, A. tuberosum*); Corn salad, or mâche (*Valerianello locusta*); Dandelion (*Taraxacum officinale*); Endive (*Cichorium endivia*); Fennel (*Foeniculum vulgare* var. *azoricum*); Garden cress, or peppergrass (*Lepidium sativum*); Good King Henry (*Chenopodium bonushenricus*); Green onion (*Allium cepa*); Johnny-jump-up (*Viola tricolor*); Kale (*Brassica oleracea* var. *acephala*); Lamb's quarter (*Chenopodium album*); Leaf lettuce (*Lactuca sativa*); Lovage (*Levisticum offcinale*); Miner's lettuce, or claytonia (*Montia perfoliata*); Mizuna (*Brassica juncea* var. *japonica*); Mustard (*Brassica juncea*, various groups); Nasturtium (*Tropaeolum majus*); New Zealand spinach (*Tetragonia teragoniodes*); Orach (*Atriplex hortensis*); Parsley (*Petroselinum crispum* var. *crispum*); Plantain (*Plantago major*); Purslane (*Portulaca oleracea*); Radicchio (*Cichorium intybus*); Radish greens (*Raphanus sativus*); Salad burnet (*Sanguisorba minor*); Sorrel (*Rumex acetosa, R. scutatus*); Spinach (*Spinacea oleracea*); Sweet cicely (*Myrrhis odorata*); Swiss chard (*Beta vulgais* var. *cicla*); Tyfon (*Brassica rapa*); Violet (*Viola odorata*) Watercress (*Rorippa nasturtium aquaticum*).

ABOUT
Description: Mesclun is a mix of tender, young salad green leaves. (Mesclun is the French word for "mixture.") Mesclun seed mixes usually include a variety of lettuces and European and Asian salad greens that grow under similar conditions, have similar rates of maturity, and taste good together. Greens can be mixed by season, by flavor, by color, or by where they are grown. Mesclun leaves are usually clipped when only a few inches (centimeters) tall.

TYPES OF MESCULN
Seasonal mixes are grown for spring or early harvest; midseason harvest; and autumn harvest. Here are some seasonal mixes:
- **Spring harvest mix** might contain leaf lettuce, spinach, arugula, bok choy, radish, and mustard greens.
- **Midseason harvest mix** might include chervil, onion, lamb's lettuce, borage, arugula, parsley, lettuce, and beet greens.
- **Autumn harvest** mix might include mustard, garden cress, chive, lettuce, onion, radish and chicory.

Flavor mixes can be mild or spicy.
- **Mild blends** might include leaf lettuce with small amounts of more flavorful greens such as endive, arugula, orach, purslane, spinach, claytonia, or chervil.
- **Spicy blends** might include mustard greens, arugula, garden cress, chicory, kale, endive, and radish instead of lettuce.

Color mixes might include shades of green, plus reds, purples, and near yellows.

Textured mixes could include leaves that are large, small, mid-size, lobed, wavy, frilled, and savoyed.

Traditional French Mixes:
- **Provencal Mesclun** (originated in Provence, France): includes lettuce, curly endive, rocket, and chervil. The traditional recipe calls for one part arugula, two parts chervil, one part curly endive, and four parts lettuce. It is made up entirely of leaves, mild-tasting or zesty.
- **Mesclun** (originated in northern France): Various lettuces and endive cultivars and cress, corn salad, and spinach.
- **Nicoise** (originated in Nice, France): Mediterranean salad leaves including dandelion, upland cress, rocket, chicory, lettuce and curly endive.

KITCHEN

Serve: Raw is the only way that mesclun is served. Serve alone or mixed with tomatoes, onion, celery, mushrooms, sweet bell pepper, avocado, citrus fruits, blanched almonds, toasted bred crumbs, hard boiled egg, bacon or ham, cooked shellfish, poultry, or meats. Season mesclun with virtually all herbs, onions, or garlic. Top mesclun with vinegar or vinaigrette dressing or plain or flavored mayonnaise.

BASICS

Seed planting depth: 1/8 –¼ inch (3–6 mm); mix the seed well before sowing
Germination soil temperature: 45–75°F (7–24°C); optimum 68°F (20°C)
Days to germination: 2–10
Sowing indoors: 4 weeks before transplanting
Sowing outdoors: When soil can be worked
Days to maturity: 28–42
Soil pH range: 6.5–6.8
Growing soil temperature: 40–75°F (4–24°C)
Spacing of plants: About ½ inch (13 mm) apart in a 2–4 inch (5–10 cm) wide band
Light: Full sun for best yield
Water: Keep soil evenly moist

Nutrients: Feed with compost tea every 3 weeks
Succession planting: Every 2 weeks for continuous harvest
Rotating crops: Avoid following radicchio, endive, escarole, artichokes
Companion crops: Everything
Incompatible crops: None

SITE

Best climate: All growing zones; cool weather
Soil preparation: Well-drained, rich soil, high in organic matter
Container growing: Use a container at least 12 inches (30 cm) wide and deep with good bottom drainage; fill with good potting soil.

PLANTING

Sow seed at a depth of ⅛–¼ inch (3–6 mm) deep after mixing the seed well.
Planting time:
- Spring when the ground can be worked for spring and summer harvest
- Midsummer for autumn harvest
- Late autumn and winter: grow in a coldframe or cool greenhouse for winter harvest

CARE

- Keep beds weed free.
- Place shade cloth above plants to protect crops from summer heat.

HARVEST

Begin cutting mesclun leaves when they reach 3–6 inches (7.5–15 cm) long; cut leaves about 1 inch (2.5 cm) above the soil surface. Many will re-grow for a second harvest. Or harvest just the outer leaves. Or harvest the entire bed and replant.
Storage: Wash in cold water and dry between soft towels; store in plastic bags in the refrigerator.

Mint

Common name: Mint; See below.
World names: *Mentha piperita* (peppermint): menthe poivrée (French); Pfefferminze (German); menta piperina (Italian); la menta (Spanish). *Mentha spicata* (spearmint): menthe verte, menthe douce (French); Grüne Minze, Ährenminze (German); menta ricciuta (Italian)
Botanical name: *Mentha* species, *Mentha piperita* (peppermint); *Mentha spicata* (spearmint); *M. suaveolens* (apple mint); *M.* x *gracilis* (Golden apple mint); *M requienii* (Corsican mint, Jewel mint of Corsica); *M. arvensis* var. *piperescens* (Japanese mint)
Pronounced MEN-thuh
Family: Mint family—*Lamiaceae (Labiatae)*

ABOUT

Type of plant: Perennial
Origin: Mediterranean region. Mint has been cultivated since Biblical times.
Description: Square stems with smooth lance-like leaves; leaves can be smooth, hairy, crinkled and variegated. Spreads by rhizomes, or underground stems.
• **Peppermint** *(Mentha piperita)*: reddish purple, hairless stems and dark green pointed leaves; lilac flowers clustered at stem tips; leaves a cooling sensation in mouth and throat; use to flavor sweets.
• **Spearmint** *(Mentha spicata)*: dark green, toothed leaves. Use fresh or dried to flavor food or drinks. Curly mint *(Mentha spicata)* 'Crispa.'
• **Apple mint** *(Mentha suaveolens)*: 18-36 inches (45–90cm), round, slightly hairy green-gray leaves. 'Variegata': pineapple mint; leaves with white markings.
• **Golden apple mint, Austrian mint, Vietnamese mint** *(Mentha* x *gracilis)*: to 24 inches (60cm) tall; smooth deep green leaves with yellow variegation; spicy apple fragrance; inconspicuous flower; flavor foods.
• **Corsican mint, Jewel mint of Corsica** *(Menta requienii)*: small leaves on a plant to 1 inch (2.5 cm) tall.
• **Chocolate mint** *(Mentha* x *piperita* 'Chocolate').
• **Orange mint or bergamot mint** *(Mentha* x *p. citrata)*: grows to 24 inches (60cm) high; has broad 2 inch (5cm) long leaves; small lavender flowers; use to flavor foods.
• **Field mint** *(Mentha arvensis)*; **Japanese mint** *(M.a.* var. *piperescens)*.
Height: 12–36 inches (30–90 cm)
Breadth: 12–48 inches (30–122 cm)

MINT

Root depth: Shallow rooted to 2 inches (5 cm)
Bloom time and flower: Mid-summer; small, purple, pink, or white blossoms in whorls on terminal spikes
Edible parts: Leaves

KITCHEN

Serve: Use mint fresh or dried to flavor vegetables—cabbage, carrots, cucumbers, eggplants, peas, potatoes, tomatoes, and zucchini. Add fresh mint to cold and hot soups and beverages.

BASICS

Seed planting depth: ¼ inch (6 mm)
Germination soil temperature: 65–70°F (16–21°C)
Days to germination: 7–10
Planting divisions or cuttings: Set plants so the roots are just beneath the surface of the soil.
Sow indoors: Grow to maturity indoors, about 8 weeks
Sow outdoors: After last frost in spring
Days to maturity: 60
Soil pH range: 6.0–7.0.
Growing soil temperature: 55–70°F (13–21°C)
Spacing of plants: 12–18 inches (30–45 cm) apart in all directions
Water: Keep soil moist
Light: Full sun or partial shade
Nutrients: Low nitrogen, phosphorus, and potassium
Companion crops: Asparagus, carrots, celery, cucumbers, onions, parsley, peppers, tomatoes
Incompatible crops: Mint can be invasive; control its spread.
Propagation: Root divisions, stem cuttings, or layering. Take root or stem cuttings, or divide mint in spring and autumn. In summer, root stem cuttings in water. Division in spring or autumn; cuttings in spring or summer. Stem cuttings root easily in water, vermiculite or perlite.
Seed vitality: 2–3 years
Seed weight: 512,000 seeds per ounce (18,000 per gram)

SITE

Best climate: Growing zones 5–9
Frost tolerance: Hardy to –20°F (–30°C)
Soil preparation: Moist, well-drained soil; do not top-dress with manure or too much compost.
Container growing: Plant in a container to control spread of roots; mint can take over a garden if not controlled. In cold-winter regions, move container to a protected area such as

a patio or garage to over-winter. Choose a container at least 8–10 inches (20–25 cm) deep. Mint needs to be divided and repotted every year to stay healthy.

PLANTING

Sow mint seed at a depth of ¼ inch (6 mm).

Spring planting: Divide established clumps before growth starts. After growth begins, root stem-tip cuttings in water or moist soil.

Autumn planting time: Divide and replant established plants in early autumn.

GROWING

Nutrients: Light feeder; top-dress with compost or well-rotted manure in autumn.

Side dressing: Spray plant with liquid seaweed extract 2–3 times during the growing season.

CARE

Common problems: Grow in large pots above ground or sunk to the rim to restrain invasive roots or sink plastic, metal or masonry barriers 12 inches (30 cm) deep on all sides of the plant.

- Remove flowers to prevent cross-pollination.
- Keep mint pinched back for fuller growth. Prune back the top half or more of the plant in the late spring and again in midsummer. In the late autumn, after final harvest, cut the plant back to the ground. If the plant is not cut back frequently and severely, it will become woody after several years.
- Avoid letting the flowers bloom; blossoming affects the oil content of the leaves.

Pests: Aphids, spider mites, loopers, flea beetles.

- Control aphids and mites with a strong spray of water or with a botanical insecticidal soap.
- Exclude loopers and beetles with floating row covers.

Diseases: Verticillium wilt, mint rust.

- Thin crowded clumps for good air circulation to prevent root and foliage diseases.
- Remove all dead stems and leaves from the bed before winter.

HARVEST

Mint will grow to maturity and is ready for harvest in about 60 days from sowing. Cut top, tender fresh leaves as needed. To dry, cut stalks just before blooming then hang in bunches to dry.

Storage: Store in air-tight containers. Preserve by drying or freezing.

Mustard Greens

Common name: Mustard, mustard greens
World names: bao xin jie cai, chang jiao cai, kai-choi (Chinese); moutarde chou (French); Breiblättriger Senf (German); setsuriko (Japanese); mostaza de la china (Spanish)
Botanical name: *Brassica juncea* var. *rugosa*
Pronounced BRASS-ih-kuh
Family: Mustard or cabbage family—*Brassicaceae (Cruciferae)*

TYPES OF MUSTARD

Mustard, Chinese mustard, leaf mustard, cabbage leaf mustard, mustard greens, Oriental mustard. Hardy species are also widely known as Indian, brown, or yellow mustard.
(The classification for members of *B. juncea* is confusing because there are many different forms.)

- Southern or American mustard: also called curled mustard, Southern curled mustard.
- Wrapped heart mustard: also called dai gai choy and variations (Chinese), swatow mustard cabbage, heading mustard. Forms a dense, rounded heart. Also placed in the newer scientific name: *B. juncea* subsp. *integrifolia*.
- Bamboo or leaf mustard: also called juk gai choy and variations (Chinese), small gai choy, and stick-leaf mustard
- Red-in-snow mustard: also called green-in-snow mustard, hseuh li hung and variations (Chinese)
- Giant-leafed mustard: also called Japanese mustard, purple mustard, red mustard, aka takana (Japanese)
- Garlic mustard: also called hedge garlic, jack-by-the-hedge, sauce-alone

ABOUT

Type of plant: Cool-season perennial grown as an annual
Origin: Central Asia near the Himalaya foothills, Mustard has been in cultivation since 200 B.C.
Description: Mustards varieties include heading, large leaf, small leaf, curled leaf, large petiole, green petiole, root, big stem, multi-shoot. Mature plants resemble spinach in their growth. Mustard spinach: smooth dark green leaves, large, crinkled leaves with strong red shading.
Height: 18 inches (45 cm)

Breadth: 12 inches (30 cm)
Root depth: 18 inches (45 cm),
Bloom time and flower: Spring, small yellow flowers
Edible parts: Leaves

KITCHEN

Serve: Use young, tender mustard leaves alone in a salad or mixed with other greens. Mustard greens dress well with a little olive oil and vinegar.

BASICS

Seed planting depth: ¼ inch (6 mm)
Germination soil temperature: 65–70°F (18–21°C)
Days to germination: 4–6
Sow indoors: 2 weeks before last frost
Sow outdoors: Every 3 weeks from spring to summer and late summer to early fall
Days to maturity: 30–40
Soil pH range: 5.5–6.8
Growing soil temperature: 45–75°F (7–24°C); optimum 60°F (16°C). Mustard leaves become inedible when daily temperatures begin to rise above 85°F (29°C).
Spacing of plants: 1 inch (2.5 cm); thin successful plants to 4–6 inches (10–15 cm) apart in all directions. Mustard grows well even if overcrowded.
Light: Full sun
Water: Keep soil moist.
Nutrients: Prepare soil with plenty of organic matter, no fertilizer necessary
Rotating crops: Do not follow or precede cabbage family crops.
Companion crops: English peas, snap beans, beets, carrots, celery, chamomile, cucumbers, dill, hyssop, lettuce, mint, onion family, potatoes, rosemary, sage, spinach, thyme
Propagation: Seed
Seed vitality: 4 years; store in an airtight cool, dark place.
Seed weight: 14,000 seeds per ounce (494 per gram)

SITE

Best climate: Growth zone 2 and warmer
Soil preparation: Humus rich, moisture retentive soil; mix in well-rotted manure; high nitrogen needs; moderate phosphorus and potassium needs
Container growing: Mustard grows well in containers.

PLANTING

Sow mustard seed ¼ inch (6 mm) deep.
Spring planting time: Early spring; sow outdoors 4–6 weeks before the last expected frost. In short-season regions, start seeds indoors on damp newspaper or paper towels then

transplant or sow in a coldframe. Long, hot summer days will force the plant to bolt and go to seed. For autumn harvest, sow in late summer.

Autumn planting time: Sow seed 6–8 weeks before the first frost date.

Reverse-season and mild-winter regions planting time: Sow in autumn or early winter

Succession plantings: Every 4–6 weeks

CARE

Pests: Aphids, cabbage loopers, flea beetles.
- Handpick or hose insects off plants.
- Exclude loopers and beetle with floating row covers.

Diseases: Downy mildew, white rust
- Remove and destroy plants infected with mildew.
- Water from below and avoid handling plants when they are wet.

HARVEST

Mustard leaves will mature 30–40 days after sowing. When bottom leaves are 6–8 inches (15–20 cm) long, harvest the inner leaves that are 3–4 inches (7.5–10 cm) long. Harvest the entire plant before sustained warm weather comes. Cut leaves or entire plant just below the head.

Storage: In refrigerator for up to one week. Freeze, can, or dry.

VARIETIES

Choose from these mustard varieties: 'Florida Broad Leaf' has large, smooth leaves and a mild flavor; 'Osaka Purple' has frilly, purple-tinted leaves and a pungent flavor; 'Red Giant' has large red-purple leaves. Mizuna is a feathery and is mild tasting salad green which originated in Japan. Tatsoi, also called spoon mustard, has dark green, spoon-shaped leaves.

Okra

Common name: Okra, lady's fingers, gumbo, bhindi, gombo, ochro. The name okra derives from the West African language Ashanti. Gumbo, another common name for the plant, comes from the Bantu language of South Africa.
World names: jiao dou, ka fei huang kui (Chinese); gombo, bamia, bamya (French); Okra, Gombo (German); bhindi (Hindi); ocra (Italian); okura (Japanese); kachang bendi (Malay); quimgombó (Spanish)
Botanical name: *Abelmoschus esculentus*
Pronounced ah-bel-MOS-kus es-kyoo-LEN-tus
Family: Mallow family—*Malvaceae*

ABOUT

Type of plant: Annual, warm season
Origin: Ethiopia, tropical West Africa and Asia. Okra has been grown in parts of Africa for centuries. It arrived in Central and North America during the era of the slave trade.
Description: Herbaceous bushy shrub-like; hairy stems and large maple-like lobed leaves 6-10 inches (15–25 cm) across; produces long, slender pods in leaf joints.
Height: 48–72 inches (122–183 cm); dwarf variety 24–48 inches (60–122 cm)
Breadth: 48–72 inches (122–183 cm)
Root depth: 48–54 inches (122–137 cm)
Bloom time and flowers: Summer; flowers are hibiscus-like creamy-white, yellow or red and yellow, 2–3 inches (5–7.5 cm) across. Short-day lengths stimulate flowering of most cultivars. Flowering begins at a very early stage of growth at day lengths of less than 11 hours; with longer days, the flower buds tend to abort.
Edible parts: Pods; blossoms also are edible

KITCHEN

Serve: Use okra raw or cooked. Okra can be steamed, boiled, sautéed, baked, deep-fried, braised or made into soup or cut raw into salad.

BASICS

Seed planting depth: ½ inch (12 mm)
Germination soil temperature: 80–95°F (27–35°C)
Days to germination: 7–12

OKRA

Sow indoors: 5 weeks before last frost
Sow outdoors: After last frost
Days to maturity: 55–65 frost free days. If pods mature, plant growth will decline and few flowers will develop. With continued harvesting, the plant continues to set fruit.
Soil pH range: 6.0–6.8
Growing soil temperature: 65–95°F (18–35°C); optimum 85°F (29°)
Spacing of plants: 12 inches (30 cm) apart in all directions
Water: Low
Light: Full sun
Nutrients: Moderate nitrogen, phosphorus, and potassium
Rotating crops: Do not rotate with other plants.
Companion crops: Basil, cucumbers, eggplant, melons, peppers, southern peas
Propagation: Seed; soak seed overnight before planting to speed germination or soak seed in a water bath at 113°F (45°C) for 1½ hours.
Seed vitality: 2 years
Seeds weight: 500 seeds per ounce (18 per gram)

SITE

Okra grows best in growth zones 5–11. Warm humid summer weather with hot nights is ideal for growing okra.
Frost tolerance: Very tender; will not tolerate frost
Soil preparation: Humus-rich, loamy soil, well-drained. If ground is slow to warm in spring, plant in a raised bed.

PLANTING

Plant okra after all danger of frost has passed, and in summer. Okra requires midsummer heat and almost tropical heat for best growth. Best when soil temperature has reached 75°F (24°C); pre-warm soil with black plastic mulch to speed germination.
Planting in short-season areas: Start indoors 4–6 weeks before transplanting. Sow in 2 inch (5 cm) pots or plug trays, 3 seeds per pot ¼ inch (6 mm) deep. Keep soil mix temperature 80–90°F (27–32°C) for fast germination. Thin to one plant per pot. Do not disturb roots during transplanting.
Protected cropping: In cool regions, plant in heated greenhouse or plastic tunnels from early spring to mid-spring.
Day-length sensitive: Short-day lengths stimulate flowering of most cultivars. Flowering begins at a very early stage of growth at day lengths of less than 11 hours; flowers tend to abort when days grow longer.

GROWING

Water: Keep moist, but do not over water.
Nutrients: Moderate nitrogen, phosphorus, and potassium needs. Apply complete fertilizer when first pods set, again when plants are 48 inches (1.22 m) tall.

Side dressing: Fertilize twice during the growing season with fish emulsion, once just after flowering. Apply a high-potash fertilizer after plants are established.

CARE
- Keep soil weed free.
- Place a stake next to the plant when planting.
- Pinch out growing tip when the plant reaches 9 inches (23 cm) tall to encourage bushy growth.

Pests: Aphids (sign of water stress), corn earworms, flea beetles, mites, nematodes.
- Treat caterpillars with Bacillus thuringiensis (Bt).
- Flea beetles, aphids, and mites can be knocked off with a strong stream of water, or pinch out aphid-infested vegetation.
- Use collars around transplanted seedlings to protect against cutworms.

Diseases: Verticillium, fusarium wilt
- Keep garden clean to help cut down the incidence of disease.
- Remove infected plants before they can spread disease to healthy plants.
- Rotate crops to prevent the buildup of disease in the soil.

HARVEST
Okra is ready for harvest 55–65 days after planting. Snap or cut immature pods when they are 2–4 inches (5–10 cm) long, tender and colored pale green, green, or purplish. (Larger, mature pods will be dark brown and woody.) Pick every other day using a sharp knife or scissors. Clip pods regularly to keep plant productive.

Harvest note: Wear gloves when harvesting okra to prevent potential skin irritation from prickles on pods. Pods contain a sticky sap that may be difficult to remove from clothing and utensils.

Storage: Use okra fresh if possible. Pods will store in the refrigerator for 7–10 days at 36–55°F (2–13°C) and 90% relative humidity. Keep wrapped in a plastic bag. You can also freeze, can, or dry them.

VARIETIES
Choose from these okra varieties: 'Blondie' and 'Clemson Spineless' are top-performing favorites; 'Cajun Delight' is a short-season variety good for cool regions; 'Burgundy' and 'Red Velvet' have red pods and stems; 'Baby Bubba' is a dwarf variety for small spaces.

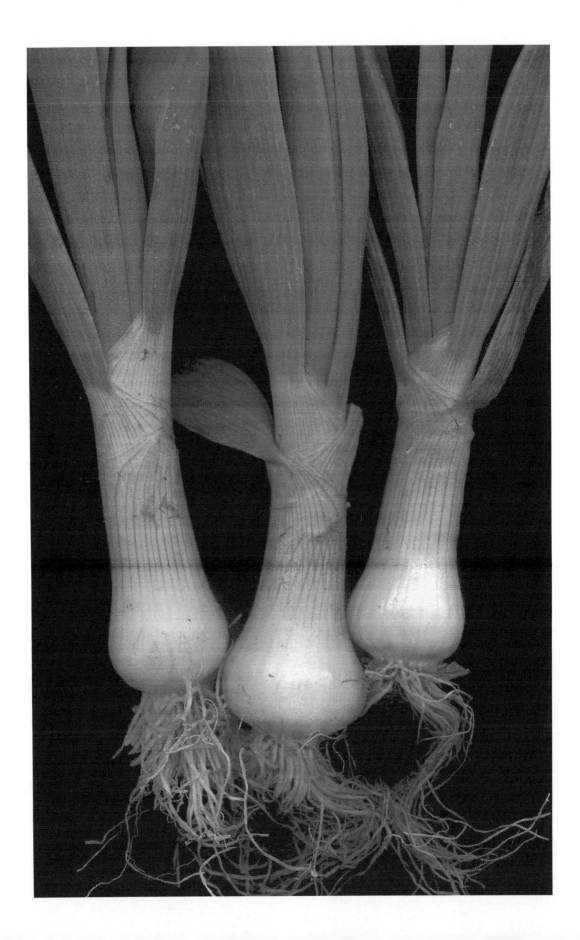

Onions

Common name: Onion
World names: cong tou, yang cong (Chinese); oignon (French); Küchenzwiebel (German); cipolla (Italian); tama negi (Japanese); cebola (Portuguese); cebolla (Spanish)
Botanical name: *Allium cepa*
Pronounced AL-lee-um SEE-puh
Family: Onion family—*Alliaceae (Liliaceae)*

ABOUT
Type of plant: Biennial grown as annual, cool season
Origin: Central and Southwest Asia. Onions have been in cultivation for more than 5,000 years.
Description: Hollow green to dark green leaves, the base of which enlarges to form a bulb; mature bulb has a papery sheath covering layer upon layer of pungent flesh; flower stalk is also hollow
Height: 24–36 inches (60–90 cm)
Breadth: 6–8 inches (15–20 cm)
Root depth: Superficial root system extending only 12 inches (30 cm) from the soil surface
Bloom time and flowers: Summer; clusters of white or lavender flowers
Edible parts: Bulbs; leaves

KITCHEN
Serve: Use fresh onions raw when mild in salads, soups, sauces, stews, and curries. Use onions as a condiment raw or cooked, chopped, minced, or sliced.

BASICS
Planting depth: Seed, ¼–½ inch (6–13 mm). Sets, about 1 inch (2.5 cm).
Germination soil temperature: 65–80°F (18–27°C); optimum 70°F (21°)
Days to germination: 4–12
Sow indoors: 8 weeks before last frost
Sow outdoors: Spring
Days to maturity: 80–120 after direct seeding; 30–40 from sets. Scallions from sets may be harvested in as few as 35 days.

Soil pH range: 6–6.8
Growing soil temperature: 55–75°F (13–24°C)
Spacing of seed: ½ inch (13 mm) apart; thin to 3–4 inches (7.5–10 cm) apart for large onions and 4 inches (10 cm) apart for sweet mild types
Spacing of sets: Bulbs, 3–5 inches (7.5–13 cm). Scallions or bunching, 2–3 inches (5–13 cm) apart in all directions
Water: Medium and even
Light: Full sun
Nutrients: Moderate nitrogen, phosphorus, and potassium
Rotating crops: Follow squash or lettuce. Do not plant onions in beds used for garlic during previous seasons.
Companion crops: Beets, cabbage family, carrots, kohlrabi, early lettuce, parsnips, peppers, spinach, strawberries, summer savory, tomatoes
Incompatible crops: All beans, asparagus, peas, sage
Propagation: Seed, seedling, sets (onions grown from small bulbs are called "sets")

- Seed is very small and can be difficult to work with; seeds are often started indoors and transplanted out as seedlings. Onions started from seed grow large and store longer.
- Onion sets are small, immature bulbs about ½–1⅛ inches (13–19 mm) in diameter grown from thickly planted seed of the previous season. Sets are usually taken from the field in autumn and planted in late winter or early spring for production of green onions or bulbs.
- Bulbs less than an 1 inch (2.5 cm) are best for planting because larger bulbs tend to produce flowers and seed more quickly. Sets are easier and faster to grow but are more subject to bolting and rot.
- Multipliers are tiny bulblets which develop in the leaf sheath of the mother bulb and are later sown to grow mature onions.

Seed vitality: 1–2 years; store in an airtight container in a cool, dark place.
Seed weight: 6,500 seeds per ounce (230 per gram)

SITE

All growth zones for scallions or "green onions'; growth zones 3–11 for bulb onions.
Frost tolerance: Hardy; can survive some light frosts
Soil preparation: Onions grow best in well-drained, humus rich, sandy to loam soil; add well-rotted manure, muck or peat the previous autumn. Avoid planting in heavy clay and coarse sand.
Container growing: Onions are a good container crop. Plant sets in containers on 6-inch (15 cm) centers in containers 10–12 inches (25–30 cm) deep

PLANTING

Plant onion seed, seedlings, and sets (onions grown from small bulbs are called "sets".

- Onion seed is very small and can be difficult to work with; seeds are often started indoors

and transplanted out as seedlings. Onions started from seed grow large and store longer.
- Onion sets are small, immature bulbs about ½–1⅛ inches (13–19 mm) in diameter grown from thickly planted seed of the previous season. Sets are usually taken from the field in autumn and planted in late winter or early spring for production of green onions or bulbs. Bulbs less than an 1 inch (2.5 cm) are best for planting because the larger bulbs tend to produce flowers and seed more quickly. Sets are easier and faster to grow but are subject to bolting and rot.
- Multipliers are tiny bulblets which develop in the leaf sheath of the mother bulb and are later sown to grow mature onions.

Planting depth: Seed, ¼–½ inch (6–13 mm). Sets, about 1 inch (2.5 cm). To harvest mature dry onions plant just deep enough to cover the set. To harvest green onions, use larger sets and plant them fully 2 inches (5 cm) below the surface.
- Small bulb size is the result of planting seeds closely together.
- Thin to 1½–2 inches (3.8–5 cm) apart for highest yields. Thin to 3–4 inches (7.5–10 cm) apart for larger onions and 4 inches (10 cm) apart for the "sweet mild" type.

Sowing seed indoors for transplanting: Sow seed indoors in flats in early spring, broadcast ½ inch (13 mm) apart, covered ¼ inch (6 mm); clip tops when they reach 5 inches (13 cm) tall. Transplant to the garden 4 inches (10 cm) apart.

Spring seed planting time indoors: Sow seeds indoors 4–6 weeks before the last expected frost; transplant to the garden as soon as the soil can be worked.

Weeks to transplanting: 4–8; keep seedling tops trimmed to ½–1 inch (1.3–2.5 cm) until a week before planting outdoors.

Spring direct seeding outdoors: As soon as the soil can be prepared in early spring

Planting onion sets (onions grown from small bulbs are called "sets"): To harvest green onions, plant sets 3–4 weeks before the desired harvest. To harvest mature bulbs, plant sets 3–4 months before the desired harvest.

Planting in mild-winter and reverse-season climate: Sow in late autumn.

Succession planting: Plant a second crop 8 weeks after the spring planting for autumn scallions.

GROWING

Water: Keep soil moist; dry soil will cause the onion to form two bulbs instead of one. Withhold water one week before harvest.

Nutrients: Apply moderate levels of nitrogen, phosphorus, and potassium.

Work compost into the bed before planting. Use fish emulsion or compost tea to encourage good early growth.

Side dressing: Apply nutrients when plants have grown 4–6 leaves. Feed every 2–3 weeks with fish emulsion or liquid kelp or side dress with dried blood or other high-nitrogen fertilizer for bulbing types, stop fertilizing once bulbs begin to swell.

CARE

- Choose the proper onion variety for your region; use appropriate planting methods; plant at the right time.
- Keep weed free; use shallow cultivation; mulch with grass clippings or straw to control weeds.
- In severe-winter climates, mulch heavily with straw and a covering layer of soil to propagate for the following season.

Common Problems: Failure to form bulbs usually indicates an unsuitable cultivar for your area.

Pests: Japanese beetles, onion eelworms, onion maggots, slugs, thrips, wireworms.

- Thrips attack onion tops. Spray away with a strong, stream of water.
- Larvae feed under the epidermis of onion leaves causing reductions in yields.
- Cutworms feed at night; cut off damaged young plants at the base.
- Nematodes, onion eelworm, wireworms attack the roots. Solarize the soil.
- Onion maggots infest sets and bulbs. Sprinkle diatomaceous earth or wood ashes into the soil near the base of the plants.

Diseases: Botrytis, damping off, pink rot, smut, storage rot, white rot, bulb and root rot, downy mildew

- Plant disease resistant varieties.
- Remove infected plants before they can spread disease to healthy plants.
- Downy mildew can infect onion foliage in humid climates.
- Black mold, fusarium basal rot, smut, and white rot are fungal diseases of leaves and bulb scales.
- Pink root is a fungal disease that causes the pinking of roots which eventually die.
- Yellow dwarf, and aphid-transmitted viral disease can result in chlorotic streaking, stunting, and distorted flattening of leaves.
- Botrytis can cause neck rot in harvested bulbs.
- Soft rot, caused by bacteria, first appears as water-soaked areas in the bulb tissue and then becomes odorous, soft, and watery.
- Plant in well-drained soil. Avoid over watering and allowing water to collect in planting beds.

Disease note: Onions grown from sets are more prone to disease than seed grown onions. Plant seeds and sets in different locations to avoid the spread of disease.

HARVEST

Onions will be ready for harvest 80–120 after direct seeding; 30–40 days from planting sets. Scallions from sets may be harvested in as few as 35 days.

Harvest preparation: Bulb formation can be hastened by bending or creasing stalks to the ground to halt foliage development; this is called "lodging". Lodge stalks after immature flower buds begin to open atop the plants. Do not leave onions in the soil throughout flowering; bulbs will turn mushy and may divide. For bunching onions, trim off the flowers after they have died and remove any brown stalks.

Harvest: Onions are ready to harvest when the stalks fall over. In cool, humid regions, harvest when the entire stalk falls over. In cool, dry regions, harvest when about half of the stalk has fallen. In warm regions, harvest when a quarter to a third of the top falls over. Pull scallions and onions for fresh use as needed. Allow them to cure in the sun for about a week before use. Seedlings that were planted early will produce larger plants and larger mature bulbs than those that emerged later in the season.

Harvest specifics:

Days to maturity: 80–120 after direct seeding; 30–40 from sets. Scallions from sets may be harvested in as few as 35 days.

- **Sets:** harvest in early spring for sets; young, partially developed onions grown from sets can be pulled about 4–6 weeks after planting; serve as spring or green onions (actually the bulbous growth is only partly grown at this stage and a good part of the stem is edible); the remaining bulbs can be allowed to mature for use during the summer and autumn.
- **Green onions and scallions** (immature green and white stems): harvest when bulbs are no more than ½ inch (13 mm) in diameter.
- **Bunching varieties:** harvest when bulb divisions reach 1–2 inches (2.5–5 cm), by splitting them off from the outside of the bunch.
- **Mature bulbs:** harvest when tops become withered and brown and bulbs are 3–5 inches (7.5–13 cm) in diameter.

Curing: Cure onions to prevent rot-causing organisms from entering the bulb through the neck. Air dry bulbs outdoors or in window for 10–12 days. Protect bulbs from the sun to prevent scalding, but allow for air circulation. Clip off dried or partially dried tops.

Storage: Onions store best at low temperatures of 32–45°F (0–7°C) or high temperature of 77–95°F (25–35°C) for 3–6 months without sprouting. Poorest storage is at room temperature in the range of 60–70°F (15–21°C). Dry, clip off tops and store in onion bags or shallow boxes at 65–70% humidity.

- **Green and bunching varieties:** in vegetable compartment of refrigerator for 2–3 weeks.
- **Bulbs:** cut 1½ inches (4 cm) above the bulb, or leave tops on and braid into strands. Dry for 10–20 days in moderately warm, dry area, then hang or store in a cool, dry place.
- **Chopped onions:** fresh in bags or frozen for use in cooking; dried in a plastic container.

TYPES AND CLASSIFICATIONS

Choose from these onion types and classifications:

Color classification of onions:

- **Yellow or golden varieties:** best for storing; early crop for mid-summer harvest.
- **Red varieties:** sweet tasting, early crop for mid-summer harvest.
- **Whites:** mild flavored bulb onions.

Other onion classifications:
- **Long storing:** choose American type, yellow, white or red onions.
- **Tiny and round:** choose pearl or pickling onions.
- **Large, sweet for slicing:** choose Bermuda or Spanish onions.
- **Scallions:** harvest onions at scallion size or grow bunching onions.
- **Onion sets:** dwarfed, dried bulbs (yellow, red, or white) of quick-growing varieties used to start crops.

Day-length classifications: different types form bulbs in response to varying day lengths:
- **Short-day varieties:** require equal amounts of darkness and light (about 10–12 hours of each) to set bulbs; in the Northern Hemisphere best grown in southern regions where the summer daylight period is shorter than in the north; they bulb too soon in the north as the days lengthen. Best for southern latitudes; plant in autumn or early winter with bulbs forming in spring. Varieties include: 'Bermuda', 'California Red', 'Granex', 'Grano Super Sweet'. Short-day varieties do not store well.
- **Long-day varieties:** require about 14–15 hours of light and 9–10 hours of darkness; in the Northern Hemisphere, best suited to the northern regions where summer daylight lasts longer. Varieties include: 'Early Yellow Globe', 'Ebenezer', 'Ruby', 'Southport White Globe', 'Sweet Spanish'.
- **Intermediate-day-length varieties:** requires about 13½ to 14 hours of daylight to bulb. Varieties include: 'Autumn Spice', 'Red Torpedo', 'Ringmaker'.

Day-length note: Plants are actually sensitive to the length of the dark period, not the length of day light, in order to initiate good bulb development. Bulbs are formed under favorable conditions of daylight length and temperature when the plants have reached a certain stage of growth.

Oregano

Common name: Oregano, wild marjoram, pot marjoram
World names: origan (French); Echter Dost (German); origano (Italian); orégano (Spanish)
Botanical name: *Origanum vulgare. O.* x *hirtum* (Greek oregano). *O.* x *majoricum* (Italian marjoram). *O. onites* (pot marjoram). There are about 30 species.
Pronounced Or-IG-ah-num vul-GARE-ay HEER-tum
Family: Mint family—*Lamiaceae (Labiatae)*

ABOUT
Type of plant: Perennial herb
Origin: Northern Europe and Mediterranean region
Description: Herbaceous upright to lax shrub with aromatic oval, dark green leaves 1½ inches (3.8cm) long and ¾ inch (19mm) wide; square reddish stems.
Height: 12–24 inches (30–60 cm)
Breadth: 12–18 inches (30–45 cm)
Root depth: Shallow
Bloom time and flower: Mid- to late summer; tubular blossom clusters of ¼ inch (6 mm) edible mauve-white to reddish purple flowers
Edible parts: Leaves

KITCHEN
Serve: Use Oregano leaves with salads, cheese, eggs, tomato dishes and sauces, marinated vegetables, roasted and stewed beef, poultry, game, beans, shellfish, soups, vinegars, or pastas. Add fresh oregano toward the end of cooking. Sprinkle on cooked vegetables.

BASICS
Seed planting depth: Scatter oregano seed on soil surface, does not need cover.
Germination soil temperature: 60–70°F (16–21°C)
Days to germination: 10–21
Sowing indoors: 4 weeks before setting out
Sowing outdoors: After the last frost in spring
Day to maturity: 50–60
Soil pH range: 6.0–7.0

Growing soil temperature: 55–80°F (13–27°C)
Spacing of plants: 18–24 inches (45–60 cm) apart in all directions
Light: Full sun to light shade
Water: Water sparingly
Nutrients: Low nitrogen, phosphorus, and potassium
Rotating crops: Avoid rotating oregano and marjoram with each other.
Companion crops: Grows well with almost all vegetables and herbs
Incompatible crops: None
Propagation: Cuttings taken in the summer or divisions in the spring or autumn. Propagate only the most flavorful plants.
Seed vitality: 1–2 years
Seed weight: 250,000 seeds per ounce (8,825 per gram)

SITE

Best climate: Growing zones 5–9
Frost tolerance: Hardy to –30°F (-34°C)
Soil preparation: Light, well-drained soil
Container growing: Minimum soil depth of 6 inches (15 cm); will produce enough leaves to use as flavoring if grown in a 4-inch (10 cm) pot on a south windowsill in the winter. Container-grow as an annual or over-winter in an unheated garage or patio.

PLANTING

Oregano can be scattered on the soil surface where light will help it germinate.
Spring planting time: Sow indoors 4 weeks before setting out; set plants outdoors after all danger of frost is past; sow in groups of three seeds.
Autumn planting time: Divide roots and bring indoors in pots to a cool location, replanting outdoors in early spring.
Winter growing: Grow in pot indoors in sunny windowsill.

CARE

Nutrients: Low nitrogen, phosphorus, and potassium
Side dressing: Spray plants with liquid seaweed extract 2–3 times during the growing season.
- Keep blossoms cut off and plant trimmed to encourage fresh growth. Cut back severely just before blooming, to induce bushy growth for harvest; use the prunings in cooking, or dry them for storage.

Pests: Aphids, spider mites, but generally no serious pest problems. Wash away aphids and mites with a strong stream of water from the garden hose.
Diseases: Botrytis rot, damping off, root rot where there is prolonged wet weather. Plant in well-drained soil. Avoid over-watering and allowing water to collect in planting beds.

HARVEST

Oregano is ready for harvest 50 days after sowing. Snip fresh sprigs as needed all summer; cut the whole plant in early summer and again in late summer, cut back to 3 inches (7.5 cm) just before flowering.

Storage: Keep oregano fresh in a plastic bag in the refrigerator for 3–4 days. Store dried in an air-tight container. Freeze or dry leaves.

VARIETIES

Choose from these oregano varieties: 'Aureum' is also called creeping golden marjoram; 'Aureum Crispum' has curly golden leaves; 'Compactum' is creeping oregano; 'Thumbles Variety' is low growing; 'Kaliteri' has silver gray leaves and is spicy; 'White Anniversary' is tender.

Parsley

Common name: Parsley
World names: fan yan sui (Chinese); persil (French); Petersilie (German); prezzemolo (Italian); perejil (Spanish)
Botanical name: *Petroselinum crispum* (curly leafed parsley); *Petroselinum crispum* var. *neapolitanum* (flat or plain-leaved parsley, also called Italian parsley or celery-leaved parsley). A related variety is *P. c.* var. *tuberosum* (Hamburg parsley or turnip-rooted parsley) which is cooked and eaten like celeriac.
Pronounced peh-tro-she-LY-um KRIS-pum
Family: Carrot and parsley family—*Apiaceae* (*Umbelliferae*)

ABOUT

Type of plant: Biennial grown as annual
Origin: Mediterranean. Parsley was known in ancient Greece but not used as a seasoning until the Middle Ages.
Description: Tufted finely cut dark green leaves
- **Curly leaf:** Finely divided, ruffled leaves, on a stalk to 8–12 inches (20–30 cm) tall.
- **Flat-leaf:** Flat, bright green leaves resembling celery on a long stalk to 18–24 inches (45–60 cm) tall; clusters of tiny yellow green flowers appear during the second year of growth.

Height: 8–24 inches (20–60 cm) depending on variety
Breadth: 12–18 inches (30–45 cm)
Root depth: Taproot to 8 inches (20 cm)
Bloom time and flower: Early summer of second year; umbels of tiny, greenish yellow blossoms
Edible parts: Leaves

KITCHEN

Serve: Use parsley fresh, dried, frozen, or marinated. It's best used fresh. Parsley added at the last minute to cooked foods will be crisper, tastier, and greener.

BASICS

Seed planting depth: ¼ inch (6 mm)
Germination soil temperature: 50–75°F (10–24°C)

Days to germination: 5–6 weeks to emerge from the soil; soak seed overnight in warm water before sowing or pour boiling water in drill at planting time.
Sowing indoors: Late winter to early spring
Sowing outdoors: Early spring before the last frost
Days to maturity: 70–90
Soil pH range: 5.5–6.7
Growing soil temperature: 60–65°F (16–18°C)
Spacing of plants: 6–8 inches (15–20 cm) apart in all directions
Water: Keep soil moist
Light: Full sun to partial shade
Nutrients: High nitrogen, phosphorus, and potassium
Companion crops: Asparagus, sweet corn, peppers, tomatoes
Incompatible crops: Carrots, celery, parsnips
Propagation: Seed
Seed vitality: 3 years; store in an airtight container in a cool, dark place.
Seed weight: 9,800 seeds per ounce (345 per gram)

SITE

Best climate: Growth zones 2 and warmer
Frost tolerance: Very hardy
Soil preparation: Moderately rich, well-drained soil
Container growing: Grows and yields well in a container; bring indoors for winter harvests. Container at least 12 inches (30 cm) wide and deep.

PLANTING

Sow parsley seed ¼ inches (6 mm) deep.
Spring planting time: Sow in garden after the danger of frost has passed.
Spring planting indoors: Sow seeds indoors 4–6 weeks before the last frost; maintain soil temperature of 60–85°F (16–29°C) for germination. Transplant seedlings outside after the danger of frost has passed.
Over-wintering in mild climates: Plants will over winter, but the leaves will be tough.

CARE

Nutrients: Heavy feeder
Side dressing: Spray plants with liquid seaweed extract 2–3 times during the growing season. Side-dress with compost in midseason.
Care: Remove flower stalks that form and prune away dead leaves.
Pests: Cabbage loopers, carrot rust flies, carrot weevils, nematodes, parsley worms, spider mites.
- Handpick worms off plants. Exclude pests from plants with floating row covers.
- Use a fence to keep rabbits out of the garden.

Diseases: Crown rot, leaf spot; but usually no serious diseases. Plant in well-drained soil.

HARVEST

Parsley will be ready for harvest 70–90 days after sowing. Cut outer leaf stalks at the base for fresh foliage (inner leaves will continue to grow). Cut the whole plant at once and it will re-grow. Collect seeds when ripe. Plants will provide greens through the year from one planting in the early spring.

Storage: Cut for fresh use; freeze whole or chopped; hang in bunches to dry in the shade.

VARIETIES

Choose from these parsley varieties: 'Giant Italian' and 'Giant of Naples' are flat-leaf Italian parsley for cooking; 'Moss Curled' and 'Extra Curled' are curly-leaf parsleys.

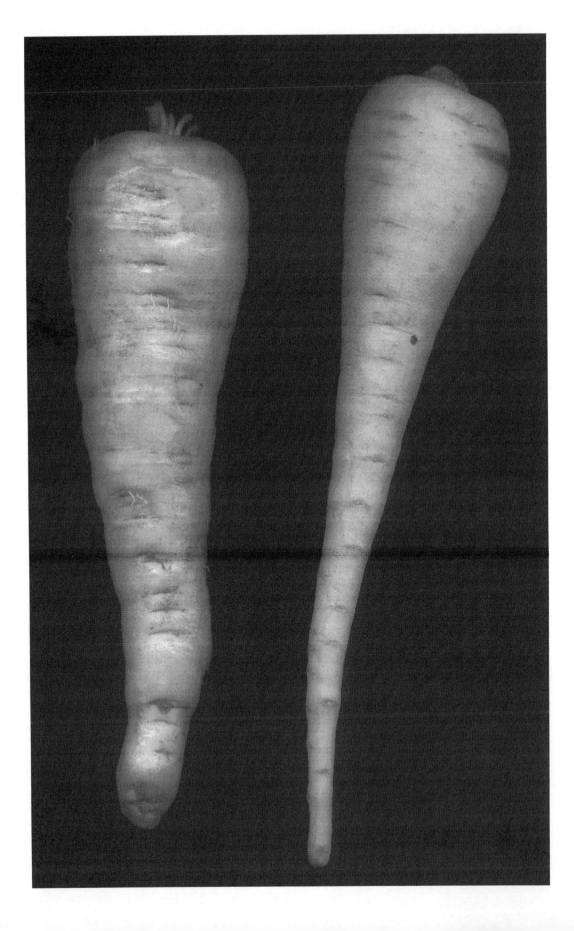

Parsnips

Common name: Parsnips
World names: panais, patenais (French); Hammelmöhre, Pastinak (German); pastinaca (Italian); pastinaca, chirivia (Portuguese); chirivía (Spanish)
Botanical name: *Pastinaca sativa*
Pronounced pah-stih-NAH-kuh suh-TY-vuh
Family: Carrot and parsley family—*Apiaceae (Umbelliferae)*

ABOUT

Type of plant: Cool-season biennial usually grown as an annual
Origin: Europe and Western Asia. Parsnips were grown for food in Europe as early as the Middle Ages.
Description: Rosette of compound celery-like leaves growing atop a cream to light rust colored fleshy root 4–9 inches (10–23 cm) long and 2 inches (5 cm) in diameter at their tops, tapering down to a pointed tip. The carrot-like taproots are yellowish to creamy white in color.
Height: 12–18 inches (30–45 cm)
Breadth: 10–15 inches (25–38 cm)
Root depth: Taproot usually to 15 inches (38cm) with some fibrous roots reaching down to 60 inches (152 cm), but most roots are limited to 24 inches (60 cm) long.
Bloom time and flowers: Summer; umbels of small yellow flowers
Edible parts: Roots

KITCHEN

Serve: Parsnips are usually eaten cooked—parboiled, steamed, or added to soup—and can be prepared as you would carrots, salsify, or turnips. Parsnips will replace those vegetables in most recipes.

BASICS

Seed planting depth: ¼–½ inch (6–13mm)
Germination soil temperature: 40–75°F (4–24°C)
Days to germination: 5–28; about 21 days at 60°F (16°C)
Sow indoors: Not recommended
Sow outdoors: Spring as soon as the soil can be worked

Days to maturity: 95–120
Soil pH range: 6.0–6.8
Growing soil temperature: 45–75°F (7–24°C); optimum 65°F (18°C)
Spacing of plants: 1 inch (2.5 cm) apart; thin successful plants to 3–4 inches (7.5–10 cm) apart in all directions
Water: Moderate
Light: Full sun to partial shade; needs only 5 hours of shade a day
Nutrients: High nitrogen, low phosphorus and potassium
Rotating crops: Avoid following carrots, parsley, or celery.
Companion crops: Bush beans, beets, carrots, garlic, onions, peas, peppers, potatoes, radishes, rutabagas, and other root vegetables
Incompatible crops: Tomatoes, tomatillos, cole vegetables such as broccoli, Brussels sprouts, cabbage, kale
Propagation: Seed
Seed vitality: 1 year; store in an airtight container in a cool, dark place.
Seed weight: 4,900 seeds per ounce (172 per gram)

SITE

Best climate: Growing zones 3–10
Frost tolerance: Hardy; heavy frost or freezing is required to improve the flavor of roots.
Soil preparation: Parsnips prefer humus-rich, slightly sandy, friable, cultivated soil free of rocks to a depth of 18 inches (45 cm). Cultivate or double dig soil to 16 inches (41 cm).
Container growing: The leafy tops of parsnips produce well in a container, but the roots do not grow satisfactorily unless the soil is deep.

PLANTING

Plant parsnip seed ¼–½ inch (6–13mm) deep. Parsnips can be slow to germinate from 5–28 days; about 21 days at 60°F (16°C). To improve germination, soak seed in water for a day before planting.
Planting time in cold-winter region: Late spring 2–4 weeks before the last expected frost to 4 weeks after the last frost for autumn harvest. Sow in spring for harvest in autumn.
Planting time in mild-winter region: Early summer for winter harvest; in autumn for harvest in spring.
Planting time in reverse-season climates: Late autumn for harvest the following spring

GROWING

Water: Water frequently and consistently during the early stages of root growth to prevent the roots from splitting.
Nutrients: Parsnips require high levels of nitrogen and low applications of phosphorus and potassium; too rich fertilizer will cause hairy roots.

Side dressing: Carefully work well-rotted manure around the plants 4–6 weeks after seeds are sown. Apply fish emulsion once a month during the growing season

CARE
- Keep weed free, especially when plants are young.
- In severe-winter climates before the first hard freeze, mulch the bed with 6–10 inches (15–25 cm) of straw or loose wood chips then cover it with 4–6 inches (10–15 cm) of soil; in milder climates, simply mulch the patch to protect the ground from freezing.
- Keep well watered to prevent celery blight.

Pests: Armyworms, cabbage root maggots, carrot rust flies, flea beetles, leafhoppers, nematodes, onion maggots.
- Discourage root maggot flies from laying eggs near plants by putting a 3–4 inch (7–10 cm) square of plastic around each plant.
- Delay planting a few weeks until the insect cycle is over or cover young plants with a floating row cover.

Diseases: Parsnips have no serious disease problems.

HARVEST
Parsnips will be ready for harvest 95–120 days after sowing, autumn onwards and as needed after the first frost. The sweetest roots are dug after heavy frosts in late autumn. Complete harvest by early spring before top growth begins. Trim or mow tops then use a garden fork to carefully remove the parsnips without damage. During winter harvest, keep unharvested crops covered with mulch. Roots left in the ground all winter will have the best flavor; sugar content increases with cold weather. Do not leave roots in the ground a second season as they will be too fibrous to eat. In mild-winter and reverse-season climates, complete harvest before the onset of hot weather. Mature roots left in the ground will continue to grow and may become tough and woody.

Storage: Keep parsnips in the refrigerator for 2–4 months in perforated bags or bins, but some flavor and texture will be lost. For storage in ground, see above.

VARIETIES
Choose from these parsnip varieties: 'Hollow Crown' also called 'Long Guernsey Smooth' has a good yield; 'Harris Model' has snow-white flesh and smooth texture; 'Lancer' and 'Gladiator' are sweet flavored; 'White Gem' grows in all soils; 'Premium' is short rooted for short seasons; 'Cobham Improved' can be over-wintered.

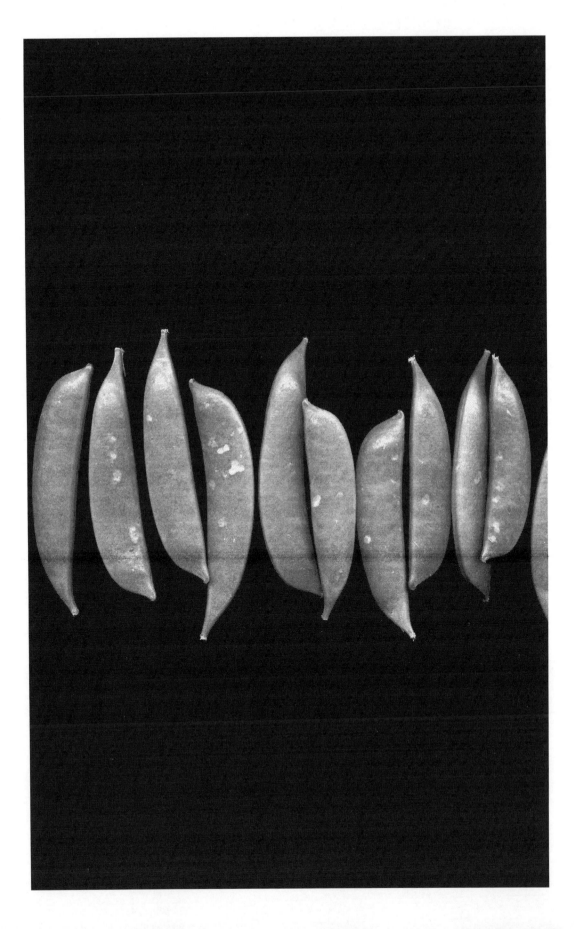

Peas

Common name: Garden pea, English pea, green pea
World names: he lan dou, tian wan dou (Chinese); pois (French); Gartenerbse (German); pisello (Italian); piisu (Japanese); ervilha (Portuguese); guisante (Spanish)
Botanical name edible-pod pea: *Pisum sativum*
Botanical name shell pea: *Pisum sativum* var. *macrocarpon*
Pronounced PY-sum sub-TY-vum
Family: Legume family—*Fabaceae (Leguminosae)*

ABOUT

Type of plant: Annual, cool season
Origin: Eastern Mediterranean, northeast Africa and the Middle East, China. Peas have been grown in China for more than 4,000 years.
Description: Weak-stemmed, climbing vine or knee-high bush with compound leaves with one to three pairs of leaflets ending in branched tendrils used for climbing; pod fruit 4–6 inches (10–15 cm) long containing 4–10 seeds, either smooth or wrinkled depending on the variety.
- Smooth seed types are more adapted to cool weather conditions than the wrinkled types.
- Smooth seed coated types are starchy; wrinkled seed coated types are sweeter.
- Peas are indeterminate (climbing) types or determinate (bush or dwarf) types.
- Varieties are classified as dwarf, medium, and tall; the taller they grow the larger the yield. Tall peas require a fairly long, cool spring and often do not mature until summer, at least 3 weeks later than other varieties. Grow tall peas on poles, fences, or trellises. Pods are larger than other varieties and filled with larger peas. Medium-tall varieties give a larger crop and higher quality than the dwarf, but require support for the vines.

Height: 24 inches–6 feet (60cm–1.8 m)
Breadth: 6–10 inches (15–25 cm)
Root depth: Shallow to 36 inches (90 cm)
Bloom time and flower: Spring; white, streaked, or colored flowers
Edible parts: There are three subclasses of the garden pea, English pea or green pea:
(1) Some are for shelling, shelled seeds; (2) some have edible pods; (3) others can be eaten either way.
- Shelling peas are sometimes used as dry or soup peas and are also called pod or field peas. Shell peas are left on the vine to fully mature, rather than picked at the green stage. Dry peas date back at least 7,000 years.

- Some peas for shelling are picked when immature. The shelled peas are referred to as fresh peas. They are cooked as a vegetable.
- Small-seeded peas are called *petit pois* or "baby peas." They include any garden pea picked early. *Petit pois* are a delicacy in France known for their tenderness and sweet flavor. Some are genetically smaller, 2–3 inches (5–7.5cm) long at maturity; 6–9 peas per pod. Varieties include 'Waverex' and 'Precovelle'.
- Edible pod peas are called snow or sugar peas. Varieties include 'Mammoth Melting Sugar'.
- Shelling and edible pod peas can be eaten either when the pods are still immature (pods and peas eaten together) or later at maturity after shelling. Varieties include: 'Sugar Snap' (tall), 'Super Sugar Snap' (tall), 'Sugar Ann' (bush)

KITCHEN

Serve: Shelled garden peas or green peas can be served raw or cooked. Snow peas can be served whole raw or cooked. Sugar snaps can be served whole raw or only briefly cooked to retain their crispness.

BASICS

Seed planting depth: ½–1 inch (1.3–2.5 cm)
Germination soil temperature: 45–75°F (7–24°C); optimum 75°F (24°C)
Days to germination: 5–7
Sow indoors: Not recommended
Sow outdoors: Spring as soon as the soil can be worked; late summer
Days to maturity: 55–70
Soil pH range: 5.5–6.8
Growing soil temperature: 50–75°F (10–24°C)
Spacing of plants: Sow 2 seeds, 2–3 inches (5–7.5 cm) apart; thin successful plants to 4 inches (10 cm) apart in all directions
Water: Moderate until flowering, then low
Light: Full sun
Nutrients: Low nitrogen, phosphorus, and potassium
Rotating crops: Rotate peas each year to avoid disease and to benefit other crops by nitrogen fixation. Kale can follow peas.
Companion crops: Beans, carrots, celery, chicory, coriander, corn, cucumbers, eggplant, parsley, early potatoes, radishes, spinach, strawberries, sweet peppers, turnips
Incompatible crops: Garlic, onions, late potatoes

Propagation: Seed
Seed viability: 3 years; store in airtight containers in a cool, dark place.
Seed weight: 115–140 sees per ounce (4–5 per gram)

SITE

Peas grow best in growth zones 2 and warmer. Choose a site with full sun and good air circulation.

Frost tolerance: Very hardy, not harmed by late frosts

Soil preparation: Loose, humus-rich, well-drained soil; peas do not tolerate soggy or water-soaked conditions.

Site preparation: Do not crowd peas. Raise rows 6–8 inches (15–20 cm); install wire or strong supports between posts for bush varieties, sturdy poles, wire fence or trellis supported by posts for pole varieties. Support vines with 24–48 inches (91–122 cm) tall wire or fencing.

Container growing: Peas will grow in a container, but it takes space to produce a reasonable crop. Choose a container at least 12 inches (30 cm) deep.

PLANTING

Seed planting depth: ½–1 inch (1.3–2.5 cm) in winter for spring; 1–2 inches (2.5–5 cm); 2 inches (5 cm) for autumn crop; 2 inches (5 cm) deep in light soil; ½–1 inch (1.3–2.5 cm) deep in heavy soil.

Distance between plants: Sow 2 seeds, 2–3 inches (5–7.5 cm) apart; thin successful plants to 4 inches (10 cm) apart

Planting in rows: Between rows allow 18–24 inches (45–60 cm) for dwarf type; 36–48 inches (90–122 cm) for bush peas.

Planting around poles: Sow 1 seed at a time 2 inches (5 cm) deep, 2 inches (5 cm) apart, in a circle 8–10 inches (20–25 cm) from the pole; thin to 8 successful plants around each pole.

Planting time cold-winter climates: Early spring as soon as the soil can be prepared; sow seeds 6–8 weeks before the last frost date. Peas must mature before the weather gets hot. Late planting can cause poor results. For an autumn crop, sow seeds about 12 weeks before the first frost date in autumn.

Planting time in mild-winter climates: Usually late autumn and early winter where there is little or no frost. For autumn and winter crops, sow seeds from late summer through autumn. For a spring crop, sow seeds in spring 6–8 weeks before the last frost date.

Planting time in reverse-season climates: Mid- to late-autumn where summer temperatures regularly exceed 80°F (27°C). In Growing zones 7 and warmer, seed planted in late autumn often over-winter and germinate in early spring.

Succession planting: Plant every 3 weeks until late spring, and again in late summer.

Autumn crop: Choose powdery mildew resistant varieties for autumn crops; plant 2 months before the first frost.

GROWING

Types of peas: Peas are indeterminate (climbing) types or determinate (bush or dwarf) types.

- Varieties are classified as dwarf, medium, and tall; the taller they grow the larger the yield. Tall peas require a fairly long, cool spring and often do not mature until summer, at least 3 weeks later than other varieties. Grow tall peas on poles, fences, or trellises. Pods are larger than other varieties and filled with larger peas. Medium-tall varieties give a larger crop and higher quality than the dwarf, but require support for the vines.

Water: Moderate water; shallow watering is said to increase germination.

Nutrients: Light feeder; low need for nitrogen, phosphorus, and potassium. In light soil, give a complete fertilizer 6 weeks after planting. Peas supply their own nitrogen. No fertilizing is necessary in soil prepared well with well-rotted manure and bone meal. Use the proper bacterial inoculant to promote nitrogen fixation. A high-nitrogen fertilizer will prevent blooms from setting pods.

Side dressing: When vines are about 6 inches (15 cm) tall, apply compost or fish emulsion.

CARE

- Keep soil moist along each side of the rows or in each basin around poles.
- Use porous shade cloth erected on wooden supports to protect peas from early heat in hot climates.

Pests: Most pests affect seedlings: aphids, cabbage loopers, cabbage maggots, corn earworms, corn maggots, cucumber beetles, cutworms, garden webworms, flea beetles, slugs, snails, thrips, webworms, weevil wireworms, rabbits, birds.

- Control aphids by pinching out infested foliage or by hosing them off the vines.
- Exclude beetles by covering crop with floating row cover.
- Wireworms attack germinating seed. Solarize the soil in the spring.
- Nematodes can infest the roots: nodules should not be confused with nematode galls on the roots. Solarize the soil in the spring.
- Fence out rabbits and discourage birds with bird netting or bird tape.

Diseases: Bacterial blight, downy mildew, enation mosaic, fusarium wilt, leaf curl, powdery mildew, root rot, seed rot

- Ascochyta blight is seed borne and is characterized by purplish to black, streaky, and irregularly shaped lesions on the stem.
- Septoria blight, a fungus, causes the leaves to appear yellowish and shrunken.
- Bacterial blight produces water-soaked lesions on all parts of the plant, which may appear creamy and slimy under highly humid conditions.
- Remove and destroy plants infected with blight. Solarize the soil with black plastic.
- Pea mosaic, a viral disease, induces severe stunting and mottling of leaves with streaks of yellowing on the stems. Early infection causes the plant to die. Crop rotation is recommended for control.
- Powdery and downy mildew. Spray foliage thoroughly with a baking soda solution (1 teaspoon per quart/liter of water).

- Pea root rot causes browning and drying of the foliage from the ground up. Gardens that have this problem with peas each year are said to have "pea sick" soil. Ensure well-drained soil and rotate crops.

General disease treatments:
- Plant disease resistant varieties.
- Avoid handling vines when wet.
- Remove and destroy infected plants.

HARVEST

Peas will be ready for harvest 55–70 days after sowing, summer to early fall.
- **Garden, green, or English peas** mature 55–70 days after seeding, summer to early autumn. Pick when pods are bulging but before they are full size to encourage regrowth. Pick daily as plant reaches maturity so that new pods will form. Under cool temperatures, peas do not mature rapidly and can be harvested for several days. Under warm temperatures, the seeds accumulate starch rapidly, and harvest should be completed in a day or two. Shell early for sweetest texture and flavor. Any withered or yellowed pods may be harvested for dried peas. Midsummer pickings are not as heavy or as good as cool or mild weather harvests.
- **Snow peas** also called Chinese peas are harvested when the pods reach full size but before the seeds become enlarged.
- **Snap peas also called sugar snap peas** are harvested when pods are 1½– 2½ inches (3.8–6.4 cm) long and peas are just barely visible within the pods.
- **Peas for shelling** are harvested when pods have swollen to cylindrical shape but before they lose their bright green color. Harvest edible pods when 2–3 inches (5–7.5cm) long before seeds begin to swell.

Storage: Peas will keep in a plastic bag in the refrigerator for 1–2 weeks. Shelled peas should be cooled as quickly as possible to 32°F (0°C) to prevent conversion of sugars to starch and to reduce the respiration rate. Snow pea varieties also may be blanched in boiling water, chilled in an ice water bath, dried, and stored in the freezer for up to 3 months; some texture will be lost. Dried peas can be stored in a cool, dry place for 10 to 12 months.

VARIETIES

Choose from these pea types and varieties:
- **Garden peas, green peas, or English peas:** 'Knight' and 'Dakota' is an early pea; 'Lincoln' is a sweet heirloom; 'Green Arrow' is a flavorful climber; 'Alderman' ('Tall Telephone') is sweet climber; 'Maestro' and 'Eclipse' are good in warm regions; 'Alaska' is a short-season variety; 'Little Marvel' and 'Wando' are small garden, bush varieties. Small-seeded green peas are called *petit pois* or "baby peas": varieties include 'Waverex' and 'Precovelle'.

- **Snow peas:** 'Corgi' is flavorful; 'Oregon Giant' is large podded; 'Sugar Pod 2' is good for cool regions; 'Norli' is sweet; 'Dwarf Gray Sugar' is a bush type; 'Mammoth Melting Sugar' is a long-podded climber.
- **Sugar peas and sugar snap peas:** 'Super Sugar Mel' is a favorite; 'Super Sugar Snap' is a sweet climber. Other favorites include: 'Sugar Snap' (tall) and 'Sugar Ann' (bush). 'Sugar Pop' and 'Sugar Daddy' are stringless varieties.

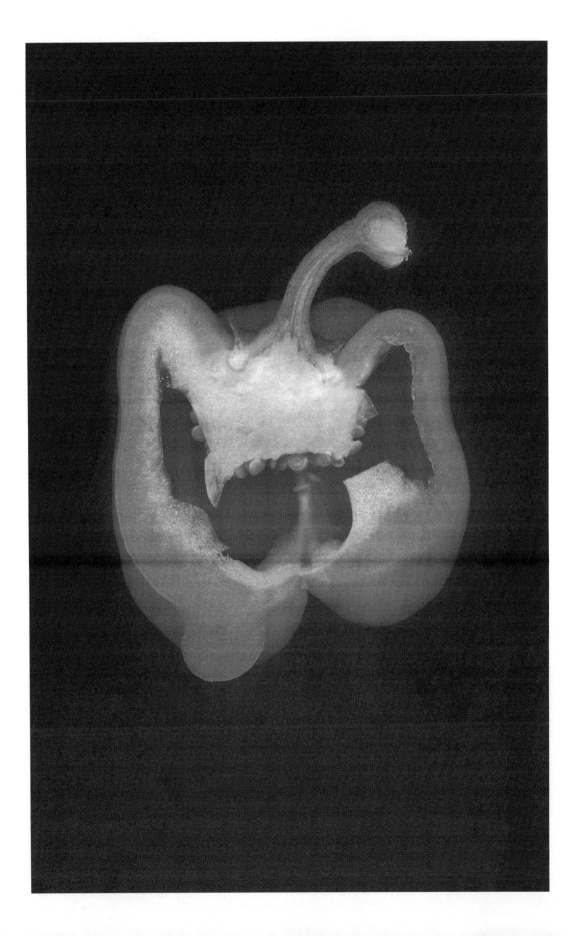

Peppers

Common names: Sweet pepper, hot pepper, chili
World names Sweet Peppers: tian jiao (Chinese); poivron (French) Gewürzpaprika, Spanischer Pfeffer (German); hara mirch (Hindi); pimento, pepperone (Italian); peppaa (Japanese); cabai (Malay); pimiento picante (Spanish); phrik (Thai).
World names Hot or Chili Peppers: la jiao (Chinese); piment, cayenne (French); Chili, Tabasco (German); mirch (Hindi); peperoncino arbustivo (Italian); kidachi tougarashi (Japanese); lada merah (Malay); guindilla (Spanish); phrik kheenuu (Thai).
Botanical name: *Capsicum annum* (mostly sweet peppers), *Capsicum chinense, Capsicum frutescens* (hot or chili peppers)
Pronounced KAP-sih-kum AN-yoo-um
Family: Nightshade or potato family—*Solanaceae*

ABOUT

Type of plant: Annual, warm season; perennial in tropical climates
Origin: New World tropics, West Indies. Peppers were among the first plants cultivated in South America, perhaps as long as 5,000 years ago.
Overview of peppers: There are two basic kinds of peppers: sweet and hot. Sweet peppers are mild in flavor. They include stuffing and salad peppers usually called bell peppers. Sweet peppers ripen to red, yellow, orange, purple and brown. Hot peppers are pungent and range in flavor from mildly spicy to extremely hot. They vary in size from very small to 6–7 inches (15–18cm) long.
General description: Erect herbaceous plants usually becoming woody at the stem base; multi-branched with smooth oval to lance-like deep-green leaves 2–4 inches (5–10 cm) long. Fruits range in size from 1–7 inches (2.5–10 cm) long and vary in color from green, yellow or even purple when young to a mixture of glossy red, orange, and yellow at maturity; pod size varies from short and long to fat and round to skinny and long. The sweet or hot taste of a pepper is affected by the level of capsaicin contained in the pepper's seeds and outer skin membrane.
Height: 6–48 inches (15–122cm) tall depending upon variety
Breadth: 24 inches (60 cm).
Root depth: The fibrous spreading roots of peppers generally reach down to about 8 inches (20 cm), but sometimes extend 48 inches (122 cm) deep.

Bloom time and flower: Summer; flowers are insignificant, colors vary from white to greenish-white, and lavender to purple

Edible parts: Pod fruits

KITCHEN

Serve: Eat sweet peppers raw or cooked. Fresh hot or chili peppers can be baked, roasted, grilled, stuffed, or eaten raw.

BASICS

Seed planting depth: ¼–½ inch (6–13 mm)

Germination soil temperature: 75–95°F (24–35°C); optimum 85°F (29°C)

Days to germination: 7–10

Sow indoors: 8 weeks before last frost

Sow outdoors: Not recommended

Days to maturity: 60–95 days: 55–80 days from transplanting for green peppers; 15–20 days more for mature peppers

Soil pH range: 5.5–6.8

Growing soil temperature: Set out seedlings when the average night temperature is at least 55°F (13°C) and the soil temperature has reached 60°F (16°C) or above; however, the optimum soil temperature range is from 70–80°F (21–27°C).

Spacing of plants: 12–15 inches (30–37 cm). Plant two seeds in each hole; thin out the weakest of each planting pair. Plant a staggered pattern across a 36-inch (90 cm) bed so that leaves will touch at maturity.

Water: Moderate and even until fruit set; less after

Light: Full sun

Nutrients: High nitrogen, phosphorus, and potassium

Rotating crops: Do not follow with tomatoes, eggplant, potatoes

Companion crops: Basil, carrots, eggplants, onions, parsley, parsnip, peas, tomatoes

Incompatible crops: Fennel, kohlrabi

Propagation: Seed

Seed viability: 2 years; store in an airtight container in a cool, dark place.

Seed weight: 3,920 seeds per ounce (138 per gram)

SITE

Peppers grow best in growth zones 4–12. Peppers require a warm, long growing season and are sensitive to cool, wet weather.

Frost tolerance: Very tender; peppers do not tolerate frost.

Soil preparation: Light, well-drained fertile soil, not overly humus-rich

PLANTING

Starting plants indoors: Sow indoors 6–8 weeks before the last spring frost or 6–8 weeks before the average night time temperature is expected to stay above 55°F (13°C). Sow seeds indoors, under glass, broadcasting seed 5–8 inches (12–20 cm) apart in a planting tray 4–6 inches (10–35 cm) deep filled with loose potting soil. Grow at 70°F (21°C); keep night time temperature above 62°F (17°C). When the first true leaves just show, transplant seedlings 2–3 inches apart in flats or 2-inch (5 cm) cell-type containers. Reduce moisture slightly to harden. Never let plants wilt. Ideal seedlings have buds, but no open flowers. The plants should receive full sunlight. After 4 weeks adjust the temperature to 70°F (21°C) day and night. Transplant to the garden after the last frost when the soil has warmed and plants are 4–6 inches (10–15 cm) tall. Well-developed root systems are important to the success of young transplants. Water-in transplants using a high phosphorus solution. Do not mulch until the soil is thoroughly warm.

Planting site note: Avoid planting hot peppers in the same part of the garden as sweet peppers so that they cannot cross pollinate.

Planting time in cold-winter and short-season climates: Spring; direct sow after all danger of frost has past and night time temperatures stay above 55°F (13°C).

Planting time in warm and hot climates: Sow seed or set out seedlings in late spring when the soil has warmed, about 90 days before the hottest summer temperatures. Best to grow plants when the day time temperatures are above 70°F (21°C) and night time temperatures above 60°F (16°C).

Row covers: Protect early plants from cold weather by using mulch in combination with lightweight fabric row cover supported by wire hoops. Cold nights will cause blossoms to drop producing bushy plants without peppers. Remove row covers when there is sunny weather above 85°F (29°C) to prevent heat damage.

Succession plantings: Every 3–4 weeks until the peak of summer heat

GROWING

Water: Keep soil moist. Do not let plants wilt. Irrigate in dry spells.

Nutrients: Peppers are medium to heavy feeders. Add rotted manure or compost to bed before planting. Magnesium is important for peppers; scatter 1 teaspoon (5 ml) of Epsom salts around the base of each plant.

Side dressing: Apply liquid seaweed at blossom time and 2–3 times per season.

CARE

- Water frequently when fruits begin to form. Allow soil to nearly dry between watering.
- Shade plants in hot midsummer climates or blossoms may drop without setting peppers.
- Water heavily 4–8 hours before harvest for milder peppers; withhold watering to increase spiciness.
- Sunscald is caused by inadequate foliage.
- Prevent blossom end rot with adequate soil calcium and regular moisture.
- Too much nitrogen can result in big, bushy plants with few peppers.

- Do not plant where peppers or other nightshade family members, such as tomatoes and eggplants, have grown during the past two years.
- If you smoke, wash your hands before working with the plants to avoid spreading tobacco mosaic virus.

Common problems: Blossom end rot and sunscald can cause dry, sunken patches on the fruit.

Pests: Aphids, armyworms, Colorado potato beetles, corn borers, corn earworms, cut worms, flea beetles, leaf miners, mites, slugs, snails, tomato hornworms, vegetable weevils, wireworms.

- Do not plant where peppers or other nightshade family members, such as tomatoes and eggplants, have grown during the past 2 years.
- Protect young plants from cutworms with cardboard or foil collars.
- Hand-pick hornworms off of plants.
- You can partially control flea beetles and aphids by hosing them off the plants and pinching out aphid-infested foliage.

Diseases: Rot, blossom end rot, anthracnose, tobacco mosaic virus, bacterial spot, leaf spot, soft rot, southern blight, tobacco mosaic, mildew.

- Plant disease-resistant varieties and maintain garden sanitation.
- Remove and destroy infected plants.
- If you smoke, wash your hands before working with the plants to avoid spreading tobacco mosaic virus.
- To prevent bacterial spot and phytopthora, drip irrigate only, plant only in well-drained soil, minimize soil compaction, and follow a 4-year crop rotation.
- Western yellow or curly top virus causes old leaves to curl upwards and turn yellow. Control curly top by excluding leafhoppers with floating row covers.
- Nematodes attack the roots causing gall formations. Solarize the soil with black plastic.
- Phytophthora root rot causes rotting of roots under high temperatures and high soil moisture. It can be controlled by careful regulation of soil moisture.

HARVEST

Harvest Warning: Capsaicin is an oily, alkaloid-like substance that clings to the outer skin, juice, and seeds of fresh and dried hot peppers. It is a skin and eye irritant. Use disposable rubber gloves when handling peppers to prevent burns to the skin. Do not rub your face with your hands after handling peppers or their plants. Use milk to wash the hot pepper's sting from skin.

Harvest: Peppers are ready for harvest 60–95 days after seeding, midsummer onwards. Pick promptly when full size. Pick mature peppers when 50–75 percent colored; they will finish ripening in 1–2 days at room temperature. If you pick fruit at the green stage, instead of letting them ripen to red, the plant will continue to set new fruit. Bell peppers are harvested when they have attained full size and are still green. Allow hot peppers to ripen on the vine to reach full pungency. The ripening process is similar to the tomato.

Storage: Keep peppers in a plastic bag in the refrigerator for up to 1 week, or in a cool, dry spot for up to 2 weeks. If roasted, peeled, and stored in the freezer, for up to 6 months. If dried, whether in a vegetable dehydrator, hung in garlands, or laid out loose in flats in the sun, for up to 1 year. If pickled whole, cooked, and canned, for up to 2 years.

CLASSIFICATION AND VARIETIES

Overview of peppers: There are two basic kinds of peppers: sweet and hot. Sweet peppers ripen to red, yellow, orange, purple and brown. Hot or chili peppers are pungent and range in flavor from mildly spicy to extremely hot. They vary in size from very small to 6–7 inches (15–18 cm) long.

• **Common names and descriptions of *C. annuum* varieties:**

Ancho: large, heart-shaped fruit colored green, dark brown or red at maturity; mildly pungent flavor. Ancho is the dried version of the Pablano pepper. Used for stuffing and drying. Use 'Ancho 101'.

Banana: Also known as pepperoncini, Tuscan peppers, and sweet Italian peppers. Try 'Banana Supreme'. All purpose pepper.

Bell: large blocky fruit with a blunt end of three or four lobes; fruit harvested green at maturity, some red at maturity, others are gold, yellow, or orange colored; usually sweet flavor. Green bell pepper varieties include: 'California Wonder', 'Whopper Improved'. Yellow bell pepper: 'Labrador.' Orange bell: 'Ariane'. Red bell peppers at maturity include: 'Big Early', 'Ace', 'Lipstick', 'Blushing Beauty', 'Tequila', 'Roumainian Rainbow'.

Cayenne: Tapered, slender, and wrinkled; usually red at harvest; highly pungent; 'Sweet Cayenne', 'Jimmy Nardello', 'Cayenne II'.

Cheese: Small- to medium-sized round fruit; yellow or green fruit matures to red; usually not pungent.

Cherry: Small spherical to somewhat flattened fruit; harvested at either green or red stage; sweet or pungent; 'Cherry Pick', 'Cherry Bomb'.

Chiltepin: Very small, egg-shaped fruit; oval to elongated fruits are known as *chilipiquin*; highly pungent. An old wild pepper sometimes called the "mother of all peppers."

Cubanelle (Cuban): Irregular blunt shape; harvested when yellow or green or after becoming red; mildly pungent. Popular frying pepper.

Jalapeño: Small, cylindrical with rounded ends, russeted skin; usually harvested green; very pungent. Used in Mexican and Southwestern cuisine. 'Jaloro' is a yellow jalapeño. 'Mucho Nacho' is a green to red ripening jalapeño.

Long Wax: Long and tapered to a point, although some are blunt; tolerates low and high temperatures; harvested at green, yellow, and red stages; mildly pungent.

New Mexican: Long, slender fruit; harvested green and red; moderately pungent, though some are sweet. 'Anaheim' is a popular cultivar.

Pimiento (Pimento): Large, cone- or heart-shape; harvested red; mild flavor; 'Pimento L', 'Pimento Perfection'. Used for salads, stuffing, roasting, pickling, or canning.

Serrano: Elongated, short, nearly blunt; usually harvested green; very pungent. Often used for pickling and sauce. Choose 'Serrano' or 'Serrano del Sol'.

Squash: Flattened scallop shape; usually pungent.

- **Common name and description of *C. chinense* (a form of *C. frutescens*) variety:**

Habañero: Small thin, puffy walled, lantern shaped; extremely pungent; considered the hottest of all peppers. Excellent for sauce. Choose 'Habañero' or 'Jamaican Hot Chocolate', a habañero type pepper.

Scotch bonnet: Small, changes from green to orange and scarlet. Used to make hot sauce.

- **Common name and description of *C. frutescens* variety:**

Tabasco: Erect, slender, short fruit; usually harvested at the red stage; highly pungent. Used to make the Louisiana hot sauce.

Potatoes

Common name: Potato, white potato, Irish potato
World names: ma ling shu (Chinese); pommes de terre (French); Kartoffel (German); patate (Italian); ubi kenteng (Malay); batata (Portuguese); papa (Spanish)
Botanical name: *Solanum tuberosum*
Pronounced So–LAY–num too–ber–OH–sum
Family: Nightshade or potato family—*Solanaceae*

ABOUT

Type of plant: Perennial grown as annual, cool season
Origin: Chile, Peru, Bolivia, Mexico. Potatoes have been cultivated in the Andes of Peru and Bolivia for as long as 7,000 years.
Description: Sprawling weak-stemmed plant with hairy, dark green divided leaves similar in appearance to tomato leaves, producing swollen tubers that grow underground from the plant's roots. Tubers can be red, purple, brown, tan, and yellow. Shapes are primarily oval or round, though unusual varieties grow in finger- and cluster-like shapes. Individual sizes range from bite size to about 1 pound (0.4 kg).
Varieties include early, midseason, and late-season potatoes. Usually, two crops can be grown: one for late summer harvesting and the second to store for winter use.
Varieties can be divided for culinary purposes according to their starch content:
- Floury in texture: high in starch content; used for baking, frying, and mashing.
- Waxy in texture: low in starch content; high water content; hold together well when boiled.

Height: 24–30 inches (60–76 cm)
Breadth: 24 inches (60 cm)
Root depth: 18–24 inches (45–60 cm)
Bloom time and flowers: Summer; 1 inch (2.5cm) wide pale blue flowers in clusters.
Edible parts: Tuber

KITCHEN

Serve: Potatoes are served cooked. They be can boiled, steamed, baked, fried, mashed, roasted, sautéed, or cooked au gratin. Potatoes must be served cooked because they contain high levels of indigestible starch. That starch is converted to sugar during cooking.

BASICS

Tuber planting depth: 2–4 inches (5–10 cm)
Soil temperature for planting: 60–65°F (16–18°C); sprouts will emerge slowly in cooler soil temperatures (30–35 days for complete emergence at mean soil temperature of 52°F/ 12°C). Tuber formation decreases at soil temperatures slightly above 68°F (20°C) and is almost completely inhibited above 84°F (29°C).
Planting tubers outdoors: 3 weeks before last frost
Days to maturity: Planted in early season: 90–110 days. Planted mid-season: 100–120 days. Planted late in season: 110–140 days.
Soil pH range: 5.0–6.5
Growing air temperature: 60–80°F (16–26°C); optimum 65°F (18°C). Potatoes differ widely in their growing temperature requirements according to variety.
Spacing of plants in beds: 12–18 inches (30–45cm) apart in all directions
Spacing of plants in rows: 12–15 inches (30–37 cm) apart and in all directions in wide beds
Spacing between rows: 24 inches (60 cm)
Water: Moderate
Light: Full sun
Nutrients: High nitrogen, phosphorus, and potassium
Rotating crops: Do not follow with tomato family plants.
Companion crops: Brassicas or cabbage family plants, corn, marigolds, beans, cabbage, eggplant, horseradish
Incompatible crops: Cucumbers, peas, pumpkins, raspberries, spinach, squash, sunflowers, tomatoes

SITE

Potatoes grow best in growth zones 3–11.
Frost tolerance: Very tender; cannot tolerate any frost
Soil preparation: Potatoes prefer loose, well-drained sandy-loam, loam, silt loam or peat at least 2–3 feet (60–100 cm) deep. Soil should be slightly acidic soil with plenty of potash. Tubers will become deformed in heavy, poorly drained soil.
Container growing: Use a container 30 inches (76 cm) deep and 20 inches (51 cm) across. Place 10 inches (25 cm) of soil at the bottom of the container then place the sprouted potatoes on top of the soil and cover with 2 inches (5 cm) of soil. Using the "hilling" process, allow the plants to grow to 6 inches (15 cm) then cover again with 2–3 inches (5–7 cm) of soil. Continue this process of allowing the plants to grow and then cover half of the leaves with soil. Harvest will come in about two months.

PLANTING

"Seed potatoes." Potatoes are not grown from seed but rather from pieces of the tubers called "seed potatoes" that are grown the previous year. Each tuber piece should be about the size of an egg and have at least two "eyes," or dormant buds. Cut seed potatoes to size and let the pieces dry for one day to prevent rotting in the ground. (Cut pieces into 1½ inch/3.8 cm cubes with at least 2 eyes or use mini-tubers planted whole.) Treat seed potatoes with a light dusting of agricultural sulfur to protect against fungal disease. Plants are clones of the parent plant. (Potato blossoms sometimes produce a small fruit which contains seed but they do not grow true-to-type.)

Before planting: Place tubers in a well lit, well ventilated place, spread out in a single layer, with the eye-side upward for 4–5 weeks. The tubers will begin to sprout. Choose those tubers that sprout stubby shoots, not thin or spindly shoots. Cut the tubers into pieces roughly 1½ inches (3.8 cm) in diameter, weighing 1½–2 ounces (40–60 g), with at least one strong "eye" on each piece. Dust the cut surfaces of seed potatoes with garden lime or allow the surfaces to dry for up to a day before planting.

Planting in trenches or "hilling": Dig trench 6 inches (15 cm) wide, 4–8 inches (10–20 cm) deep, and space trenches 30–36 inches (76–90 cm) apart. Place seed pieces 9–12 inches (25–30 cm) apart at the bottom of the trench and place 2 inches (5 cm) of soil atop the trench. When the plants are 12 inches (30 cm) tall, draw soil up around them ("hilling") so just a few inches (5 cm) of the plant is seen. Hilling will protect potatoes from sunburn and from turning green.

Planting time in cold-winter climates: Spring as soon as soil can be worked. For summer crop where soil temperatures do not climb above 85°F (29°C), plant cuttings of early-maturing varieties in spring 2–3 weeks before the last frost date. For autumn crop, plant late-maturing varieties in late spring. Potatoes are tolerant of cool soil and moderate frost.

Planting time in mild-winter climates: Early spring for winter into spring crop. For summer crop, plant in late winter or early spring 4–6 weeks before the last frost date. For winter-into-spring crop, plant in late summer or early autumn.

GROWING

Water: Keep soil moist, but do not saturate the soil.

Nutrients: In advance of planting, work rotted manure, compost, and rock fertilizers into the soil. Avoid overusing nitrogen, which will encourage foliage growth at the expense of tuber development.

Side dressing: Apply high-phosphorus blended organic fertilizer after 1 month of growth.

CARE

When sprouts emerge, add 2 inches (5 cm) of soil to the trench. As tubers grow, form a large hill around the base of each plant to protect developing tubers from sunburn and to prevent greening. When plants are about a 12 inches (30 cm) tall, hill them with a continuous 6–8 inch (15–20 cm) high mound of soil by hoeing from each side; "hill" again 2–3 weeks later. Hilling ensures potatoes will grow protected from sunlight which causes "greening", green patches that contain the toxic alkaloid solanine.

- Carefully cultivate to remove weeds until the plants form flowers.

Pests: Aphids, cabbage loopers, Colorado potato beetles, corn borers, corn earworms, cucumber beetles, cutworms, earwigs, flea beetles, Japanese beetles, lace bugs, leafhoppers, leaf miners, nematodes, slugs, snails, tomato hornworms, white grubs, wireworms.

- Covering plants with row covers or dusting them with ground limestone helps deter beetles. Control potato beetle larvae with Bacillus thuringiensis (Bt).
- Look for yellow potato beetle eggs on leaf undersides and crush them.
- Hand pick slugs, snails, and hornworm eggs and larvae. Spray away aphids with a strong stream of water.

Diseases: Black leg, early blight, fusarium wilt, late blight, mosaic, powdery mildew, yellows, root rot, ring rot, scab, verticillium wilt

- Scab—scabby patches or curly roughness of the skin—does not affect the eating quality of the potato. Avoid scab by not allowing soil to dry out.
- At least 10 viruses are transmitted by aphids and insects. Spray away aphids with a strong stream of water. Exclude pests with row covers.
- Plant resistant varieties.
- Use seed certified as true to type and free of disease.
- Remove infected plants and destroy them.
- The best disease control is fertile soil and irrigation when needed to keep the crop growing strongly.

HARVEST

Potatoes planted in early season will be ready for harvest in 90–110 days; planted mid-season, 100–120 days; planted late in season, 110–140 days. Dig early for "new potatoes" when plants begin to bloom and fade; dig for mature, full-size potatoes when the vines yellow and die. To harden the potato skin, water for the last time 2 weeks before harvest; 10 days later, cut the foliage away; 4 days later harvest during a cool part of the day. Dig carefully with a garden fork, starting 8–10 inches (20–25 cm) away from the plant, then work closer to the vine until all the potatoes have been gathered. Brush but do not wash clinging soil from the tubers.

- Young, small, "new" potatoes can be harvested beginning about 7–8 weeks after planting. To harvest "new" potatoes, cut or beat down the vines a few days before digging to "set" the skin. Tubers should be dug and carefully handled to avoid bruising and the subsequent formation of black spot.
- Mature potatoes can remain in the ground where the ground does not freeze. Harvest all potatoes before they start growing again.

Storage: Allow surfaces to dry before putting into storage containers. Cure for a period of 4–5 days at 60–70°F (16–21°C) in high humidity; this will allow cuts and surface injuries of the tuber to "heal." Store at 40–50°F (4–10°C) at relative humidity of 90%. Store in a dark, well-ventilated area for up to 6 months. Do not refrigerate. Prepared or new potatoes freeze well and potatoes can also be dried. Well-matured potatoes without defect are the best keepers.

Toxins: When potato tubers are exposed to light, an alkaloid, solanine, forms. The amount depends on the length of exposure, intensity, and quality of light. Solanine tastes bitter; the ingestion of large amounts can cause sickness and in extreme cases, death.

TYPES OF POTATOES

- **Russet potatoes:** Also called old potatoes, baking potatoes, or Idaho potatoes (if they were grown in Idaho)—have an oblong, elliptical shape, and a rough, netted, brown skin with numerous eyes and white flesh. Russets grow from 4–6 inches (10–15 cm) long and about 2 inches (5 cm) in diameter. Russets are low in moisture and high in starch so they cook up dry and fluffy. Russets are suited for baking, mashing, and deep frying (French fries). Top varieties are russet 'Burbank', russet 'Norkotahs', russet 'Arcadia', and russet 'Butte'.

- **Long white potatoes:** Also called white rose or California long whites (because they were developed in California)—have an elliptical shape and a thin ivory white to pale gray-brown skin with imperceptible eyes. Long whites grow from 4–6 inches (10–15 cm) long and about 2 inches (5 cm) in diameter. Long whites have a medium to low starch content and are moister than russets. You can use long whites for boiling, baking, or deep frying. Long whites keep their shape when cooked.

- **Fingerlings:** Are thumb-sized potatoes that grow to about 3 inches (7.5 cm) long and 1 inch (2.5 cm) wide. Fingerlings are thin skinned and can be cooked unpeeled—baked, boiled, steamed, fried, and roasted. They are low in starch with a waxy texture and hold together well after cooking. They are yellow fleshed with a rich, buttery texture. Fingerling varieties include 'Ruby' crescent fingerlings, 'Russian Banana' fingerlings, 'Long White' fingerlings, and 'Purple Peruvian' fingerlings.

- **Yellow potatoes:** Are usually round to slightly oblong shaped potatoes with thin, yellowish light brown skins, and buttery yellow to golden waxy flesh. Yellow potatoes are low to medium in starch and have a moist, creamy, succulent texture with a buttery flavor. They are well suited for boiling, steaming, mashing, roasting, grilling, and au gratin dishes. Yellow flesh potato varieties include 'Yukon Gold', 'Yellow Finn', 'German Butterball', 'Carola', 'Nicola', and 'Alby's Gold'.

- **Round white potatoes:** Are medium-sized, round with a light tan to freckled brown skin and waxy to creamy textured flesh. Round whites are moist with low to medium starch. They are well suited for boiling, roasting, frying, and mashing. Round whites hold their shaped after cooking. Round whites are grown mostly in the Northeastern United States. Round white varieties include 'Kennebec', 'Superior', and 'Atlantic'.

- **Round red potatoes:** Also called new potatoes (because they are small), red bliss potatoes and boiling potatoes are medium-sized, round, rose to reddish-brown skinned potatoes with a dense, crisp white flesh. Round reds are low in starch and are sweeter tasting than round whites. Choose round reds for boiling, roasting, grilling, sautés, stews, salads, and au gratin dishes. You can serve round reds cooked whole. Round reds are mostly grown in the Northwestern United States. Round red varieties include red 'Norland' and red 'Pontiac'.

- **Purple potatoes or blue potatoes:** Are heirloom potatoes with grayish-blue to purple skins and usually inky blue flesh. They are delicate flavored. Purple and blue skinned potatoes are low in starch and can be boiled, steamed, roasted, fried, mashed, or served in stews, salads, and au gratin dishes. Blue and purple potatoes are probably descended from the original potatoes from Peru which were the same color. Purple flesh potato varieties include 'All Blue' which is dry and good for roasting; 'Purple Peruvian' which is good fried; and 'Purple Viking' which has good flavor and is good mashed.

- **Other heirloom potatoes:** Include two red skinned and red fleshed potatoes: 'Huckleberry' and 'Blossom'. Both of these potatoes are low in starch and can be boiled, steamed, roasted, fried, mashed, or served in stews, salads, and au gratin dishes.

- **New potatoes:** Is a term for any variety of potato that has been harvested before it has reached maturity. (However, mature round red potatoes are also called new potatoes simply because they are small.) New potatoes are also called baby potatoes and sometimes creamers. They can be as small as marble-sized.

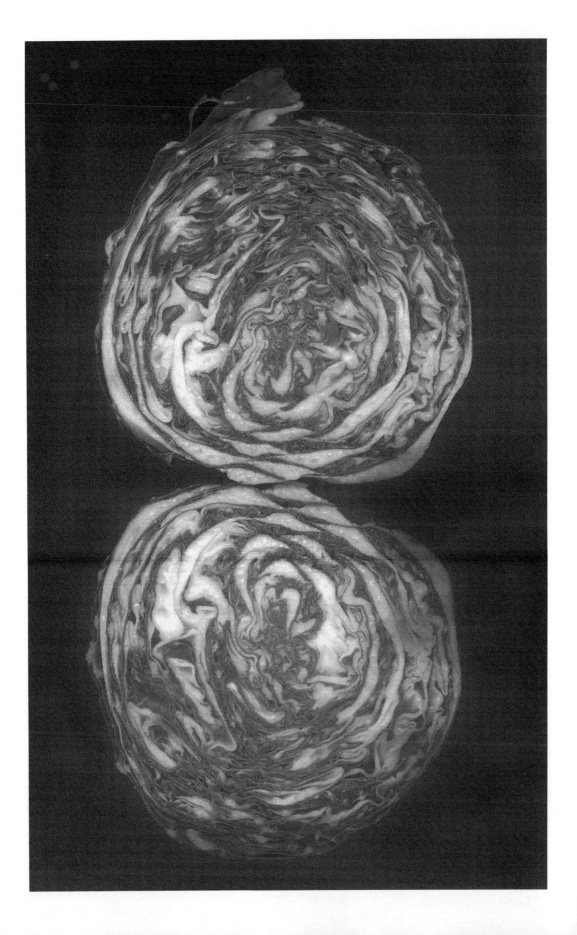

Radicchio

Pronounced rah–DEEK–eeyo
Common name: Radicchio, Italian chicory, heading chicory, rosette chicory, spring chicory, leaf chicory, Italian dandelion; red-leafed chicories grown for salads
World names: ju ju (Chinese); chicofee à café (French); Wurzelzichorie, Kaffeezichorie (German); cicoria (Italian); kiku nigana (Japanese); achicoria (Spanish)
Botanical name: *Cichorium intybus*
Pronounced sih–KO–ree–um
Family: Sunflower family—*Asteraceae (Compositae)*

ABOUT
Type of plant: Perennial, cool weather
Origin: Northern Italy. Radicchio originated in the Veneto region of Italy where it has been cultivated since the sixteenth century.
Description: Lettuce like heads that color to a deep rosy red as weather grows cold in autumn or winter. Most cultivars form small, tight heads with elongated leaves similar to romaine lettuce; some can form a softball-size head. The slightly bitter taste sweetens with cooler day temperatures.
There are five northern Italian varieties that are well known:
- 'Chioggia' (Rosa di Chioggia): rounded, compact, Chianti-colored; bittersweet to bitter leaves.
- 'Verona': elongated leaves, bright colored
- 'Early Treviso': resembles a small reddish-purple romaine, slender and tapered, with white ribs
- 'Late Treviso': leaves swirl; flavor similar to Belgian endive
- 'Castelfranco': lettuce-like leaves, yellow with rose speckles; tender, mild taste

Height: 4–6 inches (10–15 cm)
Breadth: 4–6 inches (10–15 cm)
Root depth: 3–4 inches (7.5–10 cm)
Bloom time and flower: Late spring or autumn, blue flowers
Edible parts: Leaves

RADICCHIO

KITCHEN
Serve: Eat radicchio raw or cooked. You can use radicchio in place of chicory and escarole in most recipes.

BASICS
Seed planting depth: ¼ inch (6 mm)
Germination soil temperature: 60–65°F (7–18°C)
Days to germination: 5–7
Sowing indoors: 8 weeks before the last frost
Sowing outdoors: 2 weeks before last frost and 2 months before the first frost
Days to maturity: 75–110 days.
Soil pH range: 5.0–6.8
Growing soil temperature: 45–65°F (7–18°C)
Spacing of plants: 8–10 inches (20–25 mm) apart in all directions
Water: Keep soil moist
Light: Full sun to partial shade
Nutrients: Moderate nitrogen, phosphorus, and potassium
Rotating crops: Do not follow escarole and endive
Companion crops: Lettuce
Propagation: Seed
Seed vitality: 5 years
Seed weight: 15,000 seeds per ounce (530 per gram)

SITE
Best climate: Growth zone 8 and above
Soil preparation: Fertile, well-drained soil
Container growing: Radicchio will grow in containers. Choose a container at least 12 inches (30 cm) wide and deep.

PLANTING
Sow radicchio seed ¼ inch (6 mm) deep.
Planting time in cold-winter climates: Spring; sow seeds 6–8 weeks after the last frost for early summer harvest.
Planting time in mild-winter climates: Sow in late summer for autumn or winter harvest; thin plants to12 inches (30 cm).
Planting time in reverse-season climates: Autumn; plants tend to bolt if days are too long when heads begin to form. Cool weather causes radicchio to develop its distinctive purplish-red coloration and become milder in taste.
Succession planting: Plant new crops every 10–14 days

CARE

- Keep soil free of weeds
- Feed with fish emulsion every 3 weeks. Moderate nitrogen, phosphorus, and potassium

Common problems: Provide shade in hot spells to prevent brown, crisp ends of leaves.

Pests: Aphids, armyworms, flea beetles, leafhoppers, slugs, snails.

- Control slugs with pans of beer set into the soil (they will drown) or handpick and destroy.
- Exclude beetles and leafhoppers with floating row covers Spray with insecticidal soap.
- Spray away aphids with a strong, steady stream of water.

Diseases: Downy mildew

- Provide good air circulation to avoid molds

HARVEST

Radicchio is ready for harvest 75–110 days after sowing. Cut off outer leaves; harvest before frost. Cut full heads as soon as they are firm.

Storage: Refrigerate for 2–3 days wrapped in a paper towel in a plastic bag.

VARIETIES

Choose radicchio from these varieties: 'Rossa di Treviso' and 'Rossa de Verona' are favorites; 'Giulio' for spring crops; 'Augusto' for fall and winter crops.

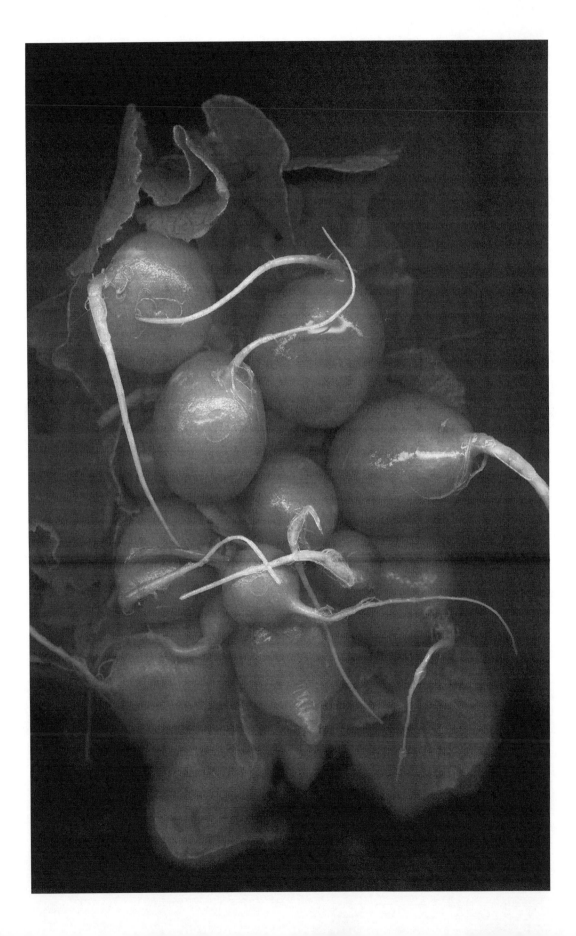

Radishes

Common names: Radish
World names: luo bo (Chinese); radis (French); Rettich, Radieschen (German); ravanello (Italian); radeisshu (Japanese); lobak (Malay); rabanete (Portuguese); rabanito (Spanish)
Botanical name: *Raphanus sativus*
Pronounced RAF–an–us suh–TY–vus
Family: Mustard or cabbage family—*Brassicaceae (Cruciferae)*

ABOUT

Type of plant: Biennial grown as annual, cool season
Origin: China, Japan, and Mediterranean countries
Description: Grown for swollen roots, white, red, purple, cream, yellow, or black, and stems under a rosette of lobed and irregularly toothed leaves.
Height: 6–8 inches (15–20 cm)
Breadth: 6 inches (15 cm)
Root depth: 2–8 inches (5–20 cm)
Bloom time and flowers: Second year, white or pink flowers
Edible parts: Roots

KITCHEN

Serve: Radishes can be served raw in appetizers, salads, sandwiches or with dip. Cooked radishes can be added to soups, stews, omelets, and stir-fries. Radish greens can be prepared like spinach when they are fresh and tender.

BASICS

Seed planting depth: ½ inch (12 mm)
Germination soil temperature: 45–85°F (7–29°C); optimum 85°F (29°C)
Days to germination: 4–10
Sow indoors: Not recommended
Sow outdoors: Early spring and autumn in cool regions; winter in hot regions
Days to maturity: 21–35 days for spring radishes; 50–60 days for winter radishes
Soil pH range: 5.5–6.5
Growing soil temperature: 50–75°F (10–24°C)

Spacing of plants: 1 inch (2.5 cm) apart; thin successful plants to 4 inches (10 cm) apart in all directions
Water: Moderate and even
Light: Full sun, tolerate partial shade
Rotating crops: Precede with a legume cover crop
Companion crops: Beans, beets, carrots, cucumbers, lettuce, nasturtiums, peas, peppers, and spinach. Plant radishes with carrots, they will be ready to harvest shortly before the baby carrots need thinning.
Incompatible crops: Fennel
Propagation: Seed
Seed vitality: 5 years; store in an airtight container in a cool, dark place.
Seed weight: 2,240 seeds per ounce (155 per gram)

SITE

Radishes grow well in all growth zones; grow as a winter vegetable in mild areas.
Frost tolerance: Hardy; withstands moderate frost
Soil preparation: Radishes prefer loose, moisture-retentive, but well-drained soil. Mix in well-rotted manure. There should be no obstacles such as stones in the bed to impede root growth.
Container growing: Radishes do well in a container with a minimum depth of 4 inches (10 cm). In a round container, plant radishes in concentric circles; in a larger container, plant in wide rows.

PLANTING

Plant radishes 1 inch (2.5 cm) apart; thin successful plants to 4 inches (10 cm) apart.
Spring planting time: 4–6 weeks before the last expected frost and soon as ground can be worked
Autumn planting time: 7 weeks before the first expected frost
Succession planting: Every 10 days until warm weather arrives (average air temperatures over 70°F (21°C), and then start again in the late summer for autumn successions, planting every 10 days
Planting time in mild-winter and reverse-season climates: For winter crop sow in late autumn and early winter. Sow in intervals in autumn and winter for harvest then.
Planting note: Fast growing radishes are a good "nurse crop." Use them to mark the rows of slower growing crops such as parsley, carrots, or parsnips; radishes will help shade the seedlings of those crops. Radishes are a good filler crop.
Day length note:
- Rounder roots and shorter tops are controlled by short or medium short days, cool harvest conditions and sandy soil.

- Plants will bolt to seed if grown in hot weather or under long day lengths of 15 hours.
- Long days and hot weather can result in roots that are misshaped, cracked, rough, colorless, hot, and pithy.

CARE

Water: Keep the soil moist. For mild and tender radishes, grow rapidly with plenty of moisture. If growth is interrupted, roots will be hot, tough, and pithy. Mulch between rows to keep soil moist in hot weather.

Nutrients: Light feeder; low applications of nitrogen, phosphorus, and potassium. Add ample well-rotted compost to the soil before planting. High-nitrogen fertilizers or green manure will encourage excessive foliage growth at the expense of root development.

Side dressing: Feed with liquid fertilizer beside row 10 days after planting.

Common problems:
- Spring radishes can become pithy and hollow when over-mature.
- Radishes may bolt, or go to seed, if they receive more than 8 hours of sunlight.

Cover the plants in midsummer so they only get 8 hours of sunlight; a 12-hour day produces flowers and seeds but no radishes.

Pests: Aphids, cabbage root maggots, cabbage loopers, flea beetles, wireworms, cut worms, harlequin bugs, diamondback moths, white butterflies, leaf miners, nematodes.
- Use floating row covers at the time of planting for insect-free radishes.

Diseases: Clubroot, black leg, root rot, phytophthora, wire stem, powdery and downy mildews, black spot, black rot, yellows, white rust, and verticillium wilt. Plant in well-drained soil; avoid collecting water in the planting beds. Usually radishes grow so quickly that they are not affected by diseases.

HARVEST

Spring planted radishes will be ready for harvest in 21–35 days; winter radishes in 50–60 days. Harvest when roots have swollen to 1 inch (2.5 cm) in diameter and have attained full color. Harvest as soon as they reach maturity; radishes will become pithy and bitter if left in the ground too long.
- Pull winter radishes as needed when they reach eating size; harvest all roots before a hard freeze.
- Daikon radishes are brittle; fork and lift these roots taking care not to gouge or break them.

Storage: Topped radishes will keep 3–4 weeks in good crisp condition. Store near freezing in high humidity in semi–permeable containers.

TYPES AND VARIETIES

- **Small, round types** also called table radish, small radish, spring or summer radish, or European radish. These are grouped in the *R.s.* Radiculata Group. The roots can be round, olive-shaped, oblong, or icicle-shaped up to 1 inch (2.5 cm) in diameter with the small long types up to 3 inches (7 cm) long. Roots vary in color including white, pale rose, lavender, or crimson. Leaves of both grow to about 5 inches (13 cm) tall. Round types, such as 'Champion' and 'Cherry Belle' and hybrids are grown early in the season.
- **Large, long types** also called Asian or Oriental radishes, autumn, winter and overwintering radishes, and daikon (Japanese), mooli (Indian), moo or mu (Korean), lo bok (also lo pak) or luo bo (Chinese). These are grouped in the *R.s.* Longipinnatus Group. These torpedo- to turnip-shaped, large rooted varieties may be more than 9 inches (23 cm) in diameter and up to 24 inches (60 cm) long. The skin and flesh can vary in color: green, pink, red or white. Large type varieties take about two months to mature. The tops of these varieties may grow to 24 inches (60cm) tall with a spread of 18 inches (45 cm). Large, long radishes can be grown in hot weather and during the long mid-summer days of the year when round types cannot be grown for harvest. Also grouped in the large type of radish is *R.s.* Caudatus Group called the rat tail radish.

Radishes typed by season of harvest:

- **Early-season or spring radish:** grown for spring crops; red and white, varieties from the Radiculata Group. Red varieties include: 'Comet', 'Cherry Belle', 'Red Ball'. White varieties include: 'White Icicle', 'Burpee White'. Bicolored include: 'French Breakfast', 'D'Avignon', and 'Easter Egg'.
- **Late summer or winter radish:** long tapering, carrot shaped, red-skinned; usually planted for late summer, autumn, and winter use. From the Longipinnatus Group. Varieties include: 'Round Black Spanish', 'Long Black Spanish', 'Chinese White', 'Chinese Rose'. Japanese varieties include: 'Summer Cross', 'April Cross', 'Tama', 'All Season', 'Minowase', and 'Miyashige'.

Rhubarb

Common name: Rhubarb, garden rhubarb, pie plant
World names: da huang (Chinese); rhubarbe (French); Rhabarber (German); rabarbaro (Italian); ruibarbo (Portuguese, Spanish)
Botanical name: *Rheum rhabarbarum* syns. *Rheum* x *cultorum*, *Rheum* x *hybridum*
Pronounced ROOM kul–TOR–um
Family: Knotweed family—*Polygonaceae*

ABOUT

Type of plant: Perennial, hardy cool season
Origin: Southern Siberia. Rhubarb varieties known today were popularized in the nineteenth century,
Description: Large deep green, wavy leaves to as much as 18 inches (45 cm) wide; red or green stalks to 10–15 inches (35–38 cm) long. Big crinkled leave with elongated heart shape on thick red-tinted stalks.
Height: 24–36 inches (60–90 cm)
Breadth: 48 inches (122 cm)
Root depth: Several feet (.3 m) out and several feet deep
Bloom time and flowers: Summer; insignificant flowers in spike-like clusters; flowers are greenish or reddish on tall spikes
Edible parts: Stalks

KITCHEN

Serve: Rhubarb can be stewed or baked. It is used to make sauces, jams, and desserts such as pies, cakes and muffins. It is commonly cooked and made into compote, marmalade, or marinades and it is also incorporated into sorbets, ice cream, and punches.

BASICS

Root or crown planting depth: 1–3 inches (2.5–7.5 cm)
Soil planting temperature: 40–75°F (4–24°C)
Plant outdoors: Early spring
Time to maturity: 2–4 years to attain its first full harvest; can live 10–15 years or longer
Soil pH range: 6.0–6.8
Soil growing temperature: 35–80°F (2–27°C); optimum 65°F (18°C)
Spacing of plants: 24–36 inches (60–90 cm) apart in all directions

RHUBARB

Water: Moderate and even
Light: Partial shade to full sun
Nutrients: Low nitrogen, phosphorus, and potassium
Rotating crops: Long lived perennial do not rotate
Companion crops: Other perennial bed crops such as artichokes and asparagus. Also cole vegetables such as Brussels sprouts, cabbage, sprouts, and kale but not legume or root vegetables.
Propagation: Root divisions called crowns. Planting from seed is not recommended.

SITE

Rhubarb grows best in growth zones 3–9, in regions where the ground freezes each winter. Winter chill results in thick stems and red color. Rhubarb is not productive in areas with very hot summers.
Frost tolerance: Hardy
Soil preparation: Rhubarb prefers well-drained, fertile soil. Apply abundant organic compost to native soil. Add sand or gypsum to heavy clay soil.
Planting site: Choose a permanent site for this perennial which can produce for 10 or more years; plant on the sunny side of an asparagus bed.
Container growing: Rhubarb is a perennial that needs a cold dormancy period and is therefore not suitable for containers.

PLANTING

Crown planting depth: Set crowns 1 inch (2.5 cm) below the surface of mounds raised 6–8 inches (15–20 cm) and 36 inches (90 cm) apart in rows 60 inches (152 cm) apart. Plant the crown bud side up. Firmly tamp down the soil and water crowns to prevent dry pockets around the crowns.
Planting time: Early spring; plant the crown as soon as the soil is workable; plant divisions containing at least one bud in late winter or early spring.
Planting time in mild-winter climates: Autumn after the summer heat has broken; not easily grown in desert and hot-summer climates or in warm-winter regions; treat rhubarb as cool season annual and plant in autumn for winter-into-spring harvest (plants may rot in heat of late spring and summer)

GROWING

Water: Keep soil moist, but never waterlog the soil.
Nutrients: Rhubarb is a heavy feeder. Work bone meal and rock potash into the root zone area at the time of planting to help roots become established. Fertilize each spring with well-rotted manure, compost, or low-nitrogen fertilizer. Mulch the soil with organic compost in autumn.

CARE

- Cut and remove flower stalks when they appear to keep plant growing strongly.
- Remove dead leaves in spring.
- Use shade cloth to shield rhubarb whenever temperatures are expected to exceed 85°F (29°C).

Care in severe-winter climates: Cut the stems to the crown in autumn, mulch with 1–2 feet (30–60 cm) of straw, and cover with 1–2 inches (5–50 mm) of soil to protect the crown from freezing. Remove the straw in spring after air and soil temperatures have warmed.

Division: Divide the plant's root crowns in the autumn of the third year and replant in another area of the garden to sustain the planting. Use a sharp shovel to slice the crown. Division will rejuvenate plants.

Pests: Aphids, flea beetles, leafhoppers; however, generally pest free.

Diseases: Rhubarb has no serious disease problems. Some old clumps may develop crown rot, but this can be avoided by dividing the clumps before they get too large.

HARVEST

Let rhubarb grow for 2 seasons before harvesting in the third season, harvest leaf stalks for 4–5 weeks in spring; older plants can take 8 weeks of harvest, called pulling.

Harvest note: Do not eat rhubarb leaves which contain poisonous concentrations of oxalic acid.

Harvest calendar:

- First year: Do not harvest.
- Second year: Late spring or summer, harvest when leaf stalks are 1 inch (2.5 cm) or more in diameter and stems about 24 inches (60 cm) in length, plants will be about 36 inches (90 cm) in diameter. Grasp each stalk near the base, pull outwards and twist sideways; cut outer stalks at the base leaving a few young central leaves to replenish the crowns. To keep the plant going strong, do not cut more than a third of the leaves in any year.
- Third year and following: Harvest all stalks 1 inch (2.5 cm) or more in diameter for 6–8 weeks. Leave smaller stalks to make food for the crown and the following year's production. Harvest by snapping or cutting the stalks at the base. Remove seed stalks.
- Do not remove all leaves from single plant; stop harvest when slender leafstalks appear.
- Every 3–5 years: divide plants.

Storage: In refrigerator for 2–4 weeks; remove leaves first. Cut and blanched in the freezer for 3–4 months. Canned, for up to 1 year. Freeze or make preserves.

VARIETIES

Choose from these rhubarb varieties: 'Valentine' and 'Strawberry' are vivid red colored and require less sweetening than other cultivars; 'Canada Red' stays red after cooking; 'Cherry Giant' likes warmer weather; 'Victoria' can be grown from seed and has green stalks; 'MacDonald' grows well in heavy soil.

Rosemary

Common name: Rosemary
World names: romarin (French); Rosmarin (German); romarino (Italian); roméro (Spanish)
Botanical name: *Rosmarinus officinalis*
Pronounced ros–muh–RY–nus off–iss–ih–NAY–lis
Family: Mint family—*Lamiaceae (Labiatae)*

ABOUT
Type of plant: Perennial
Origin: Mediterranean region near the sea. Rosemary has been in cultivation since ancient Roman and Egyptian times.
Description: Woody, evergreen perennial with scaly bark and dark green resinous aromatic, needle-like leaves, gray underneath. Form varies from stiff and upright to rounded and spreading shrubs. Narrow leaves 1–1¼ inches (2.5–3.1cm) long
Height: 12–72 inches (30–183 cm)
Breadth: 12–24 inches (30–60 cm)
Root depth: 12–18 inches (30–45 cm)
Bloom time and flowers: Winter through spring; ¼–½ inch (6–13 mm) lavender to blue blooms in clusters along branches
Edible parts: Leaves

KITCHEN
Serve: Use rosemary leaves to season meat dishes such as lamb, pork, poultry, and fish.

BASICS
Seed panting depth: ¼ inch
Germination soil temperature: 65–75°F (18–24°C)
Days to germination: 21
Sow indoors: Early spring or layer stems in summer
Sow outdoors: Transplant to pots outdoors
Days to maturity: 60
Growing soil temperature: At least 10°F (–12°C)
Soil pH range: 6.5 to 7.0
Spacing of plants: 18–36 inches (45–90 cm) apart in all directions

Water: Water infrequently once established
Light: Full sun
Nutrients: Low nitrogen, phosphorus, and potassium
Rotating crops: Perennial plant requires a permanent home
Companion crops: All members of the cabbage family, beans, carrot, sage
Incompatible crops: Cucumber
Propagation: Seed difficult to germinate. Start cuttings in spring or late summer; layer stems in early summer. To start cuttings, snip 3-inch (7.5 cm) cuttings from the tops of several branches and remove the leaves from the lower third of each piece. Plant three to six cuttings firmly in a 4-inch (10 cm) pot filled with seed starting mix. To root cuttings in winter, provide them with a bottom heat of 70°F (21°C) and good light.
Seed vitality: 2–3 years
Seed weight: 21,000 seeds per ounce (864 per gram)

SITE

Best climate: Growth zones 8–10
Frost tolerance: Withstands light frosts, but not hard freezes; in cold climates, winter potted plants in a cool, sunny window indoors
Soil preparation: Light, well-drained soil
Container growing: Can be container-grown as an annual or grown in the garden and taken into a protected area such as an unheated garage or patio to over winter. Choose a container at least 12 inches (30 cm) in diameter or larger, at least 8 inches (20 cm) deep.

PLANTING

Sow rosemary seed ¼ inches (6 mm) deep.
Planting time: Sow seed in spring; start cuttings from new growth in spring or late summer; layer stems during summer

CARE

Nutrients: Light feeder
Side dressing: Apply foliar spray of liquid seaweed or kelp extract 2–3 times during the growing season.
Pests: Mealybugs, scale. Rosemary has no serious pest problems. Indoors, watch for scale pests and wipe them from foliage with cotton soaked with rubbing alcohol.
Diseases: Rosemary has no serious disease problems. In humid climates, watch for fungal root rot.

HARVEST

Rosemary will be ready for leaf harvest 60 days after sowing. Snip fresh foliage as needed all year.

Storage: Dry sprigs and branches; strip off leaves before storing. Preserve by drying or freezing.

VARIETIES

Choose from these rosemary varieties: 'Blue Boy' is a compact dwarf variety suited for containers; 'Rexford' has good flavor; 'Arp' has gray-green foliage; 'Madalene Hill' has dark green leaves.

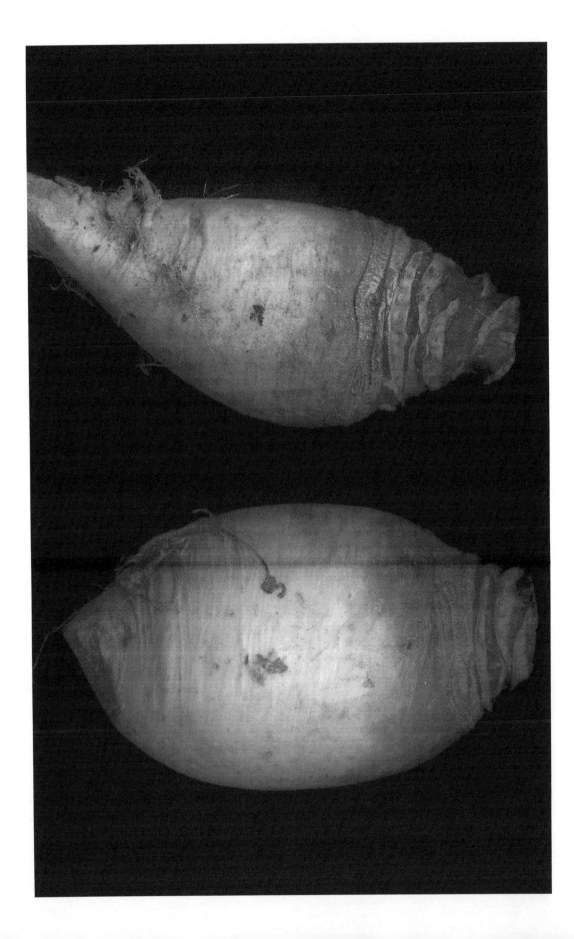

Rutabaga

Common name: Rutabaga, Swede, Swedish turnip, Russian turnip, yellow turnip, Canadian turnip; chou-navet jaune (French and French Canadian)
World names: yang you cai (Chinese); chou colza, navette (French); Raps, Ölsaat (German); cavolo colza, napo oleifera (Italian); colza (Portuguese) colza, nabo (Spanish)
Botanical name: *Brassica napus*
Pronounced BRASS–ih–kuh NAP–us
Family: Mustard or cabbage family—*Brassicaceae (Cruciferae)*

ABOUT

Type of plant: Biennial grown as an annual, cool season
Origin: North Central Europe and Russia. It is likely that the rutabaga began as a random cross between carrots and cabbages in Europe during the Middle Ages.
Description: Round, slightly squat yellowish root resembles a turnip; flesh is firm and golden yellow to white; skin yellow deepening to purple at the top; rosette of smooth, grayish-green, deeply-lobed leaves that grow from the swollen stem. Roots often reach 3–5 pounds (1.1–1.8 kg), larger than turnips. Grown for autumn use and winter storage; take a month longer than turnips to mature.
Height: 15 inches (37 cm) tall foliage
Breadth: 15 inches (37 cm) across foliage
Root depth: 24–36 inches. (60–90 cm)
Bloom time and flower: Summer, yellow flowers on sparse flowering branches
Edible parts: Roots; young leaves

KITCHEN

Serve: Serve rutabagas raw or cooked like you would turnips. Rutabagas can replace turnips in recipes. Shred or julienne new crop rutabagas to serve raw or marinated in salads. Use rutabagas in stews and soups.

BASICS

Seed planting depth: ½ inch (13 mm); sow ¼ inch (6 mm) deep in early spring
Germination soil temperature: 65–85°F (18–29°C); optimum 85°F (29°C)
Days to germination: 7–15
Sow indoors: Not recommended

RUTABAGA

Sow outdoors: Early spring
Days to maturity: 90–120
Soil pH range: 5.5–6.8
Growing soil temperature: 60–75°F 16–24°C); optimum 60°F (16°C)
Spacing of plants: 1 inch (25 mm) apart; thin successful plants to 6–8 inches (15–20 cm) apart allowing ample room for plants to reach full size
Water: Moderate
Light: Full sun
Nutrients: Low nitrogen, moderate phosphorus and potassium
Rotating crops: Succession crop to follow onion or scallions
Companion crops: Beets, carrots, nasturtium, peas, turnips
Incompatible crops: Potatoes
Propagation: Seed
Seed vitality: 4 years
Seeds weight: 9,000 seeds per ounce (320 per gram)

SITE

Rutabaga grows best in growth zones 3 and warmer; grow as a winter vegetable in mild areas.
Frost tolerance: Hardy, will withstand severe frost
Soil preparation: Rutabaga prefers light, sandy loam, well drained; work compost and leaf mold into the soil before sowing. Turn green manure into the bed before the end of the prior season.
Container growing: Like many root crops, rutabagas do not grow well in containers.

PLANTING

Plant rutabaga 1 inch (25 mm) apart; thin successful plants to 6–8 inches (15–20 cm) apart allowing ample room for plants to reach full size.
Planting time in cold-winter climates: Early spring for early summer crop, plant in the garden 4–6 weeks before the last frost. For autumn crop and winter use, in early- to midsummer, 16 weeks before first expected frost or about 90 days before intended use. Late maturing varieties store well in the ground; flavor improves with light frost.
Planting time in mild-winter climates: Spring for summer harvest; then again in early autumn for winter-into-spring harvest
Planting time in reverse-season climates: Late autumn for winter harvest

GROWING

Water: Keep soil moist; avoid sporadic watering which may crack developing roots. Mulch to prevent soil from drying out.
Nutrients: Low nitrogen, moderate phosphorus and potassium
Side dressing: Feed with a light application of organic nitrogen when plants are about 5 inches (13 cm) high

CARE

- Keep soil weed free.
- When the root begins to swell, trim the outer foliage or bend the stalks of the plants to the ground to halt foliage development and enhance root development and sweetness (called "lodging").
- A boron deficiency can cause a brown discoloration of the roots.

Common problems: Rutabagas that mature in hot weather may be tough.

Pests: Armyworms, cabbage root maggots, flea beetles.

- Rotate rutabaga and other root crops to avoid root maggots.
- Exclude flea beetles and cabbage root maggots with row covers.
- Control aphids by pinching out infested foliage or hosing the aphids off the plants.

Diseases: Black rot, turnip mosaic virus

- Soft brown interior root spot indicates soil boron deficiency, corrected by good compost.
- Practice crop rotation.
- Dispose of infected plants and do not allow any to survive the winter to infect new crop.

HARVEST

Rutabaga is ready for harvest 90–120 days after planting, autumn onwards; best after first frost. Grasp tops and pull up when tops are 12 inches (30 cm) tall and tubers are 3–5 inches (7.5–12 cm) in diameter. If soil is dense and pulling causes top to break off, carefully dig roots with a garden fork. To extend harvest in cold regions, mulch heavily. Young rutabaga leaves may be used in the same manner as turnip greens.

Storage: In the ground as long as possible, unless temperatures drop below 24°F (–4°C) or exceed 80°F (27°C). In refrigerator, for 2–4 months: cut tops and store washed or unwashed at 32°F (0°C) and 95 percent humidity. If diced and frozen, for 3–4 months, though some flavor and texture will be lost.

VARIETIES

Choose from these rutabaga varieties: 'York' has a smooth, rich flavor; 'Thomson Laurentian' stores well; 'Gilfeather' is sweet heirloom; 'Joan' and 'American Purple Top' has a sweet flavor; 'Altaweet' is mild flavored.

Sage

Common name: Sage
World names: sauge officinale, sauge commune (French); Echter Salbei, Gartensalbei (German); salvia (Italian); salvia officinal (Spanish)
Botanical name: *Salvia officinalis*
Mint family (*Labiatae*)
Family: Mint family—*Lamiaceae (Labiatae)*

ABOUT

Type of plant: Perennial, hardy cool season
Origin: Southern Siberia. Sage varieties known today were popularized in the nineteenth century.
Description: Large deep green, wavy leaves to as much as 18 inches (45 cm) wide; red or green stalks to 10–15 inches (35–38 cm) long. Big crinkled leave with elongated heart shape on thick red–tinted stalks.
Height: 24–36 inches (60–90 cm)
Breadth: 48 inches (122 cm)
Root depth: Several feet (.3 m) out and several feet deep
Bloom time and flowers: Summer; insignificant flowers in spike-like clusters; flowers are greenish or reddish on tall spikes
Edible parts: Fresh or dried leaves

KITCHEN

Serve: Use sage fresh or cook with liver, beef, pork, veal, fish lamb, poultry, duck, goose, artichokes, tomatoes asparagus, carrots, squash, corn, potatoes, eggplants, snap bans, leeks, onions, Brussels sprouts, cabbage, oranges, lemons garlic, cheese, lentils, and shell beans.

BASICS

Seed planting depth: Surface or lightly cover
Germination soil temperature: 65–70°F (18–21°C)
Days to germination: 7–21
Sow indoors: 6–8 weeks before last frost
Sow outdoors: Not recommended
Days to maturity: 75–80
Soil pH range: 5.5–7.0

Growing soil temperature: 55–80°F (13–27°C)
Spacing of plants: 20–24 inches (50–60 cm) apart in all directions
Water: Light
Light: Full sun to part shade
Nutrients: Low nitrogen, phosphorus, and potassium
Rotating crops: Replace every 4–5 years. Avoid rotating with cabbage, carrot, cauliflower, kale, and kohlrabi
Companion crops: Broccoli, Brussels sprouts, cabbage, carrot, cauliflower, kale, kohlrabi
Incompatible crops: Cucumber
Seed vitality: 2 years
Seed weight: 3,400 per ounce (120 per gram)

SITE
Best climate: Hardy in growing zones 4–8
Soil preparation: Sage requires well-drained garden soil.

PLANTING
Planting time: Sow outdoors in late spring or indoors in late winter.

CARE
Nutrients: Light feeder
Side dressing: Spray plants with liquid seaweed extract 2–3 times during the growing season.
- Cut back in autumn.
- Protect in winter with straw or mulch.
- Divide and replant every three years to maintain vigor.
- Prune away flower stems for best flavor.
- To grow indoors in winter, pot young plants in summer, cutting foliage to just above the soil. Seal pot in a plastic bag, and refrigerate to mimic winter. In autumn, unwrap and place in a sunny window for winter harvests. French tarragon requires a cold weather resting period.

Pests: No serious pest problems.
Diseases: Downy mildew, powdery mildew, root rot; but usually no serious disease problems. Don't handle plants when wet. Don't allow water to collect in the garden. Water from below.

HARVEST
Sage is ready for harvest 75–80 days after sowing. Gather sage as needed during the growing season. Sage is the most flavorful just before flowering. Refrain from harvesting sage the first year.

Storage: Fresh sage leaves can be kept in a paper towel in a plastic bag in the refrigerator for 2 or 3 days.

VARIETIES

Choose from these sages:

Tricolor sage (*S. o.* 'Tricolor'): mottled green, cream, and pink leaves with blue flowers and gentle flavor.

Black currant sage (*S. microphylla*): broad, deep green leaves with purple-pink flowers, has a rich black currant scent.

Green sage (*S. fruitcosa*): large, gray-green leaves, strongly aromatic; use sparingly in cooking or to make tea.

Clary sage (*S. sclarea*): broad pebbly deep green leaves with bitter, balsam-like flavor; use for garnish or to make fritters.

Variegated golden sage (*S.o.* 'Icterina'): gold and green leaves with a mild flavor.

Pineapple sage (*S. elegans*): long leaves with red flowers in autumn, pineapple scent.

Purple sage (*S. o. pupurea*): purple-green leaves with a musky, spicy aroma.

Salsify

Common name: Salsify, oyster plant, vegetable oyster, white salsify
World names: salsifis (French); Haferwurzel (German); salsifi blanco (Italian, Spanish)
Botanical name: *Tragopogon porrifolius*
Pronounced trag–o–PO–gon
Family: Sunflower family—*Asteraceae (Compositae)*

ABOUT

Type of plant: Biennial grown as an annual, cool season
Origin: Southern Europe, North Africa. Salsify has been known for more than 2,000 years but did not come into general cultivation until the seventeenth century.
Description: Long, grass-like leaves resemble parsnips with forked, slender, white taproot resembling a long thin carrot in shape with scraggly tiny rootlets
Height: 24–48 inches (60–122 cm)
Breadth: 12 inches (30 cm)
Root depth: 8–12 inches (20–30 cm); 1½ inch (3.8 cm) in diameter
Bloom time and flower: In the second year, ball-shaped, bluish-purple flowers which close at midday
Edible parts: Roots

KITCHEN

Serve: Young salsify can be added raw to salads. It can be cooked unpeeled cut into large pieces. After cooking, it is easy to remove the skin.

BASICS

Seed planting depth: ½ inch (13 mm)
Germination soil temperature: 50–65°F (10–18°C)
Days to germination: 7–14
Sow indoors: Not recommended
Sow outdoors: Spring as soon as the soil can be worked
Days to maturity: 120–150
Soil pH range: 6.0–6.8
Growing soil temperature: 45–85°F (7–29°C); optimum 65°F (18°C)

SALSIFY

Spacing of plants: ½ inch (13 mm) apart; thin successful plants to 3–4 inches (7.5–10 cm) apart
Water: Moderate
Light: Full sun
Nutrients: High nitrogen, low phosphorus and potassium
Rotating crops: Avoid following parsley, or celery.
Companion crops: Carrots, turnips, rutabaga, potatoes, sweet potatoes
Incompatible crops: Tomatoes, tomatillos, cole vegetables such as broccoli, Brussels sprouts, cabbage, kale
Propagation: Seed
Seed vitality: 4 years; store in an airtight container in a cool, dark place
Seed weight: 2,800 seeds per ounce (100 per gram)

SITE

Salsify grows best in growth zones 3–10 and needs at least 100 frost-free days.
Soil preparation: Deep, loose, rich loam, with no manure or stones; apply abundant organic compost to a depth of 18 inches (45 cm). (Manure at the time of planting will cause root to split.)
Container growing: Does not grow well in containers

PLANTING

Sow salsify seed ½ inch (13 mm) deep.
Planting time: Spring, sow seeds 2–4 weeks after the last expected frost or as soon as soil is workable
Planting time in mild-winter and reverse-season climates: Early autumn for late autumn and winter harvests

GROWING

Water: Keep soil moist
Nutrients: High nitrogen, low phosphorus and potassium

CARE

Weed regularly
Pests: Armyworms, flea beetles, leafhoppers.
• Exclude pests by covering crop with floating row cover early in season.
Diseases: No serious disease problems

HARVEST

Salsify will be ready for harvest 120–150 days after sowing. Harvest autumn and winter when 12–18 inches (30–45 cm) long, or lift as needed. Harvest if the soil temperature warms above 85°F (29°C). If harvest is planned after freezing temperatures, mulch the bed with 12–24 inches (30–60 cm) of straw and 1–2 inches (2.5–5 cm) of soil late in autumn; roots are winter-hardy and freezing does not injure them. Mulched roots can overwinter for spring harvest. Lift the roots with a garden fork to avoid breaking them.

Storage: In refrigerator for 3–4 weeks, or store in a cold, moist place for two to four months. Stores well in the ground, even after frost.

VARIETIES

'Mammoth Sandwich Island' is a favorite salsify variety.

Savory

Common name: Summer savory (*S. hortensis*); Winter savory (*S. montana*).
World names: sarriette (French); Bohnenkraut (German); santoreggia (Italian); ajedrea (Spanish)
Botanical name: *Satureja hortensis* (summer savory); *S. montana* (winter savory)
Pronounced sat–yew–REE–yuh hor–TEN–siss
Family: Mint family—*Lamiaceae (Labiatae)*

ABOUT

Type of plant: Summer savory is an annual. Winter savory is a perennial.
Origin: Mediterranean, Southern Europe. Savory has been cultivated for more than 2,000 years.
Description:
- **Summer savory:** fast-growing annual; upright to 18 inches (45cm) with loose open form; aromatic, narrow oblong, needle-like to 1 inch (2.5 cm) long gray-green leaves. Square, hairy stem, branching and green, turning reddish-brown; woody in second season.
- **Winter savory:** semi-evergreen shrubby perennial to 15 feet high and 2 feet wide; stiff narrow 1 inch (2.5 cm) long, dark green leaves; spikes of ¼ inch (6 mm) white to lavender flowers; strong more piney flavor than sweeter flavored summer savory.

Height: Summer savory, 12–18 inches (30–45 cm); winter savory, 12–15 inches (30–38 cm)
Breadth: 12–18 inches (30–45 cm), summer and winter
Root depth: 12 inches (30 cm)
Bloom time and flower: Mid- to late-summer; white or pale pink ¼ inch (6 mm) flowers. Summer savory has whorls of tiny pinkish white to rose flowers in summer; winter savory blooms in summer with whorls of small white to lilac flowers.
Edible parts: Leaves

KITCHEN

Serve: Use annual summer savory to flavor meat, fish, eggs, soup, beans, peas, and lentils. Finely chop summer savory to season omelets, scrambled eggs, and deviled eggs.
Use perennial winter savory in salads, soups, dressings, sausage, roast poultry, fish, beef and braised meats, pork, and bean dishes. Use dried or winter savory to flavor crumbs for breading meat, fish, or vegetables.

BASICS

Seed planting depth: Surface of the soil
Germination soil temperature: 60–70°F (16–21°C)
Days to germination: 14–21 for winter savory; 7 days for summer savory
Sowing indoors: Grow indoors for harvest; transplant out after last frost.
Sowing outdoors: After last frost
Days to maturity: 60–70
Soil pH range: 6.5 to 7.0
Growing soil temperature: 50–75°F (10–24°C)
Spacing of plants: Summer savory, 10 inches (25 cm) apart; winter savory, 10–12 inches (25–30 cm) apart in all directions
Water: Occasional water
Light: Full sun
Nutrients: Light feeder; low nitrogen, phosphorus, and potassium
Rotating crops: Savory is a soil improver and can follow any crop.
Companion crops: Beans, corn, lettuce, peas, onions, garlic, radish
Propagation: Seed or cuttings. Use fresh seeds, because they do not store well for more than a year. Winter savory tends to die out after 2 or 3 years. Root vigorous tip cuttings in summer to keep replacements coming. Seed germinates slowly.
Seed vitality: 3 years
Seed weight: 70,000 seeds per ounce (2,880 per gram)

SITE

Best climate: Growing zones 5–9
Frost tolerance: Winter savory is hardy to Zone 6
Soil preparation: Sandy, well-drained, loam enriched with humus
Container growing: Either species of savory can be grown in containers at least 6 inches deep.

PLANTING

Sow savory seeds on the soil surface.
Planting time: Early spring; sow seeds of both species indoors 6–8 weeks before last frost. Do not cover the seeds with soil. Transplant seedlings outdoors after the last expected frost. Summer savory can also be direct-seeded in the garden after the last frost date. Divide plant in spring or autumn. Winter savory also propagates readily by cuttings in spring.

CARE

Prune back the top half of the plant in midsummer or early autumn before flowering. Clip at the start of flowering for drying.
Pests: No serious pest problems
Diseases: No serious disease problems

HARVEST

Cut fresh as needed, or cut and dry foliage just before flowering.
Storage: Preserve by drying

VARIETIES

Choose from these savory varieties: 'Aromata' is a peppery summer savory; 'Nana' is a dwarf variety of winter savory.

Shallots

Common name: Shallot, griselle, French grey shallot
World names: cong tou, yang cong (Chinese); oignon (French); Küchenzwiebel (German); cipolla (Italian); tama negi (Japanese); cebola (Portuguese); cebolla (Spanish)
Botanical name: *Allium cepa* var. *ascalonicum*; *Allium oschaninii* (Asian variety)
Pronounced AL–le–um SEE–puh
Family: Onion family—*Alliaceae (Liliaceae)*

ABOUT

Type of plants: Biennial grown as an annual; perennial bulb
Origin: Western and Central Asia. Shallots have been widely cultivated since ancient Greek and Roman times.
Description: Onion-shaped red, brown, or gray bulbs each about 1 inch (2.5 cm) or so in diameter; narrow green leaves. Bulbs are divided into cloves that grow on a common base. Dutch shallots have a golden brown skin and white cloves. Red shallots have a coppery skin and purple cloves.
Height: 8 inches (20 cm) leaves
Breadth: 2 inches (5 cm)
Root depth: Shallow, fibrous roots
Bloom time and flower: Summer; small white flowers borne in round clusters
Edible parts: Bulbs; young green shoots used fresh as scallions

KITCHEN

Serve: Shallots can be served raw or cooked—roasted, stewed, caramelized, and double-poached. The greens of immature shallots can be chopped and used like chives. Shallot cloves can be diced and lightly added to green salads.

BASICS

Bulb or set planting depth: Plant stock cloves, broad end down, pointed end up, 4–8 inches (10–20cm) apart, covering the tips with ½ inch (13 mm) of soil. Each set will multiply 6–10 or more times, depending on fertility and planting time, with earlier plantings more productive. Sets may be planted in late summer through early autumn for spring green onions and earlier mature shallots.
Planting soil temperature: 35–90°F (2–32°C)
Sow outdoors: Spring

Days to maturity: Bulbs in 90–120 days; shoots in 60 days
Soil pH range: 6–6.8
Growing soil temperature: 40–85°F (4–29°C); optimum 65°F (18°C). Shallots require a dormant period lasting at least 1 month soon after planting, with temperatures 32–50°F (0–10°C).
Spacing between bulbs: 5–8 inches (12–20 cm) to form clusters; sown ½–¾ inch (13–19 mm) apart in 2–4 inch (5–10 cm) wide bands single shallots will form
Water: Medium and even
Light: Full sun
Nutrients: Moderate nitrogen, phosphorus, and potassium
Rotating crops: Follow squash or lettuce. Do not plant onions in beds used for garlic during previous seasons.
Companion crops: Beets, cabbage family, carrots, kohlrabi, early lettuce, parsnips, peppers, spinach, strawberries, summer savory, tomatoes
Incompatible crops: All beans, asparagus, peas, sage
Propagation: Bulblets or "sets." Shallots rarely produce seed. Each set will produce 8–10 shallots; choose the largest and best clumps. Also cloves, the sections of bulbs.

SITE

Shallots grow well in all growth zones; may be autumn-planted in growing zones 6 and warmer.
Frost tolerance: Withstands moderate frost
Soil preparation: Shallots prefer humus rich, well-drained soil. Add well-rotted manure, organic compost and peat to soil during the autumn before planting.
Container growing: Good choice for container growing. An 8 inch (20 cm) pot will accommodate two or three shallot cloves.

PLANTING

Bulb or set planting depth: Plant stock cloves, broad end down, pointed end up, 4–8 inches (10–20cm) apart, covering the tips with ½ inch (13 mm) of soil. Each set will multiply 6–10 or more times, depending on fertility and planting time, with earlier plantings more productive. Sets may be planted in late summer through early autumn for spring green onions and earlier mature shallots.
Planting time in cold-winter climates: Early spring 2–4 weeks before the first frost-free date and as soon as the soil is workable for a summer crop for green shoots in summer; for bulbs plant in autumn.
Planting time in mild-winter climates: Autumn after soil temperatures have dropped to 50°F (10°C) or lower for harvest in spring, or in late winter for harvest in mid-spring. Plant in autumn for harvest of green tops through winter and early spring; bulbs can be harvest in late spring and summer.
Day lengths: Shallots, like onions, are day length sensitive. Bulb formation is triggered by long days. Time sowing so the plantlet has at least 3–4 leaves before the longest day.

Temperature sensitive: Bolting is induced by exposure to cold temperatures after the plant has 3–5 leaves.

GROWING

Water: Keep soil moist

Nutrients: Apply moderate levels of nitrogen, phosphorus, and potassium.

Work compost into the bed before planting. Use fish emulsion or compost tea to encourage good early growth.

CARE

- Keep soil weed free.
- For a quicker harvest, "lodge" the stalks when they have reached 16–18 inches (40–45 cm) in height, which will force the bulbs to mature in 3–4 weeks. (Bulb formation can be hastened by bending or creasing stalks to the ground to halt foliage development; this is called "lodging".)
- Control weeds: mulch with grass clippings or straw and cultivate carefully to control weeds.

Common problems: Dry conditions or poor soil produces scrawny shallots. Work in plenty of compost or well-rotted manure and water regularly.

Pests: Thrips, onion fly maggots. Do not plant where shallots or relatives, such as onions or leeks, have grown the previous year.

- Most pests, such as thrips, can be washed off with a hose.
- Early seedlings can be troubled by onion maggots causing them to rot. Sprinkle diatomaceous earth or wood ashes around the base of the plant and work it into the soil.

Diseases: No serious disease problems

HARVEST

Harvest shallots mid-summer when tops are yellow and dry and begin to fall. For scallions harvest green shoots or leaves before they develop bulbs. To harvest pull up clumps and separate bulbs.

Storage: In the refrigerator for up to one week. Allow harvested bulbs to dry for a month in a cool, dry area before use or storage. Or clip stems and store bulbs in mesh bags. Mince and pack into ice cube trays, frozen, then sealed in plastic bags and stored in the freezer for up to 8 months; each cube contains approximately 2 tablespoons (25 ml).

VARIETIES

Choose from these shallot varieties: 'Ambition', 'Dutch Yellow Shallot', 'French Red Shallot', 'French Shallot", 'Gray Shallot', 'Pikant', 'Success'.

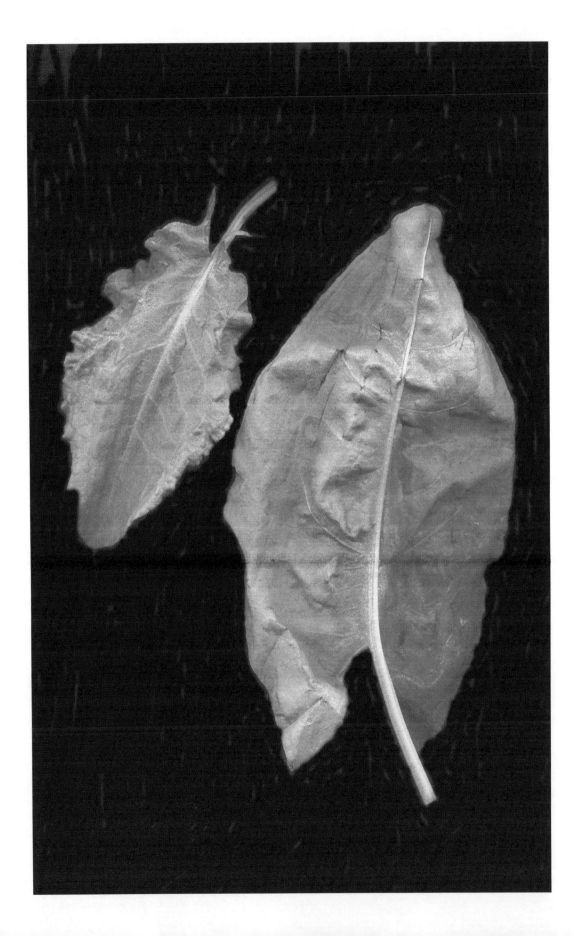

Sorrel

Common names: Common sorrel, garden sorrel, broad-leaved sorrel (*Rumex acetosa*); French sorrel, white sorrel, lettuce sorrel, blonde sorrel (*Rumex scutatus*); mountain sorrel, monk's sorrel, maiden sorrel (*Rumex alpinus*); sheep sorrel, sour grass (*Rumex acetosella*); curly dock, yellow dock, sour dock (*Rumex crispus*); broadleaf dock, bitter dock (*Rumex obtusifoliu*); herb patience, spinach dock (*Rumex patientia*); spinach rhubarb (*Rumex abyssinicus*).
World names: oseille (French); Sauerampfer (German); acetosa (Italian); acedera (Spanish)
Botanical names: *Rumex acetosa* and *Rumex scutatus*
Pronounced ROO–meks
Family: Knotweed family—*Polygonaceae*

ABOUT
Type of plant: Perennial can also be grown as an annual, hardy
Origin: Europe and northern Asia. Sorrel has been cultivated for more than 2,000 years. It is an important ingredient in French and English culinary traditions.
Descriptions:
- **French sorrel** (*Rumex scutatus*) is sprawling growing to 12–18 inches (30–45 cm) tall; its broad, fiddle-shaped, gray-green leaves make good salad greens with a mild lemon flavor.
- **Common sorrel** (*Rumex acetosa*) grows to about 36 inches (90 cm) tall; produces leaves to 6 inches (15 cm) long that are good used fresh in salads.
- **Spinach dock** (*Rumex patientia*) is a much taller plant with leaves that can be used either fresh or cooked.
- **Spinach rhubarb** (*Rumex abyssinicus*) grows up to eight feet (2.4 m) tall.

Bloom time and flowers: Spring; inconspicuous red-brown flowers on stalks
Edible parts: Leaves

KITCHEN
Serve: Sorrel can be served raw or cooked. Use raw whole French sorrel and shredded garden sorrel in salads. Add sorrel to creamy dishes and sauces.

BASICS
Seed planting depth: ¼ inch (6 mm)
Germination soil temperature: 55–70°F (13–21°C)

Days to germination: 14–21
Sow indoors: Grow indoors for winter harvest
Sow outdoors: Late spring
Days to maturity: 60
Soil pH range: 5.0–6.8
Growing soil temperature: 55–70°F (13–21°C)
Spacing of plants: 1 inch (2.5 cm) apart; thin seedlings to 8 inches (20 cm) apart in all directions
Water: Keep soil moist
Light: Full sun or partial shade
Nutrients: Side-dress with compost or well-rotted manure each spring.
Rotating crops: Do not follow legumes
Companions crops: Chard, spinach
Incompatible crops: Avoid tall plants such as corn or pole beans also potatoes
Propagation: Division; vegetative propagation is recommended
Seed vitality: 3 years
Seed weight: 81,000 seeds per ounce (3,300 per gram)

SITE

Best climate: Zones 3–9. Plants go dormant in winter if the ground freezes, but revive in spring.
Soil preparation: Humus-rich, well-drained soil
Container growing: Sorrel grows well in a container; plant a single sorrel plant in a 6 inch (15 cm) pot or several in a larger container on 8-inch (30 cm) centers.

PLANTING

Sow sorrel seed ¼ inch (6 mm) deep.
Planting time: Early spring, sow seed about 2 weeks after last frost date; start earlier indoors

CARE

- Weed regularly.
- Cut off flower and seed stalks to encourage new leaves and quality.
- Replace perennial plantings every 3–4 years by seed or division.

Pests: Aphids. Control aphids by pinching out infested areas or hosing them off the plant.
Diseases: Sorrel has no serious disease problems.

HARVEST

Sorrel is ready for harvest 60 days after seeding. Pick tender leaves when big enough to use, about 60 days after sowing seeds or when leaves are big enough to use. Continue harvesting individual leaves throughout the growing season.

Storage: Use fresh or store leaves in the refrigerator for 1–2 weeks. Refrigerate unwashed. Freeze or dry the leaves as herbs.

VARIETIES

'Large Belleville' is a favorite sorrel variety.

Spinach

Common name: Spinach
World names: bo cai (Chinese); épinard (French); Spinat (German); paalak (Hindi); spinacio (Italian); hourensou (Japanese); espinafre (Portuguese); espinaca (Spanish)
Botanical name: *Spinacea oleracea*
Pronounced spin–ACH–ee–uh oh–ler–AY–see–uh
Family: Beet family—*Chenopodiaceae*

ABOUT

Type of plant: Annual, cool season
Origin: Eastern Himalayas, southwestern Asia (Iraq). Spinach was first used in Persia and later introduced into European cookery by the Moors during the Middle Ages.
Description: Rosette of dark green leaves; leaves may be crinkled ('Savoy type') or smooth. Smooth leaf cultivars have thin, tender, sweetly flavored leaves. Crinkle or savoy-leaved spinaches have broader, thicker leaves which hold up better when cooked.
Height: 4–6 inches (10–15 cm)
Breadth: 6–8 inches (15–20 cm)
Root depth: Usually limited to the upper 12 inches (30 cm) of soil, but the taproot measures up to 60 inches (152 cm) long
Edible parts: Leaves

KITCHEN

Serve: Spinach can be eaten raw or cooked. The dark green leaves of fresh spinach will add color to a lettuce salad. Spinach can be pan-steamed in the water it is rinsed with.

BASICS

Seed planting wide depth: ¼ inch (6 mm)
Germination soil temperature: 55–70°F (13–21°C)
Days to germination: 6–14
Sow indoors: 3–4 weeks before last frost
Sow outdoors: Early spring
Days to maturity: 40–50; slow maturing autumn, winter and spring
Soil pH range: 6.0–6.8
Growing soil temperature: 60–70°F (15–21°C)

SPINACH

Spacing of plants: 2 inches (5 cm); thin successful plants to 4–6 inches (10–15 cm) apart in all directions
Water: Light but even
Light: Full sun in cool regions or partial shade in warm regions
Nutrients: Moderate nitrogen, phosphorus, and potassium
Rotating crops: Do not follow legumes
Companion crops: All beans, brassicas or cabbage family plants, celery, legumes, lettuce, onions, peas, radishes, strawberries
Incompatible crops: Avoid tall plants such as corn or pole beans also potatoes
Propagation: Seed. Refrigerate seed 1 week before sowing to help germination.
Seed vitality: 2 years; store in airtight container in a cool, dark place.
Seed weight: 2,240 seeds per ounce (80 per gram)

SITE

Spinach grows best in growth zones 5–10.
Frost tolerance: Hardy; will withstand moderate frost
Soil preparation: Spinach prefers moist, humus-rich, fertile soil; thoroughly worked with plenty of organic matter added. Light sandy soils with good drainage are best in regions of high rainfall.
Container growing: Choose a container 4–6 inches (10–15 cm) deep for two or three plants.

PLANTING

Sow spinach seed 2 inches (5 cm); thin successful plants to 4–6 inches (10–15 cm). For salad mix (small clipped leaves): Sow in 2–4 inch (5–10 cm) wide band, ¾ inch (19 mm) apart, about 40 seeds per 12 inches (30 cm). Clip small leaves in 3–5 weeks, depending on time of year and speed of growth.
Planting time in cold-winter climates: Early spring; sow seed 4–6 weeks before the last frost date. For autumn crop, sow seeds in autumn 4–6 weeks before the first frost date. Plant from late summer until freezing for an early harvest the following spring; use floating row covers for winter protection.
Planting time in mild-winter and reverse-season climates: Late autumn for winter harvest. Seed autumn crops heavily; spinach germinates poorly in warm soil. Prefers cool medium day lengths of 40°F (4°C) and 10–12 hours. Longer hotter days cause bolting to seed.
Succession planting: Plant spinach every 2–3 weeks in early spring until the temperatures rise above 65°F (18°C) and the days lengthen. Start succession again in late summer for an autumn crop. For a continuous supply, sow every 7 days.

GROWING

Water: Keep soil moist.
Nutrients: Apply moderate applications of nitrogen, phosphorus, and potassium. Prepare soil with plenty of organic matter.

Side dressing: Apply balanced, high-nitrogen fertilizer such as blood meal or kelp meal at midseason or use dilute foliar fertilizer every 1–2 weeks. Use fish emulsion or 1 tablespoon (15 ml) of blood meal mixed in 1 gallon (4.5 liters) of water.

CARE
- Keep soil moist, without wetting leaves, unless the plant will dry quickly before nightfall.
- Weed regularly. Crowding of plants produces bolters sooner.

Common problems: Spinach is light- and heat-sensitive. Hot weather—above 75°F (24°C)—and lengthening days (more than 12–13 hours of sunlight) can cause plants to bolt. Use heat-resistant cultivars and sow spring crops early. An early-maturing variety is 'Tyee.'

Pests: Aphids, beet leafhoppers, cabbage loopers, cabbage worms, flea beetles, leaf miners, slugs, snails.
- Pinch out or hose off aphid-infested foliage. Hand pick and destroy slugs and snails.
- Remove leaves on which leafminers have laid their eggs; look for the eggs on the underside of the leaves.
- Use row covers to exclude early season pests and beetles.

Diseases: Curly top virus, damping off, downy mildew, fusarium wilt, leaf spot, mosaic virus, spinach blight, rust
- Plant disease resistant varieties.
- Remove and destroy infected plants before the disease can spread to other plants.
- Plant in well-draining soil and avoid allowing water to sit in the garden.

HARVEST
Harvest spinach 35–70 days after planting when leaves are 4–7 inches (10–18 cm) long on heads with 6–8 leaves; thin leaves from the outside to allow central growth bud to continue producing leaves. If leaves are picked too late, they will have a gritty texture. When plant begins to bolt, cut 3 inches (7.5 cm) above the soil to force re-growth.

Storage: In refrigerator for 10–14 days at 32°F (0°C) and 95% humidity. If blanched and chilled, store in the freezer for 4–6 months.

VARIETIES
Choose from these spinach types and varieties:
- **Curly or savoy spinach:** Crisp, curly leaves with root ends that are often reddish. The firm texture makes curly spinach a good choice for cooking or serving raw in salads. 'Winter Bloomsdale' is a savoyed variety. Semi-savoyed varieties include: 'Tyee'. 'Space', and 'Melody'.

- **Flat-leaf spinach:** Large, smooth leaves that are more tender than curly spinach. Good cooked. Try 'Olympia' in cool regions.
- **Baby spinach:** Immature flat-leaf spinach. Very tender and great for salads.
- **New Zealand spinach:** This is not a true spinach but a different genus and species, *Tetragonia tetragonioides*. The leaves of this plant can be cooked just like true spinach.
- **Malabar spinach:** A tropical spinach-like perennial (*Basella alba* 'Rubra').

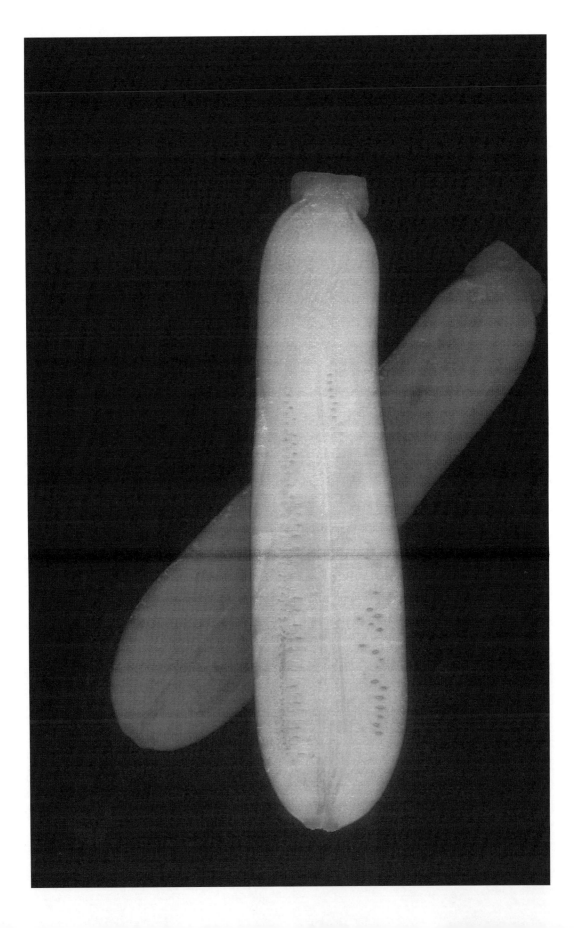

Summer Squash

Common summer squash names: crookneck, pattypan, staightneck, scallop, vegetable marrow, zucchini. (Summer squash in Great Britain is called "vegetable marrow"; the word "marrow" is used for either mature fruits of *Cucurbita pepo* or *Cucurbita maxima*, a winter squash, served boiled or stewed.)

World names: xi hu lu, xi hu gua (Chinese); potiron , courgette (French); Gartenkürbis, Zucchini (German); zucca, zucchino (Italian); pepo kabotcha, zukkiini (Japanese); abóbora, abóborinha (Portuguese); calabaza común, calabacín (Spanish).

Botanical name: *Cucurbita pepo*

Pronounced kew–KUR–bih–tuh

Family: Cucurbits or gourd family—*Cucurbitaceae*

ABOUT

Type of plant: Annual, tender

Origin: Mexico and American tropics. Squashes have been in cultivation for more than 10,000 years.

Description summer squash: Weak stemmed, tender annuals with large, lobed cucumber-like leaves and separate male and female flowers; usually grows as a bush, rather than a vine. Both stems and leaves are covered in small prickles. Fruits have thin, tender skin and are generally eaten in the immature state before the skin hardens. Summer squash are for warm weather harvest and are eaten when immature. Varieties include scalloped white squash (called patty pan), yellow crookneck, straightneck, cylindrical, green or gray zucchini or Italian squash.

Height: 12–15 inches (30–38 cm)

Breadth: 12–20 square feet (3.7–6.1 sq m), depending on variety.

Root depth: Most of the roots of winter squash are in the top 12 inches (30 cm) of the soil, but the taproot can grow from 24–36 inches (60–90 cm)

Bloom time and flower: Summer; large brilliant yellow-petaled flowers borne singly in the leaf axils; separate male and female flowers appear on the same plant.

Edible parts: Fruits

KITCHEN

Serve: Tender, summer squash can be eaten raw or cooked. Use raw tender squash as an addition to crudités trays and salads.

SUMMER SQUASH

BASICS

Seed planting depth: ½ inch–1 inch (13mm–2.5 cm)
Germination soil temperature: 70°F (21°C); minimum 59°F (15°C)
Days to germination: 7–10
Sow indoors: 3–4 weeks before last frost
Sow outdoors: When soil temperature reaches 70°F (21°C)
Days to maturity: 50–65 frost free days and bears for weeks
Soil pH range: 5.5–6.8
Growing soil temperature: 62–85°F (17–29°C)
Spacing of plants: 12–18 inches (30–45 cm) for bush varieties; thin successful plants to 36 inches (90 cm) apart in all directions
Water: Heavy and even
Light: Full sun
Nutrients: High nitrogen, moderate phosphorus and potassium
Rotating crops: Avoid following winter squash, pumpkins, cucumbers, melons
Companion crops: Celeriac, celery, corn, nasturtiums melon, onions, radish, peas, beans
Incompatible crops: Potatoes, pumpkins, tall plants
Propagation: Seed
Seed vitality: 6 years; store in an airtight container in a cool, dark place.
Seed weight: 176–300 seeds per ounce (6–10 per gram)

SITE

Tender squash grows best in growth zones 3 and warmer; bush forms can be grown and fruited in cool or short summer regions; long, vining varieties require a growing season of 4–5 months of warm to hot weather.
Frost tolerance: Tender
Situation: Full sun with good air circulation
Soil preparation: Humus-rich, well-drained soil; work in organic compost the autumn before planting.
Container growing: Bush-types grow best in containers. Plant 2–3 seeds in the center of a 10-inch (25 cm) deep container and thin to the strongest plant when the seedlings have two true leaves, leaving the strongest seedling to grow. Move the pot indoors on cool nights when frost is expected.

PLANTING

Sow squash seed ½–1 inch (13mm–2.5 cm) deep; warm the soil in spring by covering with black plastic; remove plastic before sowing. Allow 12–18 inches (30–45 cm) between bush varieties; thin successful plants to 36 inches (90 cm) apart.
Spacing using hills: Sow 4–5 seeds 2–3 inches (5–7.5 cm) deep, 3–4 inches (7.5–10 cm) apart in hills raised 12 inches (30 cm) spaced 6–8 feet (1.8–2.4 m) apart. Thin to 2 successful plants per hill. If plants are supported on wooden tripods space hills 4 feet (1.2 m) apart.

Planting time: Spring after soil has warmed (minimum 62°F /17°C for treated seeds and 70°F/21°C for untreated seeds) and danger of frost has passed; seeds will rot in cool soil, especially cool, wet soil.

Starting indoors: Sow seed indoors in peat pots or large plastic cells about 3–4 weeks before plants are to be set outside, 2 seeds per pot. Move seedlings outdoors 10 days before transplanting; transplant carefully to avoid breaking roots.

Cold protection: Heavy grade floating row covers will provide about 4° of frost protection, and add warmth for vigor and earlier harvest.

Planting time in reverse-season climates: Late summer

Intercropping: Corn

GROWING

Water: Keep well watered; water deeply. Avoid overhead watering.

Nutrients: Heavy feeder; apply lots of compost. Apply nitrogen before blooming. Soil should be rich in phosphorus.

CARE

Keep soil basin around each hill or alongside each row saturated with water and weed free.

- If not supported on vertical tripods, place developing squash on wood planks to prevent direct soil contact.
- If night temperatures fall below 65°F (18°C) cover the plants with floating row covers. Floating row covers will provide about 4° of frost protection, and add warmth for vigor and earlier harvest.
- Use row covers to protect plants from cucumber beetles and squash borers; remove covers when the plants bloom.
- Downy mildew may occur in cool, damp weather powdery mildew in hot, droughty periods and in late summer.

Pollination problems: Poor pollination can result in yield reduction and misshapen fruit. Fruit that turns black and rots before reaching picking size has not been pollinated. This can happen in cool spells or when pollinating insects are less active.

Pests: Aphids, cucumber beetles, leaf miners, mites, nematodes, pickle and melon worms, squash bugs, squash vine borers.

- Use rows covers to protect young plants from cucumber beetles and squash borers; remove covers when the plants bloom.
- Control beetles by hand-picking or hosing them off the plants.
- Locate and crush squash bug eggs laid on the underside of leaves.
- Keep surrounding borders well mowed.
- Clean up refuse at the end of the season, and turn the soil in spring to bury insect pupae.

Diseases: Bacterial wilt, mosaic virus, mildew, blight, curly top
- Bacterial wilt infects leaves and is spread by cucumber beetles. Control beetles.
- Root rot starts as soft rot of the stem at the soil surface; the plant wilts as the disease worsens.
- Squash mosaic is transmitted by cucumber beetles; use virus-free seed and control beetles row covers to suppress the disease.
- Curly top is spread by leafhoppers; it kills seedlings and leaves older plants dwarfed with leaves turning yellow and curled at the edges. Exclude leafhoppers with row covers.
- Downy mildew may occur in cool, damp weather; powdery mildew in hot, droughty periods and in late summer. Plant in well-draining soil.
- Plant disease resistant varieties.
- Keep water off the foliage. Don't handle plants when wet to help control fungal disease.
- Remove and destroy infected plants.

HARVEST

Tender squash is ready for harvest 50–65 frost free days after sowing and bears for weeks, midsummer onwards when still tender. For all varieties, harvest when the rind is tender and before the seeds have developed. Fruits should be harvested 2–3 times a week once plants begin bearing. Harvest immature fruits as small as possible for cooking. Break fruit from the plant, or use a knife. Clean knife after each use to avoid spread of disease to other plants. Avoid bruising or cutting harvested fruits.
- Zucchini and crookneck: when 5–10 inches (13–25 cm) long for slicing into rounds; 3–5 inches (7.5–13 cm) long for use whole.
- Yellow varieties: when 4–7 inches (10–18 cm) long
- Scallop or pattypan varieties: when 3–5 inches (7.5–13 cm) in diameter.

Storage: 1 week at 50°F (10°C); 2–4 days at 40°F (4°C); chilling injury occurs if held for several days at temperatures below 50°F (10°C). Also freeze, can, pickle, or dry. If cooked, store in the freezer for 6–8 months.

SUMMER VARIETIES

Varieties include scalloped white squash (called patty pan), yellow crookneck, straightneck, cylindrical, green or gray zucchini or Italian squash.
- **Zucchini:** glossy dark green or yellow cylindrical squash measuring 2½–8 inches (6.4–20 cm) long; this is the classic zucchini. Varieties: 'Gold Rush', 'Spacemaster', 'Eightball'.
- **Costata Romanesca** (ribbed Roman zucchini): slightly belled squash, pale raised ribs green variety measuring 10–15 inches (25–38 cm) long and about 5 inches (13 cm) thick; green skin marked with lighter stripes running the length; also called cocozelle or Italian vegetable marrow.

- **Middle Eastern-type zucchini** (also called Lebanese, Egyptian, Cousa, Kuta, and Magda): usually stocky, pale green tapering cylinder about 5 inches (13 cm) long with a thick dark green stem; smooth skinned and shiny.
- **Round zucchini or globe squash:** about 5 inches (13 cm) in diameter varying shades of green, seedless and smooth textured.
- **Tatume (and oval types):** dense smooth flesh, about 5 inches (13 cm) long, seedless.
- **Scallop or pattypan** (also called custard squash or cymling): scalloped or crimped pie-like circumference, flattened or bell shaped; cream, yellow, pistachio, mottled colors. Varieties: 'Sunburst', 'Starship', 'Golden Scallopini Bush'.
- **Yellow or summer crookneck and yellow or summer straightneck**: warted yellow-skinned types, crooked, semi-crooked, or straight necked. Straightneck varieties: 'Zephyr', 'Saffron'; Crookneck varieties: 'Horn of Plenty'.
- **Baby squash or mini-squash:** any squash harvested when very young.

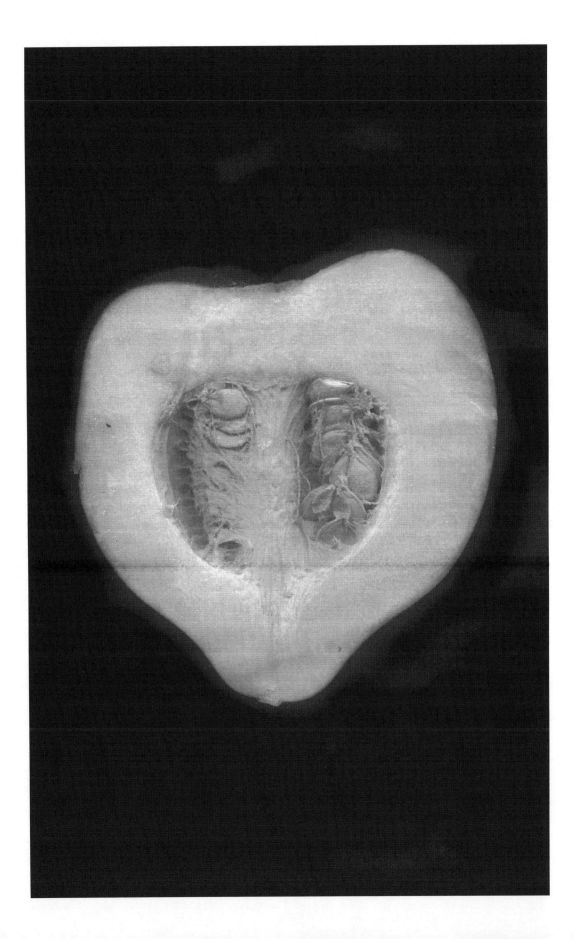

Winter Squash and Pumpkin

Common winter squash names: Acorn, banana (*maxima*), buttercup (*pepo*), butternut (*moschata*), cushaw delicious, Hubbard (*maxima*), marrow (*pepo*), pumpkin, spaghetti (*pepo*), turban.
World names: sun gua, yang gua (Chinese); courge d'hiver (French); Riesenkürbis (German); zucca (Italian); seiyou kabotcha (Japanese); abóbora-menina, abóbora-moranga (Portuguese); calabaza grande (Spanish)
Botanical name: *Cucurbita maxima* and *Cucurbita moschata*, *Cucurbita pepo*
Pronounced kew–KUR–bih–tuh
Family: Cucurbits or gourd family—*Cucurbitaceae*

ABOUT
Type of plant: Annual, tender
Origin: Mexico and American tropics. Squashes have been in cultivation for more than 10,000 years.
Description winter squash: Weak-stemmed trailing vines with tendrils and alternate, large rounded leaves; stems are rounded; some varieties have been bred to have a more compact, bushy form of growth. Winter squashes are larger than summer squashes requiring more room to grow; fruits have hard skins when they are harvested and eaten.
Height: 12–15 inches (30–38 cm)
Breadth: 12–20 square feet (3.7–6.1 sq m), depending on variety.
Root depth: Most of the roots of winter squash are in the top 12 inches (30 cm) of the soil, but the taproot can grow from 24–36 inches (60–90 cm)
Bloom time and flower: Summer; large brilliant yellow-petaled flowers borne singly in the leaf axils; separate male and female flowers appear on the same plant.
Edible parts: Fruits

KITCHEN
Serve: Winter squashes are drier and more fibrous than summer squashes. They should be harvested when fully ripe and require cooking.

BASICS
Seed planting depth: ½–1 inch (1.3–2.5 cm)
Germination soil temperature: 65–85°F (18–29°C)

Days to germination: 4–10
Sow indoors: 3–4 weeks before last frost
Sow outdoors: When soil temperature reaches 70°F (21°C)
Days to maturity: 60–100 frost free days from seed; 60–80 after transplanting
Soil pH range: 6.5–7
Growing soil temperature: 75–85°F (24–29°C)
Spacing of plants: Sow 2–3 seeds every 18 inches (45 cm), 24–36 inches (60–90 cm) for large-fruited varieties, or sow about 6 inches (15 cm) apart. Thin to 1 plant per spot.
Water: Heavy and even
Light: Full sun
Nutrients: High nitrogen, moderate phosphorus and potassium
Rotating crops: Avoid following summer squash, cucumbers, and melons.
Companion crops: Celeriac, celery, corn, onions, nasturtiums, bush peas, beans
Incompatible crops: Cabbage or other cole vegetables, potato
Seed vitality: 6 years; store in an airtight container in a cool, dark place
Seed weight: 300 seeds per ounce (11 seeds per g)

KITCHEN
Serve: Winter squash must be cooked. Add winter squash to soups, stews, couscous, and curries. Use winter squash to make pies, cakes, muffins, cookies, pudding, soufflés, and cream desserts.

SITE
Winter squash grows best in growth zones 3 and warmer.
Frost tolerance: Very tender; cannot tolerate frost
Situation: Full sun in a site with good air circulation
Soil preparation: Winter squash prefers humus-rich, well-composted, well-drained soil.

PLANTING
Sow seed ½–1 inch (1.3–2.5 cm) deep. Sow 2–3 seeds 18 inches (45 cm) apart, 24–36 inches (60–90 cm) for large-fruited varieties, or sow about 6 inches (15 cm) apart. Thin to 1 plant per spot.
Planting on hills: Raise hills 12 inches (30 cm), 20 inches (50 cm) in diameter, and 6–8 feet (1.8–2.4 m) apart if plants are allowed to spread, or 4–5 feet (1.2–1.5 m) apart if plants are supported on sturdy wooden tripods. Sow 4–5 seeds 2–3 inches (5–7.5 cm) deep, 3–4 inches (7.5–10 cm) apart. Thin to 2 successful plants per hill.
Supporting plants: Most winter squashes grow as vines; cage or train vines to climb up a fence or trellis to save space. Set the supports in place at the time of planting.
Spring planting time: 2 weeks after the last expected frost when all danger of frost is past; start indoors 2–3 weeks before the last frost in individual pots; transplant carefully to avoid breaking roots. Winter squash requires 3 months of frost-free weather.

Direct seeding: Sow in late spring after frost danger is past when the soil is warm, minimum soil temperature of 62°F (17°C) for treated seeds and 70°F (21°C) for untreated seeds. Seeds will rot in cool soil; especially cool, wet soil.

Sowing indoors for transplanting: Sow in 1 ½–2 inch (3.8–5 cm) containers or flats; thin to 1–2 plants per container with scissors; harden plants 4–7 days by reducing fertilizer, water, and temperature, moving flats outside if there is no frost danger. Transplant after danger of frost is past or earlier if plants are to be covered with floating row covers. Transplant about 18 inches (45 cm) apart for bush and small fruited varieties, and 24–36 inches (60–90 cm) apart for large fruited varieties; do not disturb roots.

Autumn planting time: 13 weeks before first expected frost

Planting time in reverse-season climates: Plant a second crop in early autumn for harvest in winter

GROWING

Water: Plenty of water; water deeply. Avoid overhead watering.

Nutrients: Squash will accept high applications of nitrogen and moderate applications of phosphorus and potassium; fertilize with nitrogen only during the growth period before blooming. Winter squash benefits from compost or manure.

CARE

- Keep soil basin around each hill or alongside each row saturated with water and weed free.
- Avoid direct soil contact with fruit; support on tripods, hang fruit in nylon netting, place fruit on wood planks, shingle or piece of plastic to prevent direct soil contact.
- Use black plastic sheeting to warm soil in cool-weather regions; leave it in place to maintain soil temperature.
- Use rows covers to protect young plants from cucumber beetles and squash borers; remove covers when the plants bloom.

Spring cold protection: Use a heavy grade floating row cover to provide about 4° of frost protection; plants will not tolerate near freezing temperatures.

Autumn frost: Frost can damage fruits and cause spotting and poor storage. Mature fruits can usually tolerate 1 and sometimes 2 or 3 light frosts without substantial damage. Sprinkler irrigation wards off moderate frost damage to fruits.

Pollination problems: Poor pollination can result in yield reduction and misshapen fruits. Fruit that turns black and rots before reaching picking size has not been pollinated. This often happens when male blossoms appear, or in cool spells, when pollinating insects are less active.

Pests and Disease: See information under Summer Squash.

HARVEST

Winter squash are ready for harvest in autumn 60–100 frost free days from seed; 60–80 days after transplanting. Allow winter squashes to mature fully on the vine until their skins are extremely hard. Cut the stems 2–4 inches (5–10 cm) above the fruit for longer storage using pruning shears. Wipe off any clinging soil but do not wash. Harvest before frost.

Cure: Outdoors: dry and toughen skins by exposing fruits to sun for 5–7 days; cover in the evening if frost is likely or in a warm, protected area; afterwards, place the squash in a cool, dry ventilated area for 5–6 months. Indoors: expose squash to 80–90°F (27–32°C) heat with ventilation for 3–5 days.

Storage: Indefinitely at 50–59°F (10–15°C) and 60% relative humidity. If stored at temperatures greater than 59°F (15°C) respiration rate is high and the fruit will begin to shrink. Maintain good air circulation do not place fruit on top of each other. High humidity will result in decay. If cooked, store squash in the freezer for 4–6 months. Winter squash can be frozen or dried.

VARIETIES

Botanical species with descriptions:
Cucurbita maxima: trailer-climber with almost round leaves; includes pumpkin types, hubbard squash, and banana types.
Cucurbita moschata: long trailer with large, soft, shallow lobed leaves; some bush forms; includes butternut squashes, trombone pumpkin type, and pumpkin "cheese" types.
Cucurbita pepo: Includes zucchini or courgettes and custard or scallop squash; also includes winter squashes such as turban shaped, buttercup-type squash, spaghetti vegetable, sweet potato squash, vegetable marrows, and crookneck squash.
Common names: Acorn, banana (*maxima*), buttercup (*pepo*), butternut (*moschata*), cushaw delicious, hubbard (*maxima*), marrow (*pepo*), spaghetti (*pepo*), turban.

- **Acorn** varieties: acorn shaped, dark green fruit, some mottled with white and green to about 2 pounds (0.9 kg); best baked. Varieties: 'Heart of Gold', 'Tuffy', 'Table Top'.
- **Banana** (Pink) (*C. maxima*): smooth gray-green skin and light orange flesh, sometimes to18 inches (45 cm) long.
- **Butternut** (*C. moschata*): squat acorn shape; blackish-green rind with yellow orange flesh; all seeds are in the blossom end; noted for fine quality and flavor. Varieties: 'Early Butternut', 'Long Island Cheese', 'Waltham'.
- **Calabaza, Caribbean pumpkin, West Indian pumpkin, Cuban** *squash* (*C. moschata*): rounded to pear shaped, mottled skin green, orange, amber or buff; smooth and hard shelled, 9–10 inches (23–25 cm) in diameter.
- **Cheese pumpkin** (*C. moschata*): tan, lobed, flattened pumpkin, 10–12 inches (25–30 cm) in diameter.
- **Cushaw** (Green-striped) (*C. maxima*): gourd shaped 10–15 inches (25–38 cm) long; striped yellow-white-green skin.

- **Hubbard squash** (Blue and Golden) (*C. maxima*): bluish, gray, orange or dark to light green; mottled or not; smooth or warty; 10–11 inches (25–28 cm) long. Varieties: 'Blue Hubbard', 'Blue Ballet', 'Warted Green Hubbard'.
- **Jarrahdale or Australian pumpkin** (*C. maxima*): 13–15 inches (33–38 cm) in diameter, brilliant yellow flesh
- **Kuri (Red) or Uchiki Kuri or Orange Hokkaido** (*C. maxima*): 5–6 inches (13–15 cm) in diameter, orange skin and flesh, tear drop or pear shaped.
- **Queensland Blue** (*C. maxima*): dark green skin, yellow flesh, 8 inches (20 cm) in diameter
- **Rouge Vif d'Etampes, Red Etampes, or Cinderella** (*C. maxima*): classic orange pumpkin, deep yellow flesh, 15–30 pounds (7–14 kg), 11 inches (28 cm) in diameter. Varieties: 'Atlantic Giant', 'The Great Pumpkin', 'Howden', 'New England Pie', 'Wee-B-Little'.
- **Turban or Turk's Cap** (*C. maxima*): bright-colored shells, 6–7 inches (15–18 cm) in diameter, often used for decoration buy yellow, moist flesh can be eaten
- **Valenciano** (*C. maxima*): white pumpkin, 10 inches (25 cm) in diameter

Alpine Strawberries

Common name: Alpine strawberry, European wild strawberry
World names: cao mei (Chinese); fraisier (French); Erdbeere (German); fragola (Italian); ichigo. sutoroberii (Japanese); morango (Portuguese); fresa (Spanish)
Botanical name: *Fragaria vesca*
Pronounced fra–GARE–ee–uh
Family: Rose family—*Rosaceae*
Other cultivated species: *Fragaria ananassa*, pineapple strawberry; *Fragaria chiloensis*, Chilean strawberry; *Fragaria virginiana*, North American strawberry; *Fragaria moschata*, musk strawberry or hautbois strawberry

ABOUT
Type of plant: Perennial
Origin: North and South America, Europe. The development of modern cultivated strawberries began in the early eighteenth century through the crossing of wild strawberry varieties.
Description: Toothed, roundish, medium green leaves; spreads by runners. Reddish false fruits follow flowers.
- **June-bearing types** produce one crop per year in late spring or early summer
- **Everbearing or day-neutral types** flower and set fruit over a long season with harvest peaking in early summer and continuing unevenly through autumn; everbearers put out fewer runner than June bearers

Height: 6–8 inches (15–20 cm)
Breadth: 12 inches (30 cm)
Root depth: 2 inches (5 cm)
Bloom time and flower: Spring and summer; white flowers
Edible parts: Fruit

KITCHEN
Serve: Use strawberries fresh as a dessert fruit or serve with cream and a little sugar or in fruit salads, mousses and ice cream. Use strawberries in pies, cakes, and soufflés. Process strawberries into jams, jellies, preserves, sweets, and fruit juices. Steep them in wine, champagne, brandy, or liqueur.

BASICS
Seed planting depth: $1/8$–$1/4$ inch (3–6 mm)

Crown planting: Crown leaves should be just above soil level.
Germination soil temperature: 65–75°F (18–24°C)
Days to germination: 7–14
Sow indoors: 8 weeks before setting out in early spring or autumn
Soil pH range: 5.5–7.0
Growing soil temperature: 60–80°F (16–27°C)
Space of plants: 12–14 inches (30–36 cm); offsets should be planted 7–10 inches (18–25cm) apart for larger yields
Water: Moderate
Light: Full sun to partial shade
Nutrients: Moderate nitrogen, phosphorus, and potassium
Rotating crops: Avoid following beets, corn, peas, peppers, tomatoes
Companion crops: Melons
Incompatible crops: Broccoli, cabbage family plants
Propagation: Seed; by runners called "offsets"
Seed vitality: 1 year
Seeds weight: 70,000 seeds per ounce (2,471 per gram)

SITE

Strawberries grow best in growth zones 3–10.
Soil preparation: Strawberries prefer well drained acidic soil; plant on a mound 5–6 inches (13–15cm) if soil drains poorly.
Container growing: Strawberries grow well in containers. Choose a container at least 6 inches (15cm) deep.

PLANTING

Sow seed or set out bareroot crowns 12–14 inches (30–36 cm) apart; offsets should be planted 7–10 inches (18–25cm) apart for larger yields. Crown leaves should be just above soil level; a buried crown will rot; the topmost roots should be ¼ inch (6 mm) beneath the soil.
Hill planting: Plant on hills for fewer runners and larger plants. Grow everbearing varieties on hills.
Planting time in cool climates: Sow indoors 8 weeks before setting out in early spring. Plant outdoors after all danger of frost has passed.
Planting time in warm climates: Set out June bearers in late summer or autumn for harvest the next spring. Set out everbearing plants in spring for summer and autumn harvest.

GROWING

Water: Moderate, do not let soil dry out.
Nutrients: Feed June bearers two times a year; lightly when growth starts and again more heavily after fruiting. Everbearers prefer consistent light feeding. Heavy feeding will lead to excessive growth, soft rot and fruit rot.

CARE

- Mulch under fruit with straw or other organic material to prevent fruit rot and to deter weeds.
- Pinch out early blooms and runners to get large plants with smaller yields of larger berries.
- Use clear or black plastic mulch and floating row covers (vent for pollination).
- Replace older plants every few years.
- Mulch in cold climates; cover plants with 4–6 inches (10–15 cm) of straw in the winter; remove the mulch when temperatures begin to warm in the spring.
- Plant as an annual in summer or early autumn for generally healthier, bigger plants and berries; do not allow offsets to develop; use plastic mulch for ripening and remove the plants after harvest. Use June bearers such as 'Chandler' for this method.
- June bearers grown as perennials should be renewed. After harvest cut off the foliage with a lawn mower; then water and fertilize to encourage new growth. Reduce dense planting by removing old "mother" plants and leave younger more productive plants.

Pests: Birds and mice; protect crop with floating row cover or netting.
Diseases: Botrytis fruit rot, leaf spot, leaf scorch. Control with clean cultivation. Plant in well-draining soil.

HARVEST

Harvest strawberries when the fruit turns crimson and is soft and aromatic, from spring to autumn.

Storage: Strawberries are best eaten fresh. They will keep in the refrigerator for 2–3 days in a sealed container. Pack lightly so that they do not bruise or rot.

VARIETIES

Choose from these strawberry types and varieties:

- **June-bearing types** produce one crop per year in late spring or early summer. Varieties include: 'Allstar', 'Benton', 'Chandler', 'Earliglow', 'Guardian', 'Jewel', 'Lateglow', 'Robinson', 'Sequoia', 'Surecrop', 'Sparkle', and 'Winona'.
- **Everbearing or day-neutral types** flower and set fruit over a long season with harvest peaking in early summer and continuing unevenly through autumn; everbearers put out fewer runner than June bearers. Varieties include: 'Alexandria', 'Fort Laramie', 'Ogalla', 'Ozark Beauty', 'Quinault', 'Tristar', and 'Tribune'.
- **Cultivated varieties** of alpine and wild strawberries include 'Baron Solemacher', 'Pineapple Alpine Rugen', and 'Yellow Alpine'.

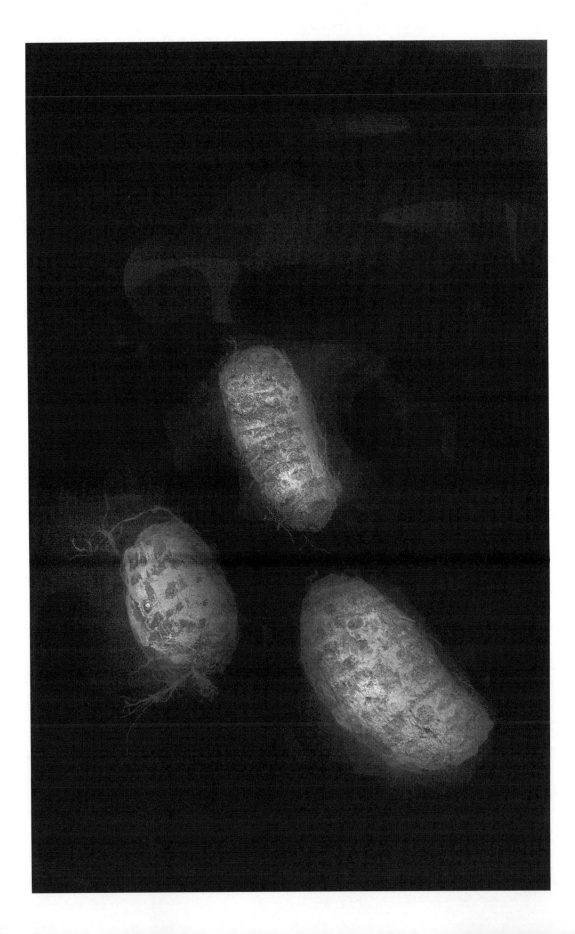

Sunchokes

Common name: Sunchoke, Jerusalem artichoke, sunroot, girasole.
(An edible variety of the perennial sunflower but not related to the globe artichoke. The name "Jerusalem" is believed to be an English corruption of the French name for sunflower, "girasole.")
World names: ju yu (Chinese); topinambour (French); Topinambur, Erdbirne, Jerusalem Artischocke (German); topinambur, carciofo di gerusalemme (Italian); kiku imo (Japanese); pataca (Spanish)
Botanical name: *Helianthus tuberosus*
Pronounced hee–lee–AN–thus too–bur–OH–sus
Family: Sunflower family—*Asteraceae (Compositae)*

ABOUT

Type of plant: Perennial
Origin: North America. Sunchokes were brought to Europe in the sixteenth century by New World explorers. (So-called Jerusalem artichokes were not introduced to Europe from Jerusalem by Crusaders during the Middle Ages as some stories say.)
Description: Tall plant with coarse, dark-green, oval leaves that are 6–8 inches (15–20 cm) long. Produces a potato-like knobby tuber about 1¼–2½ inches (3–6 cm) in thickness and 3–4 inches (7–10 cm) long. Tuber color varies with variety: white, yellow, red and blue.
Height: 6–7 feet (180–210 cm)
Breadth: 2–3 feet (30–60 cm)
Root depth: 6–8 inches (15–20 cm)
Bloom time and flower: Late summer to early autumn; masses of bright daisy-like yellow flowers are medium-size 3–5 inches (7.5–13 cm) across with a chocolate scent.
Edible parts: Tubers

KITCHEN

Serve: Sunchokes can be eaten raw in salads but are best cooked or marinated, puréed, or prepared au gratin.

BASICS

Tuber planting depth: 4 inches (10 cm)
Planting soil temperature: 50–60°F (10–16°C)
Days to germination: 7–14

Sow indoors: Not applicable; sunchokes grow best outdoors
Plant outdoors: After last frost
Days to maturity: 110–150
Soil pH range: 5.8–6.2
Growing soil temperature: 65–90°F (18–32°C)
Spacing of plants: 12–24 inches (30–60 cm) apart in all directions
Water: Moderate to heavy
Light: Full sun
Nutrients: Moderate nitrogen, phosphorus, and potassium
Rotating crops: Do not rotate
Companion crops: Grow in a special bed because of its vigorous growth
Incompatible crops: Don't grow with other crops
Propagation: Vegetatively propagated from whole or cut tubers with 2–3 prominent buds or eyes

SITE

Sunchokes grow best in growth zones 4–10; yields are smaller in very warm regions. Choose a permanent location for this crop because they are difficult to eliminate once established.
Frost tolerance: Frost hardy; will survive a hard freeze if protected by an over layer of soil or mulch
Soil preparation: Sunchokes prefer fertile, well-drained sandy loam soil. Supplement the site with sand or abundant organic compost to keep soil loose and ensure easy harvesting. Heavy soils will decrease yield.
Container growing: Does not grow well in containers

PLANTING

Set tubers in a trench about 4–6 inches (10–15 cm) deep. Cut or break tubers to one or two eyes per piece. Do not allow cut seed pieces to dry out before planting.
Planting time in cold-winter climates: In spring, 4–6 weeks after the last frost for an autumn harvest; a 4½ month growing season is required.
Planting time in mild-winter climate: Late winter
Planting time in reverse-season climate: Winter

GROWING

Water: Keep the soil moist.
Nutrients: No additional fertilizer necessary if planted in humus-rich soil; needs moderate amounts of nitrogen, phosphorus, and potassium.

CARE

- Limit spread of roots by installing wood, plastic, metal, or masonry barriers at least 24 inches (60 cm) deep in soil. Tubers may reach 8–16 inches (20–40 cm) beyond the outer

edge of the foliage and should not be cut. Stray tubers left in the garden will sprout the following season.
- Keep growing area free of weeds, but do not cultivate too deeply.
- When leaves turn yellow, trim stalks to 3 inches (7.5 cm) in height.

Pests: Mites, gophers. Spray mites with insecticidal soap. Trap gophers.
Diseases: No serious disease problems

HARVEST

Harvest sunchokes in summer to late autumn as needed. Dig tubers after leaves die back and the tubers are 3–4 inches (7.5–10 cm) in diameter. Sunchokes tend to have a sweeter flavor if harvested after a light frost.

Storage: Keep in the refrigerator for 2–3 weeks at 32–36°F (0–2°C) in plastic bags or in a cool, moist location for up to 6 months. Tubers may be left in the ground where the ground does not freeze; keep them moist to prevent shriveling. Plant the next crop from harvested tubers or you can leave some in the ground to grow again.

VARIETIES

Choose from these sunchoke varieties: 'Stampede' produces large, white tuber; 'Boston Red' produced red-skinned tubers; 'Mammoth French White' grows well in all regions.

Sunflowers

Common name: Sunflower
World names: xiang ri kui (Chinese); soleil, tournesol (French); Sonnenblume (German); corona del sole, girasole (Italian); himawari, koujitsuki (Japanese); girassol (Portuguese); girasol (Spanish)
Botanical name: *Helianthus annuus*
Pronounced hee–lee–AN–thus
Family: Sunflower family—*Asteraceae (Compositae)*

ABOUT

Type of plant: Annuals and perennials
Origin: North and South America, Russia. Sunflowers have been in cultivation for more than 5,000 years.
Description: Numerous, coarse, hairy stem from 3–10 feet (1–3 m) tall depending upon variety; coarse, heart-shaped leaves; leaf-like bracts surround the seed disc
Height: Up to 12 feet (3.7 m) in some varieties
Breadth: 9–15 inches (23–38 cm)
Root depth: 8–12 inches (20–30 cm)
Bloom time and flower: Summer; daisy-like flower heads are flattened discs that may grow to a foot in diameter; the outer circle in each head is a row of large yellow petals but may also be orange, red or copper colored; other petals are small, tubular flowers which form row after row of circles in the center of the head.
Edible parts: Seed

KITCHEN

Serve: Use sunflower seeds plain or roasted, whole or chopped, ground or sprouted.

BASICS

Seed planting depth: 1 inch (2.5 cm)
Germination soil temperature: 75–80°F (24–27°C); optimum 75°F (24°C)
Days to germination: 5–10
Sow indoors: 3 weeks before last frost
Sow outdoors: After last frost
Days to maturity: 50–90 days depending upon variety.

SUNFLOWERS

Soil pH range: 6.8–7.0
Growing soil temperature: 50–80°F (10–27°C)
Space of plants: 6 inches (15 cm); thin to 18–24 inches (45–60 cm)
Water: Heavy until a few inches tall, then moderate
Light: Full sun
Nutrients: Low nitrogen, phosphorus, and potassium
Rotating crops: Avoid following artichokes and other members of the sunflower family.
Companion crops: Cucumbers, melons
Incompatible crops: Pole beans
Propagation: Seed
Seed vitality: 6 years; store in an airtight container in a cool, dark place
Seed weight: 560 to 1,120 seeds per ounce (20–40 per gram)

SITE

Sunflowers grow best in growth zones 3–11.
Soil preparation: Sunflowers prefer humus rich soil.
Container growing: Choose a container at least 12 inches (30 cm) deep. Choose small cultivars such as 'Big Smile', 'Sunset' or 'Sunspot'.

PLANTING

Sow sunflowers 6 inches (15 cm) apart; thin to 18–24 inches (45–60 cm).
Planting time in short-season regions: Spring; direct sow after all danger of frost has past. To start seed indoors; sow indoors 3 weeks before last frost; use 4-inch (10 cm) pots under artificial light; transplant to garden after all danger of frost has passed.
Succession planting: A new row every 2–3 weeks

GROWING

Water: Regular water; can withstand dry conditions
Nutrients: Low applications of nitrogen, phosphorus, and potassium

CARE

- Plant on the north side of garden so that they do not shade other plants.
- Mulch to retain moisture.
- Support tall plants as necessary.

Pollination: Some varieties are self-compatible though requiring the assistance of bees while others require cross-pollination between plants.
Pests: Birds, caterpillars, beetles, weevils, cutworms.

- Cover maturing heads with netting or paper bags to deter birds.
- Handpick caterpillars, beetles, and cutworms. Use row covers early in the season to exclude pests.

- Use paper stem collars or diatomaceous earth sprinkled around the base of each plant to control cutworms.

Diseases: Downy mildew, powdery mildew, rust, fungal leaf spot
- Remove and destroy infected plants.
- Water from below. Don't touch plants when wet, to avoid spreading disease.

HARVEST

Sunflowers are ready for harvest 50–90 days after sowing depending upon variety. Cut flower heads with 24 inches (60 cm) of stalk attached as soon as backside of the seed head begins to turn from green to brown. Hang heads in a dry, airy place until seeds dry, about a week. Rub seeds off of dried heads.
Storage: Store dry seed in a glass jar

VARIETIES

Choose from these sunflower varieties:
Semi-dwarf: 4–8 feet (1.2–2.4 m). 'Arrowhead', 'Sunrich Lemon', 'Peredovik'. Yellow gold blooms with dark centers.
Multi-stem: Also called branched sunflowers; bear small flowers rather than a single blossom. Tall varieties include 'Primrose Yellow' and 'Henry Wilde'; semi-dwarf varieties include 'Sunrise' and 'Valentine'.
Doubles: Dandelion-like double blooms made up of elongated disk flowers. Include 'Sol d'Or', 'Teddy Bear', 'Sun Gold'.
Dwarf: Not taller than 18 inches (45 cm). Includes 'Big Smile', 'Sunspot', 'Sebulon'. With single full-size bloom.
For cut flowers: 'Italian White', 'Inca Jewels', 'Music Box', 'Sunrich Lemon', 'Valentine'.
For seeds: 'Russian Mammoth', 'Big Smile', 'Giant Grey Stripe'.

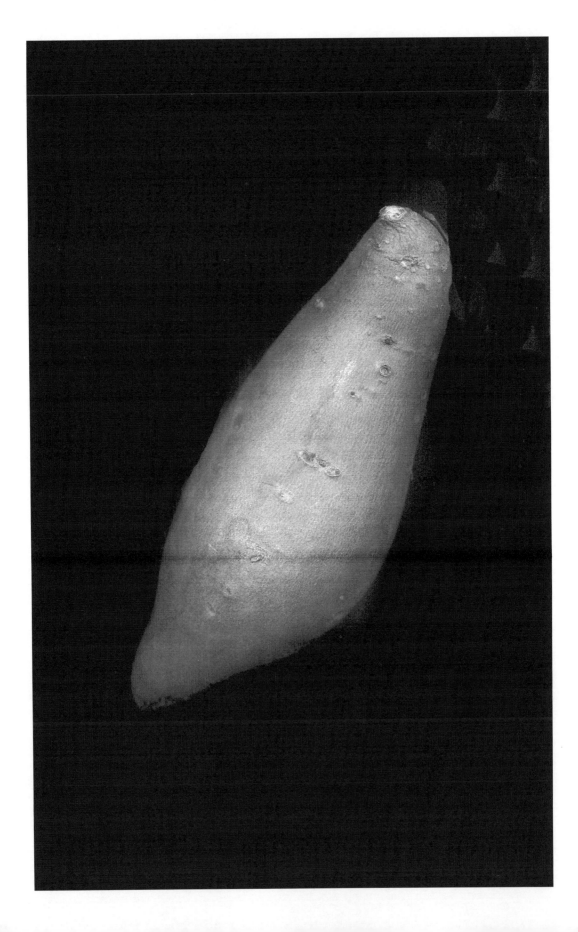

Sweet Potatoes

Common names: Sweet potato, kumara, batata (The moist type of sweet potato is incorrectly called a yam in some parts of the United States.)
World names: fan shu (Chinese); patate douce (French); Süßkartoffel, Batate (German); patata dolce (Italian); satsuma imo, kan sho (Japanese); ubi keladek (Malay); batata doce (Portuguese), batata (Spanish); man thet (Thai)
Botanical name: *Ipomoea batatas.* The yam is a different plant, *Dioscorea* species.
Pronounced ip–oh–MEE–uh bah–TAH–tas
Family: Bindweed or morning glory family—*Convolvulaceae*

ABOUT

Type of plant: Perennial grown as an annual, warm season
Origin: Tropical America and Caribbean. Sweet potatoes were cultivated in Peru as long as 10,000 years ago.
Description: Vine or semi-erect perennial; leaves vary from oval to lobed, 4–6 inches (10–15 cm) long; skin of swollen fleshy tubers range in color from light brown to red; sweet flesh is yellow or gold. There are two classes of sweet potatoes. The first is the so-called "moist" types with soft, sugary, yellowish orange flesh – commonly called yams (although the true yam, *Dioscorea* species, is an entirely different plant found in tropical countries). The second class of sweet potato is a firm and "dry" tuber with whitish flesh. (In fact, some dry varieties have higher moisture content than some moist ones.) The dry type tends to do best in cooler climates.
Height: 10–12 inches (25–30 cm)
Breadth: 4–8 square feet (1.2–2.4 sq. m)
Root depth: 6–8 inches (15–20 cm)
Bloom time and flowers: Summer; sparse, small white, pink, or red-purple flowers
Edible parts: Roots; thickened root

KITCHEN

Serve: Sweet potatoes are served cooked. Mash boiled sweet potatoes for extra smoothness. Sweet potatoes can be peeled before or after they are cooked.

BASICS

Planting depth: Set cuttings (called slips or draws) 2–3 inches (5–7.5 cm) deep

SWEET POTATOES

Planting outdoors: 2 weeks after last frost
Days to maturity: 150–175 after setting out cutting; 100–125 after transplanting
Soil pH range: 5.0–6.5
Growing soil temperature: 60–85°F (16–29°C)
Spacing of plants: 10–12 inches (25–30 cm) apart in all directions
Water: Low
Light: Full sun.
Nutrients: Low nitrogen, phosphorus, and potassium
Rotating crops: Avoid following root crops
Companion crops: Marigold
Incompatible crops: Long-cycle root vegetables such as beets, parsnips, salsify
Propagation: Slips, cuttings (also called "draws" or "seed roots"). To grow slips, begin about 3 months before they will be transplanted outdoors. Set a sweet potato in a glass jar half filled with water, submerging one-third of the tuber. Place in a warm, sunny location until it sprouts. When sprouts are 6 inches (15 cm) long, pull them off the potato and set them in water or damp sand until they root. Slips can be planted out 2–4 weeks after the last frost when soil and night time temperatures are above 60°F (16°C).

SITE

Sweet potatoes grow best in growth zones 6–12. They prefer a long, hot, frost-free growing season.
Frost tolerance: Very tender, cannot tolerate any frost.
Soil preparation: Sweet potatoes prefer well drained, fertile; light, sandy loam, amended with compost.
Container growing: Semi-trailing varieties can be grown in containers draping over the edges

PLANTING

Sweet potatoes are grown from rooted cuttings, also called "slips" or "draws." Set cuttings 2–3 inches (5–7.5 cm) deep. With a rake make a ridge of soil 6–10 inches (15–20 cm) wide. Plant slips into the ridge about 12 inches (30 cm) apart. Set slips so only the stem tips and leaves are exposed. Mound soil onto the ridge at least once before the vining plants make further cultivation impossible.
Planting time in mild-winter climates: For summer crop, plant slips in spring when soil has warmed to 70°F (21°C) but does not exceed 85°F (29°C).
Planting time in cold-winter climates: Early spring; start seed tubers indoors 6–8 weeks before soil has warmed. Dust the cut surfaces with garden lime, then cover each cutting with 4 inches (10 cm) of moist sand and maintain at a temperature of 80°F (27°C) for 3–4 weeks. Reduce the temperature to 70°F (21°C) when sprouts are 3–4 inches (7.5–10 cm) long. Plant out in garden after frost danger is past. Sweet potatoes require a long, hot growing season to flourish. Long days promote vine growth. Short days induce root enlargement and flowering.

GROWING

Water: Keep soil moist until newly set slips begin to grow. Don't let water stand. During growing season, allow soil to dry between watering.

Nutrients: Low requirements for nitrogen, phosphorus, and potassium. Add fish emulsion only to the planting soil. Too much nitrogen produces leafy growth.

CARE

- Do not pinch or cut the vines back.
- Row covers add heat and keep out pests.
- Let vines sprawl or train vines onto vertical supports made of lattice or wire strung between sturdy poles. Lift vines so that secondary roots do not establish and compete with main roots.
- Avoid using high-nitrogen fertilizer, which will result in lush foliage but poorly developed sweet potatoes.

Pests: Aphids, flea beetles, leafhoppers, nematodes, weevils, wireworms.

- Rotate plantings and keep soil organic matter high to reduce nematode, weevil, and wireworm damage.
- Use floating row covers to deter flea beetles.
- Deer will eat leaves and shoots; fence them out of the garden.

Diseases: Fungus disease: black rot, root rot, soil rot, stem rot, soft rot, dry rot Virus diseases: internal cork, chlorotic leaf spot, yellow dwarf, russet crack.

- Plant disease resistant varieties.
- Remove infected plants before disease can spread.
- Rotate crops to avoid planting in the same soil for 4 years.
- Plant in well-draining soil; don't allow water to collect in garden; water from below.

HARVEST

Sweet potato tubers should be fully developed potatoes 100–140 days after planting or when vines begin to wither and leaves turn yellow. If there is frost, harvest immediately. Tubers are damaged by freezing or cold soils, so dig up sweet potatoes early rather than late, before the first frost. Best to harvest before soil temperature gets below 50°F (10°C). Cut back vines then dig carefully with a garden fork, 8–10 inches (20–25 cm) away from the plant. Take care not to cut or bruise thin-skinned tubers.

Storage: Dry harvested tubers in sun for a day; cure in a shady and warm place for a week. Let dry until soil can be brushed off, curing for 10–14 days in a warm place at about 85°F (29°C). After curing temperatures should be lowered to 55–60°F (13–16°C) at relative humidity of 85–90%; store for 4–6 months. You can also freeze, can, or dry them. Flavor improves in storage as starch is converted to sugar.

TYPES AND VARIETIES

There are two classes of sweet potatoes:
- **Soft, sugary, yellow-orange flesh:** varieties include 'Allgold', 'Beauregard', 'Centennial', 'Jewel', 'Kona-B', 'Vardamen', 'Vineless Puerto Rico'.
- **Firm, dry, whitish flesh:** varieties include 'Onokeo', 'Waimanalo Red', 'Yellow Jersey'.

Tarragon

Common name: French tarragon, true tarragon
World name: estragon (French); Esdragon, Estragon (German); estragon (Italian); estragon (Spanish)
Botanical name: *Artemisia dracunculus*
Pronounced ar–tih–MIZ–ee–uh druh–KUN–kyoo–lus suh–TY–vuh
French tarragon may be labeled "sativa"; Russian tarragon may be labeled "indodorus"
Family: Sunflower family—*Asteraceae (Compositae)*

ABOUT

Type of plant: Perennial
Origin: Caspian Sea, Siberia. Tarragon was introduced to Europe by the Crusaders returning from the Near East during the Middle Ages.
Description: Sprawling, long branched green stems, slender, spiky dark green leaves rarely more than an inch (2.5 cm) long; leaves are aromatic
Height: Up to 24 inches (60 cm)
Breadth: 24 inches (60 cm)
Root depth: 6–10 inches (15–25 cm)
Bloom time and flowers: Summer, may not bloom in all climates; inconspicuous yellow or whitish green flowers
Edible parts: Leaves, seeds

KITCHEN

Serve: Tarragon can be used raw, dried or cooked. Use tarragon sparingly to impart its distinctive licorice-like flavor. Add fresh leaves to meat dishes and stews. Add leaves to mayonnaise for fish dishes, salad dressings, light soups, tomatoes, omelets, or scrambled eggs.

BASICS

Seed planting depth: Tarragon is not grown from seed, but from cuttings
Germination soil temperature: 75–80°F (24–27°C); optimum 75°F (24°C)
Days to germination: 5–10
Sow indoors: Not grown from seed
Sow outdoors: Transplant

TARRAGON

Days to maturity: Leaves can be gathered 2 months after transplanting
Soil pH range: 6.5–7.0
Growing soil temperature: 50–80°F (10–27°C)
Spacing of plants: 18 inches (45 cm) apart in all directions
Water: Low
Light: Full sun to partial shade
Nutrients: Light feeder
Rotating crops: Avoid rotating with sunflower family plants.
Companion crops: Tarragon is believed to enhance the growth of many vegetables.
Incompatible crops: None
Propagation: Cuttings, division. Divide mature plants in spring or take stem cuttings anytime during the growing season. French tarragon is not propagated by seed.
Seed vitality: 1 year
Seed weight: 145,800 seeds per ounce (6,000 per gram)

SITE

Best climate: Growth zones 4–8; does not grow well in hot, humid areas
Frost tolerance: Hardy; apply winter mulch in colder climates to prevent heaving.
Soil preparation: Prefers rich, sandy, well-drained loam; never plant tarragon in a wet or acid soil.
Container growing: Grow in pot at least 12 inches (30 cm) deep and wide.

PLANTING

Spring planting time: Spring; plant rooted cuttings outdoors after all danger of frost is past. Divide old clumps before growth starts. Divide older plants in spring every 3 years.
Autumn planting time: Take cuttings from new growth in autumn, over-winter young plants indoors until the following spring

CARE

Nutrients: Light feeder
Side dressing: Spray plants with liquid seaweed extract 2–3 times during the growing season.
- Cut back in autumn.
- Protect in winter with straw or mulch.
- Divide and replant every three years to maintain vigor.
- Prune away flower stems for best flavor.
- To grow indoors in winter, pot young plants in summer, cutting foliage to just above the soil. Seal pot in a plastic bag, and refrigerate to mimic winter. In autumn, unwrap and place in a sunny window for winter harvests. French tarragon requires a cold weather resting period.

Pests: Tarragon has no serious pest problems.
Diseases: Downy mildew, powdery mildew, root rot; but usually no serious disease problems. Don't handle plants when wet. Don't allow water to collect in the garden. Water from below.

HARVEST

Clip tarragon foliage as needed all summer, or indoors in winter. Do not cut branches more than one-third to allow for re-growth. Tarragon is most flavorful before the plant flowers.
Storage: Fresh foliage lasts several weeks in the refrigerator when wrapped in paper towels, then placed in a plastic bag. Preserve by freezing or drying or in vinegar.

VARIETIES

French tarragon is preferred for cooking, *Artemisia dracunculus* var. *sativa*. Russian tarragon *A. d.* var. *inordora* is coarse and bitter tasting and is not recommended. Mexican tarragon, a species of marigold, *Tagetes lucida*, is sometimes used in cookery.

Thyme

Common name: Thyme, common thyme
World names: thym (French); Gartenthymian (German); timo (Italian); tomillo (Spanish)
Botanical name: *Thymus vulgaris*
Pronounced TY–mus vul–GARE–is
Family: Mint family—*Lamiaceae (Labiatae)*

ABOUT
Type of plant: Perennial
Origin: Mediterranean. Thyme has been in use since the time of ancient Egypt.
Description: Small prostrate sub-shrub with tiny, oval, pointed, aromatic gray-green leaves ¼ inch (6 mm) long on wiry stems; sometimes evergreen.
Height: 6–15 inches (15–38 cm)
Breadth: 18–24 inches (45–60 cm)
Root depth: 6–10 inches (15–25 cm)
Bloom time and flowers: Late spring to early summer; tiny, tubular white, lilac, pink, or red blossoms in clusters
Edible parts: Leaves

KITCHEN
Serve: Thyme is known as the "blending" herb because it pulls flavors together. Use leaves with beef, pork, poultry, seafood, sausages, vegetables, lentils, cheeses, eggs, rice, grains, breads, beans, stuffings, and soups.

BASICS
Seed planting depth: 0– ¼ inch (6 mm)
Germination soil temperature: 65–70°F (18–21°C)
Days to germination: 8–21
Sow indoors: 6–8 weeks before last frost
Sow outdoors: After last frost
Days to maturity: 70
Soil pH range: 5.5–7
Growing soil temperature: 55–70°F (13–21°C)
Spacing of plants: 6–12 inches (15–30 cm) apart in all directions

THYME

Water: Even water allowing soil to dry between watering
Light: Full sun
Nutrients: Low nitrogen, phosphorus, and potassium
Companion crops: All cabbage family plants, eggplants, potatoes, strawberries, tomatoes. Thyme is said to benefit the growth of eggplants, potatoes, and tomatoes; it also repels cabbage worms and whiteflies.
Incompatible crops: Cucumbers
Propagation: Cuttings, divisions, layering, seed. Divide or take cuttings from established plants anytime from mid-spring to early summer, but preferably in spring.
Seed vitality: 2–3 years
Seed weight: 180,000 seeds per ounce (7,400 per gram)

SITE

Best climate: Growth zones 4 and warmer
Frost tolerance: Thyme is hardy in cold climates.
Light: Full sun to partial shade
Soil Preparation: Light, well-drained soil
Container growing: Good container plant. Minimum soil depth of the container should be 6 inches (15 cm). Root prune if plant becomes pot bound.

PLANTING

Plant seed no more than ¼ inch (6 mm) deep; or sow them in a very shallow furrow without covering and allow soil to wash over them when they are watered.
Planting time: Late spring, sow outdoors. To start indoors, sow seed in late winter at 70–80°F (21–27°C) about a month before the last frost date; transplant outdoors in late spring.
Greenhouse growing: Grows well in a cool greenhouse if the matted foliage is kept dry to prevent rot. When the plant starts growing out in all directions and the tiny leaves on the bottom begin to dry up, clip it down to the main stems to make it bushy again.

CARE

Nutrients: Low nitrogen, phosphorus, and potassium
Side dressing: Benefits from some supplemental fertilizer once a month. In addition, spray the plants with liquid seaweed extract 2–3 times during the growing season.
- In winter mulch with a light material like straw.
- Replace plants every 3–4 years to control woody growth.

Pests: Aphids, spider mites; but usually has no serious pest problems.
- Spray away aphids and spider mites with a strong stream of water.

Diseases: Botrytis rot; but usually no serious disease problems. Plant in well-draining soil.

HARVEST

Thyme will be ready for harvest about 70 days after sowing. Snip foliage as needed during the summer, or harvest entirely twice per season, leaving at least 3 inches (7.5 cm) of growth.

VARIETIES

Here are additional varieties with their botanical name and description:

- **Creeping thyme** (*T. praecox arcticus*): height to 4 inches (10 cm); forms dense, dark green groundcover; flower color (rose, purple, crimson or white) varies with cultivar; also called mother-of-thyme and used in herb mixes.
- **Lemon thyme** (*T. x citriodorus*): height to 12 inches (30 cm); leaves are dark green or variegated, glossy, and lemon-scented; combines well with chicken or fish dishes.
- **Bushy French thyme** (*T. vulgaris*): also called common thyme; sweeter than English thyme with gray-green foliage. Dark green on the upper side and whitish underneath with a warm, sharp taste.
- **Caraway thyme** (*T. herba-barona*): to 1 inch (2.5 cm) tall and especially good in stir-fry and with meat.
- **Nutmeg thyme** (*T. herba-barona*): adds a nutmeg note to cooking.
- **Silver thyme** (thyme (*T. vulgaris* 'Argentus'): has a strong lemon scent, excellent for cooking.
- **Orange thyme** (*T. vulgaris* 'OrangeBalsam') narrow, orange-scented leaves good with stir-fries and poultry.

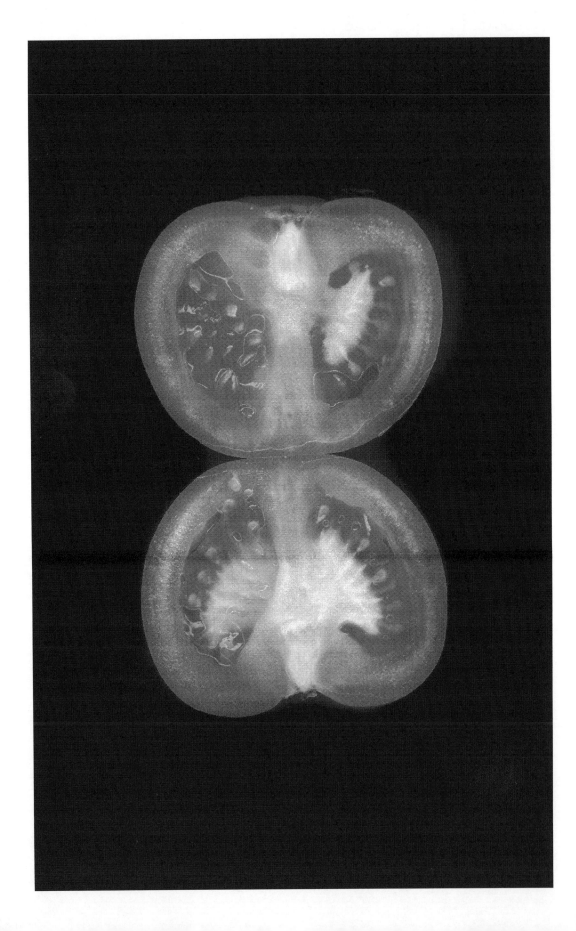

Tomatoes

Common name: Tomato. Small tomatoes are sometimes called cherry tomatoes; large tomatoes are referred to as beef tomatoes; egg-shaped tomatoes are called paste or jam tomatoes; oblong tomatoes are referred to as Italian tomatoes.
World names: fan qie (Chinese); tomate (French); Tomate (German); tamatar (Hindi); pomodoro (Italian); tomate (Portuguese, Spanish)
Botanical name: *Lycopersicon esculentum*
Pronounced ly–ko–PER–si–con es–kew–LEN–tum
Family: Nightshade or potato family—*Solanaceae*

ABOUT

Type of plant: Short-lived perennial usually grown as an annual
Origin: South America. The wild tomato (*Lycopersicon esculentum* syn. *L. lycopersicum*) was introduced to Europe in the sixteenth century.
Description: There are more than 1,000 tomato varieties; most are red, others are yellow, striped, pink, orange, whitish-green shades; most are round, others are pear-shaped, oblong, or tear-drop shaped. Tomatoes are sprawling plants that can not climb but are referred to as a vine. The plant has aromatic compound leaves.
Height: 24–60 inches (60–152 cm)
Breadth: 18–24 inches (45–60 cm)
Root depth: 18 inches (45 cm)
Bloom time and flower: Summer; yellow flowers borne on clusters on trailing stems up to 6 feet (2 m) long.
Edible parts: Fruit

KITCHEN

Serve: Use tomatoes raw or cooked. Eat tomatoes raw without dressing or added to salads, appetizers, and sandwiches.

BASICS

Seed planting depth: ½ inch (13 mm)
Germination soil temperature: 65–86°F (18–30°C); optimum is 86°F (30°C)
Days to germination: 5–7
Sow indoors: 6–7 weeks before last frost
Transplant outdoors: After all danger of frost is past

Days to maturity: 50–90
Soil pH range: 5.5–6.8
Growing soil temperature: 55–85°F (13–29°C)
Space of plants: 18–48 inches (45–122 cm) apart, thinning successful plants to 36–42 inches (90–107 cm) apart in all directions.
Water: Moderate to high during growth, low during harvest
Light: Full sun
Nutrients: High nitrogen, phosphorus, and potassium
Rotating crops: Avoid following potatoes, peppers, and eggplants.
Companion crops: Asparagus, basil, brassicas or cabbage family plants, bush beans, carrots, celery, chives, cucumbers, garlic, head lettuce, marigolds, melons, mint, nasturtiums, onions, parsley, peas, and peppers
Incompatible crops: Corn, dill, fennel, kohlrabi, potatoes, walnuts
Propagation: Seed
Seed vitality: 4 years; store in airtight container in a cool, dark place.
Seed weight: 8,400 seeds per ounce (300 per gram)

SITE

Tomatoes grow best in growth zones 3 and warmer.
Frost tolerance: Tender
Light and situation: Plant in full sun. In cool regions, plant near a wall or the side of a house or building that faces west or south. The wall will soak up the day's heat and release it at night keeping tomatoes warm.
Soil preparation: Tomatoes prefer light, loose, fertile, well-drained soil with plenty of organic matter. Prepare beds in the spring by digging compost in to a depth of 36 inches (90 cm). Add a handful of bone meal to each planting hole. Prepare future tomato beds each autumn by digging in plenty of well-rotted manure and chopped leaves. Warm soil by placing black plastic on the bed a few weeks before planting.
Container growing: Grow in containers indoors year-round. Minimum container depth should be 12–18 inches deep and just as wide Indoors use ultraviolet "grow lights" to promote flowering and fruiting—tomatoes require a minimum of 6 equivalent full-sun hours per day. For container plants, install a cage at the time of planting to support the plants' foliage and fruits

PLANTING

Sow tomato seed ½ inch (13 mm) deep and 18–48 inches (45–122 cm) apart, thinning successful plants to 36–42 inches (90–107 cm) apart.
Direct sowing: When sowing directly in the garden, plant 4 or 5 seeds in a group; when the seedlings have 2–3 sets of true leaves, clip off all but one of the seedlings in each group.

Starting indoors: Sow in pots of light soil mix 5–7 weeks before you intend to set out plants. Use soilless starting mix sowing seeds ½ inch (13 mm) deep and an inch (2.5 cm) apart. (Cuttings treated with rooting hormone can be used for propagation.) The ideal temperature for germination is 75–90°F (24–32°C); optimum seed starting temperature is 85°F (29°C). Place under grow lights or in a sunny window after germination. If you use grow lights, keep the bulbs about 2 inches (5 cm) above the plants. Start several seeds in a small pot to begin and then thin to the best plant. Transplant to 2 inch (5 cm) growing cell or pot after 10 days or when the first true leaves develop. Clip away leaves to 1 inch (2.5 cm) and replant. Fertilize with fish emulsion. Grow seedlings at 60–70°F (16–21°C). Water enough to keep the mix from drying. Fertilize with fish emulsion or a soluble complete fertilizer. After two more weeks, about 24 days after germination, transplant seedlings once again, this time into 4-inch pots. Trim off all of the leaves below the top 2 inches and again set each seedling in its new pot up to the bottom leaf.

Selecting garden center seedlings: Select plants 6–8 weeks old, usually in a 4-inch (10 cm) pot. Check bottom of pot to make sure roots are not growing through and plant is not root bound.

Transplanting: Soil temperature should be 55–60°F (13–16°C) and night temperature should not fall below 45°F (7°C). Transplant into medium rich garden soil 12–24 inches (30–60 cm) apart for determinate varieties, 24–36 inches (30–90 cm) apart for indeterminate, unstaked varieties, and 14–20 inches (36–51 cm) for staking. Transplant into a 6-inch (15 cm) hole, allowing 4 inches (10 cm) of plant to remain above the soil. Clip off leaves below soil line. The plant will form added roots on the buried stem. In the bottom of your planting hole put a layer of compost with a handful of bone meal and 1 teaspoon (5 ml) of Epsom salts. Firm plant gently into soil and water. Water seedling with a high-phosphate fertilizer solution. Transplant again after 2 more weeks to 4-inch (10 cm) pot. Bury all but top 2 inches (5 cm). The best seedlings are short bushy plants with dark foliage and no flowers. Harden off plant 2 weeks before planting into garden to minimize shock.

Planting time: Choose varieties suited to your climate: varieties for cool weather, hot and humid weather, and hot and dry weather. Set out in the garden after the danger of frost has passed and the soil has warmed.

Planting time in short-season climates: Choose extra-hardy, early-maturing varieties. Start indoors 6–8 weeks before the soil is expected to warm; harden seedlings 7–10 days before transplanting outdoors, or transplant nursery-grown seedlings 4–6 weeks after all danger or frost has passed.

Planting time in long-season (mild winter) climates: After soil has warmed to above 55°F (13°C), fruit will not set at lower temperature; in the hottest climates, in late spring, 6 weeks before the last spring frost.

Succession planting: Plant early, midseason and late varieties or plant in spring and again in summer where the summer is long enough.

GROWING

Water: Keep soil moist but not wet; maintain even moisture throughout growth period; over-watering is detrimental so soil should drain easily. Water heavily enough to reach the plant's deepest roots, about 1–2 inches (2.5–5 cm) of water every week.

Nutrients: Tomatoes require a moderate amount of nitrogen and ample amounts of phosphorus and potassium. Abundant soil phosphorus is important for early high yields. Too much nitrogen will encourage leaf growth, but not flowers and fruit or soft fruit susceptible to rot.

Side dressing: Do not fertilize until the plant is well established and in full blossom. Then give weak compost tea or fish emulsion. Apply light application of fish emulsion every 2 weeks from the first blossoms set until the end of harvest.

Staking: Determinate (bush) varieties can be grown without support although cages may be used. Indeterminate (climbing) varieties should be staked, trellised, or caged, and pruned for best results. Train indeterminate tomatoes using a 2-by-2-inch (5 cm) 6-foot-long (1.8 m) stake, a wire tomato cage or cylinder with opening large enough to put your hand through, or trellis. Set support in place at planting time. Set the support in the ground before setting out plants. Anchor cages to a pair of 4-foot (1.2 m) stakes driven into the ground before planting. Use soft ties to train the plant to a stake, or train branches through the cage as the plant grows. Tie the main stem every foot or so with soft twine or horticultural tape. Tie up the main stem of indeterminate varieties once a week. Do not let fruit lie on the ground where it could suffer rot, pest damage, and discoloration.

Pruning: Indeterminate vines should be pruned so that only one or two main stems develop. Pinch off suckers that grow between the main stem and the branches. (Suckers are non-flowering shoots that grow in the angle between the main stem and leaf stalks.) Pruning allows nutrients to be used for fruit development. Pinch out the growing tips when the plant reaches the top of its support.

Growing air temperature: 65–90°F (18–32°); optimum 75°F (24°C); fruit may not set in temperatures exceeding 85°F (29°C) and may require shade covers to prevent sunburn in direct sunlight areas exceeding 90°F (32°C). The mean temperature must be above 60°F (16°C); when temperature drops below 53°F (12°C) plant gets chilled; prolonged chilling will result in injury of the tissues and fruit may not ripen. In cool climates, where the growing season is short or where inclement weather makes vine ripening difficult, green tomatoes may be picked and ripened indoors in a warm spot.

CARE

- Keep soil moist; do not wet the fruit, vines, or foliage.
- Mulch after the soil warms to maintain soil temperature at night; this will aid root development.
- A 2-inch (5 cm) layer of mulch will keep down weeds; do not cultivate around tomato plants to avoid disturbing roots.

- Blossom-end rot is caused in part by a lack of calcium in the soil; add crushed eggshells (about six or so) to the soil every 2 weeks.
- Use row covers to maintain warmth; remove covers if temperatures reach 85°F (29°C).
- In areas where nights are cool and chilly, select cold-tolerant varieties.
- In extreme heat, shade plants with porous shade fabric installed on wooden supports.
- Use row covers to deter insects.
- Remove suckers to increase fruit size.
- If you plant early and frost is possible, place a brown paper bag, open at each end, into the planting hole about 6 inches deep; place planting mix into the open ended bag and set tomato plants inside. The bag will protect the plants from insects and cool temperatures; close the top on chilly nights with a clip or clothespin. When frost danger is past, cut off the bag near ground level.

Pests: Aphids, beet leafhoppers, cabbage loopers, Colorado potato beetles, corn borers, corn earworms, cucumber beetles, flea beetles, fruit worms, gophers, Japanese beetles, lace bugs, leaf-footed bugs, mites, nematodes, slugs, snails, stink bugs, thrips, tobacco budworms, tomato hornworms, whiteflies, cutworms, leaf miners.

- Protect young plants from cutworms with cardboard, plastic, or metal collars.
- Handpick tomato hornworms or use Bacillus thuringiensis (Bt).
- Spray away aphids, thrips, and mites with a strong stream of water.
- Handpick and destroy snails and slugs.
- Use nematode resistant cultivars.
- Encourage birds in the garden.

Diseases: Alternaria, anthracnose, bacterial canker, bacterial spot, bacterial wilt, botrytis fruit rot, curly top, damping off, early blight, fusarium wilt, late blight, psyllid yellows, leaf spot, soft rot, southern blight, spotted wilt, sunscald, tobacco mosaic, verticillium wilt, mosaic virus.

- Tomatoes are subject to a variety of plant diseases, both viral and fungal. Plant geneticists have developed disease-resistant varieties, identified by the letter "V" (verticillium wilt), "F" (fusarium wilt), "N" (nematodes, a microorganism that causes cankers on the roots), and "T" (tobacco mosaic virus—tomatoes are a relative of the tobacco plant, and subject to viral diseases of that plant species). Select resistant varieties; use young, healthy transplants.
- Early blight or alternaria blight cause dark spots with concentric rings inside on leaves and sunken lesions with a ring pattern on fruit. Control early blight with liquid copper fungicide spray.
- Verticillium wilt, a fungus, causes yellowing of old crown leaves and sometimes causes mottling of the stem.
- Fusarium wilt, a fungus, causes yellowing of leaves and the vascular system of the stem turns a reddish-brown color.

- Phytophthora root rot, caused by a soil fungus, is due to wet soil and is most prevalent in soil high in clay.
- Tobacco mosaic virus-infected leaves show blotchy yellow and green spots. The virus is transmitted by seed and handling especially by tobacco smokers.
- Spotted wilt is transmitted by thrips; the virus causes dark brown spots and streaks to appear on the stem near the growing point giving the shoots a bronzing effect. Irregular dark brown steaks appear on newly formed leaves.
- Curly top, a virus disease, causes leaves to roll with some twisting. With progress of the diseases the veins turn purple and the leaf color turn yellow. Infected plants cease growth and subsequently die. Some cultivars have naturally curly leaves which are sometimes confused with curly top.
- Yellow leaf curl, a viral disease, is transmitted by whiteflies.
- Remove and destroy infected plants.
- Ensure good soil drainage. Water plants from below.
- Plow under or bury tomato plant refuse at the end of the season.
- Rotate crops.
- Do not handle tobacco or smoke before handling plants.
- Avoid overhead irrigation.
- Fungicides can reduce certain diseases.
- Prevent blossom end rot by providing abundant soil calcium and an even supply of soil moisture.
- Soil with nematodes and bacterial wilt causing organisms should be avoided.

HARVEST

Harvest tomatoes in late summer 50–90 frost free days after planting. Pick the fruit when it is evenly colored but still firm. For determinate varieties, harvest when clusters of fruit reach full color and desired size. For indeterminate varieties, harvest the fruit at the peak of color and before it turns soft. Support the vine in one hand and gently pull the fruit to prevent damage to the plant.
- A month before the first expected frost, start plucking new flowers off the plants. This will direct the plant's energy into ripening tomatoes already on the vine.
- Harvest all fruit when a frost is predicted.

Cherry tomato yield: Allow 1–4 plants of each variety; mix early and late cultivars
Cooking tomato yield: Allow 3–6 plants of each variety; mix early and late cultivars; will yield 8–10 quarts (7–9 liters).
Slicing tomato yield: Allow 1–4 plants of each variety; mix early and late cultivars; double the number of plantings if the fruit is intended to be crushed for juice.
Storage: Ripe red tomatoes should be stored at 38–40°F (3–4°C); at higher temperatures, the fruit continues to ripen and quality deteriorates rapidly. Store at room temperature for

7–10 days. Keep harvested tomatoes out of sunlight. Picked tomatoes placed in the sun will overheat and ripen unevenly. They will spoil more quickly. To redden up harvested tomatoes, place them in a paper bag with an apple or a banana. Ethylene gas given off by the fruit will speed the ripening.

- Refrigerated tomatoes should be placed in the butter compartment or the vegetable crisper, where they are protected from some of the cold. If tomatoes become overripe, freeze them or use immediately. Do not can overripe tomatoes because they may have lost their natural acidic balance which increases the risk of botulism, even if processed in a pressure cooker. If cut and packaged, store in the freezer for 3–4 months. If canned for up to 2 years. If pickled, for up to 2 years; pick green for pickling. Tomatoes picked at the peak of ripeness will retain their flavor and nutrients if canned or frozen.

TYPES

There are more than 1,000 tomato varieties; most are red, others are yellow, striped, pink, orange, whitish-green shades; most are round, others are pear-shaped, oblong, or tear drop shaped.

Categories of use: There are three major tomato categories based on use: cherry or miniature, cooking, and slicing and eating.

- **Cherry or miniature:** smallest ranging in size from ¾–1½ inches (1.9–3.8 cm) in diameter and in hues of red, yellow, and zebra-stripe green. Use in salads or for snacking.
- **Cooking:** usually oblong or pear shaped, with meatier, less juicy flesh than the eating varieties; sweeter flavor; generally ripen at the same time providing quantities for canning and sauces.
- **Slicing and eating:** generally the largest, juiciest, most flavorful tomatoes

They come in both early-season and longer-developing varieties; those with longer growth periods have enhanced taste and texture.

Categories based on growth form or habit

- **Determinate:** bush type grows to genetically predetermined size and then stops; flowers at the end of the stalk; bears fruit early; the fruits ripen all at once usually for a period of 6 weeks, the plant then dies; suited to cool-climate gardens (sow seeds 6 week before the last frost date); use as an early crop in warm climates then follow with indeterminate varieties. Generally less disease resistant. Does not need to be staked or trellised.
- **Indeterminate:** sprawling vine-like plant; long bearing period producing a succession of fruits at the tips of branching spurs which form beneath the foliage; continues to grow until frost kills the plant; start 8 weeks before the last frost date; usually more resistant to disease; requires training on a stake, in a cage, or on a trellis; the majority of heirloom tomatoes are indeterminate.

VARIETIES AND COMMON NAMES

You are apt to see tomatoes labeled in a multitude of ways. And since there are more than 1,000 varieties of tomatoes, here is a short guide common tomato names and varieties:

- **Beefsteak tomato:** is a slicing or eating tomato that can be eaten raw or cooked. These are large, bright red tomatoes with a slightly elliptical shape. The beefsteak is the classic sandwich or hamburger tomato. It is so large and juicy with such a large seed cavity that it usually does not hold its shape when cooked.
- **Bicolored tomato:** is a two colored, usually striped tomato. Bicolored tomatoes are often heirloom varieties.
- **Black tomato:** is a black or deep-purple skinned tomato variety. Black tomato varieties include 'Black Cherry', and the globe tomatoes 'Black Krim' and 'Black Russian'.
- **Cherry tomato:** about 1 inch (2.5 cm) in diameter, red or yellow-gold in color for snacking, adding to salads, or eating raw. Also use the cherry tomato as a garnish. It has excellent flavor. Well known varieties include: 'Sweet 100 Plus', 'Sun Gold', 'Matt's Wild Cherry'.
- **Cool-summer tomato:** is a tomato variety that will ripen where the accumulated heat over the course of the growing season is too low for most tomatoes. Cool-summer tomatoes are suited for cool-summer regions. Cool-summer tomato varieties include 'San Francisco Fog', 'Moskvich', 'Oregon Pride', 'Oregon Spring', and 'Seattle Best of All'.
- **Currant tomato:** is smaller than a cherry tomato, about ½ to ¾ inches (13–19 mm) in diameter and weighs about ⅛ ounce. Currant tomatoes are sometimes called "mini cherry tomatoes." Currant tomatoes are usually red or yellow and are sweet and crisp for snacking or using on salads.
- **Early tomato:** is a tomato variety that sets fruit at lower night temperatures than a main crop tomato. Early tomato varieties are grown in short-season regions and often in high-elevation areas. Early tomato varieties include 'Early Girl'. 'Burpee's Early Pick', 'Quick Pick', and 'Stupice'.
- **Globe tomato:** is a medium-size, round, usually red tomato that is firm and juicy. The globe tomato is similar to the beefsteak tomato. It is good raw for slicing and eating out of hand and cooked.
- **Grape tomato:** is an elliptical, egg- or pear-shaped tomato about the size of a grape. The grape tomato can be a baby Roma or a variety such as 'Juliet' which produces grapelike clusters of small fruit. The 'Roma' is a tomato variety that is meaty, with few seeds, red or yellow and most often used as a canning or sauce tomato.
- **Green tomato:** are tomato varieties that are green when mature. Some green tomato varieties are globe tomatoes and some are beefsteak. These tomatoes have a piquant flavor and are best used for frying, broiling, and adding to relishes. Green tomato varieties include 'Aunt Ruby's German Green', 'Emerald Evergreen', and 'Green Bell Pepper'.
- **Hawaiian tomato:** is a tomato variety developed for growing especially in Hawaii where many tomato diseases flourish. Hawaiian tomato varieties include 'Anahu', 'Healani', 'Kalohi', and 'Puunui'.

- **Heirloom tomato:** vary in size and appearance. Heirloom tomatoes are old tomato varieties, some in cultivation for hundreds of years. Heirloom tomatoes come in a rainbow of colors, textures, and tastes. Most are the size and shape of a globe or beefsteak tomato. Well known varieties include: 'Rose', 'German', 'Brandywine'.
- **Hybrid tomato:** are first-generation tomatoes from controlled parent lines. Hybrids grow to a uniform size and often are very similar in quality. The seed of hybrid tomatoes do not breed true.
- **Hydroponic tomato:** is a tomato grown in water without soil in greenhouse. Hydroponic tomatoes often lack flavor.
- **Large-fruited tomato:** is a tomato variety that grows a large tomato. Large-fruited tomato varieties include 'Beefsteak', 'Beefmaster', 'Big Beef', and 'Burpee's Supersteak Hybrid'. Large-fruited tomatoes are often used for slicing.
- **Main crop tomato:** is a tomato variety that grows to full size in regions where the days and nights are warm and well-suited for tomato growing. 'Celebrity', 'Big Beef', 'Big Boy', and 'Better Boy' are main crop tomatoes. Main crop tomatoes are also called standard tomatoes.
- **Orange tomato:** is an orange-skinned tomato variety. Orange tomato varieties include 'Amana Orange', 'Ida Gold', and 'Orange Jubilee'.
- **Paste tomato:** is a small, oval, thick-meated tomato with the maximum amount of flesh and virtually no seed cavity. Paste tomatoes are used to make tomato paste or for sun-drying. Paste tomatoes are sometimes called plum tomatoes. See a list of varieties under "Sauce Tomato."
- **Pear tomato:** is smaller than a cherry tomato, egg- or pear shaped, and looks like a small plum tomato. The pear tomato is used like a cherry tomato for snacking or on salads.
- **Pink tomato:** is a pink-skinned tomato variety. 'Brandywine' and 'New Big Dwarf' are beefsteak-size tomatoes with pinkish colored skins. 'Dwarf champion', 'Giant Belgium Pink', and 'Pink Beefsteak' are globe-sized pink tomatoes.
- **Plum tomato:** is also called Italian plum tomato and Roma tomato. The plum tomato is egg-shaped, red or yellow, and flavorful. The plum tomato can be 2–4 inches (5–10 cm) long and 1–2 inches (2.5–5 cm) in diameter. The plum tomato is thick and meaty, not juicy, and contains few seeds. It is sometimes called a paste tomato.
- **Purple tomato:** is an heirloom tomato with a purple skin. Purple-skinned tomato varieties include 'Purple Calabash', 'Brandywine', and 'Cherokee Purple.' Purple tomatoes can be dusky pink with purple shoulders to dusky rose-purple all over. Purple tomatoes are usually the size of a globe or beefsteak tomato.
- **Round tomato:** is a globular or oval tomato 2–5 inches (5–13 cm) in diameter, usually red, pink, orange, yellow, or green colored. The round or common round tomato is usually firm and juicy and used for slicing, eating out of hand, or cooking.
- **Sauce tomato:** is usually a plum tomato, Roma tomato, Italian tomato, or paste tomato. Sauce tomatoes are usually egg-shaped with thick meat and few seeds. Sauce tomatoes

are excellent for sauce making. Their thick flesh holds shape when canned. Well known varieties include: 'Juliet', 'Tuscany', 'Milano', 'Amish Paste', and 'San Remo'.

- **Slicing tomato**: is a large slightly squat shaped tomato used for slicing. The large seed cavity of the slicing tomato contains lots of juice. The beefsteak tomato is a slicing tomato, up to 6 inches (15 cm) in diameter. The slicing tomato is used raw, not cooked.
- **Standard tomato**: is a main crop tomato variety suited for growing in warm weather regions. See "Main crop tomato."
- **Striped tomato**: is a tomato striped, sometimes red and yellow, sometimes red and green, sometimes red and white, as well as other colors. Striped tomatoes are often heirloom tomato varieties. Striped tomato varieties include 'Marvel Striped', 'Big White Pink Stripe', 'Hillbilly', 'Green Zebra', and 'Mister Stripey'.
- **White tomato**: is a tomato variety that has a white skin. White tomato varieties include 'White Wonder' and 'Snow White Cherry'.
- **Yellow cherry tomato**: the same size as its red counterpart but slightly less acidic and usually blander in flavor. Cook the yellow cherry tomato as a side dish or sauté it with herbs.
- **Yellow pear tomato**: is the yellow version of the pear tomato: slightly smaller than a cherry tomato and resembles a tiny pear. The yellow pear tomato may be blander tasting than the red pear tomato.
- **Yellow tomato**: is a yellow-skinned tomato variety. Yellow tomato varieties include 'Azoychka', 'Banana Legs', 'Garden Peach Tomato', and 'Yellow Brandywine'.

Turnips

Common Names: Turnip
World names: man jing, wu jing (Chinese); raap (Dutch); navet (French); Weiße Rübe (German); navone (Italian); kabu (Japanese); nabo (Spanish)
Botanical name: *Brassica rapa* var. *rapa*
Pronounced BRASS–ih–kuh RAY–puh ray–pih–FAIR–uh
Family: Mustard or cabbage family—*Brassicaceae (Cruciferae)*

ABOUT

Type of plant: Biennial grown as an annual, cool season
Origin: Northeastern Europe, Siberia. Turnips have been in cultivation for more than 4,000 years and were used in ancient Greece and Rome.
Description: Squat round shaped root similar to a spinning top with a rosette of hairy, compound, bright green leaves growing from the root—which is actually a swelling at the base of the stem. Greens and bulbous white-fleshed root-stem are edible. Radish-shaped, lilac-topped white turnip is common. The Tokyo turnip (also called Tokyo-type or kobaku-type) is all white and about radish size with buttery flavor. Root colors are white, white with purple on upper part. Shapes are globe and flattened globe.
Height: 10–15 inches (25–38 inches)
Breadth: 6–8 inches (15–20 inches)
Root depth: 6–10 inches (15–25 cm)
Bloom time and flower: Spring or autumn in mild-winter areas; flower color is correlated with the flesh color of the roots; white-flesh rooted plants have bright yellow petals and the yellow-fleshed roots have pale orange-yellow petals.
Edible parts: Roots, leaves; baby turnips are especially tender.

KITCHEN

Serve: Turnips can be eaten raw, baked, boiled, or mashed. Prepare them as you would carrots.

BASICS

Planting seed depth: ½ inch (12mm)
Germination soil temperature: 70–85°F (21–29°C)
Days to germination: 3–10

Sow indoors: Not recommended
Sow outdoors: Early spring to midsummer
Days to maturity: 30–50 days
Soil pH range: 5.5–6.8
Growing soil temperature: 40–75°F (4–24°C); optimum 60°F (16°C)
Spacing of plants: 2–6 inches (5–15cm) apart for roots; 1–4 inches (2.5–10cm) for greens
Water: Moderate
Light: Full sun; tolerates light shade
Nutrients: Low nitrogen, phosphorus, and potassium
Rotating crops: Avoid following cabbage family crops.
Companion crops: Bush beans, peas, and southern peas. Interplant with tomatoes, peppers, cucumbers, squash
Incompatible crops: Potato
Propagation: Seed
Seed vitality: 4 years; store in airtight container in a cool, dark place.
Seed weight: 8,500 seeds per ounce (300 per gram)

SITE

Turnips grow well in all growth zones. They are best grown as a winter vegetable in mild climates.
Frost tolerance: Hardy; will withstand light frost, which also makes the taste sweeter
Soil preparation: Turnips prefer loose, deep humus-rich soil; best in loamy soil. Soil is best if green manure or organic compost is dug into the bed before the end of the prior season.
Container growing: Turnips can be grown in containers; choose any variety. Choose a container 10–12 inches (25–30 cm) deep.

PLANTING

Sow turnips seed depth ½ inch (12 mm) deep spacing plants 2–6 inches (5–15 cm) for roots; 1–4 inches (2.5–10 cm) for greens. Two crops of turnips can be grown, the first to be planted in early spring and the second in late summer for winter storage.
Spring planting time: Early spring; 4–6 weeks before the first expected frost for summer crop.
Autumn planting time: 6–8 weeks before the first expected frost for autumn crop
Planting time in cold-winter regions: Early spring for early summer harvest; summer for autumn harvest
Planting time in mild-winter regions: Plant in autumn for winter crop
Planting time in reverse-season climate: Late autumn for winter harvest; sow autumn crop 8–10 weeks before the first autumn frost.
Succession planting: Plant every 3 weeks until midsummer

GROWING

Water: Keep well watered; water regularly for fast growth in spring; roots are milder if the soil is kept moist; more pungent in dry conditions.

Nutrients: Light application nitrogen, phosphorus, and potassium.

Side dressing: Bone meal or other phosphorus fertilizer improves yields; organic nitrogen when the plants are 5–6 inches (13–15 cm) high.

CARE

- Keep soil weed free.
- Mulch with loose straw to protect the tops of the root from sunburn.
- Do not leave turnips in the ground past maturity; this will cause turnips to become woody and lose flavor.
- Floating rows covers installed on the day of sowing will keep turnips free of insect pests, including flea beetles and root maggots.

Common problems: Turnips that mature in hot weather may be fibrous or strong-flavored. For spring crops, choose quick maturing cultivars.

Pests: Cabbage roots maggots, flea beetles, aphids.

- Exclude flea beetles and roots maggots by using floating rows covers installed on the day of sowing.
- Reduce root maggot damage by not planting where other root crops have grown the previous year.
- Control aphids by pinching out infested foliage or spraying off with a strong stream of water.

Diseases: Most cultivars are disease resistant.

HARVEST

Young radish-size turnips will be ready for harvest about 30 days after sowing, full size in 40–50 days. Roots are smoothest when small. When greens are 12 inches (30cm) long and roots are 2–3 inches (5–7.5 cm) in diameter. Dig carefully with a garden fork. For greens, thin the outside leaves, leaving the central growth bud to re-sprout. Turnips are damaged by hard frost. Turnip greens sometimes are grown as the only crop, either by harvesting before the root forms or by planting varieties that do not develop swollen roots.

Storage: Roots in the refrigerator at 32°F (0°C) and 95% humidity for 7–10 days. Roots also store well in the ground at soil temperatures of 35–80°F (2–27°C). Greens can be wrapped in damp towels, then in a plastic bag, and kept in the refrigerator for a few days. Both the roots and the greens can be canned or dried.

VARIETIES

Choose from these turnip varieties: 'De Milan' and 'Tokyo' has tender roots and mature early; 'Purple Top White Globe' is a favorite for autumn crop; 'Aberdeen' is a yellow variety; for turnip greens choose 'Just Right' and 'All Top'.

Growing Season Information for the Untied States and Canadian Provinces

The dates and growing season days listed here are estimates or averages based on our compilation of information from the Untied States Department of Agriculture and several other sources. This information should be used only as estimated guidelines. Climate, weather, and growing season days in your region can change from month to month and year to year. For more information on growing season days and average temperatures, contact your Cooperative Extension Service.

The hardiness zones or "zones" listed here are also guidelines. Hardiness zones, also called growing zones, are guides to help you know which plants will grow where you live. These are guidelines to help determine the lowest sustained temperature a particular type of plant can withstand. Growing plants requires more than knowledge of growing zones; successful growing is also determined by the garden soil type, rainfall or irrigation, daytime temperature, nighttime temperature, day length, wind, humidity, and heat. Climates and growing conditions can vary even if they are in the same growing zone. Use the zones as a starting point, not as the final determinant of what will grow in your garden.

There are 11 growing zones, 1-11; 1 having the coldest annual minimum temperatures and 11 the warmest. The growing zones are further divided here into "A" and "B"; "A" is the less warm region of the zone and "B" is the warmer region of the zone.

USDA zones are given for all regions of the United States and Canada. The USDA zones are also given for other parts of the world. Note that many countries, such as Australia, have adopted their own growing zone designations. Consult agricultural officials in your region of the world to obtain the most accurate information.

GROWING SEASON INFORMATION

State and city	Average date of last frost	Average date of first frost	Growing days	Zone	Average minimum temp
United States					
Alabama					
Birmingham	March 19	November 14	241	7B	5F to 10°F
Mobile	February 17	December 12	298	8A	10F to 15°F
Montgomery	February 27	December 3	279	8A	10F to 15°F
Alaska					
Anchorage	May 18	September 13	118	4	−20F to −30°F
Barrow	June 27	July 5	8	4	−20F to −30°F
Cordova	May 10	October 2	145	4	−20F to −30°F
Fairbanks	May 24	August 29	97	4	−20F to −30°F
Arizona					
Flagstaff	June 8	October 2	116	5B	−10F to −15°F
Phoenix	January 27	December 11	317	9A	20F to 25°F
Tucson	March 12	November 21	225	8A	10F to 15°F
Winslow	April 28	October 21	176	5B	−10F to −15°F
Arkansas					
Fort Smith	March 23	November 9	231	8B	15F to 20°F
Little Rock	March 16	November 15	244	7A	0F to 5°F
Pine Bluff	March 26	November 5	224	7B	5F to 10°F
Texarkana	March 21	November 19	233	7B	5F to 10°F
California					
Bakersfield	February 14	November 28	287	8B	15F to 20°F
Eureka	March 10	November 18	253	8B	15F to 20°F
Fresno	February 3	December 3	303	8A	10F to 15°F
Los Angeles	January 3	December 28	359	10	30F to 40°F
Marysville	February 21	November 21	273	7B	5F to 10°F
Palm Springs	January 8	December 18	334	9B	25F to 30°F
Pasadena	February 3	December 13	313	9B	25F to 30°F
Red Bluff	March 6	December 5	274	7B	5F to 10°F
Riverside	March 6	November 26	265	8B	15F to 20°F
Sacramento	January 24	December 11	321	8B	15F to 20°F
San Diego	no frost	no frost	365	10	30F to 40°F
San Francisco	January 7	December 29	356	8B	15F to 20°F
San Jose	February 10	January 6	299	8B	15F to 20°F
Santa Barbara	January 22	December 19	331	8B	15F to 20°F
Santa Rosa	April 10	November 3	207	8B	15F to 20°F

Colorado

Denver	May 2	October 14	165	5A	−15F to −20°F
Grand Junction	April 20	October 9	173	6A	−5F to −10°F
Pueblo	April 28	October 12	167	5B	−10F to −15°F

Connecticut

Bridgeport	April 26	October 16	174	6A	−5F to −10°F
Hartford	April 22	October 19	180	5A	−15F to −20°F
New Haven	April 15	October 25	193	6A	−5F to −10°F

Delaware

Dover	April 17	October 22	188	7A	0F to 5°F
Newark	April 20	October 17	180	7A	0F to 5°F
Wilmington	April 18	October 26	191	7A	0F to 5°F

District of Columbia

Washington	April 10	October 28	200	9A	0F to 5°F

Florida

Jacksonville	February 6	December 16	313	8B	15F to 20°F
Miami	irregular frost	irregular frost	365	10	30F to 40°F
Orlando	January 31	December 17	319	9B	25F to 30°F
Tallahassee	February 26	December 3	280	8B	15F to 20°F
Tampa	January 10	December 26	349	9A	20F to 25°F

Georgia

Atlanta	March 20	November 19	244	7B	5F to 10°F
Augusta	March 14	November 1	249	7B	5F to 10°F
Macon	March 12	November 19	252	7B	5F to 10°F
Savannah	February 21	December 9	291	8B	15F to 20°F

Hawaii

Hilo	no frost	no frost	365	10	30F to 40°F
Honolulu	no frost	no frost	365	10	30F to 40°F

Idaho

Boise	April 29	October 16	171	6A	−5F to −10°F
Coeur d'Alene	May 12	October 14	155	5B	−10F to −15°F
Pocatello	May 8	September 20	155	4	−20F to −30°F

Illinois

Cairo	March 23	November 11	233	6A	−5F to −10°F
Chicago	April 19	October 28	192	5B	−10F to −15°F
Peoria	April 22	October 20	181	5A	−15F to −20°F
Rockford	May 7	October 11	157	5A	−15F to −20°F
Springfield	April 8	October 30	205	5B	−10F to −15°F
Urbana	April 22	October 20	151	5B	−10F to −15°F

Indiana
Evansville	April 2	November 4	216	6A	−5F to −10°F
Fort Wayne	April 24	October 20	179	5B	−10F to −15°F
Indianapolis	April 17	October 27	193	5B	−10F to −15°F

Iowa
Des Moines	April 20	October 19	183	5A	−15F to −20°F
Dubuque	April 19	October 19	184	5A	−15F to −20°F
Mason City	April 25	September 25	153	4	−20F to −30°F
Sioux City	April 27	October 13	169	4	−20F to −30°F

Kansas
Concordia	April 16	October 24	191	5B	−10F to −15°F
Topeka	April 9	October 26	200	5B	−10F to −15°F
Wichita	April 5	November 11	210	6A	−5F to −10°F

Kentucky
Lexington	April 13	October 28	198	6A	−5F to −10°F
Louisville	April 1	November 7	220	6B	0F to −5°F

Louisiana
Lake Charles	February 18	December 6	291	8B	15F to 20°F
New Orleans	February 13	December 12	302	9A	20F to 25°F
Shreveport	March 1	November 27	272	8A	10F to 15°F

Maine
Bangor	May 1	October 4	156	5A	−15F to −20°F
Caribou	May 19	September 21	125	4	−20F to −30°F
Greenville	May 27	September 20	116	5A	−15F to −20°F
Portland	April 29	October 15	169	5A	−15F to −20°F
Presque Isle	May 31	September 18	110	4	−20F to −30°F

Maryland
Baltimore	March 28	November 17	234	7A	0F to 5°F
Cumberland	May 1	October 10	163	6A	−5F to −20°F
Salisbury	April 20	October 20	183	7A	0F to 5°F

Massachusetts
Amherst	May 12	September 19	130	5B	−10F to −15°F
Boston	April 16	October 25	192	6A	−5F to −10°F
Fall River	April 22	October 23	184	6A	−5F to −10°F
Nantucket	April 12	November 16	219	6A	−5F to −10°F
Pittsfield	May 12	September 27	138	5B	−10F to −15°F
Worcester	May 7	October 2	148	5B	−10F to −15°F

Michigan
Detroit	April 25	October 23	181	5B	−10F to −15°F
Escanaba	May 14	October 6	145	4	−20F to −30°F

Grand Rapids	April 25	October 30	190	5B	−10F to −15°F
Lansing	May 6	October 8	155	5B	−10F to −15°F
Marquette	May 13	October 19	159	4	−20F to −30°F
Minnesota					
Albert Lea	May 3	October 6	156	4	−20F to −30°F
Duluth	May 22	September 24	125	3	−30F to −40°F
Minneapolis	April 30	October 13	166	4	−20F to −30°F
Virginia	May 29	September 14	108	3	−30F to −40°F
Mississippi					
Biloxi	February 22	November 28	279	8B	15F to 20°F
Jackson	March 10	November 13	248	7B	5F to 10°F
Tupelo	March 31	October 28	211	7B	5F to 10°F
Vicksburg	March 8	November 15	252	7B	5F to 10°F
Missouri					
Columbia	April 9	October 24	198	5B	−10F to −15°F
Kansas City	April 5	October 31	210	5B	−10F to −15°F
Saint Joseph	April 11	October 14	186	5B	−10F to −15°F
St. Louis	April 2	November 8	220	5B	−10F to −15°F
Springfield	April 13	October 20	190	6A	−5F to −10°F
Montana					
Billings	May 15	September 24	132	4	−20F to −30°F
Glasgow	May 19	September 20	124	3	−30F to −40°F
Great Falls	May 9	September 25	139	4	−20F to −30°F
Havre	May 9	September 23	138	4	−20F to −30°F
Nebraska					
Lincoln	April 20	October 17	180	5A	−15F to −20°F
Norfolk	May 4	October 3	152	5A	−15F to −20°F
North Platte	April 30	October 7	160	5A	−15F to −20°F
Omaha	April 14	October 20	189	5A	−15F to −20°F
Nevada					
Elko	June 6	September 3	89	5A	−15F to −20°F
Las Vegas	March 13	November 13	245	7A	0F to 5°F
Reno	May 14	October 2	141	5B	−10F to −15°F
New Hampshire					
Berlin	May 29	September 15	109	4	−20F to −30°F
Concord	May 11	October 1	143	5A	−15F to −20°F
Errol	June 1	September 5	96	4	−20F to −30°F
New Jersey					
Atlantic City	March 31	November 11	225	6B	0F to −5°F
Cape May	April 4	November 13	222	6B	0F to −5°F

New Brunswick	April 21	October 19	179	6A	−5F to −10°F
Newark	April 3	November 8	219	6A	−5F to −10°F
Trenton	April 8	November 5	211	6B	0F to −5°F
New Mexico					
Albuquerque	April 16	October 29	196	7A	0F to 5°F
Roswell	April 9	November 2	208	7A	0F to 5°F
Santa Fe	April 23	October 19	179	5A	−15F to −20°F
New York					
Albany	April 27	October 13	169	5A	−15F to −20°F
Binghamton	May 4	October 6	154	5A	−15F to −20°F
Buffalo	April 29	October 23	178	5B	−10F to −15°F
New York City	April 7	November 12	219	6B	0F to −5°F
Syracuse	April 30	October 15	168	5A	−15F to −20°F
Watertown	May 7	October 4	151	5A	−15F to −20°F
North Carolina					
Asheville	April 12	October 24	195	7A	0F to 5°F
Charlotte	March 21	November 15	239	7B	5F to 10°F
Raleigh	March 24	November 16	237	7B	5F to 10°F
Wilmington	March 15	November 19	274	7B	5F to 10°F
Winston Salem	April 14	October 24	193	7A	0F to 5°F
North Dakota					
Bismarck	May 11	September 24	136	4	−20F to −30F
Fargo	May 13	September 27	137	4	−20F to −30F
Williston	May 14	September 23	132	3	−30F to −40°F
Ohio					
Cincinnati	April 15	October 25	192	6A	−5F to −10°F
Cleveland	April 21	November 2	195	5B	−10F to −15°F
Columbus	April 17	October 30	196	5B	−10F to −15°F
Dayton	April 20	October 21	184	5B	−10F to −15°F
Toledo	April 24	October 25	184	5B	−10F to −15°F
Oklahoma					
Miami	April 7	October 26	202	6A	−5F to −10°F
Oklahoma City	March 28	November 7	223	7A	0F to 5°F
Tulsa	March 31	November 2	216	6B	0F to −5°F
Oregon					
Bend	June 8	September 7	91	5B	−10F to −15°F
Eugene	April 13	November 4	205	7B	5F to 10°F

Medford	April 25	October 20	178	7B	5F to 10°F
Portland	February 25	December 1	279	8A	10F to 15°F
Salem	April 14	October 27	197	7B	5F to 10°F
Pennsylvania					
Altoona	May 6	October 4	151	5B	−10F to −15°F
Erie	May 1	October 11	163	5A	−15F to −20°F
Harrisburg	April 10	October 28	201	6A	−5F to −10°F
Philadelphia	March 30	November 17	232	6B	0F to −5°F
Pittsburgh	April 20	October 23	187	6A	−5F to −10°F
Scranton	April 24	October 14	174	5B	−10F to −15°F
Williamsport	May 3	October 13	164	5B	−10F to −15°F
Rhode Island					
Kingston	May 1	October 14	166	6A	−5F to −10°F
Providence	April 13	October 27	197	6A	−5F to −10°F
South Carolina					
Charleston	February 19	December 10	294	8A	10F to 15°F
Columbia	March 14	November 21	252	7B	5F to 10°F
Greenville	March 23	November 17	239	7B	5F to 10°F
South Dakota					
Huron	May 4	September 30	149	5A	−15F to −20°F
Rapid City	May 7	October 4	150	5A	−15F to −20°F
Sioux Falls	May 5	October 3	152	5A	−15F to −20°F
Tennessee					
Chattanooga	March 26	November 11	229	7A	0F to 5°F
Knoxville	March 31	November 6	220	6B	0F to −5°F
Memphis	March 20	November 12	237	7A	0F to 5°F
Nashville	March 28	November 7	224	6B	0F to −5°F
Texas					
Brownsville	February 15	December 10	298	9A	20F to 25°F
Corpus Christi	January 26	December 27	335	9A	20F to 25°F
Dallas	March 18	November 22	249	8A	10F to 15°F
El Paso	March 26	November 14	238	8B	15F to 20°F
Houston	February 5	December 11	309	8B	15F to 20°F
Lubbock	April 1	November 9	205	7A	0F to 5°F
Plainview	April 10	November 6	211	7B	5F to 10°F
Utah					
Blanding	May 18	October 14	148	6B	0F to −5°F
Logan	May 15	October 6	144	6B	0F to −5°F
Ogden	April 13	October 22	192	6B	0F to −5°F
Salt Lake City	April 12	November 1	202	6B	0F to −5°F

Vermont

Bennington	May 15	October 4	142	5A	−15F to −20°F
Burlington	May 8	October 3	148	4	−20F to −30°F
St. Johnsbury	May 22	September 25	126	3	−30F to −40°F

Virginia

Norfolk	March 18	November 27	254	7B	5F to 10°F
Richmond	April 2	November 8	220	7A	0F to 5°F
Roanoke	April 20	October 24	187	7A	0F to 5°F

Washington

Centralia	April 27	October `7	173	7B	5F to 10°F
Seattle	February 23	December 1	281	7B	5F to 10°F
Spokane	April 20	October 12	175	5B	−10F to −15°F
Walla Walla	April 3	November 1	211	5B	−10F to −15°F
Yakima	April 15	October 22	190	6A	−5F to −10°F

West Virginia

Charleston	April 18	October 28	193	6B	0F to −5°F
Martinsburg	April 29	October 16	170	6B	0F to −5°F
Parkersburg	April 16	October 21	189	6A	−5F to −10°F

Wisconsin

Green Bay	May 6	October 13	161	5A	−15F to −20°F
Lacrosse	May 1	October 8	161	4	−20F to −30°F
Madison	April 26	October 19	177	5A	−15F to −20°F
Milwaukee	April 20	October 25	188	5B	−10F to −15°F

Wyoming

Casper	May 18	September 25	130	4	−20F to −30°F
Cheyenne	May 20	September 27	130	4	−20F to −30°F
Sheridan	May 21	September 21	123	4	−20F to −30°F

Puerto Rico

All locations	no frost	no frost	365	10	30F to 40°F

Virgin Islands

All locations	no frost	no frost	365	10	30F to 40°F

Canada

Alberta

Calgary	May 28	September 9	104	3	−30F to −40°F
Edmonton	May 14	September 14	123	3	−30F to −40°F

British Columbia

Prince George	June 10	August 28	79	3	−30F to −40°F
Victoria	February 28	December 9	284	7B	5F to 10°F

Manitoba						
	Churchill	June 26	September 12	82	2	−50F to −40°F
	Winnipeg	May 25	September 21	119	3	−30F to −40°F
New Brunswick						
	Fredericton	May 18	September 26	130	4	−20F to −30°F
Newfoundland						
	Saint John's	June 3	October 12	131	5A	−15F to −20°F
Northwest Territories						
	Yellow Knife	May 30	September 16	109	2	−50F to −40°F
Nova Scotia						
	Halifax	May 15	October 15	153	5B	−10F to −15°F
Ontario						
	Toronto	April 20	October 30	193	5B	−10F to −15°F
Prince Edward Island						
	Charlottetown	May 17	October 15	151	5A	−15F to −20°F
Quebec						
	Montreal	May 3	October 17	155	4	−20F to −30°F
	Quebec City	May 18	September 18	123	4	−20F to −30°F
Saskatchewan						
	Regina	May 27	September 12	108	5B	−10F to −15°F
Yukon						
	Dawson	May 26	August 27	93	4	−20F to −30°F

Growing Zones throughout the World

(see introductory note on page 359)

Country and city	Zone	Minimum annual temperature
Argentina		
Buenos Aires	9	–7C to –1°C / 20F to 30°F
Cordoba	9	–7C to –1°C / 20F to 30°F
Australia		
Adelaide	10	–1C to 5°C / 30F to 40°F (Australia zone 4)
Brisbane	10	–1C to 5°C / 30F to 40°F (Australia zone 4)
Melbourne	10	–1C to 5°C / 30F to 40°F (Australia zone 4)
Perth	10	–1C to 5°C / 30F to 40°F (Australia zone 4)
Sydney	10	–1C to 5°C / 30F to 40°F Australia zone 4
Austria		
Vienna	6	–23C to –18°C / –10F to 0°F
Belgium		
Brussels	8	–12C to –7°C / 10F to 20°F
Chile		
Santiago	10	–1C to 5°C / 30F to 40°F
China		
Beijing	7	–18 to –12°C / 0–10°F
Hong Kong	10	–1C to 5°C / 30F to 40°F
Shanghai	9	–7C to –1°C / 20F to 30°F
France		
Lyon	8	–12C to –7°C / 10F to 20°F
Paris	8	–12C to –7°C / 10F to 20°F
Marseille	9	–7C to –1°C / 20F to 30°F
Germany		
Berlin	6	–23C to –18°C / –10F to 0°F
Frankfurt	7	–18 to –12°C / 0–10°F

	Hamburg	7	−18 to −12°C / 0–10°F
	Munich	6	−23C to −18°C / −10F to 0°F
Ireland			
	Belfast	9	−7C to −1°C / 20F to 30°F
	Dublin	8	−12C to −7°C / 10F to 20°F
	Galway	9	−7C to −1°C / 20F to 30°F
Italy			
	Florence	9	−7C to −1°C / 20F to 30°F
	Milan	8	−12C to −7°C / 10F to 20°F
	Palermo	10	−1C to 5°C / 30F to 40°F
	Rome	9	−7C to −1°C / 20F to 30°F
	Venice	8	−12C to −7°C / 10F to 20°F
Japan			
	Sapporo	6	−23C to −18°C / −10F to 0°F
	Kyoto	9	−7C to −1°C / 20F to 30°F
	Tokyo	9	−7C to −1°C / 20F to 30°F
New Zealand			
	Auckland	10	−1C to 5°C / 30F to 40°F
	Christchurch	9	−7C to −1°C / 20F to 30°F
	Wellington	10	−1C to 5°C / 30F to 40°F
South Africa			
	Cape Town	11	4°C and above / 40°F and above
	Durban	11	4°C and above / 40°F and above
	Johannesburg	9	−7C to −1°C / 20F to 30°F
Spain			
	Barcelona	10	−1C to 5°C / 30F to 40°F
	Cordoba	9	−7C to −1°C / 20F to 30°F
	Madrid	9	−7C to −1°C / 20F to 30°F
	Seville	10	−1C to 5°C / 30F to 40°F
	Valencia	10	−1C to 5°C / 30F to 40°F
United Kingdom			
	Bristol	9	−7C to −1°C / 20F to 30°F
	Glasgow	8	−12C to −7°C / 10F to 20°F
	Inverness	8	−12C to −7°C / 10F to 20°F
	Leeds	8	−12C to −7°C / 10F to 20°F
	Liverpool	9	−7C to −1°C / 20F to 30°F
	London	8	−12C to −7°C / 10F to 20°F
Uruguay			
	Montevideo	10	−1C to 5°C / 30F to 40°F

Glossary

A

Alternaria. A fungus whose spores are borne in soil and water that can cause plants to decompose.

Annual. A plant whose life cycle of germination, flowering, and seeding occurs within one growing season.

Anthracnose. A group of fungal diseases that create black, sunken dead areas on leaves, stems, or fruit. It is spread by rain, overhead irrigation, or the handling of plants.

Aphid. A very small soft-bodied insect that damages plants by sucking the sap. Aphids are usually seen in large numbers on new plant growth. Symptoms: colony of small insects on leaves; honeydew or excrement is sticky. Control: hose off with water, use a soap solution or sticky yellow traps.

Armyworm. A caterpillar similar to a cutworm. Armyworms gather in large numbers. Symptom: small plants cut off at soil level at night. Control: put paper collar around lower stem of plant extending into soil.

B

Bacillus thuringiensis (Bt). A soil dwelling bacterium used as a biological control, mainly for caterpillars. Spores and insecticidal proteins produced by Bacillus thuringiensis are used as insecticides which are regarded as environmentally friendly because they have little effect on humans, wildlife, pollinators, and most beneficial insects.

Beetle. Small insect with chewing mouthparts and wing parts that form protective convex shells. Beetles include the bark beetle, leaf beetle, Colorado potato beetle, Japanese beetle, and flea beetle. The immature larvae are generally soft-bodied grubs. Symptom: shoots channeled; holes eaten in leaves by larvae or beetles. Control: pick off, pyrethrum.

Biennial. A plant completing its life cycle in a two-year period. Biennials flower and seed in the second season following germination. Some biennials are treated as annuals, for example carrots.

Black rot. A descriptive term for several diseases usually caused by a seed-borne fungus which causes seedlings to rot or leaves or stems to take on a water-soaked appearance followed by a dark colored decay. Control: Plant resistant varieties in well-drained soil and rotate crops.

Black leg. A descriptive term for certain fungal or bacterium caused diseases which results in the base of the plant stem turning black with decay. Canker is also called black leg.

Blanch. A practice that excludes light from a plant's leaves and stems to prevent the development of green coloration and makes the plant more palatable. Celery, leeks, chicory, and endive are sometimes blanched.

Blight. A loose term for a plant disease that results in the sudden withering of leaves and shoots. Many kinds of blight are caused by bacteria or fungi. Circular yellow spots first appear which later turn gray or black. Control: garden sanitation and the removal of infected plants are the most effective countermeasure.

Blood meal. Dried, powdered, slaughterhouse blood used as a high nitrogen fertilizer. Blood meal can be mixed with water and applied to plants as a liquid fertilizer.

Bolting. The premature production of flowers or seed especially in vegetables, often a reaction to heat, insufficient moisture, or the lack of nutrients.

Bone meal. Ground bone used to improve soil fertility. Bone meal or bone manure is a source of phosphorus, consisting mostly of calcium phosphate. The bones are usually steamed or heated to remove fats and pathogens.

Borer. A chewing insect, usually the larva of certain beetles or moths. Symptom: leaves and stems tunneled by larvae. Control: pick off, pyrethrum, remove the infested plant.

Botanical name. The two Latin words that comprise the scientific or botanical name of a plant. The first word identifies the genus and the second the species.

Botrytis. A fungus responsible for several diseases. Symptoms can include rot or gray mold on stems, leaves, or fruits. Adequate spacing and the disposal of infected plants will limit the hazard.

Brassica. A member of the mustard or cabbage family (Brassicaceae).

Broadcast. To scatter granular substances such as seeds or dry fertilizer over an area of ground.

Bug. A common term for an insect pest. True bugs of the Hemiptera family have sucking mouth parts leathery upper wings and membranous lower wings. Examples: harlequin bug, lace bug, squash bug.

Bulb. Modified plants stem and bud with swollen leaves acting as a storage organ, usually underground.

Bulbil or bulblet. A small bulb or bulb-like growth rising above the ground in the axil of a leaf or bract.

C

Canker. A diseased and often depressed or darkened area of a root or stem caused by fungus or bacteria. Canker is sometimes called black leg.

Caterpillar. A larva of a butterfly or a moth. Caterpillars have biting mouthparts. Symptom: holes eaten in leaves, and stems. Control: pick off, Bacillus thuringiensis (Bt), pyrethrum.

Cloche. A small, low portable structure, often made of plastic or glass, used to protect early crops grown outdoors.

Clubroot. A fungus disease which causes a distortion of roots and causes plants to become stunted. Clubroot particularly affects brassicas. Crop rotation is the best control.

Coldframe. A low-lying rectangular unheated structure with a glass or plastic lid.

Companion plants. Plants grown together on the premise that they will benefit each other, for instance, having the beneficial effect of repelling insects or deterring disease.

Compost. Decomposed organic material used as soil conditioner, mulch, potting or seed-sowing medium. Compost will improve soil fertility, structure, and water-holding capacity. Finished compost contains roughly two part nitrogen, one part phosphorus, and one part potassium, with a pH of 7.

Compost tea or compost water. Compost dissolved in water which offers nutrients in solution that are easily absorbed by plant roots. To make compost tea, fill a watering can half with well-rotted compost and half with water, stir gently a dozen times and pour near plant roots. The compost can be used several times.

Cool-season crop. A vegetable that grows best in temperatures ranging from 60-65°F (16-18°C). Cool-season crops can tolerate light to moderate frosts but can not tolerate warm summer weather. Cool-season crops are usually grown for their vegetative parts: roots, leaves, stems, and immature flowers. Cool-season crops include broccoli, cabbage, cauliflower, Chinese leaves, kale, kohlrabi, lettuce, mustard greens, peas, radish, rutabaga, spinach, turnips. Other crops that can be planted in cool weather include beets, carrots, chard, parsley, parsnips.

Cottonseed meal. A slow-release acidic, organic fertilizer containing about 7 percent nitrogen, 3 per cent phosphoric acid, and 2 percent potash.

Cotyledon. The plant's first leaf, called a seed leaf, folded within the seed.

Crown. The part of a plant where the roots and stem meet at soil level.

Crown rot. A fungus disease which attacks a plant at the soil level resulting in the plant's death.

Cultivar. A contraction of the phrase "cultivated variety"; a group of cultivated plants propagated for their desirable characteristics.

Cucurbit. A garden term denoting members of the gourd family, Cucurbitaceae. Cucurbits include cucumbers, gourds, squashes, melons, and pumpkins.

Curly dwarf. A plant virus that reduces plant growth and vigor and causes plants to become stunted. Control: garden and greenhouse sanitation are important controls; dispose of infected plants.

Cutworm. One of many brown or gray caterpillars, the larvae of various moths that attack plants at soil level. Cutworms attack lettuce, onions, brassicas, carrots, celery, beets, potatoes, and strawberries. Symptom: small plants cut off at soil level at night; mature plant stems girdled. Control: put paper collar around lower stem of plant, extending into soil.

D

Damping off. A soilborne fungus disease that causes seedlings to wilt, rot, and die at soil level. Caused by several fungi that thrive in wet conditions. Crowding, excessive moisture, poor ventilation, and too much shade contribute to the spread of the disease.

Deciduous. Plants that lose their leaves at the end of the growing season and regrow them the following year.

Determinate. A term applied to plants whose main growth is stopped by the production of a terminal flower and fruit at its apex. Determinate crops flower and then bear nearly their entire crop at one time which is an advantage in short-season regions. Some tomatoes and beans are determinate.

Division. A method of increasing the number of plants; the parent plant is divided into parts, each portion bearing some roots of its own.

Dormant; dormant period, dormancy. Temporary cessation of growth in living plants as a result of seasonal changes or physiological factors. In the temperate zone, dormancy usually coincides with winter, but can also be caused by lack of water.

Downy mildew. Gray, lavender, or white downy spots usually on the undersides of leaves caused by mold fungi.

Drill. A shallow furrow for planting seeds or transplants, or the act of planting seeds rather than broadcasting.

Dust, dusting. Pest control applied to plants or the soil as a finely ground powder or dust. Dusts can be applied to the undersides and tops of leaves and especially adhere well to plants with waxy foliage.

Dwarf. Plant varieties that grow to a lesser height than other varieties.

E

Early. A crop produced early in the season or a crop variety that matures in a shorter period of time than other varieties.

Earwig. A beetle-like insect growing to 1 inch (25 cm) long armed with forceps at the rear end. Earwigs are nocturnal and hide in holes or under debris during the daytime. Symptom: earwigs make irregularly shaped holes in leaves. Control: trap earwigs under cardboard or in a rolled up newspaper and destroy them; also pyrethrum.

Evergreen. A plant that retains its leaves throughout the year.

F

Family. A group of plants above the category of genus with similar flowers and fruits.

Fertile. A term used to mean capable of being productive. Fertile soil contains abundant plant nutrients, is well structured, well-drained, and aerated.

Fertilizer. Any material organic or in inorganic—produced naturally or synthetically—used to increase the supply of available nutrients for plant growth.

First frost. The first frost or freezing temperature usually in autumn that ends the warm growing season. See 'Growing season'.

Flea beetle. A small (1/8 inch/3 mm) mostly black round beetle that eats small round holes in leaves. Flea beetles spring away like fleas when disturbed. Symptom: small holes in plant leaves and stems; spreads certain plant diseases. Control: pick off, sticky yellow traps, pyrethrum.

Floating row cover. Sheets of flexible lightweight fabric or plastic placed loosely over plants to provide protection from low temperatures and pests.

Flies. A large group of insects. Adults have wings. The larval states are legless maggots which dwell in the soil or bore into plant tissue or fruit causing rot. Examples are cabbage-root fly, carrot fly, celery fly, fruit flies, onion fly, and leaf miners. Control: sticky traps for mature flies.

Foliar feeding. Application of a diluted fertilizer solution to the foliage and stems of a plant. Often used for supplemental feeding.

Forcing. Process to encourage the early growth of foliage, flowers, or fruit ahead of the normal season. Rhubarb and chicory are commonly forced.

Friable. Used to describe soil with a crumbly workable texture that can be used for seeding.

Fruit. Botanically a fertilized and ripened ovary of a seed plant. 'Fruit' commonly refers to plant parts that have a more or less sweet pulp.

Fungicide. A substance or chemical used for the control of diseases caused by fungi. Fungicides can work on contact or systemically. Crop rotation, good drainage, and garden sanitation can mitigate fungal attacks.

Fungus. A lower class of organism that is not plant or animal. Fungi can not manufacture their own food and so must live as the parasites of other living organisms or as saprophytes of dead organic tissue. Fungi reproduce by spores. Plant diseases cause by fungi includes mildews, rusts, smuts, and molds.

Fusarium. A soil fungi. Fusarium rot is a disease that results in small, reddish-brown spots or concentric ridges or rings with water-soaked margins. Fusarium can cause plants to wilt and die.

G

Gall. Swollen plant tissue or enlarged deformity resulting from enlarged plant cells and caused by bacteria, fungus, virus, or an insect.

Genus. A taxonomic classification used to describe pant with several similar characteristics. Genus is the rank between family and species.

Germination. The physiological and structural process that causes a seed to sprout or come into active growth. The seed moves from a dormant state to growth.

Greenhouse. A structure made largely of transparent or translucent material, such as glass or plastic, for the cultivation of plants in a controlled environment.

Green manure. A rapidly maturing leafy crop grown for digging into the soil to improve its structure and fertility.

Growing season. The period during each year when crops can be grown. The growing season is determined by the crop selected, the climate, location, temperature, daylight hours (photoperiod), rainfall or availability of water, and other environmental factors. In temperate regions, the growing season usually occurs between the last frost in spring and the first frost in autumn.

Growing zone. Regions in which plants will grow and north of which they will die. Zones are based on weather statistics kept over a period of many years and are determined by the average minimum temperatures of the coldest month. Zone designations are not infallible. If a particular plant is not hardy (cold tolerant) to a particular zone, it should be assigned to the next warmest zone.

H

Half hardy. Plants that tolerate low temperatures but not frost. Half-hardy plants generally thrive after the risk of frost has passed.

Harden off. To acclimatize plants gradually to more rigorous conditions enabling them to withstand cooler conditions. Half-hardy and tender plants are hardened off before planting outside.

Hardy. Plants that can withstand frost or cold injury without protection. In subtropical and tropical regions, a hardy plant may be one that can withstand drought.

Heavy soil. A soil with a high proportion of clay particles. Heavy soil is prone to waterlogging in winter and drying in summer.

Herbaceous. Relating to plants that do not have woody stems and that die down at the end of each growing season.

Hill up. To draw the soil around the base of a plant for support or to cover the plant for the purpose of blanching

Humus. A complex mixture of organic decomposed plant material in the soil. Humus will benefit sandy soil by increasing the availability of water and clay soil by allowing particles to bond.

Hybrid. A plant resulting from the crossing of two or more genetically dissimilar and distinct species or genera.

I

Indeterminate. A plant whose terminal growth is not prevented by a flower or fruit at the end of its main stem or apex. Such plants generally continue to grow and bear until frost. Some beans and tomatoes are indeterminate plants.

Insecticide. Chemical used to kill or control insect pests.

Intercropping; interplanting. Planting rows of fast growing plants between rows of slower-maturing plants and growing the two crops simultaneously to make the maximum use of the ground. Or to combine plants with differing growth habit, such as short and tall allowing for more plants to be planted in a single bed.

K

Kitchen garden. A garden to produce edible produce such as vegetables, salad greens, herbs, and small fruits for the home table.

L

Ladybugs. Small (1/8-1/4 inch/ 3-7 mm) oval beetle with red, tan, or brown wing covers bearing black spots. Adult ladybugs and larvae eat aphids, scale insects, mealybugs, thrips, and mites.

Larva, larvae. The immature form of many insects sometimes called caterpillars, grubs, or maggots. Larvae do not resemble the adult form of the insect.

Last frost. The last frost or freezing temperature of the winter or cold season, usually in late winter or early spring. See 'Growing season'.

Leaf. A plant organ borne on a stem or shoot containing chlorophyll essential for photosynthesis.

Leaf curl. A curled leaf margin; a symptom which may be caused by disease, insects, or environmental factors.

Leafhopper. A small (1/4 inch/5 mm) sap-sucking insect related to the aphid that hops or flies a short distance when disturbed. Leafhoppers usually feed on underside of leaves causing leaf spotting on the upper surface. Leafhoppers and can transmit virus diseases. Symptoms: hopping insects; tip of leaves turn brown. Control: insecticidal soap, pyrethrum.

Leaf miner. An insect larva that lives part of its life cycle tunneling between the upper and lower epidermis of leaves. Symptom: Light-colored blisters or winding trails on leaves, sometimes called mines. Control: pyrethrum.

Leaf mold. A plant disease seen in tomatoes grown in high humidity (such as a greenhouse) that results in pale yellow patches on the upper surface of leaves. The yellow patches are caused by a green-gray fungal growth on the underside of the leaves.

Leaf mold. A substance formed by decayed and partially decayed leaves produced when leaves are composted. Leaf mold is rich in humus and can be used to enhance soil structure but is low in plant nutrients.

Leaf scorch. Browned and scorched appearance of leaf margins and plant tissue caused by poor growing conditions such as too little moisture or too much heat, wind, salt spray, chemical substances, or pathogenic organisms.

Leaf spot. A term for fungal or bacterial disease that causes discolored spots on leaves and can weaken a plant's ability to produce food.

Legume. A one-celled seed pod of the pea family and a descriptor for the pea and bean family. Legumes support bacterial nodules on their roots which enable them and the surrounding soil to benefit from atmospheric nitrogen.

Lime. Calcium compounds used to reduce soil acidity and improve soil fertility.

Loam. The term used for a soil of medium texture which is rich in fibrous organic matter, moisture retentive, and free of silt, clay, sand, or stones.

Lodge. Bending or creasing stalks to the ground to halt foliage development and enhance bulb formation; called "lodging". The stalks of onions and garlic are lodged after immature flower buds begin to open atop the plants.

Loopers. Worm-like crawling insects with several pairs of legs. Symptom: Leaves and shoots eaten. Control: hand pick, Bacillus thuringiensis (Bt), pyrethrum.

M

Maggot. The common name for the legless white or yellow larvae of flies. Maggots burrow into plant tissue and feed on roots, tubers, and bulbs and often cause the collapse or death of the plant. Symptom: stunted and sickly plants. Control: wood ash around bade of plant, beneficial nematodes.

Main crop. The largest crop produced through the main growing season. Also used to describe the varieties and cultivars grown during the main growing season.

Mealybug. A small (up to ¼ inch/ 5mm), oval, soft, sap-feeding insect covered with fine white filaments and a powdery secretion known as "meal." Mealybugs mass in leaf axils. Symptom: white powdery secretions; excrement collects soot and can debilitate plants. Control: spay off with water, insecticidal soap, pyrethrum.

Mildew. A whitish discoloration of a plant surface produced by a fungus. Downy mildew, powdery mildew, and sooty mold are caused by differing fungi.

Millipede. A straight, elongated, slender creature with two pairs of legs on mostly hard-shelled body segments. Millipedes may have as many as 50 segments. (Centipedes look similar but have only one pair of legs per each body segment.) Symptom: some, but not all millipedes, feed on seedlings and soft plant tissue. Control: cultivation and garden sanitation.

Mite. A sap-sucking arachnid with a needle-like mouthpart and four pairs of legs. Mites can be found on the undersides of leaves where they sometimes spin fine webs. Symptoms: pale, yellowish curled leaves. Control: spray away with water.

Mold. The visible growth of downy fungal spores on organic matter, especially where there is a high moisture content and high temperature.

Mosaic. Leaf discoloration—yellow, pale green, or dark green—that is a symptom of one of several viral diseases.

Moth. The adult, winged form of a caterpillar. At the larval stage they are serious pests that pupate in the soil and feed on plant roots and stems. At the larval stage they are known as bagworms, budworms, cankerworms, cutworms, earworms, fruitworms, hornworms, and tent caterpillars.

Mulch. A layer of organic or inorganic material placed over the soil to protect the soil surface, conserve moisture, deter soil-inhabiting pests, and control weeds.

N

Nematode. Microscopic wormlike creatures some of which are predators that feed on bacteria or fungi and others which are parasites that feed on plant cells. Nematodes are also known as eelworms because they can move in the thin water film between plant cells in an eel-like manner. Pest nematodes have pin-shaped mouthparts which pierce plant cells in order to feed. Pest nematodes can cause lesions of plant roots.

Neutral. Soil or compost with a pH value of 7, which is neither acid nor alkaline (see pH).

Nitrogen (abbreviation N). A major essential plant nutrient which stimulates leaf and stem growth. Bloodmeal, guano, hoof and horn meal, soybean meal, and cottonseed meal are good sources of nitrogen.

Nitrogen fixing. The conversion of atmospheric nitrogen to nitrogen compounds usable by plants. Bacteria associated with the legume family plants fix nitrogen in legume root nodules.

Nutrients. Minerals ions necessary for plant growth. Macronutrients include nitrogen (N), phosphorus (P), potassium (K), magnesium (Mg), calcium (Cu), and sulfur (S). Micronutrients or trace elements include iron (Fe), manganese (Mn), copper (Cu), zinc (Zn), boron (Bo), molybdenum (Mb), and chlorine (Cl).

O

Organic. Term used to describe substances that are derived from natural materials. Also used to denote a way of gardening that encourages life in the soil without the use of manufactured chemicals.

P

Perennial. A plant—usually herbaceous—that survives for three or more seasons.

Perlite. Heat expanded volcanic rock that is inert, sterile, and has a neutral pH value. Perlite is used as a rooting and potting mix.

pH. A measure of the acidity or alkalinity of soil or other substances. The pH scale ranges from 0 to 14, and is an indicator of the soluble calcium within a soil or growing medium. A pH of 7.0 is neutral. A pH below 7.0 is acid, and above alkaline.

Phosphorus (abbreviation P). A major plant nutrient important in plant enzyme reactions essential for cell division and tissue development. Usually placed in the root zone to assist plant root development. Mushroom compost, rock phosphate, and bonemeal are very good sources of phosphorus.

Physiological disorder. A defect in growing conditions not the result of pests or disease that adversely effects a plant's growth.

Phytophthora. Parasitic fungi sometimes soilborne that cause plant tissue to rot. In some plants such as potatoes, brown dead patches form on leaf edges followed by black patches and tissue rot. The fungi can also attack roots, plant crowns, and fruit.

Pinch out. To remove the growing tip of a plant in order to induce branching.

Planting zone. See 'Growing zone'.

Plume moth. A moth with lobed and fringed wings. Plume moth larvae mine plant leaves and feed on plant leaves, buds, and flower parts. Control with pyrethrins.

Pollination. The transfer of pollen from an anther to a stigma; necessary for fertilization and the production of viable seeds, but not always necessary for flowers or fruit production.
Potassium (abbreviation K). A major plant nutrient important in plant metabolism. Potassium is present in all soils and most abundant in clay and soils high in organic content. Wood ashes, sawdust, granite dust, cocoa shell dust, fish emulsion, and greensand are good sources of potassium. Symptoms of potassium deficiency include restricted shoot growth and small and poor quality fruit and fruit drop.
Pot up. To move a plant into a larger pot.
Powdery mildew. Whitish, powdery growth on leaves, stems, and buds caused by a number of fungi. The fungi exist mainly on the surface of the plant where it feeds on epidermal cells. Powdery mildew does not require moisture on the host plant to develop like other fungal pathogens. Control powdery mildew by removing infected plants or pruning away infected plant parts.
Propagation. The increase of plant numbers by seed or vegetative means.
Psyllid. Small ($1/8$ inch/3 mm) sap-feeding insects with two pairs of wings. Psyllids can cause tomato and potato leaves to become curled and yellow.
Pyrethrum, pyrethrin. Pyrethrum refers to members of the chrysanthemum family that are the source of an insecticide. The extracted active ingredients of pyrethrums are called pyrethrins.

R
Relay cropping. A second crop is started amidst the first crop before it has been harvested.
Reverse-season climate. A sub-tropical climate or region where the weather remains warm during autumn and winter but does not become hot and humid. Many temperate zone warm-weather crops can be planted in late autumn to grow and mature during the winter in reverse-season climates.
Rhizobia. Soil-dwelling bacteria that fixes nitrogen after it becomes established inside the root nodules of legumes. Nitrogen fixation is the conversion of atmospheric nitrogen to a form that is useable by plants. Nitrogen is a major essential plant nutrient which stimulates leaf and stem growth. Residual nitrogen is left in the soil and can benefit future crops.
Rhizome. A fleshy underground stem that acts as a storage organ.
Root. The part of the plant that is responsible for absorbing water and nutrients from the soil and also anchors the plant.
Root crops. Vegetables grown for their edible roots or tubers, like carrot, parsnip, and potatoes.
Root rot. A fungal or bacterial disease that causes the decay of plant roots.
Rosette. A circular or radiating cluster of leaves or other plant parts from a common center or crown.
Rot. Disease that cause the decay of plant tissues.

Rotation. The practice of changing the position of crops growing in a garden on a rotating cycle, usually a period of years. Rotation counters the depletion of some soil nutrients and the build-up of pathogens and insect pests that can occur when plants from the same family are grown in the same location year after year.

Rotenone. Insecticide derived from several species of mostly tropical plants; kills insects by contact or as a stomach poison. Rotenone is toxic to fish.

Runner. A trailing shoot or stolon that roots where it touches the ground.

Rust. A reddish-brown, white, or yellow powdery spore mass on foliage that weakens or stunts a plant's growth. Rust disease is caused by several kinds of fungi. Remove infected plants to reduce wind-borne spores.

S

Scab. Various fungal diseases which result in an outgrowth of scabby tissue on a vegetable or fruit.

Scale. A sap-sucking insect that feeds on plant juices. Scale insects can have either hard or soft bodies. Some scale excretions encourage the growth of sooty molds. Control: spray with horticultural oil which will smother the scale.

Seed. A ripened plant ovule containing a dormant embryo capable of forming a new plant.

Seed leaves or cotyledons. The first leaf or leaves formed by a seed after germination.

Seed viability. The ability of a seed to germinate. The viability of a seed can vary from a few days to several decades.

Seedling. A young plant grown from a seed.

Sets. Small onions, shallots, or potatoes used for planting.

Shoot. A branch, stem, or twig of a plant.

Side-dressing. A fertilizer applied in a strip or on either side or a few inches away from an established plant or row of plants.

Sideshoot. A branch stem or twig growing from a main stem of a plant.

Smut. A fungal disease characterized by masses of dark, soot-like spores that kill the plant tissue beneath the spores. Smut looks similar to slime mold. Control smut by removing and destroying diseased plants.

Snail, slug. Mollusks with rasping mouthparts. Snails have a shell; slugs do not. Snails and slugs prefer damp, shady places. Slugs will eat the underground parts of plants. Symptom: leaves and stems of plants eaten. Control: trap and destroy under boards placed in the garden.

Soil. The surface of the planet that sustains life. Composed of disintegrated rock and usually decomposed organic matter, plants and animals. Earth and dirt are synonyms for soil.

Soil amendment. An organic, mineral, or chemical material added to soil that improves its nutritive value, structure, aeration, drainage, or moisture retention.

Soil temperature. The temperature of the soil. Soil temperature can affect a plant's ability to grow and its ability to survive. Soil temperature is generally cooler than the air during the summer and warmer than the air in the winter. Mulches can keep the soil warmer in the winter and cooler in the summer.

Southern blight, southern wilt. A fungal disease in warm climates that causes rotting of the stem at soil level and, in turn, yellowing and wilting of shoots. Control: crop rotation and deep cultivation.

Species. A taxonomic classification of similar closely related plants. The category below the genus level.

Stamen. The male pollen-producing part of a plant.

Stem. The main axis of a plant, from which lateral branches appear.

Stem rot. A disease that causes the disintegration of plant stems.

Stewart's wilt. A bacterial disease that causes wilted, yellow foliage. Seen in sweet corn.

Succession cropping. The planting of a crop at regular intervals or immediately after the harvesting of another crop to ensure the continuity of supply.

Sucker. A stem originating below soil level, usually from the plant's roots or underground stem, or side growth arising from an axillary bud. Suckers take nourishment away from the parent plant.

Sunscald. Injury to tender plant stems, leaves, or fruit caused by intense sunlight.

T

Taproot. The primary anchoring root of a plant usually growing straight down in the soil. The taproot anchors the plant and conveys nutrients or stores food.

Tender. Plants that will be injured or die when exposed to low temperatures.

Tent caterpillar. A caterpillar that protects itself by webbing foliage or silk webs around itself as it feeds. Also called a webworm. Symptom: eaten leaves and shoots. Control: handpick and destroy, spray with Bacillus thuringiensis (Bt), pyrethrum.

Thinning. The selective removal of seedlings or shoots to improve the quality of those that remain. Seedlings should be thinned when they are very young.

Thrip. A small ($1/8$ inch/3 mm or less) brown, yellow, or black insect that rasp or sucks plant tissues and juices. Control: spray away with water, pyrethrum.

Tilth. A fine, crumbly surface layer of soil produced by cultivation and soil improvement well suited for seed sowing.

Top-dressing. The application of organic matter or fertilizer to the soil surface to stimulate the growth of plants already in place.

Topsoil. The upper usually most fertile layer of soil.

Transpiration. The loss or evaporation of water from plant leaves and stems.

Transplant. To move a seedling from one growing position to another.

Tuber. A swollen underground stem or root used to store moisture and nutrients.

V

Variety. A botanical classification used to describe naturally occurring plant variations or subspecies.

Vegetable. A plant grown for its edible leaves, stems, roots, bulbs, or tubers. A vegetable is usually cooked and served with the main part of the meal, and not sweet. The sweet potato is an exception. A sweetened vegetable that is often though of as a fruit is the rhubarb. Vegetables that are technically fruits include tomatoes, cucumbers, squashes, eggplants, and peppers.
Vegetative. Used to describe parts of a plant that are capable of growing.
Verticillium. A soil-borne fungal disease that causes plants to wilt and often die.
Virus. Non-cellular parasitic pathogens that can cause many plant diseases by attacking living cells. Plant viral diseases may inhibit chlorophyll and stunt or deform normal growth. Plant viruses are descriptively called yellows, mosaic, or stunt. Viruses are usually spread by humans or insects.

W

Warm-season crop. A vegetable that grows best when the air and soil temperatures have reached 65-86°F (18-30°C) and requires at least 75°F (24°C) for minimum growth. Warm-season crops require short days to germinate and long days and high temperatures to form and ripen fruit. Warm-season crops include tomatoes, eggplant, peppers, beans, corn, squash, cucumbers, melons, and pumpkins.
Webworm. A caterpillar that protects itself by webbing the foliage or a silk web around itself as if feeds. Symptom: eaten leaves and shoots. Control: handpick and destroy, spray with Bacillus thuringiensis (Bt), pyrethrum.
Weed. An unwanted plant that may compete with desired plants.
Weevil. One of a group of small (1/8 inch/ 3 mm) long beetles with elongated snouts with mouthparts at the snout tip. Adult weevils feed on foliage. Grubs, the weevil's larval stage, feed on roots. Controls: clear debris where they hide and trapping.
Whitefly. A small (2 mm) sap-sucking insect that looks like a tiny white moth. Both larvae and adult moth-like insect are found on the underside of leaves. A whitefly infestation can cause leaf spotting and the insects' excrement can result in the collection of black, sooty mold. Whiteflies are often seen in warm climates and in the greenhouse. Symptom: Leaves turn yellow and plant lacks vigor. Control: sticky traps, pyrethrum.
Wilt. A term applied to a number of plant diseases whose symptoms involve wilting or drooping of leaves and stems. Wilting can be caused by pathogens that interfere with the water-conducting system of the plant and also by too much or too little moisture. Fusarium wilt and Verticillium wilt are two fungal diseases that can affect tomatoes.
Wirestem. A fungal disease which causes the damping-off of brassicas; seen as a red-brown stem lesion at the soil level.
Wireworm. The larvae of a click beetle. The larvae are shiny golden-brown, hard-bodied grubs up to 1 inch (2.5 cm) long. Wireworms can feed in the soil damaging plant roots for up to 5 years. Control: cultivation and weed control can counter the spread of wireworms.

Worm. A term to describe the earthworm. Worm also can describe other small creatures such as nematodes or eelworms, and the larval stage of many insects such as armyworms, canker worms, and wireworms.

Y

Yellows. A term for various plant diseases which cause foliage to turn yellow and become stunted. Yellows can be caused by a virus or a fungus. Plant roots are often infected from the soil. Solution: plant resistant varieties.

Bibliography

The following books and experience were the major resources used in writing this book. If you are interested in other books or resources to help grow your kitchen garden, sign-on to Harvest to Table.com (harvesttotable.com) and send us an email. We will do all we can to help your kitchen garden be a success.

Baker, Jerry. *Fast, Easy, Vegetable Garden*. New York, NY.: Plume Book, 1985. Brief, basic growing tips for most vegetables and herbs and includes lists of popular varieties.

Ball, Jeff. *Rodale's Garden Problem Solver*. Emmaus, PA.: Rodale Press, 1988. Vegetable, fruit, and herb pests and diseases are reviewed and organic solutions are given; includes line drawings of many garden pests.

Bartholomew, Mel. *All New Square Food Gardening*. Nashville, TN.: Cool Springs Press, 2005. Small space, intensive vegetable gardening guide.

Biggs, Matthew, Jekka McVicar, Bob Flowerdew. *Vegetables, Herbs & Fruits, an Illustrated Encyclopedia*. San Diego, CA.: Laurel Glen Publishing. Vegetable, fruit and herb profiles with origins and growing tips.

Coleman, Eliot. *Four-Season Harvest: Organic Vegetables from Your Home Garden All Year Long*. Chelsea, VT.: Chelsea Green, 1999. A guide to growing vegetables year round; methods to extend the growing season in cold climates.

Consumer Guide Editors. *Vegetable & Herb Gardening*. Skokie, IL.: Publications International, 1986. Vegetable garden planning, growing, harvesting, and storing.

Cox, Jeff. *How to Grow Vegetables Organically*. Emmaus, PA.: Rodale Press, 1988. Guide to growing 40 vegetables with organic gardening tips.

Creasy, Rosalind. *The Complete Book of Edible Landscaping*. San Francisco, CA.: Sierra Club, 1982. Vegetable and herb gardening incorporated into the extended garden.

Cutler, Karan Davis. *Burpee the Complete Vegetable & Herb Gardener.* New York, NY.: Macmillan. Narrative descriptions of vegetables and herbs with an overview of gardening basics.

Denckla, Tanya L. *The Gardener's A-Z Guide to Growing.* North Adams, MA.: Storey Publishing, 2003. Organic growing guide for vegetables and fruits with organic disease and pest management suggestions and companion planting guide.

Dolezal, Robert J. *Vegetable Gardening, Your Ultimate Guide.* Minnetonka, MN.: Creative Publishing, 2000.

Facciola, Stephen. *Cornucopia.* Vista, CA.: Kampong Publications, 1990. Very comprehensive guide to the varieties and cultivars of many garden vegetables and fruits.

Fell, Derek. *Vegetables How to Select and Enjoy.* Tucson, AZ.: HPBooks, 1982. Guide to growing popular vegetables and herbs with growing basics.

Fenton-Smith, John. *A Grower's Guide to Vegetables.* New York, NY.: Crescent Books, 1997. Planting, growing, and harvesting suggestions are given for 50 common vegetables.

Frederick, Kate Carter, editor. *Miracle-Gro Guide to Growing Delicious Vegetables, Flowers & Herbs.* Des Moines, IA.: Meredith Publishing, 2005.

Halpin, Anne M. ed. *The Organic Gardener's Complete Guide to Vegetables and Fruits.* Emmaus, PA.: Rodale Press, 1982. Listing for commonly grown vegetables and fruits and suggestion for saving garden space.

Hessayon, Dr. D.G. *The Vegetable & Herb Expert.* London, England: Transworld Publishers, 2002. One paragraph to two page entries on most popular vegetables and herbs with drawings and planting calendars for gardens in Great Britain.

Hull, George F. *The Language of Gardening.* Cleveland, OH.: World Publishing Co., 1967. Gardening and horticulture terms are simply defined in this short text of 800 entries.

Hunt, Marjorie B. and Brenda Bortz. *High-Yield Gardening.* Emmaus, PA.: Rodale Press, 1986. Small space and high yield vegetable gardening suggestions.

Jeavons, John. *How to Grow More Vegetables.* Berkeley, CA.: Ten Speed Press, 2002. Biointensive vegetable gardening and farming guide.

Kowalchik, Claire and William H, Hylton, editors. *Rodale's Illustrated Encyclopedia of Herbs.* Emmaus, PA.: Rodale Press, 1987. History and uses of 140 herbs.

McLeod, Judyth. *Botanica's Organic Gardening*. San Diego, CA.: Laurel Glen, 2002. Narrative entries on raising vegetables and fruits with variety suggestions popular in Australia.

Michalak, Patricia S. *Rodale's Successful Organic Gardening Herbs*. Emmaus, PA.: Rodale Press, 1993. Concise growing and harvesting guide for herbs.

Michalak, Patricia S. *Rodale's Successful Organic Gardening Vegetables*. Emmaus, PA.: Rodale Press, 1993. Concise growing and harvesting guide for vegetables.

Newcomb, Duane. *The Backyard Vegetable Factory*. Emmaus, PA.: Rodale Press, 1988. Planting tips, disease and pests notes, and suggested varieties for many vegetables.

Newcomb, Duane and Karen. *California Vegetable Patch*. New York, NY.: Harper-Collins Publishers, 1995. Detailed listing and descriptions of vegetables varieties.

Newcomb, Duane and Karen. *The Postage Stamp Garden*. Holbrook, MA.: Adams-Media Co., 1999. Gardening tips for small space vegetables gardens including choosing planting combinations.

Norman, Jill. *Herbs & Spices, The Cook's Reference*. New York, NY.: DK Publishing, 2002. A guide to 120 herbs and spices including harvesting, storing, and tasting.

Organic Gardening Magazine staff. *The Encyclopedia of Organic Gardening*. Emmaus, PA.: Rodale Press, 1978. Entries on vegetables, fruits, herbs and how to grow them organically.

Peel, Lucy. *Harper-Collins Practical Gardner: Kitchen Garden*. New York, NY.: HarperCollins, 2003. Concise vegetable gardening guide with a planting and harvest calendar for popular varieties.

Pittenger, Dennis R. editor. *The California Master Gardener Handbook*. Oakland, CA.: University of California, 2002. Comprehensive guide to edible crop gardening with emphasis on mild region gardening.

Pleasant, Barbara and Katie Lamar Smith. *All About Vegetables*. Des Moines, IA.: 1999. Basic garden making instruction with growing tips for popular vegetables.

Raymond, Dick. *Down-to-Earth Know-How for the '90s: Vegetables and Herbs*. North Adams, MA.: Storey, 1991. Garden preparation and vegetable growing.

Schrock, Denny ed. *Encyclopedia of Plant Care*. Des Moines, IA.: Meredith Books, 2005. Short entries on vegetables and fruits; also entries on houseplants, garden flowers, grasses and trees and shrubs.

Smith, Cheryl editor. *The Ortho Home Gardener's Problem Solver*. San Ramon, CA.: Ortho Books, 1993. A chemical-based pest and disease control guide. Color photographs are useful in identifying pests and diseases.

Smith, Edward C. *The Vegetable Gardener's Bible*. North Adams, MA.: Storey Publishing. 2000. Organic vegetables growing with emphasis on wide rows and raised beds.

Smith, Miranda and Anna Carr. *Rodale's Garden Insect, Disease & Weed Identification Guide*. Emmaus, PA.: Rodale Press, 1988. A guide to insect, disease, and weed identification and organic controls.

Taylor, Norman and Gordon P. DeWolf, Jr. *Taylor's Guide to Vegetables & Herbs*. Boston, MA.: Houghton Mifflin Co., 1987. Short entries on how to grow and harvest 198 vegetables and herbs.

Tenenbaum, Frances. *Taylor's Dictionary for Gardeners*. Boston, MA.: Houghton Mifflin Co., 1997. Horticulture terms, plant anatomy, gardening techniques, pests and diseases are defined in 2,000 entries.

Van Wyk, Ben-Erik. *Food Plats of the World*. Portland, OR.: Timber Press, 2005. Descriptions of 350 food plants both temperate and tropical with color photographs of each.

Vilmorin-Andrieux, MM. *The Vegetable Garden*. Berkeley, CA.: Ten Speed Press. A re-publication of the 1885 edition of this classic vegetable gardening guide.

Walheim, Lance and the editors of Sunset Books. *Sunset Vegetable Gardening*. Menlo Park, CA.: Sunset Books, 1998. Vegetable and berry entries and vegetable gardening basics.

Index

Italic page numbers refer to pages on which there are relevant photographs. Latin botanical names are italicized. Listings for common names of plants with separate entries are followed by the Latin botanical name. Listings for the Latin botanical names are followed by the common names.

A

Abelmoschus esculentus (okra), *208*, 209-211
acorn squash, 311, 314
Allium ampeloprasum, (leeks), *176*, 177-179
Allium cepa (onion), *212*, 213-218
Allium cepa var. *ascalonicum* (shallots), *290*, 291-293
Allium porrum (leeks), *176*, 177-179
Allium sativum (garlic), *158*, 159-163
Allium schoenoprasum (common chives), *108*, 109-111
Allium tuberosum (garlic chives), 109-111
Alpine strawberry, *316*, 317-319
ancho pepper, 245
annual marjoram, 187
Apium graveolens var. *rapaceum* (celeriac), *78*, 79-81
Apium graveolens var. *dulce* (celery), *82*, 83-86
apple mint, 201
Artemisia dracunculus (tarragon), *334*, 335-337
artichoke *(Cynara scolymus)*, *10*, 11-15
arugula *(Eruca sativa)*, *16*, 17-19
Asian radish, 264
asparagus *(Asparagus officinalis)*, *20*, 21-25
asparagus chicory, 97
asparagus lettuce, 182

B

baby peas, 234
baby squash, 309

banana pepper, 245
banana squash, 311, 314
Basella alba 'Rubra' (Malabar spinach), 302
basil *(Ocimum basilicum, O. cispum, O. minimum)*, 26, 27-29
batata, 329
Batavian escarole, 151
beans *(Phaseolus vulgaris)*, 30, 31-36
beet greens, 39-43
beetroot, 39
beets *(Beta vulgaris)*, 38, 39-42
Belgian endive, 97-100
bell pepper, 245
Beta vulgaris (beets, beet greens), 38, 39-42
Beta vulgaris var. *cicla* (chard), 88, 89-91
bhindi, 209
Bibb lettuce, 181, 185
bitter dock, 295
black currant sage, 281
blue potato, 254
bok choy, 103, 106
borecole, 169
Brassica juncea var. *rugosa* (mustard greens), 204, 205-207
Brassica napus (rutabaga), 274, 275-277
Brassica oleracea var. *acephala* (collards), 116, 117-119
Brassica oleracea var. *acephala* (kale), 168, 169-171
Brassica oleracea, var. *botrytis* (cauliflower), 72, 73-77
Brassica oleracea var. *capitata* (cabbage), 56, 57-61
Brassica oleracea var. *gemmifera* (Brussels sprouts), 50, 51-54
Brassica oleracea var. *gongylodes* (kohlrabi), 172, 173-175
Brassica oleracea var. *italica* (broccoli), 44, 45-48
Brassica oleracea var. *sabellica,* (curly kale), 169
Brassica rapa var. *chinensis* (Chinese leaves: bok choy, pak choi, tat soi), 102, 103-107
Brassica rapa var. *pekinensis* (Chinese leaves: pe-tsai), 103-107
Brassica rapa var. *rapa* (turnip), 354, 355-357
broadleaf cress, 133
broad-leaved endive, 151
broccoli *(Brassica oleracea* var. *italica)*, 44, 45-48
broccoli raab, 48
broccoflower, 73
Brussels sprouts *(Brassica oleracea* var. *gemmifera)*, 50, 51-54
bulbing fennel, 155

bush beans, 33
buttercup squash, 314
butterhead lettuce, 181, 185
butternut squash, 314

C
cabbage *(Brassica oleracea* var. *capitata)*, 56, 57-61
calabaza squash. 314
calabrese, 45
Canadian turnip, 275
cantaloupe, 191, 195
Cucumis melo (melons), *190*, 191-195
Cucumis melo var. *cantaloupesis* (true cantaloupe), 191, 195
Cucumis melo var. *inodorus* (honeydew melon), 191
Cucumis sativus (cucumber), *134*, 135-138
Capsicum annuum (sweet peppers), *240*, 241-246
Capsicum chinense (hot peppers), 241-246
Capsicum frutescens (hot peppers), 241-246
cardoon *(Cynara cardunculus)*, 62, 63-65
Caribbean pumpkin, 314
carrots *(Daucus carota sativus)*, 66, 67-71
casaba melon, 191, 195
cauliflower *(Brassica oleracea,* var. *botrytis)*, 72, 73-77
cayenne pepper, 245
celeriac *(Apium graveolens* var. *rapaceum)*, 78, 79-81
celery *(Apium graveolens* var. *dulce)*, 82, 83-86
celery cabbage, 104
celery root, 79
celtuce, 182
chard *(Beta vulgaris* var. *cicla)*, 88, 89-91
Charentai melon, 191
cheese pepper, 245
cheese pumpkin, 314
cherry pepper, 245
cherry tomato, 343, 349, 350
chervil *(Anthriscus cerefolium)*, 92, 93-95
chickpea, 36
chicons, 97, 99
chicory *(Cichorium intybus* var. *foliosum)*, 96, 97-100
Chilean strawberry, 317
chili peppers, 241, 245

chilipiquin pepper, 245
chiltepin pepper, 245
Chinese cabbage, 103
Chinese chives, 109
Chinese leaves *(Brassica rapa* var. *chinensis, B. r.* var. *pekinensis)*, *102*, 103-106
Chinese mustard, 205
Chinese parsley, 113
chives *(Allium schoenoprasum, A. tuberosum)*, *108*, 109-111
chou-nevet jaune, 275
Cichorium endivia (escarole, endive, curly endive), *150*, 151-153
Cichorium intybus (radicchio), *256*, 257-259
Cichorium intybus var. *foliosum* (chicory, Belgian endive, witloof), *96*, 97-100
cilantro *(Coriandrum sativum)*, *112*, 113-115
clary sage, 281
colewort, 117
collard greens, 117
collards *(Brassica oleracea* var. *acephala)*, *116*, 117-119
common chives, 109
common sorrel, 295
coriander, 113
Coriandrum sativum (cilantro), *112*, 113-115
corn *(Zea mays* var. *rugosa)*, *120*, 121-125
corn salad *(Valerianella locusta)*, *126*, 127-129
Corsican mint, 201
Cos lettuce, 182, 185
Costata Romanesca squash, 309
Crenshaw melon, 191, 195
cress *(Lepidium sativum* and *Rorippa microphylla)*, *130*, 131-133
crisphead lettuce, 181, 185
crookneck squash, 305, 309
Cuban pepper, 245
Cubanelle pepper, 245
cucumber *(Cucumis sativus)*, *134*, 135-138
Cucumis melo (melons), *190*, 191-195
Cucumis melo var. *cantaloupesis* (cantaloupe), 191
Cucumis melo var. *inodorus* (honeydew melon, casaba melons), 191
Cucumis melo var. *reticulates* (netted muskmelon), 191
Cucumis sativus (cucumber), *134*, 135-138
Cucurbita maxima (squashes: acorn, banana, cushaw delicious, hubbard), *310*, 311-315
Cucurbita moschata (butternut squash), 311-315
Cucurbita pepo (squashes: buttercup, crookneck, marrow, pattypan, pumpkin, scallop, spaghetti, staightneck, vegetable marrow, zucchini), 305-309; 311-315

curly chicory, 151
curly cress, 133
curly dock, 295
curly endive, 151
curly kale, 169
curly leafed parsley, 225
curly spinach, 302
cushaw squash, 311, 314
Cynara cardunculus (cardoon), *62*, 63-65
Cynara scolymus (artichoke), *10*, 11-14

D
daikon, 264
Daucus carota sativus (carrot), *66*, 67-71
dill *(Anethum graveolens)*, *140*, 141-143
dry beans, 31, 35-36

E
edible-pod peas, 234
eggplant *(Solanum melongena)*, *144*, 145-148
elephant garlic, 163
endive *(Cichorium endivia)*, 151-153
English peas, *232*, *233*, 237-238
Eruca sativa (arugula), *16*, 17-19
escarole *(Cichorium endivia)*, *150*, 151-153
European chives, 109
European strawberry, 317
ever-bearing strawberry, 319

F
fava beans, 36
fennel, 155
field salad, 127
fingerling potato, 253
finocchio, 155
flat leafed parsley, 225
flat leaf spinach, 302
Florence fennel *(Foeniculum vulgare* var. *azoricum)*, *154*, 155-157
Foeniculum vulgare var. *azoricum* (Florence fennel), *154*, 155-157
Fragaria species (strawberry), 317
Fragaria ananassa (pineapple strawberry), 317
Fragaria chiloensis (Chilean strawberry), 317

Fragaria vesca (Alpine strawberry), *316*, 317
French sorrel, 295
French tarragon, 335
frisée, 151

G

garden cress, 131
garden peas, 237, 238
garden rhubarb, 267
garden rocket, 17
garden sorrel, 295
garlic *(Allium sativum)*, *158*, 159-163
garlic chives, 109
garlic mustard, 205
German greens, 169
giant-leaf mustard, 205
girasole, 321
globe artichoke, 11
golden apple mint, 201
gombo, 209
Greek oregano, 221
green beans, 31
green onions, 217
green peas, 233, 237, 238
green sage, 281
griselle, 321
guinea squash, 145
gumbo, 209

H

habañero pepper, 246
Hamburg parsley, 225
hardneck garlic, 162
hautbois strawberry, 317
heading chicory, 257
Helianthus annuus (sunflowers), 325-327
Helianthus tuberosus (sunchoke, Jerusalem artichoke), *320*, 321-323
herb patience, 295
honeydew melon, 191, 192, 195
horseradish *(Armoracia rusticana)*, *164*, 165-167
hot peppers, 241, 245

Hubbard squash, 311, 315

I
iceberg lettuce, 181, 185
Indian spinach, 89
Ipomoea batatas (sweet potatoes), *328*, 329-332
Irish potato, 249
Italian chicory, 257
Italian dandelion, 97, 257
Italian oregano, 189
Italian parsley, 225

J
jalapeño pepper, 245
Japanese mint, 201
Jarrahdale pumpkin, 315
Jerusalem artichoke, 321
jewel mint of Corsica, 201
June-bearing strawberry, 319

K
kale *(Brassica oleracea* var. *acephala)*, *168*, 169-171
knob celery, 79
knotted marjoram, 187
kohlrabi *(Brassica oleracea* var. *gongylodes)*, *172*, 173-175
kumara, 329
Kuri squash, 315

L
Lactuca sativa (lettuce), *180*, 181-185
lady's fingers, 209
lamb's lettuce, 127
late melons, 191
Latin lettuce, 182
leaf beet, 89
leaf chicory, 257
leaf lettuce, 181, 185
leaf mustard, 205
leeks *(Allium porrum, A. ampeloprasum)*, *176*, 177-179
Lepidium sativum (cress, garden cress), *130*, 131-133
lettuce *(Lactuca sativa)*, *180*, 181-185

lima bean, 36
long wax pepper, 246
long white potato, 253
loose leaf lettuce, 181, 185
Lycopersicon esculentum (tomato), *342*, 343-352

M

mâche, *126*, 127-129
Malabar spinach, 302
marjoram *(Origanum majorana, O. onites)*, *186*, 187-189
marrow, 305, 309
melons *(Cucumis melo)*, *190*, 191-195
Mentha species (mint), *200*, 201-203
Mentha piperita (peppermint), 201
Mentha spicata (spearmint), 201
mesclun, *196*, 197-199
Michihili (Michihli), 104, 106
mint *(Mentha species)*, *200*, 201-203
mizuna, 197, 207
muskmelon, 191, 195
musk strawberry, 317
mustard, 205
mustard greens *(Brassica juncea* var. *rugosa)*, *204*, 205-207

N

Napa cabbage, 103, 106
netted melon, 191
New Mexican pepper, 246
new potatoes, 255
New Zealand spinach, 302
nitrogen fixation, 33
North American strawberry, 317
nutmeg melon, 191

O

ochro, 209
Ocimum basilicum (sweet basil), *26*, 27-29
Ocimum species (basil), 27-29
okra *(Abelmoschus esculentus)*, *208*, 209-211
onions *(Allium cepa)*, *214*, 213-218
orange mint, 201

oregano *(Origanum vulgare)*, 220, 221-223
Oriental mustard, 205
Oriental radish, 264
Origanum majorana (marjoram), *186*, 187-189
Origanum onites (pot marjoram), 221
Origanum vulgare hirtum (Greek oregano), 221
oyster plant, 283

P-Q
pak choi *(Brassica rapa* var. *chinensis)*, 103
parsley *(Petroselinum crispum, P.c.* var. *neapolitanum)*, *224*, 225-227
parsnips *(Pastinaca sativa) 228*, 229-232
paste tomato, 351
Pastinaca sativa (parsnips) *228*, 229-232
pattypan squash, 305, 309
peas *(Pisum sativum, P. s.* var. *macrocarpon)*, *232*, 233-238
peppermint, 201
peppers *(Capsicum annum, C. chinense, C. frutescens)*, *240*, 241-246
Persian melon, 191
petit pois, 234
Petroselinum crispum (curly leafed parsley), 225
Petroselinum crispum var. *neapolitanum* (flat or plain leafed parsley, Italian parsley), 225
Petroselinum crispum var. *tuberosum* (Hamburg parsley, turnip-rooted parsley), 225
pe-tsai *(Brassica rapa* var. *pekinensis)*, 103, 106
Phaseolus vulgaris (beans), *30*, 31-36
pickling cucumber, 135, 138
pie plant, 267
pimiento pepper, 246
pineapple sage, 281
pineapple strawberry, 317
Pisum sativum (edible-pod peas), 233, 234
Pisum sativum var. *macrocarpon* (shell peas), 233, 234
plain leaf parsley, 225
pole beans, 32, 36
Portuguese kale, 169
potato *(Solanum tuberosum)*, *248*, 249-256
pot marjoram, 221
pumpkin, 311, 314-315
purple potato, 254
purple sage, 281

R

radicchio *(Cichorium intybus)*, 256, 257-259
radishes *(Raphine's sativus)*, 260, 261-264
Raphanus sativus (radish). 260, 261-264
red-in-snow mustard, 205
red onions, 218
Rheum rhabarbarum syns. *R.* x *cultorum, R.* x *hybridum* (rhubarb), 266, 267-269
rhubarb *(Rheum rhabarbarum* syns. *R.* x *cultorum, R.* x *hybridum)*, 266, 267-269
Rocambole garlic, 162
rocket, 17
rocket salad, 17
roquette, 17
Romanesco broccoli, 73, 77
romaine lettuce, 182, 185
Romano bean, 31
Rorippa nasturtium-aquaticum (watercress), 131-133
Rosmarinus officinalis (rosemary), 270, 271-273
rosemary *(Rosmarinus officinalis)*, 270, 271-273
rosette chicory, 257
Rouge Vif d'Etampes pumpkin, 315
round red potato, 254
round white potato, 254
Rumex species (sorrel), 294, 295-297
russet potato, 253
Russian turnip, 275
rutabaga *(Brassica napus)*, 274, 275-277

S

sage *(Salvia officinalis)*, 278, 279-281
salad chervil, 93
salsify *(Tragopogon porrifolius)*, 282, 283-285
Salvia elegans (pineapple sage), 281
Salvia officinalis (sage), 278, 279-281
Salvia species, 279-281
Satureja hortensis (summer savory), 286, 287-289
Saturea montana (winter savory), 287-289
sauce tomato, 351
savory *(Satureja hortensis, S. montana)*, 286, 287-289
savoy spinach, 302
scallop squash, 305, 309
Scotch bonnet pepper, 246

Scotch kale, 169, 171
sea kale, 89
serrano pepper, 246
shallots (*Allium cepa* var. *aggregatum*), 290, 291-293
shell beans, 31, 35-36
shelling peas, 234, 237
slicing tomato, 352
silver beets, 89
snap beans, 31-36
snap peas, 237, 238
snow peas, 237, 238
softneck garlic, 162
Solanum melongena (eggplant), *144*, 145-148
Solanum tuberosum (potato), *248*, 249-256
sorrel (*Rumex acetosa, R. scutatus*), *294*, 295-297
sour dock, 295
soybean, 36
spaghetti squash, 311, 314
spearmint, 201
Spinacea oleracea (spinach), *298*, 299-302
spinach (*Spinacea oleracea*), *298*, 299-302
spinach beet, 89
spinach dock, 295
spring chicory, 257
squash. *See* summer squash or winter squash
squash pepper, 246
stem turnip, 173
St. Josephwort, 27
straightneck squash, 305, 309
strawberry (*Fragaria vesca, F.* species), *316*, 317-319
string beans, 31
succory, 97
sugar snap peas, 234-238
summer melons, 191
summer savory, 287-289
summer squash (*Cucurbita pepo*), *304*, 305-310
sunchoke (*Helianthus tuberosus*), *320*, 321-323
sunflower (*Helianthus annuus*), 325-327
sun flower seeds, *324*
sunroot, 321
Swede, 275

Swedish turnip, 275
sweet basil, 27
sweet cicely, 93
sweet corn *(Zea mays* var. *rugosa)*, *120*, 121-125
sweet marjoram, 187
sweet peppers, 241, 245
sweet potato *(Ipomoea batatas)*, *328*, 329-332
Swiss beet, 89
Swiss chard, 89

T
Tabasco pepper, 246
tarragon *(Artemisia dracunculus)*, *334*, 335-337
tatume squash, 309
Tetragonia tetragonioides (New Zealand spinach), 302
thyme *(Thymus vulgaris)*, *338*, 339-341
Thymus species (thyme), 339-341
Thymus vulgaris (thyme, French thyme), *338*, 339-341
tomato *(Lycopersicon esculentum)*, *342*, 343-352
Tragopogon porrifolius (salsify), *282*, 283-285
tri-color sage, 281
true tarragon, 335
turban squash, 311, 315
turnip *(Brassica rapa* var. *rapa)*, *354*, 355-357
turnip cabbage, 173
turnip-rooted cabbage, 173
turnip-rooted celery, 79
turnip-rooted parsley, 225

U-V
Valenciano pumpkin, 315
Valerianella locusta (corn salad, mâche), *126*, 127-129
vegetable marrow, 305
vegetable oyster, 283

W
watercress, 131-133
wax bean, 31
white cabbage, 104
white leaf chicory, 97
white potato, 253, 254

white onion, 218
white salsify, 283
wild artichoke, 63
wild marjoram, 221
winter cress, 131
winter melons, 191
winter savory, 287
winter squash *(Cucurbita maxima, C. moschata, C. pepo)*, *310*, 311-315
witloof chicory, 97
wong bok, 103, 106

X-Y-Z

yellow dock, 295
yellow onions, 218
yellow potato, 254
yellow turnip, 275
Zea mays var. *rugosa* (sweet corn), *120*, 121-125
zucchini, 305, 309

Acknowledgements

Thank you to Bruce and David Albert for their support of this project and HarvestToTable.com. Also special thanks to Anna Heath and Becky Burad for their long encouragement and Saturday mornings at the farmers' markets. Thanks to Reuben Wolff for his advice and to Bethany Lowe, Sohalia Hernandez, and Kevin Nauss for their technical support. And, finally, thanks to Kristen, Marilyn and Robert "Bub" Albert for their help in the kitchen garden.

About the Author

Stephen Albert is editor-in-chief of the Web site Harvest to Table (harvesttotable.com), a practical guide to food in the garden, market, and kitchen. He grows vegetables and fruits in the Sonoma Valley of California and designs edible and flowering gardens for clients around the country. Stephen has lived and gardened in many regions of California and in Iowa, Florida, and Massachusetts. He teaches in both the landscape design and writing programs at the extension college of the University of California at Berkeley and is a certified California nurseryman. He has served as a director and president of the master gardeners of Sonoma County. For many years, Stephen was a journalist for Time-Warner, Inc. He earned a MFA and MA from the University of Iowa and is a graduate of the University of California and Westmont College.

You can send an email to Stephen Albert at HarvestToTable.com. He'll get back to you the same day.

About HarvestToTable.com

HarvestToTable.com is a Web site dedicated to practical information about food in the garden, market, and kitchen. If you would like a free subscription to Harvest to Table that includes regular updates on kitchen gardening, logon to harvesttotable.com and enter your email address that way you will never miss a garden, market, or kitchen tip or recipe.

We Want to Hear From You

If this book has helped you in your kitchen garden, give a copy to a friend and encourage her or him to start a kitchen garden, too. A kitchen garden can be any size, even a container or two on a stoop or apartment balcony.

To order additional copies of this book visit Amazon.com or logon to HarvestToTable.com and send us an email. The Harvest to Table online store stocks this book and many others that will make your kitchen garden a success.

Write to us at HarvestToTable.com and tell us about your kitchen garden!

Thank you!

Made in the USA
Lexington, KY
21 April 2010